BWT
BEST WATER TECHNOLOGY
LechneRacing
5 D. PEREIRA
PORSCHE
MOBIL 1 SUPERCUP
DRIVER CHAMPION 2022
CHAMPIONS
BWT

INHALT - CONTENT

TAGHEUER.COM
PORSCHE
CARRERA
TAG HEUER

KÜS

VICTORY LANE
Welcome home.
MOTUL

PORSCHE
CARRERA CUP
SCANDINAVIA

亚洲保时捷卡雷拉杯 2022
Porsche Carrera Cup Asia 2022
年度总冠军
Overall Champion
JUNJIE
骏捷车队
叶弘历
Leo YE
JUNJIE
骏捷车队

André LOTTERER 36
94 Pascal WEHRLEIN

PORSCHE
PENSKE
Ansys
BOSS
Mobil 1

5 D. PEREIRA
DRIVER CHAMPION 2022
BWT
TEAM CHAMPION 2022
17 B. BUUS
ROOKIE CHAMPION 2022

PORSCHE

PORSCHE

WEC
FIA WORLD ENDURANCE CHAMPIONSHIP

TEAM CHAMPION
CARRERA CUP
2022
3 HEINRICH
CHAMPION
2022

PRESENTED BY

PORSCHE

PORSCHE MOTORSPORT

PENSKE AUTOMOTIVE

TAG HEUER

NetApp

PORSCHE MOBIL 1 SUPERCUP

CATO NETWORKS

Mobil 1

MICHELIN

ABB
Ansys
BOSS
VELTINS
SACRED
GOURMET TEA & COFFEE
SACREDCAFE.COM
HAZET
TRILUX
SIMPLIFY YOUR LIGHT.
THURMETALL
swissmade
LOCTITE
KÜS
MANTHEY
TEAM
WEAR
.AT
ZIM SPEED
www.ck-modelcars.de
H&R
BWT
BEST WATER TECHNOLOGY
LechneRacing
Cam Shaft

ROCK IM PARK: PORSCHE BEGEISTERT BEIM GOODWOOD FESTIVAL OF SPEED

ROCK IN THE PARK: PORSCHE THRILLS AT GOODWOOD FESTIVAL OF SPEED

Porsche war diesmal zwar nicht die „Honoured Marque" beim Goodwood Festival of Speed, denn das war BMW, nicht zuletzt wegen des 50-jährigen Jubiläums der Sportdivision BMW M. Dennoch hatte auch Porsche eine große Präsenz beim weltberühmten PS-Festival rund um das Anwesen von Lord March. So startete dort der rein elektrische Porsche GT4 e-Performance in seine Welttournee. Sie soll das Potenzial des Fahrzeugkonzepts sowie die damit verbundenen Rennformate aufzeigen. Außerdem sorgten Rennsportmodelle wie der aktuelle 911 GT3 Cup, der 911 RSR und der neue LMDh-Prototyp 963 in Goodwood für Begeisterung, genau wie aktuelle und ehemalige Porsche-Rennfahrer.

Der neue Porsche GT4 e-Performance hat seine Leistungsfähigkeit beim Goodwood Festival of Speed erstmals vor Publikum unter Beweis gestellt. Die Schauläufe auf der rund 1,9 Kilometer langen Bergrennstrecke im Park des Lord March in der südenglischen Grafschaft West Sussex dienten dem vollelektrischen GT-Rennwagen zugleich als Auftakt für die GT4 e-Performance Welttournee. Sie soll den innovativen Versuchsträger in den kommenden zwei Jahren zu weiteren Stationen in Deutschland und darüber hinaus führen. Ziel ist es, Motorsport-Kundenteams, Partnern und Entscheidungsträgern aus der Rennsportszene das Potenzial des fortschrittlichen Fahrzeugkonzepts und die Möglichkeiten damit verbundener Rennformate aufzuzeigen.

Der GT4 e-Performance setzt auf die Technologiekomponenten des Mission R. Mit dieser Konzeptstudie hatte Porsche auf der IAA MOBILITY 2021 in München die Vision eines vollelektrischen GT-Rennfahrzeugs für den Kunden-Motorsport der Zukunft vorgestellt. Beide basieren auf dem Chassis des bekannten 718 GT4 Clubsport-Modells. Auch die Elektromotoren- und Batterie-Technologie des Versuchsträgers stammt vom Mission R. Dies bedeutet Maximalleistungen im Qualifikations-Modus von bis 800 kW (1.088 PS). Im simulierten Rennbetrieb stehen 450 kW (612 PS) für 30 Minuten dauerhaft bereit – also der Länge eines Carrera Cup-Rennens. In puncto Rundenzeit-Performance und Höchstgeschwindigkeit orientiert sich der GT4 e-Performance am aktuellen 911 GT3 Cup der Generation 992. Dank 900-Volt-Technologie kann das Speicherniveau des Akkus bei voller Ladeleistung in rund 15 Minuten von 5 auf 80 Prozent SoC (State of Charge/Ladezustand) hochschnellen.

Admittedly, Porsche wasn't the honoured marque in this year's Goodwood Festival of Speed, as it was BMW this time, not in the least because of the 50th anniversary of the sporting division BMW M. Nevertheless, Porsche had a large presence at the world-famous automotive festival around Lord March's estate. For instance, the fully-electric Porsche GT4 e-Performance started its worldwide tour there. It is to show the potential of the vehicle concept and racing formats connected with it. Moreover, competition models like the current 911 GT3 Cup, the 911 RSR and the new LMDh prototype 963 excited at Goodwood, together with current and former Porsche racing drivers.

The new Porsche GT4 e-Performance has demonstrated its power for the first time to the public at the Goodwood Festival of Speed. The show races on the 1.9-kilometre hill-climb track in the park owned by Lord March in the south England county of West Sussex also served as a launch for the GT4 e-Performance world tour. Over the next two years, the innovative test vehicle will travel to other places in Germany and beyond. The aim is to demonstrate the potential of the cutting-edge vehicle concept and the possibilities of racing formats associated with it to motorsport customer teams, partners and decision-makers in the motorsport scene.

The GT4 e-Performance features the technology components of the Mission R. At the 2021 IAA MOBILITY in Munich, the conceptual study outlined the vision of a fully-electric GT racing car for customer motorsport in the future. Both are based on the chassis of the proven 718 GT4 Clubsport model. The entire electric motor and battery technology also comes from the IAA conceptual study, which in qualification

PENSKE
PORSCHE
PENSKE

Mark Webber and Timo Bernhard

„Das Festival of Speed ist wirklich beeindruckend: ein riesengroßes Volksfest für Automobil-Entusiasten und ein Motorsport-Mekka, wie es in Europa kein zweites gibt", betont Porsche-Werksfahrer Richard Lietz aus Österreich, der den rein elektrischen Versuchsträger in Goodwood pilotiert hat. „Ich kannte den GT4 e-Performance bereits von den Testfahrten. Er ist extrem schnell und es macht sehr viel Spaß, ihn zu fahren – so kann ich mir das elektrisch angetriebene Kundensport-Rennfahrzeug der Zukunft vorstellen. Seine Aerodynamik zielt auf Effizienz ab, denn das Auto soll komplette Renndistanzen absolvieren können. Er ist auf der Rundstrecke eher zuhause als auf einer Bergrennstrecke, wie hier in Goodwood. Deswegen entspricht eine Fahrzeit von 45,50 Sekunden und Rang zwei in der Gesamtwertung vollauf unseren Erwartungen."

Rund 6.000 Teile hat Porsche für den GT4 e-Performance neu konstruiert. Seine Formen stammen von einem Team von Porsche Style rund um den Designer Grant Larson. Die Karosserie besteht unter anderem aus Naturfaser-Verbundwerkstoffen, deren Herstellung weniger Emissionen erzeugen soll als die Produktion vergleichbarer synthetischer Stoffe. Testweise kommen auch recycelte Karbonfasern zum Einsatz. Dank weiter ausgestellter Kotflügel ist der Rennwagen um 14 Zentimeter breiter als ein 718 Cayman GT4 Clubsport. Sie schaffen Raum für noch breitere 18-Zoll-Rennreifen von Michelin, die einen besonders hohen Anteil erneuerbarer Materialien aufweisen.

„Der GT4 e-Performance weist den Weg in den Porsche-Kundensport mit elektrisch angetriebenen Rennfahrzeugen. In einem ersten Schritt präsentieren wir dieses Konzept unseren Partnern weltweit", so Oliver Schwab, Projektleiter Vertrieb für den GT4 e-Performance. „Gemeinsam mit Fahrern, Teams, Veranstaltern, Behörden und weiteren interessierten Parteien sammeln wir dabei auch Ideen für zukünftige Rennformate von Porsche."

Der GT4 e-Performance war nicht der einzige Rennwagen von Porsche, der in Goodwood zu sehen war. Der aktuelle Porsche 911 GT3 Cup, mit 510 PS der stärkste Cup-Porsche aller Zeiten, war präsent, ebenso der Porsche 911 RSR mit der Startnummer 91, nur zwei Wochen nach dem LMGTE-Pro-Klassensieg bei den 24 Stunden von Le Mans. Viel Beachtung fand auch die Premiere des neuen Porsche LMDh-Prototypen 963, das in Goodwood erstmals in der Öffentlichkeit gezeigt wurde. Mit diesem Auto, eingesetzt von Porsche Penske Motorsport, feiert Porsche 2023 die Rückkehr in der höchsten Klasse des Langstreckensports, sowohl in der FIA-Langstrecken-WM (WEC) als auch in der nordamerikanischen IMSA-Serie. Zu den aktuellen und ehemaligen Porsche-Fahrern in Goodwood gehörten Jacky Ickx, Richard Attwood, Derek Bell, Mark Webber, Timo Bernhard und André Lotterer.

#DRIVERS OF PROGRESS
MORE THAN A RACE
ABB
#ABBFORMULAE
ABB FORMULA E | MORE THAN A RACE
Collaborating as partners for a sustainable future.
Together, we're drivers of progress.
abb.com/formula-e
OFFICIAL PARTNER
FORMULA E TEAM
TAGHeuer
PORSCHE
ABB

(l.-r.): André Lotterer, Jacky Ickx, Timo Bernhard

mode translates to a maximum output of up to 800 kW (1,088 HP). In simulated racing, a steady 450 kW (612 HP) is available for 30 minutes, i.e. the duration of a Carrera Cup race. In terms of lap times and top speed, the GT4 e-Performance is on par with the performance of the current 992-generation 911 GT3 Cup. Thanks to 900-volt technology, the state of charge (SoC) of the battery at full charging capacity jumps from 5 to 80 per cent in about 15 minutes.

"The Festival of Speed is truly impressive. It's a huge festival for car enthusiasts and a motorsport Mecca like no other in Europe," states Porsche works driver Richard Lietz from Austria, who drove the all-electric prototype in Goodwood. "I was already familiar with the GT4 e-Performance from test drives. It's extremely quick and loads of fun to drive – that's exactly how I imagine the electrically-powered customer sport racing car of the future. Its aerodynamics are designed for efficiency because the car has to be able to last the full race distance. It's more at home on circuits than at hill-climb events like here at Goodwood. So, a time of 45.50 seconds and second place in the overall rankings is in line with our expectations."

Porsche designed about 6,000 new parts for the GT4 e-Performance. Under the direction of designer Grant Larsson, a team from Porsche Style came up with the car's shape. The body is made of natural fibre composite materials, among others, with production intended to generate fewer emissions than that of comparable synthetic materials. Recycled carbon fibres are also used for testing purposes. Thanks to its flared fenders, the racing car is 14 centimetres wider than a 718 Cayman GT4 Clubsport. This allows more room for the wider 18-inch Michelin racing tyres, of which renewable materials make up a particularly high proportion.

"The GT4 e-Performance blazes a trail to Porsche customer racing with electrically-powered racing cars. As a first step, we will unveil this concept to our global partners," says Oliver Schwab, Project Manager of the GT4 e-Performance. "With drivers, teams, organisers, authorities and other interested parties, we're also gathering ideas for Porsche racing formats in the future."

The GT4 e-Performance wasn't the only Porsche race car that could be admired in Goodwood. The current Porsche 911 GT3 Cup, the strongest Porsche Cup car ever at 510 hp, was present as well, as was the Porsche 911 RSR with starting number 91, only a fortnight after its LMGTE-Pro class win in the Le Mans 24 Hours. There was also a lot of attention for the premiere of the new Porsche LMDh prototype 963, shown in public for the first time at Goodwood. With this car, run by Porsche Penske Motorsport, Porsche will be making its comeback in the top class of endurance racing in 2023, both in the FIA World Endurance Championship and in IMSA competition in North America. Current and former Porsche drivers at Goodwood included Jacky Ickx, Richard Attwood, Derek Bell, Mark Webber, Timo Bernhard and André Lotterer.

Oliver Schwab

Timo Bernhard

Porsche Racing Highlights
Porsche 911 GT3 R
Art.-Nr.: LEGT180-22002
Preis 79,95€
Porsche 935
Art.-Nr.: 187481
Preis 69,95€
Porsche 919 Hybrid
Art.-Nr.: IXOSP919-1804
Preis 79,95€
Porsche 935 K3
Art.-Nr.: S1807202
Preis 54,95€
Porsche 911 (991) RSR
Art.-Nr.: LEGT18003
Preis 79,95€
Porsche 919 Hybrid Evo
Art.-Nr.: IXOSP919-1821
Preis 79,95€
NOREV
Solido
ixo MODELS
Shipment worldwide
www.ck-modelcars.de
Jetzt direkt online bestellen!
Tel.: 06443 - 81284-28 Email: info@ck-modelcars.de
ck-modelcars Christoph Krombach e.K. • Willeckstrasse 7 • 35614 Asslar

PORSCHE CLUBS FEIERN 70-JÄHRIGES BESTEHEN

PORSCHE CLUBS CELEBRATE 70TH ANNIVERSARY

Die Marke Porsche bringt seit jeher Menschen auf der ganzen Welt zusammen. Am 26. Mai 1952 wurde vor 70 Jahren der erste Porsche Club gegründet. Heute gibt es weltweit mehr als 700 Porsche Clubs mit über 240.000 Mitgliedern in 86 Ländern.

The Porsche brand has always brought people together all over the world. The first Porsche Club was founded 70 years ago on 26 May 1952. Today, there are more than 700 Porsche Clubs worldwide with in excess of 240,000 members in 86 countries.

The Porsche brand has always brought people together all over the world.

Die traditionsreiche Markenclubwelt ist in ihrer Form und Größe herausragend in der Automobilindustrie. Anlässlich des 70-jährigen Jubiläums sind im Laufe des Jahres zahlreiche Aktivitäten und Feierlichkeiten geplant.

„Porsche wäre nicht Porsche ohne die globale Community von Freunden und Fans unserer Marke. Sie kommen weltweit zusammen, um ihre Leidenschaft für die Marke zu teilen", sagt Detlev von Platen, Vorstand für Vertrieb und Marketing bei der Porsche AG. „Die Porsche Clubs vermitteln den Mythos unserer Marke. Zugleich engagieren sich ihre Mitglieder gesellschaftlich, sportlich und sozial und vertreten damit die Werte, für die wir stehen. Das macht die Clubs für Jung und Alt attraktiv. Wir freuen uns sehr, dieses besondere Jubiläum mit Ihnen zu feiern."

Porsche Clubs: eine internationale Erfolgsgeschichte

Im Mai 1952 – nur zwei Jahre nach der ersten Auslieferung eines Sportwagens der Marke in Deutschland – hatten Porsche-Kunden den heutigen Porsche Club Westfalen (Gründungsname: Westfälischer Porsche Club Hohensyburg) gegründet. 1953 entstand in Belgien der erste internationale Porsche Club; 1955 folgte die Gründung des Porsche Club of America, dem heute größten Porsche Club weltweit. Nach wie vor entstehen jährlich rund um den Globus etwa fünf neue Clubs. Hierbei handelt es sich um eigenständige, unabhängige, eingetragene Vereine oder vergleichbare Rechtsformen. Sie werden von ihren Mitgliedern gemeinschaftlich und ehrenamtlich organisiert. Dementsprechend bietet jeder Club ein individuell ausgeprägtes Programm und Leistungsangebot – von Ausfahrten und Motorsportveranstaltungen über gesellschaftliche Events und technische Vorträge zu Fahrzeugen und E-Mobilität bis hin zum „Concours d'Élégance" und mehrtägigen Porsche-Paraden.

Die Fahrzeuge der Clubmitglieder reichen von klassischen Fahrzeugen bis hin zur aktuellen Porsche-Modellpalette. Auch der rein elektrische Taycan ist immer häufiger auf Clubtreffen zu sehen. Dem Erhalt und der Pflege der historischen Porsche-Fahrzeuge haben sich insbesondere die Classic Clubs weltweit verschrieben.

This venerable global ecosystem of marque-specific clubs is unparalleled in the automotive industry in both its form and its size. A variety of activities and celebrations are planned throughout the year to mark the 70th anniversary.

"Porsche would not be Porsche without the global community of friends and fans who come together to share their passion for our brand," says Detlev von Platen, Member of the Executive Board for Sales and Marketing at Porsche AG. "The Porsche Clubs preserve the legend of our brand, while at the same time their members are involved in social, sporting and community activities, and in this way are also representing our values. This makes the clubs attractive for young and old. We are delighted to be able to celebrate this special anniversary."

Porsche Clubs: an international success story

In May 1952, just two years after the brand's first delivery of a sports car in Germany, Porsche customers joined forces to form what is now the Porsche Club Westfalen (though its original name was Westfälischer Porsche Club Hohensyburg). The first international Porsche Club outside of Germany was established in Belgium in 1953; the Porsche Club of America, today the largest Porsche Club in the world, was born in 1955. Around the globe, roughly five new clubs are set up every year. These are autonomous, independent, registered associations or comparable legal forms and are organised jointly and on a voluntary basis by their members. Each club therefore offers a unique programme and range of services – from drives and motorsport events to social gatherings and technical lectures on vehicles and e-mobility to 'Concours d'Élégance' and multi-day Porsche parades. The vehicles of the club members range from classic cars to the current Porsche model range. Even the purely electric Taycan is increasingly being seen at club events. Classic Clubs around the world are particularly dedicated to the preservation and maintenance of historic Porsche cars.

The vehicles of the club members range from classic cars to the current Porsche model range

The venerable global ecosystem of marque-specific clubs is unparalleled in the automotive industry

DIE BEEINDRUCKENDE BILANZ DES STÄRKSTEN BOXERS IM LANGSTRECKEN-RING

THE IMPRESSIVE RÉSUMÉ OF THE STRONGEST BOXER IN THE ENDURANCE RING

Development of the new Porsche 911 RSR: Roll-out at Weissach 2019

Michael Christensen, Laurens Vanthoor, Kévin Estre – Le Mans 2018

Porsche Team Manthey – Bahrain 2015

Marc Lieb, Richard Lietz, Romain Dumas – Le Mans 2013

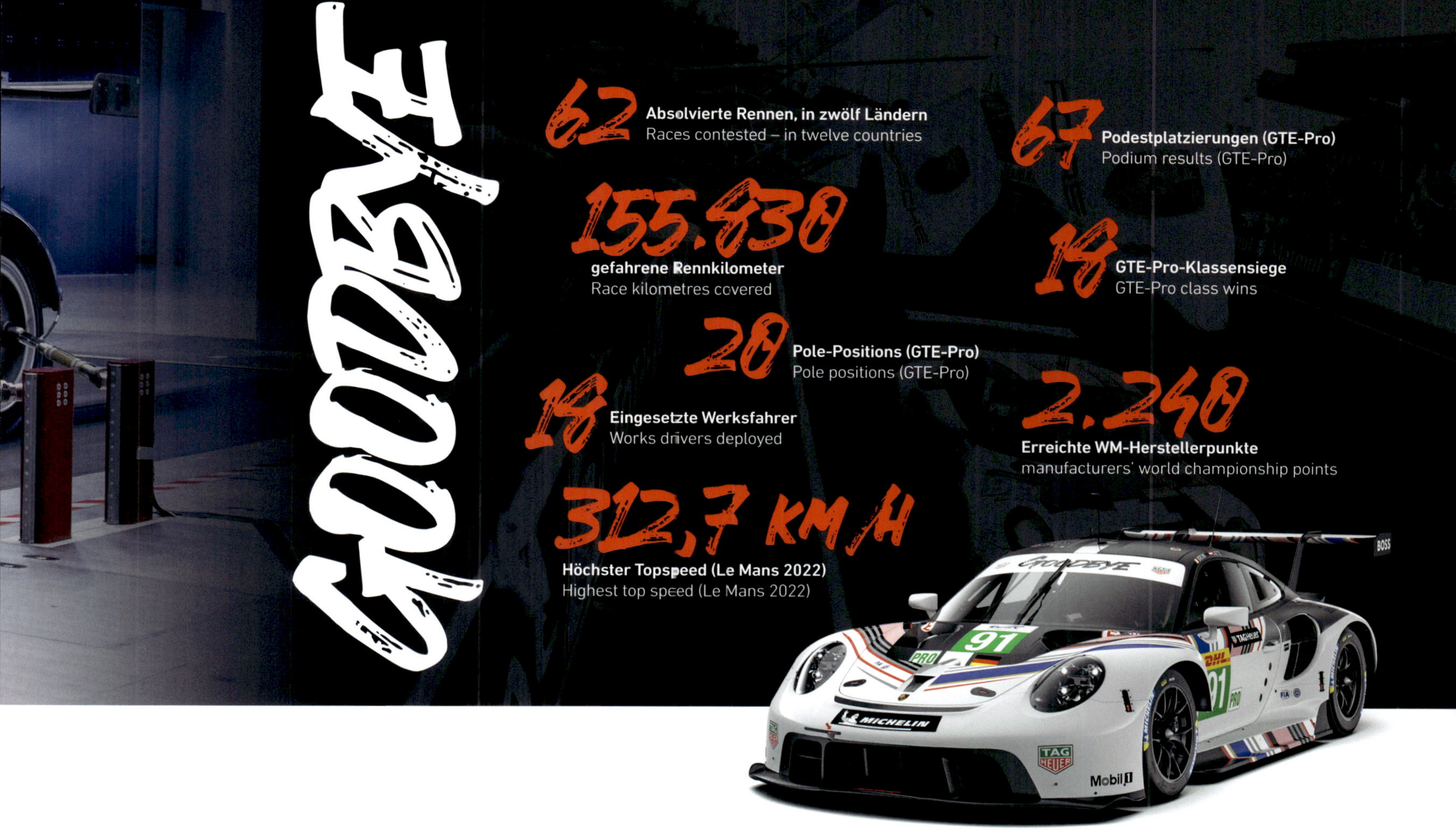

Nach 18 Renntriumphen, fünf Weltmeistertiteln und drei Klassensiegen bei den 24 Stunden von Le Mans hat Porsche sein Werks-Engagement mit dem 911 RSR in der FIA Langstrecken-Weltmeisterschaft WEC beendet.

Der stärkste Motorsport-Boxer aus dem Entwicklungszentrum in Weissach hat die zurückliegenden zehn Jahre in der hart umkämpften GTE-Pro-Klasse deutlich geprägt. In der Saison 2013 übernahm die Porsche AG 51 Prozent am Einsatzteam Manthey. Die bewährte Mannschaft aus der Eifel wurde fortan mit der Durchführung des Werkseinsatzes in der FIA Langstrecken-Weltmeisterschaft WEC (World Endurance Championship) betraut. Diese neue Konstellation führte 2013 sofort zum Erfolg: dem Klassensieg bei den 24 Stunden von Le Mans.

Der 911 RSR von 2013 basierte auf der Generation 991 und war der letzte seiner Art mit dem klassischen Sechszylinder-Boxer als Heckmotor. 2014 fuhr der Neunelfer in Silverstone und Schanghai zum Klassensieg. Im Folgejahr gelang ein weiterer großer Schritt nach vorn: Vier Triumphe in der GTE-Pro-Kategorie auf dem Nürburgring, in Austin, Schanghai und Bahrain sowie die Titelgewinne in Hersteller-, Fahrer- und Teamwertung. 2016 starteten die zwei Werksautos nur in Le Mans. Für die anschließende Saison folgte der neue GTE-Pro-Renner aus Weissach – diesmal und erstmals mit dem Antriebsaggregat vor der Hinterachse. Das neue Konzept, bei Fans weltweit wegen seines unvergleichlich beißenden Sounds sehr beliebt, erreichte große Erfolge auf vielen Rennstrecken beiderseits des Atlantiks.

2017 – 2019: Neues Fahrzeugkonzept und ein unvergesslicher Le Mans-Auftritt

2017 galt als Entwicklungsjahr, denn angesichts der veränderten Gewichtsverteilung sammelte die Mannschaft vor allem im Bereich der Reifennutzung viele neue Erkenntnisse. Der Lernprozess verlief schnell. Bereits im zweiten Einsatzjahr lieferte das FIA WEC-Werksteam in Le Mans einen sportlich wie optisch besonderen Auftritt ab: Zum 70. Geburtstag der Marke Porsche traten die beiden 911 RSR in historischen Designs an. Die in Anlehnung an die legendäre Rothmans-Lackierung folierte Startnummer 91 dominierte das Qualifying. Der italienische Werksfahrer Ginamaria Bruni stellte in der Zeitenjagd in 3:47,504 Minuten einen neuen Rekord für GTE-Fahrzeuge in Le Mans auf.

After notching up 18 race wins, five world champion titles and three class victories at the 24 Hours of Le Mans, Porsche has wrapped up its factory involvement with the 911 RSR in the FIA World Endurance Championship WEC.

Over the last decade, the most powerful racing boxer from the development centre in Weissach has left an indelible mark in the notoriously competitive GTE-Pro class. In the 2013 season, Porsche AG acquired 51 percent of the Manthey operations team. The experienced squad from Germany's Eifel region was then entrusted with running the factory engagement in the FIA World Endurance Championship WEC. This new constellation immediately brought success, with the class victory at the 2013 Le Mans 24 Hours.

Based on the 991 generation, the 911 RSR from 2013 was the last of its kind to feature the classic flat-six engine in the rear. In 2014, the nine-eleven clinched class wins at Silverstone and Shanghai. A year later, another major step was taken: four victories in the GTE-Pro class at the Nürburgring, in Austin, Shanghai and Bahrain as well as the manufacturer, driver and team championship titles. In 2016, the two works cars only contested Le Mans. The following season saw the arrival of the new GTE-Pro racer from Weissach – this time with the power unit mounted in front of the rear axle for the first time. Attracting admiration from fans around the world for its incomparably brawny sound, the new concept proved extremely successful on many racetracks on both sides of the Atlantic.

2017 – 2019: New vehicle concept and an unforgettable Le Mans performance

In view of the changed weight distribution – which gave the team a wealth of new insights, especially in terms of tyre use – 2017 was considered a development year. The learning process went fast. In just the second year of competition, the FIA WEC works team made a spectacular appearance at Le Mans – in terms of performance and design. On the occasion of the Porsche brand's 70th anniversary, the two 911 RSR featured a historic look. The No. 91 car, decked out in the style of the legendary Rothmans livery, dominated the qualifying. The Italian works driver Gianmaria Bruni set a new record for GTE vehicles at Le Mans with a lap time of 3:47.504 minutes.

2018 – 2022: Gewinn von WM-Titeln und ein weiterer Klassensieg in Le Mans

Während der Neunelfer der Generation 2017 nach dem Klassensieg in Le Mans zum GTE-Pro-Meistertitel in FIA WEC 2018/2019 fuhr, stand der Nachfolger bereits in den Startlöchern: der RSR-19 mit 4,2-Liter-Sechszylinder – dem größten Boxer, den Porsche bis dato werksseitig in einem 911-Rennfahrzeug auf die Strecke gebracht hat. Beim Debüt an der Sarthe 2019 fehlte nicht viel: Die Startnummern 91 und 93 erreichten auf den Rängen zwei und drei das Siegerpodest der hart umkämpften GTE-Pro-Klasse mit insgesamt 17 Autos von sechs verschiedenen Herstellern. 2021 folgte eine weitere Podiumsplatzierung und 2022 endlich der ersehnte Erfolg an der Sarthe. Richard Lietz, Gianmaria Bruni und Lokalmatador Frédéric Makowiecki setzten im Abschiedsjahr des Werks-Elfers noch einmal ein Glanzlicht: Klassensieg bei den 24 Stunden von Le Mans. Die letzte Saison mit den Werksfahrzeugen in der GTE-Pro-Klasse sollte noch einmal mit dem Gewinn von WM-Titeln gekrönt werden, doch beim Finale in Bahrain verpasste das Team das hoch gesteckte Ziel nur knapp.

2018 - 2022: World Championship titles and another class victory at Le Mans

While the 2017-generation 911 went on to secure the GTE-Pro championship title in the 2018-2019 FIA WEC after winning its class at Le Mans, the successor was already waiting in the wings: the RSR-19 powered by a 4.2-litre six-cylinder engine – the largest boxer that Porsche had ever planted in a works-911 racer at that stage. Its debut at the Sarthe in 2019 had it all: In a class with 17 cars from six different manufacturers, the No. 91 and 93 cars achieved podium results with second and third place in the hotly contested GTE-Pro category. Another podium finish followed in 2021, with 2022 yielding the long-awaited success at the Sarthe. Richard Lietz, Gianmaria Bruni and local hero Frédéric Makowiecki added another highlight in the final year of the factory-911, winning their class at the 24 Hours of Le Mans. The intention for the last season with the factory-run cars in the GTE-Pro class was to claim the world championship titles however the team narrowly missed out on this ambitious achievement at the finale in Bahrain.

Porsche GT Team - Bahrain 2022

Gianmaria Bruni, Richard Lietz, Frédéric Makowiecki - Le Mans 2020

Porsche GT Team - Le Mans 2018

WELTWEITER EINSATZ FÜR PORSCHE PENSKE MOTORSPORT MIT DEM NEUEN 963

GLOBAL QUEST FOR PORSCHE PENSKE MOTORSPORT WITH THE NEW 963

Das Team Porsche Penske Motorsport schickt den neuen Porsche 963 in den Kampf, um Gesamtsiege bei den weltweit größten Langstrecken-Rennen. Je zwei der Hybrid-Prototypen nach LMDh-Reglement werden ab 2023 in der FIA Langstrecken-Weltmeisterschaft WEC und der IMSA WeatherTech SportsCar Championship starten.

The Porsche Penske Motorsport team sends the new Porsche 963 to hunt for overall victories in the world's greatest endurance races. From 2023, two of the hybrid LMDh-spec prototypes will be fielded in both the FIA World Endurance Championship and the IMSA WeatherTech SportsCar Championship.

PORSCHE 963

Das am 24. Juni im britischen Goodwood präsentierte Rennfahrzeug trägt die typischen Farben von Porsche im Motorsport: Weiß, Rot und Schwarz. In den Cockpits der 500 kW (680 PS) starken Boliden wechseln sich erfahrene Prototypen-Champions mit bewährten Piloten aus dem Porsche-Werksfahrerkader ab. Porsche Penske Motorsport bereitet die Einsätze an zwei Standorten vor: Die Dependance in Mannheim (Deutschland) zeichnet für die FIA WEC verantwortlich, im US-amerikanischen Mooresville (North Carolina) werden die Fahrzeuge für die IMSA präpariert.

„Nach 7.889 Testkilometern in der ersten Jahreshälfte 2022 sehen wir uns auf einem sehr guten Weg, allerdings gibt es bis zum Start der kommenden Saison auch noch einige Arbeiten zu erledigen", betont Thomas Laudenbach, Leiter Motorsport. „Unser neuer Porsche 963 soll an die großen Erfolge legendärer Modelle wie 917, 935, 956, 962 oder 919 Hybrid anknüpfen. Ich bin sicher, dass wir im technischen Bereich bestens aufgestellt sein werden und auch auf Teamseite entsprechende Strukturen geschaffen haben, um im spannenden Wettbewerb zahlreicher Hersteller und verschiedener Konzepte siegfähig zu sein."

The racing vehicle that was unveiled on June 24th at Goodwood in England flies the typical Porsche motor racing colours: white, red and black. In the cockpits of the 500 kW (680 HP) racers, experienced and championship winning prototype drivers are paired with seasoned specialists from Porsche's works driver squad. Porsche Penske Motorsport prepares for these missions at two locations: The branch in Mannheim (Germany) is responsible for the FIA World Endurance Championship, with the IMSA WeatherTech SportsCar Championship vehicles being prepared in Mooresville, North Carolina, USA.

"After 7,889 test kilometres during the first half of 2022, we're on a very good path but there is still work to be done before the start of next season," outlines Thomas Laudenbach, Head of Porsche Motorsport. "Our new Porsche 963 should continue the legacy of legendary models such as the 917, 935, 956, 962 and the 919 Hybrid. I'm positive that we'll be well-positioned when it comes to technology and we've also created the relevant team structures to set us up for wins in the thrilling competition between many manufacturers and different concepts."

»Unser neuer Porsche 963 soll an die großen Erfolge legendärer Modelle wie 917, 935, 956, 962 oder 919 Hybrid anknüpfen.«

»Our new Porsche 963 should continue the legacy of legendary models such as the 917, 935, 956, 962 and the 919 Hybrid.«

Thomas Laudenbach, Leiter Porsche Motorsport

Das offizielle Renndebüt des Porsche 963 soll im Januar 2023 bei den 24 Stunden von Daytona in den USA stattfinden.
„Die Mitarbeiter von Porsche Motorsport und dem Team Penske sind in den vergangenen Monaten zu einer optimal funktionierenden und eingeschworenen Mannschaft, dem Porsche Penske Motorsport Team zusammengewachsen", freut sich Urs Kuratle, Leiter Werksmotorsport LMDh. „Wir werden starke Fahrerpaarungen in den insgesamt vier Werksautos haben. In der Zusammenarbeit mit unserem langjährigen Reifenpartner Michelin und dem Chassishersteller Multimatic machen wir große Fortschritte. Wir können den ersten Einsatz kaum noch erwarten."

Für die Rennen in der Langstrecken-WM FIA WEC und der IMSA WeatherTech SportsCar Championship stehen bereits jetzt die routinierten Werksfahrer Kévin Estre, Michael Christensen, André Lotterer, Laurens Vanthoor, Matt Campbell, Mathieu Jaminet sowie die beiden erfahrenen Sportwagen-Piloten Dane Cameron und Felipe Nasr fest. Während der frühen Entwicklungsphase spielte Frédéric Makowiecki eine zentrale Rolle. Der Franzose fuhr im Januar beim Roll-out in Weissach die allerersten Meter im Porsche 963 und absolvierte ebenso die ersten Runden im Simulator. Zukünftig ergänzen weitere erfahrene Piloten die Cockpitbesetzungen bei den Langstrecken-Rennen in Daytona, Sebring und Petit Le Mans.

Porsche Penske Motorsport bereitet die jeweils zwei 963 für die beiden weltweit größten Sportwagen-Rennserien an den Standorten Mooresville im US-Bundesstaat North Carolina und in Mannheim vor. Die WEC-Basis in Baden-Württemberg ist in einem ehemaligen Porsche Zentrum von Penske Automotive nach modernsten Maßstäben errichtet worden. Eine leistungsstarke Datenleitung verbindet die Teambasen in Mooresville und Mannheim mit dem Entwicklungszentrum von Porsche in Weissach. Der Datenaustausch zwischen den drei Hightech-Zentren von Porsche Penske Motorsport findet nahezu in Echtzeit statt.

The official race debut of the Porsche 963 is planned to take place in January 2023 at the 24 Hours of Daytona in the USA.
"Over the past few months, our people at Porsche Motorsport and Team Penske have grown into an efficient and committed squad – the Porsche Penske Motorsport Team," acclaims Urs Kuratle, Director Factory Racing LMDh. "We'll have powerful driver crews in the four factory cars. The collaboration with our long-standing tyre partner Michelin and the chassis manufacturer Multimatic works flawlessly. We can hardly wait for our first outing."

The drivers selected for the races in the World Endurance Championship and the IMSA WeatherTech SportsCar Championship include the experienced works drivers Kévin Estre, Michael Christensen, André Lotterer, Laurens Vanthoor, Matt Campbell, Mathieu Jaminet as well as the accomplished sportscar drivers Dane Cameron and Felipe Nasr. In the initial development phase, Frédéric Makowiecki played a key role: during the rollout at Weissach in January, the Frenchman drove the first metres in the Porsche 963 and also turned the first laps in the simulator. Other driver announcements, including those for the endurance races at Daytona, Sebring and Petit Le Mans, will be made at a later date.

Porsche Penske Motorsport prepares a total of four 963 for the world's most important sports car races at its bases in Mooresville and Mannheim. The WEC facility in Germany's Baden-Württemberg is a former Porsche Centre of Penske Automotive, built to state-of-the-art standards. The exchange of data between the three high-tech centres of Porsche Penske Motorsport occurs almost in real-time.

Ansys
PENSKE

PENSKE
PENSKE
Ansys
TAG HEUER
PORSCHE
TAGHeuer
TAGHeuer
Mobil 1
Mobil 1
Ansys
Ansys
PORSCHE

Die beiden Porsche 963 von Porsche Penske Motorsport gehen mit den Startnummern 6 und 7 in die Saison 2023 der IMSA WeatherTech SportsCar Championship. Diese Ziffern sind den Partnern, Team Penske und Porsche aus dem gemeinsamen Engagement mit dem RS Spyder bestens bekannt. Damit sind auch viele gute Erinnerungen verbunden.

Als Managing Director von Porsche Penske Motorsport fungiert Jonathan Diuguid. „Die Erwartungen sind enorm hoch", weiß der Amerikaner. „Nicht nur von der Öffentlichkeit, sondern auch von Porsche und Penske, die zusammen in der Vergangenheit großartige Geschichten im Motorsport geschrieben haben." Diuguid und Travis Law (Competition Director) leiten das globale Team Porsche Penske Motorsport und führen das Management sowohl in der Langstrecken-WM als auch in der IMSA-Serie. Das Team in der FIA WEC wird von Bernhard Demmer (General Manager) und Francis Schammo (Teammanager) geleitet, in der IMSA WeatherTech SportsCar Championship in Nordamerika zeichnet Joel Svensson (Teammanager) verantwortlich.

The two Porsche 963 from Porsche Penske Motorsport will tackle the 2023 IMSA WeatherTech SportsCar Championship flying the race numbers 6 and 7. These digits are well known to the partners, Team Penske and Porsche, from their joint effort with the RS Spyder – and are associated with many great memories for both world-class companies.

Jonathan Diuguid is the Managing Director of Porsche Penske Motorsport: "Expectations are extremely high," acknowledges the American. "Not only from the public but also from Porsche and Team Penske, who have written great motorsport chapters together in the past." Diuguid and Travis Law (Competition Director) will guide the global Porsche Penske Motorsport Team, with direct oversight and management of both the FIA WEC and IMSA programs. Daily operations of the FIA WEC team will be led by Bernhard Demmer (General Manager) and Francis Schammo (Team Manager). Joel Svensson (Team Manager) will be responsible in the IMSA championship in North America.

Der Porsche 963 basiert – wie vom LMDh-Reglement vorgegeben – auf einem Chassis der LMP2-Kategorie. Bei der neu entwickelten Fahrzeugbasis arbeitet Porsche mit dem kanadischen Hightech-Unternehmen Multimatic zusammen. Die Hybrid-Standardkomponenten steuern Bosch, Williams Advanced Engineering und Xtrac bei. Das Herz des Antriebs bildet ein 4,6 Liter großer V8-Biturbo. Die Grundlagen des Motors stammen aus dem Hochleistungs-Hybrid-Sportwagen 918 Spyder. Seine DNA reicht bis zum Rennwagen RS Spyder zurück, mit dem Porsche und das Team Penske von 2005 bis 2008 unzählige Erfolge feierten. Das Design des neuen Porsche 963 orientiert sich an den siegreichen Klassikern 956 und 962 aus den 1980er-Jahren. Am Heck bildet ein durchgehendes Leuchtband das markante Highlight der aktu-

In compliance with the LMDh regulations, the Porsche 963 is based on an LMP2-category chassis. This newly developed vehicle chassis is supplied by the Canadian high-tech company Multimatic. Bosch, Williams Advanced Engineering and Xtrac contribute the standard hybrid components. At the heart of the powertrain lies a 4.6-litre V8 Biturbo. The engine is based on the high-performance 918 Spyder hybrid sports car. Its DNA goes back to the RS Spyder racing car, with which Porsche and Team Penske notched up countless victories between 2005 and 2008. The design of the new Porsche 963 hails from the victorious 956 and 962 classics from the 1980s. A continuous strip of lighting at the rear echoes the distinctive feature of the latest 992-generation 911. The white-red-black vehicle design is a salute to Porsche's

ERSTE TESTFAHRTEN AUF INTERNATIONALER RENNSTRECKE ERFOLGREICH ABGESCHLOSSEN

FIRST TESTS ON AN INTERNATIONAL RACETRACK SUCCESSFULLY COMPLETED

Der neue LMDh-Prototyp von Porsche Penske Motorsport hat seine Feuertaufe auf internationalem Parkett bestanden. Auf dem Circuit de Catalunya nahe der spanischen Metropole Barcelona absolvierte das Fahrzeug in den vergangenen Tagen mehr als 2.000 Kilometer. Im Zentrum der Probefahrten standen die Abstimmung der Systeme, die Entwicklung von Reifen sowie die Optimierung des Zusammenspiels von V8-Turbomotor und den vom Reglement vorgeschriebenen Hybridelementen. Beim mehrtägigen Test saßen unter anderem die neuen Porsche-Werksfahrer Felipe Nasr und Dane Cameron hinter dem Steuer des rund 500 kW (680 PS) starken Boliden.

„Die erfolgreichen Testfahrten in Barcelona waren ein enorm wichtiger Schritt", fasst Thomas Laudenbach zusammen. Der Leiter Porsche Motorsport ergänzt: „Bei unseren ersten Runden auf dem Testgelände in Weissach galt es, die grundsätzliche Funktionalität des LMDh-Prototypen sicherzustellen. In Spanien zeigte sich die gesamte Bandbreite der Entwicklung: Dauerläufe, Setup-Arbeit und – ganz besonders wichtig – die Optimierung des Zusammenspiels aller Partner in diesem Projekt. Wie schnell sich die Mitarbeiter von Porsche, Penske, Michelin, Multimatic und anderen bei der Arbeit an der Teststrecke zusammengefunden haben, ist für mich höchst beeindruckend. Vielen Dank an alle, die ihren Teil dazu beigetragen haben."

The new LMDh prototype from Porsche Penske Motorsport has passed its first test on an international stage with flying colours. On the Circuit de Catalunya close to the Spanish metropolis of Barcelona, the vehicle covered more than 2,000 kilometres over the last few days. The focus of the test runs was to set up the systems, develop the tyres and optimise the interaction between the V8 Turbo engine and the hybrid elements as prescribed by the regulations. Over several days of testing, the new Porsche works drivers Felipe Nasr and Dane Cameron were among those who drove the ca. 500 kW (680 HP) car.

"The successful tests in Barcelona were an enormously important step," recaps Thomas Laudenbach, with the Head of Porsche Motorsport adding: "During our first laps on our test track in Weissach, it was critical to ensure that the basic functions of the LMDh prototype worked. In Spain, we saw the entire scope of development: endurance runs, setup work and, very importantly, the optimisation of the interaction between all partners involved in this project. I found it very impressive how quickly the employees from Porsche, Penske, Michelin, Multimatic and others came together as a unit. I'd like to thank everyone for the part they played."

Barcelona

Felipe Nasr

»Wir haben den ersten Test auf einer ‚echten' Rennstrecke absolviert und konnten die bisherige Laufleistung des neuen Porsche LMDh mit über 2.000 Kilometern mehr als verdoppeln«

»We completed the first tests on a 'real' racetrack and managed to more than double the previous mileage of the new Porsche LMDh to over 2,000 kilometres«

Urs Kuratle, Director Factory Racing LMDh

Urs Kuratle

Roger Penske

Jonathan Diuguid,
Managing Director Porsche Penske Motorsport

„Wir haben den ersten Test auf einer ‚echten' Rennstrecke absolviert und konnten die bisherige Laufleistung des neuen Porsche LMDh mit über 2.000 Kilometern mehr als verdoppeln", sagt Urs Kuratle, Leiter Werksmotorsport LMDh. „Dies zeigt, dass wir die Zeit nach den zuvor geplanten, aber abgesagten Tests sehr gut für eine intensive Vorbereitung genutzt haben. Inklusive unserer Partner waren wir mit mehr als 70 Menschen vor Ort. Das war auch organisatorisch eine Herausforderung. Wir haben mit dem Auto, aber auch in der operativen Zusammenarbeit und bei den Abläufen innerhalb von Porsche Penske Motorsport riesengroße Fortschritte erzielt. Bis wir dort sind, wo wir hinmüssen, ist es aber noch ein weiter Weg."

„Wir haben während des Tests von Tag zu Tag große Fortschritte erzielt. Die Rückmeldung der Fahrer gegenüber den Ingenieuren und des gesamten Teams war durchweg positiv", bilanziert Jonathan Diuguid, Leiter Porsche Penske Motorsport.

"We completed the first tests on a 'real' racetrack and managed to more than double the previous mileage of the new Porsche LMDh to over 2,000 kilometres," says Urs Kuratle, Director Factory Racing LMDh. "This shows that we used the time after the planned but cancelled tests very well for this intensive preparation. Including our partners, more than 70 people were at the track. From an organisation viewpoint, that was another challenge. We've made major progress not only with the car but with the operational cooperation and processes within Porsche Penske Motorsport. But we still have a long way to go before we're where we want to be."

"We made great progress from day to day during these tests. The feedback from the drivers, the engineers and the team was consistently positive," sums up Jonathan Diuguid, Managing Director Porsche Penske Motorsport.

Goodwood Festival of Speed

DIE JÜNGSTE GENERATION DES PORSCHE 911 GT3 R FEIERT PREMIERE

DEBUT FOR THE LATEST GENERATION OF THE PORSCHE 911 GT3 R

Der neue Porsche 911 GT3 R war bei den diesjährigen 24 Stunden von Spa-Francorchamps erstmals zu sehen. Porsche-Kundenteams können den Rennwagen ab der Saison 2023 bei Motorsportevents nach GT3-Reglement weltweit einsetzen. Er basiert auf der aktuellen Elfer-Generation 992. Gegenüber dem Vorgängermodell zeichnet sich der neue 911 GT3 R durch einen größeren Motor mit bis zu 416 kW (565 PS), eine konstantere Aerodynamik-Performance und eine optimierte Fahrzeug-Balance aus.

Porsche stellt mit der jüngsten Generation des 911 GT3 R einen neuen Kundensport-Rennwagen vor. Der Herausforderer für den weltweiten Einsatz in GT3-Serien basiert auf der aktuellen Generation 992 und kann mit Beginn der Saison 2023 durchstarten. Die Entwicklung begann bereits 2019. Das Hauptaugenmerk lag auf einer verbesserten Fahrbarkeit für Profis und sogenannte Gentleman-Fahrer, sowie größeren Leistungsreserven je nach Einstufung durch die „Balance of Performance" (BoP). Auch eine vereinfachte Handhabung des Rennwagens für die Teams und optimierte Laufzeitkosten standen im Mittelpunkt. Porsche Motorsport bietet den neuen 911 GT3 R ab sofort zum Preis von 511.000 Euro zuzüglich länderspezifischer Mehrwertsteuer und Optionen an.

„Der neue 911 GT3 R tritt in große Fußstapfen", sagt Michael Dreiser, Leiter Vertrieb bei Porsche Motorsport. „Sein Vorgänger hat seit 2019 in vier Saisons so gut wie alles gewonnen, was es in der GT3-Szene zu gewinnen gab. Zu seinen Erfolgen zählen Gesamtsiege bei den 24-Stunden-Rennen auf dem Nürburgring und auch in Spa-Francorchamps. Bei den 24 Stunden von Daytona und den 12-Stunden-Sebring haben unsere Kunden Klassensiege eingefahren. Das neue Modell blickt einem noch umfangreicherem Arbeitsspektrum in den Händen unserer Kundenteams entgegen."

The new Porsche 911 GT3 R was unveiled to the public at this year's 24 Hours of Spa-Francorchamps. From the 2023 season, Porsche customer teams can campaign the new racing vehicle in worldwide motorsport events that adhere to the GT3 regulations. The vehicle is based on the latest 992-generation 911. Compared to its predecessor, the new 911 GT3 R features a larger engine producing up to 416 kW (565 HP), a more constant aerodynamic performance and an optimised vehicle balance.

With the latest generation of the 911 GT3 R, Porsche unveils a new customer racing car. The new challenger for GT3 series around the world is based on the current 992 generation and will be ready to race at the beginning of the 2023 season. Development began in 2019. Priority was given to further improving the driveability for professionals and so-called gentleman drivers, as well as tapping larger performance reserves for different Balance of Performance (BoP) classifications. Another focus was streamlining the handling of the race car for the teams and reducing the running costs. Porsche Motorsport now offers the new 911 GT3 R at a price of 511,000 Euros plus country-specific VAT and optional extras.

"The new 911 GT3 R has big shoes to fill," says Michael Dreiser, Sales Director at Porsche Motorsport. "Its forerunner has won almost everything there is to win in the GT3 scene in the four seasons since 2019. Its stand-out successes include overall victories at the 24-hour races at the Nürburgring and also at Spa-Francorchamps. Raced by our customers, the predecessor scored class victories at the 24 Hours of Daytona and the 12 Hours of Sebring. The new model faces a massive workload in the hands of the Porsche customer racing teams."

Nach der Ausschreibung der GT3 Klasse in der nordamerikanischen IMSA Serie auch als Profi-Kategorie, zieht die FIA Langstrecken-Weltmeisterschaft WEC nach: Ab 2024 dürfen GT3-Rennwagen wie der neue 911 GT3 R erstmals bei den 24 Stunden von Le Mans an den Start gehen.

„Mit dem extrem erfolgreichen Vorgängermodell haben wir einen Volltreffer gelandet. Entsprechend hoch liegt nun die Messlatte für den Nachfolger", betont Sebastian Golz, Projektleiter 911 GT3 R bei Porsche Motorsport. „Dabei bestand unsere Aufgabe weniger darin, den neuen 911 GT3 R noch schneller zu machen – die Einstufung im Performance-Fenster durch die BoP gleicht diesen Vorteil schnell wieder aus. Für uns ging es in erster Linie darum, dass unsere Kunden mit dem Rennwagen länger schnell fahren können. Konstanz ist gefragt. Darum haben wir uns vor allem auf eine verbesserte Fahrbarkeit konzentriert. Dies zeigt sich jetzt in einem breiter nutzbaren Drehzahlband des neuen 4,2-Liter-Motors, einer stabileren und konstanteren Aerodynamik und entlasteten Hinterreifen, die ihr Potenzial auf diese Weise gleichmäßiger abrufen können."

Zu den Kernstücken des neuen Rennfahrzeugs zählt der seriennahe, auf der 911-Generation 992 basierende Motor. Wie beim Vorgängermodell handelt es sich um einen wassergekühlten Sechszylinder-Boxer mit Vierventil-Technologie und Benzindirekteinspritzung. Neu ist vor allem der Hubraum: Analog zum 911 RSR legte der neue 911 GT3 R von 3.997 um gut fünf Prozent auf 4.194 cm³ zu. Hierdurch ist die Spitzenleistung des Motors auf rund 416 kW (565 PS) gestiegen. In erster Linie hat Porsche aber den Drehmoment- und Leistungsverlauf über das gesamte Drehzahlband optimiert. Damit kommt der neue 4,2-Liter-Sechszylinder speziell Gentleman-Fahrern entgegen.

Der Hochdrehzahl-Sechszylinder kommt weiterhin ohne Turboaufladung zurecht und sitzt klassisch im Heck, wo er sich positiv auf Traktion und Bremsverhalten auswirkt. Er wurde um 5,5 Grad nach vorne geneigt, um mehr Freiheiten für den Unterflurdiffusor zu schaffen. Nebenaggregate, wie der Generator und der Klimakompressor, rückten gut einen Meter weiter nach vorn und tiefer in einen Freiraum vor Motor

After the GT3 class was announced as a professional category in the North American IMSA series, the FIA WEC World Endurance Championship follows suit: From 2024, GT3 racing cars such as the new 911 GT3 R will be eligible to take part in the 24 Hours of Le Mans for the first time.

"We hit the bull's eye with the enormously successful predecessor. Accordingly, the bar for its successor is high," emphasises Sebastian Golz, 911 GT3 R Project Manager at Porsche Motorsport. "Our task was less about making the new 911 GT3 R even faster – the classification within performance windows set by the BoP quickly cancels out this advantage. For us, it was primarily about our customers being able to drive the racing car fast for longer. This requires durability and that's why we focused predominantly on improved driveability. This is reflected in the new 4.2-litre engine's broader usable rev band, more stable and constant aerodynamics and lower loads on the rear tyres, which allow their potential to last longer."

At the core of the new racing car is the near-standard engine based on the 992-generation 911 power plant. Like in the previous model, it is a water-cooled flat-six engine with four-valve technology and direct fuel injection. The main new development is the displacement: like the 911 RSR, the capacity of the new 911 GT3 R has increased by a good five per cent from 3,997 to 4,194 cc. This has boosted the engine's peak output to around 416 kW (565 HP). First and foremost, however, Porsche has optimised the torque and power curve across the entire rev range. Consequently, the new 4.2-litre six-cylinder is better suited to gentleman drivers.

The high-revving six-cylinder manages without turbocharging and sits in the classic rear position, thus enhancing traction and braking. However, it has been tilted forward by 5.5 degrees, creating more leeway for the underbody diffuser. Auxiliary

und Getriebe. Dies wirkt sich positiv auf die Gewichtsbalance des 911 GT3 R aus. Das sequenzielle Sechsgang-Klauengetriebe ist eine Ableitung vom aktuellen 911 GT3 Cup. Die Lenkradwippen steuern eine elektronische Schaltwalzenaktuatorik, die besonders schnelle und präzise Gangwechsel ermöglicht.

Das vielfach im Detail modifizierte Fahrwerk des neuen 911 GT3 R unterstützt die Fahrbarkeit, präzisiert das Lenkverhalten, sorgt für einen geringeren Verschleiß der Hinterreifen und verkürzt den Zeitaufwand für Abstimmungsänderungen. Hierfür kamen zahlreiche Komponenten und Lösungen aus dem 911 RSR zum Einsatz. An der Vorderachse übernimmt ein hochmodernes Doppelquerlenker-Layout die Führung der Räder. An der Hinterachse versieht eine Mehrlenkerkonstruktion ihren Dienst. Die weiter verbesserten Rennsport-Stoßdämpfer von KW lassen sich fünffach verstellen. Für Set-up-Modifikationen stehen sogenannte Shims bereit. Diese Zielwertscheiben ermöglichen schnelle Feinjustierungen, ohne dass anschließend das Fahrwerk zeitaufwendig neu vermessen werden muss.

Die optimierte Positionierung zentraler Anlenkpunkte der Vorderachse schafft Raum für das aerodynamische „Race-Underfloor"-Konzept. Wie beim 911 RSR zielt es mit seinem höheren Unterboden auf eine störungsfreiere Anströmung des Heckdiffusors ab und verringert so die Pitch-Sensibilität des Rennwagens – also seine Reaktion auf eine verringerte Bodenfreiheit vorn, wie sie durch das einfedern beim anbremsen auftreten kann. Die Hinterräder wanderten etwas weiter zurück und verlängern den Radstand des 911 GT3 R von 2.459 auf 2.507 Millimeter. Auch dies sorgt dafür, dass weniger Gewicht auf den Hinterreifen lastet, um ihre konstante Performance im Wettbewerb am Ende längerer Stints zu erhalten.

»Mit dem extrem erfolgreichen Vorgängermodell haben wir einen Volltreffer gelandet. Entsprechend hoch liegt nun die Messlatte für den Nachfolger«

»We hit the bull's eye with the enormously successful predecessor. Accordingly, the bar for its successor is high«

Sebastian Golz, 911 GT3 R Project Manager at Porsche Motorsport

Neben den Aluminium-Monoblock-Rennbremssätteln stammen nun auch die Bremsscheiben des neuen 911 GT3 R vom Spezialisten AP. Die vorderen Stahlscheiben sind innenbelüftet und geschlitzt. Bei einem Durchmesser von 390 Millimetern werden sie von sechs Kolben umfasst. Hinten kommen 370-Millimeter-Scheiben und vier Bremskolben zum Einsatz. Eine verfeinerte Software-Applikation für das Renn-ABS der fünften Generation senkt den Reifen- und Bremsenverschleiß. Auch die Traktionskontrolle von Porsche erhielt eine Weiterentwicklung.

Der neue 911 GT3 R ist nach dem 911 GT3 Cup das zweite von Porsche Motorsport entwickelte Rennfahrzeug, das auf der aktuellen Generation 992 aufbaut. Seine Leichtbaukarosserie in intelligenter Aluminium-Stahl-Verbundbauweise basiert dabei auf der Serie, wurde für den Einsatz im 911 GT3 R aber stark modifiziert. Inklusive Front- und Motorhaube, Türen, Seitenteilen, Heckflügel und Dach bestehen nahezu alle Karosseriekomponenten aus leichtem Karbon. Für die Radhäuser kommt Aramid zum Einsatz.

Bei dem neuen 911 GT3 R steht die Funktionalität über allem. Dennoch konnte Grant Larson von Porsche Style erneut besonders schöne und harmonische Formen verwirklichen. Sie betonen das Erbgut des Elfers und vereinen es mit ausgefeilter Effizienz. Dies gilt im Besonderen für die Aerodynamik. Sie verbindet einen höher angesetzten Unterboden im Bereich vor der Vorderachse mit einem erstmals durchgängig vollverkleideten Unterboden und dem Heckdiffusor. Dies verbessert den Abtrieb, ohne den Luftwiderstand nennenswert zu erhöhen. Der Heckflügel erhält eine Schwanenhals-Aufhängung. Sie sorgt für eine ungestörtere Unterströmung und verbessert damit die aerodynamische Wirksamkeit des Bauteils.

units such as the alternator and the air conditioning compressor were moved a good metre forward and further down into a space in front of the engine and gearbox, which has a positive effect on the weight balance of the 911 GT3 R. The sequential six-speed contest-mesh gearbox is derived from the current 911 GT3 Cup. Shift paddles control an electronic shift drum actuator that enables particularly rapid and precise gear changes.

The new 911 GT3 R's suspension – many details of which have been modified – supports driveability, allows more precise steering, ensures less wear on the rear tyres and reduces the time spent on set-up changes. For this, numerous components and technical solutions were taken from the 911 RSR. At the front axle, a state-of-the-art double wishbone layout controls the wheels. The rear axle sports a multi-link design. The KW shock absorbers were further improved and offer five adjustment settings. Set-up modifications are done with so-called shims. These plates enable precision adjustments without the need for the time-consuming re-alignment of the suspension afterwards.

The optimised positioning of the central pivot points at the front axle frees up space for the aerodynamic "race underfloor" concept. Like in the 911 RSR, this elevated underbody allows for a clean flow of air to the rear diffuser and reduces the pitch sensitivity of the racing car – i.e. a high rake under braking. The rear wheels have moved a little further back, which extends the wheelbase from 2,459 to 2,507 millimetres. This also reduces the load on the rear tyres and improves the consistency of the tyres' performance over longer stints.

In addition to the aluminium monobloc racing brake callipers, the brake discs on the new 911 GT3 R are now also supplied by the specialist company AP. The internally vented and slotted front steel discs measure 390 mm in diameter and are activated by six pistons. Fitted at the rear are four-piston callipers and discs measuring 370 mm. A sophisticated software application for the fifth-generation racing ABS reduces wear on the tyres and brakes. Porsche's traction control system also received a further development.

The new 911 GT3 R is just the second racing car from Porsche Motorsport to be based on the current 992-generation 911 after the 911 GT3 Cup. Its lightweight body with an intelligent aluminium-steel composite design draws on the production model, albeit with major modifications for use in the 911 GT3 R. Almost all body components are made of lightweight carbon, including the front and rear lids, doors, side panels, rear wing and roof. The wheel arches are made of aramid fibres.

In a vehicle like the new 911 GT3 R, functionality stands at the forefront. Nevertheless, Grant Larson from Style Porsche again succeeded in creating particularly stunning and harmonious shapes. They accentuate the heritage of the nine-eleven and blend it with sophisticated efficiency. Most notably, this is reflected in the aerodynamics. The key points: an elevated underbody at the fore of the front axle, for the first time in conjunction with a smooth undertray, and a rear diffuser. This combination improves downforce without a significant increase in drag. The rear wing now features a swan-neck mount. This ensures a clean airflow under the wing and thus improves the aerodynamic efficiency of the component.

In terms of safety, the new 911 GT3 R follows an uncompromising approach. The seat has moved closer to the centre of the car. This enabled Porsche to optimally adapt the more ergonomic seat position to the improved roll cage and the newly developed FIA side impact protection. Like in the forerunner, the steering wheel and pedals can be adjusted longitudinally to suit the driver. Porsche specialists took another close look at the six-point safety harness: the tongues now slide even faster into the clasp via special ramps – saving about a second during pit stops for driver changes. The steering wheel design also received further upgrades on the previous model. It incorporates elements that have proven themselves in the latest generation 911 GT3 Cup and 911 RSR race cars. The 10.3-inch display, for example, comes from the successful one-make cup racer, with the multi-switch concept adopted from the Le Mans class winner.

The high-performance LED headlights on the 911 GT3 R rely on so-called collimator technology, which Porsche developed for the new LMDh 963 prototype, among others. This device works like a magnifying glass, only in reverse. It illuminates a particularly large area of the racetrack and is a significant improvement on the predecessor model, which was previously regarded as the class leader.

Auch in puncto Sicherheit folgt der neue 911 GT3 R einem kompromisslosen Ansatz Der Sitz rückte weiter in die Fahrzeugmitte. Hierdurch konnte Porsche die ergonomischere Sitzposition optimal auf den verbesserten Überrollkäfig und den neu entwickelten FIA-Seitenaufprallschutz abstimmen. Die Anpassung an den Fahrer geschieht wie beim Vorgängermodell über die Längsverstellung des Lenkrads und der Pedalerie. Auch den Sechspunkt-Sicherheitsgurt nahmen die Spezialisten von Porsche unter die Lupe: Über spezielle Rampen rutschen seine Zungen nun noch schneller ins eigentliche Schloss – dies kann bei einem Fahrerwechsel rund eine Sekunde an Boxenstopp-Standzeit sparen. Das Lenkradkonzept stellt eine Weiterentwicklung aus dem Vorgängermodell dar. Dabei vereint es auch Elemente, die sich im aktuellen 911 GT3 Cup und dem 911 RSR bewährt haben. Das 10,3 Zoll große Display zum Beispiel stammt aus dem erfolgreichen Markenpokalauto und das Multi-Switch-Konzept aus dem Le Mans-Klassensieger.

Die Hochleistungs-LED-Frontscheinwerfer des 911 GT3 R setzen auf die sogenannte Kollimatoren-Technik, die Porsche unter anderem für den neuen LMDh-Prototypen 963 entwickelt hat. Ihre Funktionsweise ähnelt einem Brennglas, nur im umgedrehten Sinne. Sie sorgt für eine besonders großflächige Ausleuchtung der Strecke vor dem Rennwagen und übertrifft das bisherige Modell, das bislang schon als Klassenprimus galt, nochmal deutlich.

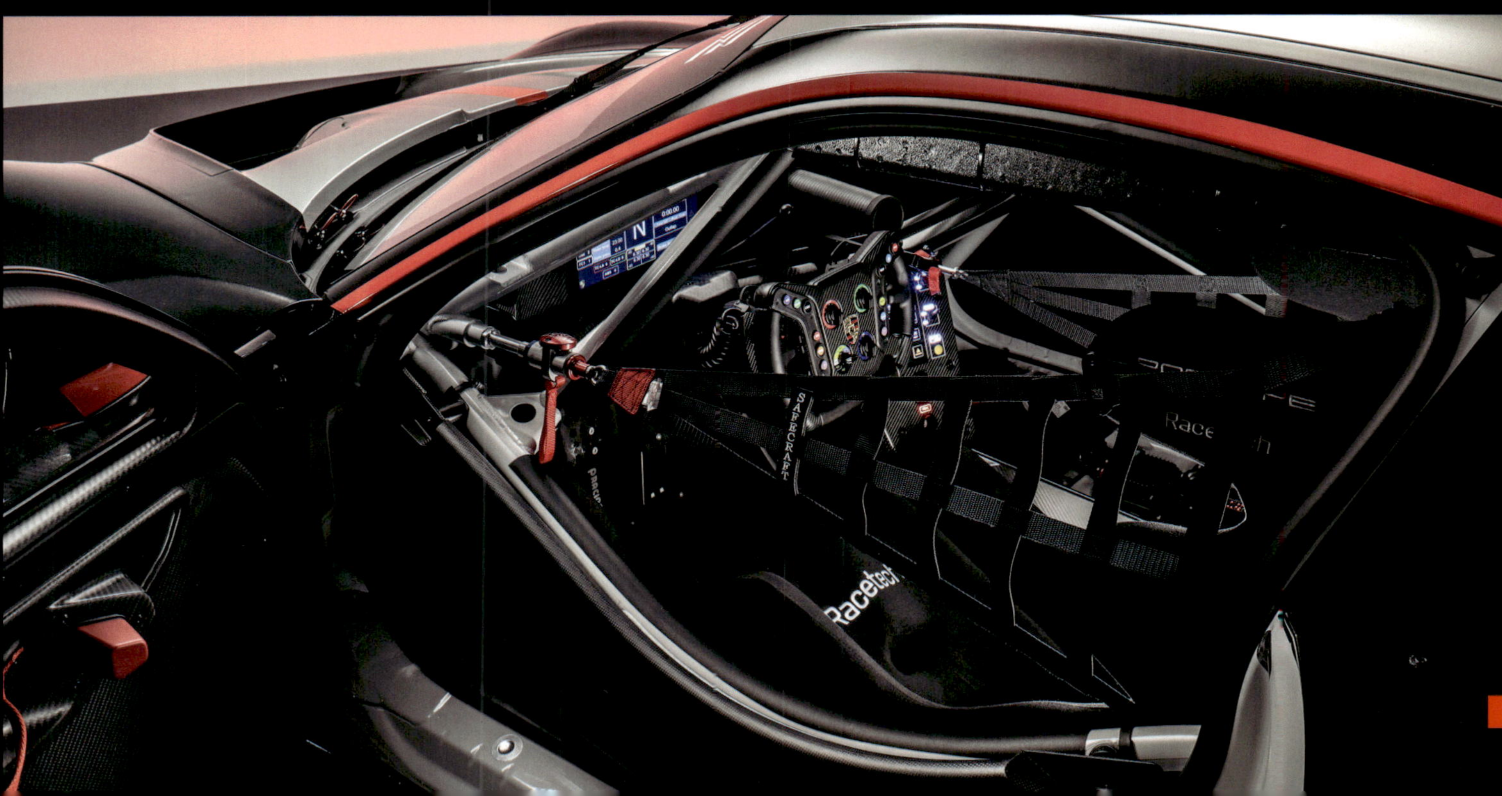

NEUER PORSCHE 911 GT3 R ERPROBT DIE NÜRBURGRING-NORDSCHLEIFE ERFOLGREICH

NEW PORSCHE 911 GT3 R SUCCESSFULLY COMPLETES FIRST RACE AT NÜRBURGRING-NORDSCHLEIFE

Frédéric Makowiecki und Julien Andlauer haben beim ersten Probeeinsatz des neu entwickelten Porsche 911 GT3 R einen Podestplatz erreicht. Die beiden Franzosen fuhren beim siebten Saisonlauf der Nürburgring Langstrecken-Serie auf Rang drei. Der neue 911 GT3 R ist der zweite Rennwagen von Porsche auf Basis der Generation 992.

Die jüngste Generation des Porsche 911 GT3 R hat ihre ersten Rennkilometer problemlos abgespult. Der neue Herausforderer für den weltweiten Einsatz in GT3-Serien ging am Samstag beim siebten Saisonlauf der Nürburgring Langstrecken-Serie (NLS) in der SP-X-Klasse an den Start. Sie ist für Fahrzeuge reserviert, die noch keine Homologation für den Motorsport besitzen. Der bis zu 416 kW (565 PS) starke Heckmotor-Hecktriebler fuhr auf Rennreifen von Michelin auf den dritten Platz der Gesamtwertung. Die schnellste Runde auf der 24,458 Kilometer langen Kombination aus Nordschleife und Kurzanbindung des Grand-Prix-Kurses drehte Frédéric Makowiecki in 7:58,942 Minuten. Der französische Werksfahrer teilte sich den Porsche mit seinem Landsmann Julien Andlauer. Auch bei den letzten beiden NLS-Rennen absolvierten die Teams Falken Motorsport und Dinamic Testeinsätze auf der Nürburgring-Nordschleife, dann auf Falken- und Pirelli-Reifen. Sein offizielles Debüt in den Händen von Kundenteams feiert der neue 911 GT3 R Mitte Januar bei dem 24-Stunden-Rennen auf dem Daytona International Speedway in Florida (USA).

„Zusammengefasst haben wir mit unserem neuen Porsche eine sehr gelungene Rennpremiere erlebt. Ich bin stolz auf jeden, der an diesem Projekt mitgearbeitet hat", fasst Projektleiter Sebastian Golz zusammen. „Die Testrunden auf der Nordschleife und die Rennen zeigen, dass die Basis des Fahrzeugs stimmt. Dank der guten Vorbereitung und Zusammenarbeit mit dem ADAC haben wir eine gute Vorstellung abgeliefert und ein positives Bild mit vielen Daten sammeln können. Mit einer sehr konstanten Performance sind wir auf Rang drei und damit auf einen Podestplatz gefahren, obwohl neue Rennwagen wie unser 911 GT3 R bei Testrennen pro Boxenstopp 30 Sekunden länger stehenbleiben müssen."

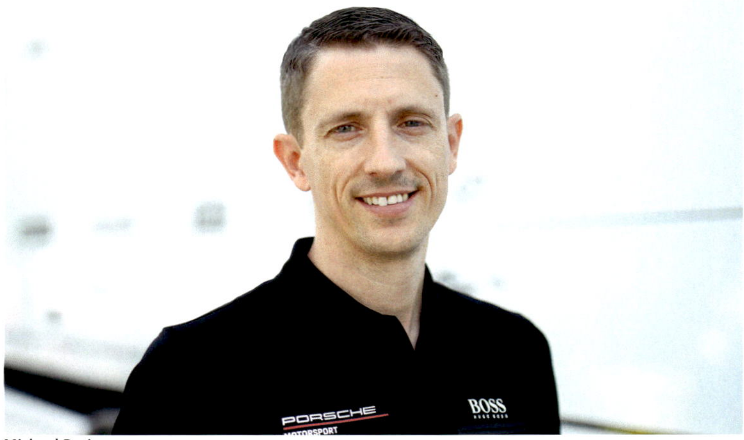

Michael Dreiser

Julien Andlauer, Matteo Cairoli

Frédéric Makowiecki and Julien Andlauer have finished on the podium at the first trial run of the newly developed Porsche 911 GT3 R. The two Frenchmen achieved third place at round seven of the Nürburgring Endurance Series. The new 911 GT3 R is the second racing car from Porsche based on the 992 generation.

The latest generation Porsche 911 GT3 R has clocked up its first race kilometres problem-free. On Saturday, the new challenger for GT3 series around the world tackled round seven of the Nürburgring Endurance Series (NLS) in the SP-X class. This category is reserved for vehicles that have not yet been homologated for motorsport. The ca. 416 kW (565 HP) rear-engine racer shod with Michelin racing tyres finished third in the overall standings. Frédéric Makowiecki turned the fastest lap on the 24.458-kilometre combination of the Nordschleife and the short version of the Grand Prix circuit in 7:58.942 minutes. The French works driver shared the Porsche with his fellow countryman Julien Andlauer. Two more tests were made from Falken Motorsport and Dinamic at the last NLS races of the season, on these occasions with racing tyres from Falken and Pirelli. The new 911 GT3 R will make its official debut in the hands of customer teams at the 24-hour race at the Daytona International Speedway in Florida in mid-January.

"All in all, we experienced a very successful race premiere with our new Porsche. I'm proud of everyone who has worked on this project," said Project Manager Sebastian Golz. "Those test laps on the Nordschleife show that the basis of the vehicle is correct. Thanks to the great preparation and cooperation with the ADAC, we performed well and managed to get a positive picture with loads of data. After a very consistent performance, we finished in third place and secured a podium spot, even though new racing cars like our 911 GT3 R must wait 30 seconds longer per pit stop at test races."

Development of the new 911 GT3 R began in 2019. Priority was given to further improving the driveability for professionals and so-called gentleman drivers, as well as tapping larger performance reserves for different Balance of Performance (BoP) classifications. Another focus was on streamlining the handling of the race car for the teams and reducing the running costs.

Klaus Bachler, Julien Andlauer

Julien Andlauer and Matteo Cairoli

Julien Andlauer, Frédéric Makowiecki

Sebastian Golz

PORSCHE 718 CAYMAN GT4 E-PERFORMANCE DECKT POTENZIAL DES MISSION R AUF

PORSCHE 718 CAYMAN GT4 E-PERFORMANCE REVEALS THE POTENTIAL OF MISSION R

Porsche hat mit dem 718 Cayman GT4 e-Performance die Erprobung der Technologiekomponenten des Mission R gestartet. Die Konzeptstudie hatte auf der IAA MOBILITY 2021 in München die Vision eines vollelektrischen GT-Rennfahrzeugs für den Kunden-Motorsport der Zukunft aufgezeigt.

Inzwischen stellt das innovative Elektro-Antriebskonzept des Mission R seine Leistungsfähigkeit auf nationalen und internationalen Strecken unter Beweis. Als Versuchsträger dient der Porsche 718 Cayman GT4 e-Performance. Wie der Mission R nutzt der allradgetriebene Rennwagen das Chassis des bekannten 718 GT4 Clubsport-Modells. Auch die komplette Elektromotoren- und Batterie-Technologie stammt von der IAA-Konzeptstudie. Dies bedeutet Maximalleistungen im Qualifikations-Modus von 735 kW (1.000 PS) und mehr. Im simulierten Rennbetrieb stehen 450 kW (612 PS) für 30 Minuten dauerhaft bereit – also der Länge eines Carrera Cup-Rennens. In puncto Rundenzeit-Performance und Höchstgeschwindigkeit orientiert sich der 718 Cayman GT4 e-Performance am aktuellen 911 GT3 Cup der Generation 992.

„Mit dem Mission R haben wir gezeigt, wie sich Porsche den nachhaltigen Kunden-Motorsport der Zukunft vorstellen kann. Der 718 Cayman GT4 e-Performance beweist nun, dass diese Vision auf der Rennstrecke funktioniert und auch begeistert", betont Matthias Scholz, Gesamtprojektleiter GT-Rennfahrzeuge. „Wir sind auf die Resonanz sehr gespannt, denn ein Markenpokal mit Elektro-Rennwagen könnte eine wichtige Ergänzung unseres bestehenden Kundensport-Programms bilden."

Porsche has begun testing the technology components of the Mission R with the 718 Cayman GT4 e-Performance. At the 2021 IAA MOBILITY in Munich, the conceptual study outlined the vision of a fully-electric GT racing car for customer motorsport in the future.

Now, the innovative electric drive concept of the Mission R is demonstrating its potential on national and international racetracks. The Porsche 718 Cayman GT4 e-Performance serves as a test vehicle. Like the Mission R, the all-wheel-drive racer uses the chassis of the proven 718 Cayman GT4 Clubsport model. The entire electric motor and battery technology also comes from the IAA conceptual study, which in qualification mode translates to a maximum output of 735 kW (1,000 HP) and more. In simulated racing, a steady 450 kW (612 HP) is available for 30 minutes, i.e. the duration of a Carrera Cup race. In terms of lap times and top speed, the 718 Cayman GT4 e-Performance is on par with the performance of the current 992-generation 911 GT3 Cup.

"With the Mission R, we've shown how Porsche envisages sustainable customer motor racing in the future. The 718 Cayman GT4 e-Performance now demonstrates that this vision works impressively on the racetrack," states Matthias Scholz, GT racing vehicle project manager. "We're very excited about the response because a one-make cup with electric racing cars could be an important addition to our existing customer racing programme."

In 2030 soll Porsche über die gesamte Wertschöpfungskette und den Lebenszyklus der neu verkauften Fahrzeuge hinweg bilanziell CO_2-neutral sein. Im selben Jahr soll der Anteil aller Neufahrzeuge mit einem vollelektrischen Antrieb bei mehr als 80 Prozent liegen.

Wie beim Mission R basiert der rein elektrische Antriebsstrang des 718 Cayman GT4 e-Performance auf je einer permanenterregten Synchronmaschine (PSM) an der Vorder- und Hinterachse. Beide zusammen verwandeln den Rennwagen in einen Allradler und können in der Spitze bis zu 800 kW (1.088 PS) erreichen. Die von Porsche entwickelte Öldirektkühlung der E-Maschinen und des Batteriepakets wirken einem thermisch bedingten Derating entgegen. „Die Integration der Ölkühlung hat das Fahrzeugkonzept maßgeblich geprägt", erläutert Björn Förster, Projektleiter GT4 e-Performance. „Das gesamte Entwicklungsteam hat mit Aero- und Thermodynamikern, Hochvoltexperten und Karosseriespezialisten eine Architektur geschaffen, in der erstmals das volle Potenzial der Batteriezellen genutzt werden kann, da sich kein thermisches Derating einstellt. Auf diese Weise steht die Power im Rennmodus über den gewünschten Zeitraum von einer halben Stunde unvermindert zur Verfügung." Dank 900-Volt-Technologie schnellt das Speicherniveau des Akkus bei voller Ladeleistung in rund 15 Minuten von fünf auf 80 Prozent SoC (State of Charge/Ladezustand).

Die Formen des 718 Cayman GT4 e-Performance hat ein Team von Porsche Style rund um den Designer Grant Larson entworfen. Der Rennwagen ist um 14 Zentimeter breiter als ein 718 Cayman GT4 Clubsport. Rund 6.000 Teile wurden für ihr neu konstruiert. Die Karosserie besteht unter anderem aus Naturfaser-Verbundwerkstoffen, deren Herstellung weniger Emissionen erzeugen soll als die Produktion vergleichbarer synthetischer Stoffe. Testweise kommen auch recycelte Karbonfasern zum Einsatz. Die gegenüber dem 718 Cayman GT4 Clubsport weiter ausgestellten Kotflügel schaffen Raum für noch breitere 18-Zoll-Rennreifen von Michelin. Sie weisen einen besonders hohen Anteil erneuerbarer Materialien auf

In 2030, Porsche aims to be CO_2 neutral across the entire value chain and life cycle of new cars sold. By then, the proportion of all new vehicles featuring all-electric drive should be more than 80 per cent.

Like with the Mission R, the fully-electric drive train of the 718 Cayman GT4 e-Performance is based on a permanently excited synchronous machine (PESM) on the front and rear axles. Together, they turn the racing car into an all-wheel-drive and can deliver a peak output of up to 800 kW (1,088 HP). The direct oil cooling of the e-motors and battery pack developed by Porsche counteracts thermally induced derating. "The integration of oil cooling has significantly impacted the vehicle concept," explains Björn Förster, GT4 e-Performance project manager. "With experts in the fields of aerodynamics and thermodynamics as well as high-voltage and bodywork specialists, the development team created an architecture to tap the full potential of the battery cells for the first time, since there is no thermal derating. In this way, the power output in racing mode remains constant for half an hour." Thanks to 900-volt technology, the state of charge (SoC) of the battery at full charging capacity jumps from 5 to 80 per cent in about 15 minutes.

Under the direction of designer Grant Larson, a team from Porsche Style came up with the shape of the 718 Cayman GT4 e-Performance. The racing car is 14 centimetres wider than a 718 Cayman GT4 Clubsport. About 6,000 parts were designed from scratch. The body is made of natural fibre composite materials, among others, with the production intended to generate fewer emissions than the production of comparable synthetic materials. Recycled carbon fibres are also used for testing purposes. Compared to the 718 Cayman GT4 Clubsport, the flared fenders allow more room for the wider 18-inch racing tyres from Michelin. Renewable materials make up a particularly high proportion of the tyres.

FORMULA E

TAG HEUER PORSCHE TEAM IN DER FORMEL E

TAG HEUER PORSCHE TEAM IN FORMULA E

28.02.–29.01.2022	*Diriyah, Saudi Arabia*
12.02.2022	*Mexico City, Mexico*
09.04.–10.04.2022	*Rome, Italy*
30.04.2022	*Monaco*
14.05.–15.05.2022	*Berlin, Germany*
04.06.2022	*Jakarta, Indonesia*
02.07.2022	*Marrakech, Morocco*
16.07.–17.07.2022	*New York City, USA*
30.07.–31.07.2022	*London, UK*
13.08.–14.08.2022	*Seoul, South Korea*

FORMULA E TEAM

TAG Heuer PORSCHE

Eine starke erste Saisonhälfte mit einem Doppelsieg in Mexiko absolvierten André Lotterer und Pascal Wehrlein mit dem TAG Heuer Porsche Formel-E-Team in der 8. Saison der ABB FIA Formel-E-Weltmeisterschaft.

Im Jahr 2022 nahm Porsche erneut an der ABB FIA Formel-E-Weltmeisterschaft teil. Am Steuer der beiden Porsche 99X Electric saßen die deutschen André Lotterer und Pascal Wehrlein, die von Januar bis August ein Programm von insgesamt 16 Rennen abspulten.

Die Saison begann mit zwei Läufen in Saudi-Arabien. Beim Diriyah E-Prix glänzte Routinier Lotterer mit einem vierten Platz im ersten Qualifying und hielt sich auch während des Rennens lange in der Spitzengruppe auf. Dabei stieß er zwischenzeitlich sogar auf Rang drei vor, doch in den Schlussrunden konnte er das Tempo der Schnellsten nicht mehr mitgehen; als 13. verpasste er die Punkteränge. Auch Wehrlein konnte keine Zähler sammeln, er verfehlte die Top Ten um eine Position.

Heat zwei an gleicher Stelle sollte vor allem für Lotterer besser laufen, wenngleich er im Zeittraining einen Rang schlechter abschnitt als beim Auftakt. Kurz vor Rennende bereitete er sich als Vierter schon auf seine Schlussattacken vor, als ein Unfall eines Rivalen für einen Safety-Car-Einsatz sorgte, der bis zum Fallen der Zielflagge andauerte. Somit gab es für ihn keine Chance mehr auf eine Positionsverbesserung und er blieb auf Rang vier. Wehrlein konnte sich auf dem Stadtkurs nahe der Hauptstadt Riad als Neunter ebenfalls WM-Punkte sichern.

A strong first half of the season with a 1-2 in Mexico and a weaker second part: that sums up Porsche's season in Formula E.

Porsche entered two 99X Electrics in the 2022 ABB Formula E World Championship programme for Germans André Lotterer and Pascal Wehrlein. The series ran from January to August, and included 16 races.

The season got underway with a pair of races in Saudi Arabia in January. At the Diriyah E-Prix, Lotterer did well to secure fourth place in first qualifying and for a long time was part of the front-running group during the race. He even briefly held third place, but was not able to hang onto it in the closing stages, and he finished 13th. Wehrlein finished two places ahead of him in 11th, also narrowly missing out on the chance to score points.

Things improved during the second race at the same venue. Although Lotterer qualified one place lower than he did for the opening round, he had a much better race. He ran fourth and was preparing to attack the cars ahead when a safety car came out, fixing the positions at the chequered flag. Wehrlein also opened his point-scoring tally as he finished ninth on the street circuit near the Arabian capital Riyadh.

SEASON 8

	André Lotterer		Pascal Wehrlein	
	Race 1	Race 2	Race 1	Race 2
Diriyah, Saudi Arabia	13	04	11	09

Pascal Wehrlein

Pascal Wehrlein

Mexico City, Mexico

André Lotterer **02** Race 3

Pascal Wehrlein **01** Race 3

André Lotterer

Weiter ging die Reise Mitte Februar nach Mexiko. Dieses Mal war es an Wehrlein, im Qualifying zu glänzen; er holte die Pole Position, Lotterer wurde Dritter. Nach der Hälfte des Rennens wurden die beiden Deutschen auf den Rängen drei und vier notiert, doch eine optimale Strategie brachte beide Porsche 99X Electric noch um jeweils zwei Plätze weiter nach vorne. Damit siegte Wehrlein vor Lotterer und das TAG Heuer Porsche Formel-E-Team durfte einen Doppelsieg bejubeln.

Es folgte eine Pause bis Anfang April, bevor Rom mit einem Doppellauf Schauplatz der ersten Europa-Station war. Durchgang eins beendete Wehrlein als Achter und Lotterer auf Rang zehn, nachdem sie im Qualifying die siebte (Wehrlein) und achte (Lotterer) Stelle eroberten.

Einen Tag später stand Heat zwei in der italienischen Hauptstadt an, den Lotterer von Startplatz drei aufnahm. Zeitweilig hatte er sogar die Führung inne, konnte diese nach einer Safety-Car-Phase aber nicht verteidigen. Als in den Schlussrunden abermals das Safety Car das Treiben neutralisierte, wurde ihm die Möglichkeiten genommen, noch einmal die Spitze zu attackieren. Lotterer blieb so auf P4. Wehrlein konnte sich von der siebten Stelle am Start um eine Position auf Rang sechs verbessern.

The next stop was Mexico in mid-February. This time, it was Wehrlein who starred in qualifying, setting fastest time to claim pole position, and he was backed up by Lotterer in third. It looked promising for Porsche as the lights turned to green, but at the mid-way point of the race they had dropped to third and fourth places respectively. However, excellent strategy from the pitwall saw them move back up to first and second positions, where they finished. Wehrlein took the victory ahead of Lotterer and the TAG Heuer Porsche Formula E Team celebrated a 1-2 finish.

There followed a short break as the cars returned to Europe, but the season continued at the beginning of April, with Rome hosting a double-header. The first race saw Wehrlein finish eighth, Lotterer tenth, having qualified their Porsches seventh and eighth on the grid respectively.

For the second race of the weekend held the following day, Lotterer started third on the grid. He managed to improve on that and even led the race, but was unable to hold the position after the safety car was deployed and he finished fourth. From seventh on the grid, Wehrlein managed to make up one place and finished sixth.

André Lotterer and Pascal Wehrlein

	André Lotterer		Pascal Wehrlein	
	Race 4	Race 5	Race 4	Race 5
Rome, Italy	10	04	08	06

Mark Webber

Ende April reiste die Formel E nach Monaco, wo das Porsche-Team nach vielversprechendem Start vor allem Enttäuschungen erlebte. Wehrlein schob sich von Startplatz zwei kommend kurz vor Rennmitte auf die erste Position und hatte bereits begonnen, sich einen Vorsprung auf die Konkurrenz aufzubauen. Doch dann wurde sein Renner plötzlich langsamer und er schied aufgrund eines technischen Defekts aus. Lotterer hatte ebenfalls wenig Glück: Als Fünfter hatte er schon zwei Plätze gewonnen, als er von einem Kontrahenten in die Streckenbegrenzung geschoben wurde; auch sein Arbeitstag war damit vorzeitig beendet.

Die beiden Auftritte Mitte Mai in Berlin beschlossen die erste Saisonhälfte. Lotterer, Fünfter im ersten Qualifying und zeitweise Führender im ersten Heat auf dem Flughafen Tempelhof, verpasste als Vierter nur knapp das Treppchen. Wehrlein sah die Zielflagge zwei Positionen hinter seinem Teamkollegen, erhielt aber noch den Zusatzpunkt für die schnellste Rennrunde.

Durchgang zwei in der deutschen Hauptstadt gestaltete sich für die beiden Porsche-Schützlinge weniger erfolgreich: Lotterer hielt, als Vierter gestartet, lange mit den Top-Piloten mit, doch in der zweiten Rennhälfte musste er abreißen lassen. Für ihn blieb am Ende die achte Stelle. Wehrlein verfehlte als Zwölfter die Punkteränge, konnte sich vom 19. Startplatz aber immerhin um sieben Positionen verbessern.

	André Lotterer	Pascal Wehrlein
Monaco, Monaco	**DNF** Race 6	**DNF** Race 6

The series then headed to Monaco at the end of April. For the Porsche team, it turned out to be a mainly disappointing affair after a promising start. From second on the grid, Wehrlein moved to lead the race just before the halfway point and had started to pull a gap. However, his car suddenly slowed and he retired due to a technical failure. Lotterer wasn't having a particularly lucky race either: running fifth having gained two places, he was forced to retire from the race after an opponent pushed him into the barriers.

	André Lotterer		Pascal Wehrlein	
Berlin, Germany	04	08	06	12
	Race 7	Race 8	Race 7	Race 8

The two races in Berlin in mid-May concluded the first half of the season. Lotterer, fifth in first qualifying and temporarily leading the first race at the former Tempelhof airport, only just missed out on the podium at the end of the race as he finished fourth. Wehrlein ended up two places further behind, but was able to score the additional championship point for the fastest race lap.

The second race in the German capital was less successful for the two Porsche drivers. Having started fourth, Lotterer kept up with the front-running group, but had to let them go in the second half of the race and he finished eighth. Wehrlein finished 12th, and so missed out on the chance to score any points, although he was encouraged at having made up seven places from 19th on the grid.

BERLIN-TEMPELHOF
BOSCH
PORSCHE
36
Mobil

Anfang Juni folgte der Jakarta E-Prix – zugleich der erste Auftritt der ABB FIA Formel-E-Weltmeisterschaft in Indonesien, wo Temperaturen von über 30 Grad Celsius und eine hohe Luftfeuchtigkeit auf die Teilnehmer warteten. Pascal Wehrlein nahm das Rennen aufgrund einer Strafe vom vorherigen Event von Rang elf auf, überholte am Start direkt drei Rivalen und wurde schließlich als Achter abgewinkt. André Lotterers Arbeitsnachweis begann am Start mit Position acht und endete als Neunter im Ziel.

Das nächste Hitzerennen sollte die FIA Formel E Anfang Juli in Marrakesch erleben. Wehrlein sorgte mit Platz vier im Qualifying für eine gute Ausgangsbasis, doch im Laufe des Rennens fiel er bis auf den 18. Rang zurück. Bis zum Zielstrich arbeitete er sich dann immerhin noch auf Position zwölf nach vorne, Punkte konnte er aber keine sammeln. Auch Lotterer blieb in Marokko ohne weitere Zähler. Er konnte wegen eines technischen Problems nicht rechtzeitig ins Qualifying einsteigen, blieb so ohne gezeitete Runde und musste das Feld von hinten aufrollen. Insgesamt sieben Positionen machte er gut, was in der Endabrechnung Rang 15 bedeutete.

Jakarta, Indonesia | André Lotterer **09** Race 9 | Pascal Wehrlein **08** Race 9

Pascal Wehrlein

Marrakesh, Morocco	André Lotterer	Pascal Wehrlein
	15	12
	Race 10	Race 10

The Jakarta E-Prix at the beginning of June marked the first visit of the ABB FIA Formula E World Championship to Indonesia. Temperatures of over 30 degrees Celsius and high humidity awaited the competitors. Having picked up a penalty in Germany, Wehrlein started from eleventh on the grid. From there, he overtook three cars at the start and went on to finish eighth. Lotterer started eighth, and finished ninth.

At Marrakech in early June, the FIA Formula E had another race in hot conditions. Fourth on the grid looked promising for Wehrlein, but he dropped back as far as 18th as the race went on. He was able to recover some of the lost ground, and was 12th at the finish, but he was again out of the points. Lotterer also failed to score. A technical issue prevented him from taking part in qualifying, so he didn't set a timed lap and had to start his recovery drive from the back of the grid. During the race, he made up seven places and finished 15th.

André Lotterer

TAGHeuer
ABB

ABB
Ansys

FORMULA E TEAM
TAGHeuer
PORSCHE
BOSS

ABB
Ansys

SACRED
LONDON

POLE POSITION
94
Julius Bär

MICHELIN
FORMULA E

New York City, USA

	André Lotterer		Pascal Wehrlein	
	16	09	06	11
	Race 11	Race 12	Race 11	Race 12

Florian Modlinger

Mitte Juli durften sich die Piloten wieder auf eine Doppelveranstaltung einstellen, dieses Mal war der Ort des Geschehens New York. Wehrlein machte als Vierter des Qualifyings eine gute Figur, während Lotterer nur als 17. notiert wurde. Das Rennen endete vorzeitig, denn wegen eines plötzlich einsetzenden Regenschauers gab es an der Spitze des Feldes eine Massenkollision. Wehrlein selbst konnte seinen Porsche trotz Aquaplaning auf der Strecke halten, wurde dann aber von einem Hintermann getroffen. Da es keinen Re-Start mehr gab, wurde er auf Rang sechs gewertet. Lotterer fand sich im Klassement auf Position 16 wieder.

Einen Tag später schien die Sonne über New York und auch Lotterer strahlte nach dem Zeittraining, das er als Dritter beendete. Doch am Start verlor er acht Positionen. Als enttäuschter Neunter kreuzte er schließlich die Ziellinie. Anders verlief der Tag bei Wehrlein, der von Startplatz 20 beginnen musste. Er konnte mit einer Aufholjagd begeistern und verpasste als Elfter nur knapp die Punkteränge.

There was another double header in mid-July, this time in New York. Wehrlein demonstrated his pace by setting fourth fastest time in qualifying while Lotterer was 17th. The race ended prematurely as a sudden downpour caused a multi-car crash at the front of the field. Despite aquaplaning, Wehrlein managed to keep his Porsche on track, but was hit by a driver coming from behind. As the race wasn't restarted, he was classified sixth. Lotterer ended the race in 16th place.

One day later, sunshine returned to New York and Lotterer was in good spirits having secured third place on the grid. At the start, however, he lost eight positions and ended up finishing ninth. Wehrlein's fortunes were slightly different. He started 20th, but put on an impressive performance during the race to finish eleventh.

Pascal Wehrlein

BAL -
LON -
BAL +
LON +
ATK
PTP
RAD
OK
PIT
FCY

TRILUX
SIMPLIFY YOUR LIGHT.
WO LICHT IST, IST LEBEN.
www.trilux.com

Zwei Wochen später war London die zweitletzte Station der ABB FIA Formel-E-WM 2022 und Wehrlein war noch immer im Modus Aufholjagd. Nach Problemen im Qualifying musste er sich mit Rang 18 in der Startaufstellung zufriedengeben, doch das hinderte ihn nicht an einer guten Leistung im Rennen. Als starker Zehnter durfte er immerhin einen Punkt mitnehmen. Lotterer konnte seine achte Startposition nicht in einen Top-Ten-Platz umwandeln, er fand sich im Ranking als Zwölfter wieder.

Auch im zweiten Heat von London zeigte ein Porsche-Pilot seine Überhol-Qualitäten, dieses Mal war es jedoch Lotterer. Er verpatzte das Qualifying, musste deshalb von Platz 21 beginnen und machte auf dem engen Kurs in den Docklands von East London im Rennen neun Positionen gut. Der Lohn in Form von Zählern blieb aber aus, denn Lotterer verpasste als Zwölfter die Top Ten. Wehrlein schaffte es vom zwölften Startplatz knapp und eroberte wie am Vortag einen Punkt.

	André Lotterer		Pascal Wehrlein	
London, UK	12	12	10	10
	Race 13	Race 14	Race 13	Race 14

A fortnight later, London served as the venue for the penultimate event of the 2022 FIA Formula E World. After problems in qualifying, Wehrlein had to make do with 18th place on the grid, but that didn't prevent him from putting in a good performance for the race. Finishing tenth he scored one point. Lotterer, meanwhile, was unable to convert eighth place on the grid into a top ten result, he was classified twelfth.

In the second race in London, a poor qualifying saw Lotterer starting 21st, but he made up nine places during the race at the narrow circuit in East London's Docklands. He finished twelfth after a sparkling drive, but even that was not good enough to score any points. Wehrlein moved up from twelfth on the grid to finish tenth, again scoring a point.

Pascal Wehrlein and
André Lotterer

André Lotterer

Seoul, South Korea	André Lotterer		Pascal Wehrlein	
	DNF	DNF	07	DNF
	Race 15	Race 16	Race 15	Race 16

Mitte August stand das große Finale mit zwei Rennen in Seoul im Kalender. In Durchgang eins startete Wehrlein von P4, musste sich aber auf den ersten Metern schon von vier Kontrahenten überholen lassen. Bis zum Ziel konnte er eine Position wieder zurückholen, sodass er als Siebter abgewinkt wurde. Für Lotterer endete der Lauf schon in Runde eins. Auf extrem nasser Piste rutschte er wie, einige andere Kontrahenten, in die Streckenbegrenzung; die Schäden an seinem Porsche 99X ließen beim Re-Start keine Teilnahme mehr zu.

Im Finalrennen einen Tag später blieb dem Porsche-Duo dann ein positives Ende der Saison verwehrt: Beide schieden ohne eigene Schuld aus. Damit schloss Wehrlein die Saison als Zehnter der Fahrerwertung ab, Lotterer erreichte in seiner letzten Saison für Porsche in der Formel E Rang zwölf der Abschlusstabelle.

(l.-r.): Thomas Laudenbach, André Lotterer, Carlo Wiggers

Two races in Seoul marked the grand finale mid-August. In the first race, Wehrlein started from fourth on the grid, but four opponents overtook him in the first few metres of the race. He managed to get one back and finished seventh. For Lotterer, the race was over on the opening lap. He slid into the barriers on an extremely wet track and was unble to make it to the restart.

In the final race of the season Porsche's drivers were unable to end the season on a high as both drivers retired, although through no fault of their own. Wehrlein ended up tenth in the drivers' standings, Lotterer was twelfth in his final season with Porsche in Formula E.

Pascal Wehrlein

Pascal Wehrlein

Pascal Wehrlein

DRIVER STANDINGS **OVERALL**

POS	NO	DRIVERS	CAR	TEAM	POINTS
1	5	Stoffel Vandoorne	Mercedes-EQ Silver Arrow 02	Mercedes-EQ Formula E Team	213
2	9	Mitch Evans	Jaguar I-Type 5	Jaguar TCS Racing	180
3	49	Edoardo Mortara	Mercedes-EQ Silver Arrow 02	ROKit Venturi Racing	169
10	**94**	**Pascal Wehrlein**	**Porsche 99X Electric**	**TAG Heuer Porsche Formula E Team**	**71**
12	**36**	**André Lotterer**	**Porsche 99X Electric**	**TAG Heuer Porsche Formula E Team**	**63**

TEAM STANDINGS **OVERALL**

POS	NO	TEAM	CAR	POINTS
1	5,17	Mercedes-EQ Formula E Team	Mercedes-EQ Silver Arrow 02	319
2	11,49	ROKit Venturi Racing	Mercedes-EQ Silver Arrow 02	295
3	13,25	DS Techeetah	DS E-Tense FE21	266
7	**36,94**	**TAG Heuer Porsche Formula E Team**	**Porsche 99X Electric**	**134**

André Lotterer

FORMULA E TEAM

TAGHeuer PORSCHE

PORSCHE 99X ELECTRIC GEN3

Mit dem Porsche 99X Electric Gen3 startet Porsche in eine neue Ära der Formel E. Der im Porsche-Entwicklungszentrum in Weissach weiterentwickelte Elektrorennwagen feierte im Porsche Experience Center im italienischen Franciacorta seine Weltpremiere. Er wird vom TAG Heuer Porsche Formel-E-Team ab der Saison 2023 in der ABB FIA Formel-E-Weltmeisterschaft eingesetzt.

Das erste Rennen für den Porsche 99X Electric Gen3 ist am 14. Januar 2023 der Mexico City E-Prix. Mit dem Einsatz der dritten Fahrzeuggeneration beginnt beim Saisonauftakt eine neue Zeitrechnung für die erste Elektrorennserie der Welt.

Die neuen Gen3-Autos, wie der Porsche 99X Electric Gen3 sind die schnellsten, leichtesten, leistungsstärksten und effizientesten Elektrorennautos, die jemals gebaut wurden. Sie wurden speziell für spannende Rad-an-Rad-Duelle auf engen Stadtkursen in faszinierenden Metropolen konstruiert, auf denen die Formel E traditionell ihre Rennen austrägt.

Das Gesamtkonzept des Porsche 99X Electric Gen3 und der anderen Fahrzeuge der neuen Formel-E-Generation ist ein großer Entwicklungsschritt. Die Fahrzeuge sind leichter geworden, der Radstand kürzer und die Spur schmaler. Die Batterie ist kleiner und zugleich leistungsstärker. Der Anteil der rekuperativen Energie ist gestiegen. Auch die Aerodynamik und das Design wurden überarbeitet. Alles in allem sind die neuen Fahrzeuge dadurch agiler, was auch die Performance auf der Rennstrecke verbessert.

Die aufregende neue Optik des Porsche 99X Electric Gen3 wurde vom Porsche Brand Purpose „Driven by Dreams" inspiriert. Sie zeichnet sich durch Individualität, Unverwechselbarkeit und einen in die Zukunft gerichteten progressiven Zeitgeist aus, der auch eine jüngere Zielgruppe anspricht.

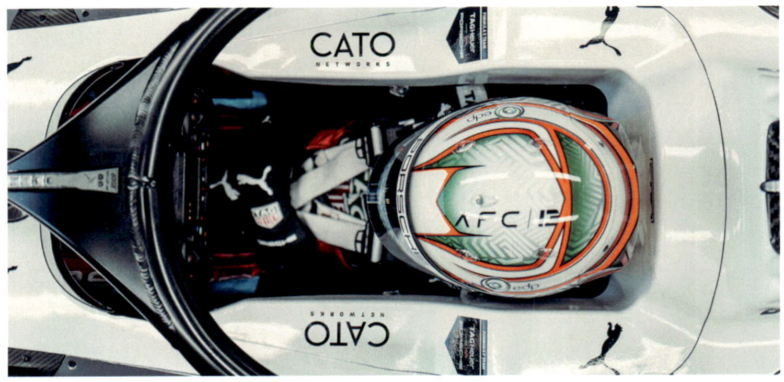

Leistung: Die Leistung der neuen Gen3-Fahrzeuge steigt von 250 auf 350 kW (476 PS).

Antriebsstrang: Eigenentwicklung von Porsche Motorsport mit einer maximalen Antriebsleistung von 350 kW auf der Hinterachse und damit 100 kW mehr als bei der vorherigen Fahrzeug-Generation (Gen2).

Bremsen: Der neue vordere Antriebsstrang erhöht die 350 kW des hinteren um weitere 250 kW und ermöglicht dadurch eine Energierückgewinnung mit einer Leistung von bis zu 600 kW – mehr als doppelt so viel wie bei den Gen2-Autos. Zusätzliche Reibungsbremse gesteuert durch eine „Brake by wire"-Einheit.

Effizienz: Die Energieeffizienz des Antriebs liegt bei etwa 95 Prozent im Vergleich zu rund 40 Prozent bei den besten Verbrennungsmotoren. Über 40 Prozent der eingesetzten Energie sollen aus der rekuperativen Energie stammen, die beim Bremsen entsteht.

Ladefähigkeit: Die Ultra-High-Speed-Ladefähigkeit der Gen3-Fahrzeuge soll während der Rennen bei 600 kW zusätzlicher Energie liegen. Damit wären die Ladegeräte der neuen Formel-E-Generation annähernd doppelt so leistungsstark wie die derzeit fortschrittlichsten kommerziellen Exemplare. Zudem soll die Fast-Charge-Technologie für eine konstant hohe Batterieleistung sorgen.

Nachhaltigkeit: Die Batteriezellen in den neuen Gen3-Autos bestehen, so die Komponentenhersteller, aus nachhaltig gewonnenen Mineralien. Nach jeder Rennsaison sollen die Batteriezellen wiederverwendet oder recycelt werden. Für den Bau der Karbonfaser-Karosserie werden nach Angaben des Herstellers recycelte Karbonfasern aus den Fahrzeugen der Vorgängergeneration verwendet. Dadurch soll der CO_2-Fußabdruck der Produktion um mehr als zehn Prozent reduziert werden. Um Maßnahmen zu bestimmen, die zur Reduzierung der Umweltauswirkungen beitragen können, wird der CO_2-Fußabdruck der neuen Fahrzeuge von der Formel E von Beginn der Designphase an gemessen. Alle unvermeidbaren Emissionen sollen als Teil der Netto-Null-CO_2-Verpflichtung der Formel E kompensiert werden.

Die Partner

Mit der Unterstützung von insgesamt 15 Partnern startet das TAG Heuer Porsche Formel-E-Team in seine vierte Saison und freut sich über zwei neue On-Car Partner bei der Weltpremiere des Porsche 99X Electric Gen3. Cato Networks, Anbieter der weltweit führenden SASE Cloud-Plattform, sowie die Schweizer Wealth-Management-Gruppe Julius Bär sind als offizielle Partner auf dem Porsche 99X Electric Gen3 sichtbar. Der Schweizer Hersteller von Luxusuhren, TAG Heuer, der das Team seit dem Start als Titel- und Timing Partner unterstützt, ist wie der Schweizer Energie- und Automatisierungstechnikkonzern ABB und Simulationssoftwarespezialist ANSYS weiterhin auf dem Rennfahrzeug präsent. ExxonMobil mit seiner Marke Mobil1 als Technologiepartner komplettiert zusammen mit dem weltweit agierende Marken- und Technologieunternehmen Henkel und seiner Marke LOCTITE, dem Modeunternehmen Hugo Boss und dem Sport-Lifestyle-Unternehmen Puma den geschätzten Kreis der insgesamt 9 On-Car Partner.

99X

With the Porsche 99X Electric Gen3, Porsche heads into a new era of Formula E. The electric racing car, which underwent an evolution in the Porsche Development Centre in Weissach, celebrated its world premiere in the Porsche Experience Center in Franciacorta, Italy. It will be fielded by the TAG Heuer Porsche Formula E Team in the ABB FIA Formula E World Championship from the 2023 season.

350 KW
476 HP
Maximum performance

2.8
SECONDS
0-100km/h

600
KW
Maximum recuperation

The Mexico City E-Prix on 14 January 2023 will be the first race for the Porsche 99X Electric Gen3. The arrival of the third vehicle generation at the start of next season heralds a new era for the world's first electric racing series.

The new Gen3 cars such as the Porsche 99X Electric Gen3 are the fastest, lightest, most powerful and efficient electric racing cars ever built. They have been specifically designed for gripping wheel-to-wheel duels on tight city circuits in fascinating major cities of the world where Formula E traditionally contests its races.

The overall concept of the Porsche 99X Electric Gen3 and the other vehicles of the new Formula E generation constitute a major evolutionary step. The vehicles have shed weight and feature a shorter wheelbase and narrower track. While the battery has shrunk in size, it is more powerful. The proportion of recuperative energy has grown. The aerodynamics and design have also undergone modifications. All in all the new vehicles are more agile, which also improves performance on the racetrack.

The striking new look of the Porsche 99X Electric Gen3 was inspired by the Porsche brand purpose "Driven by Dreams". It signifies individuality, uniqueness and a future-oriented progressive zeitgeist that also appeals to a younger target group.

Performance: The performance of the new Gen3 vehicles increases from 250 to 350 kW (476 hp).

Powertrain: Developed in-house by Porsche Motorsport with a maximum drive power of 350 kW on the rear axle – 100 kW more than the predecessor generation (Gen2).

Brakes: The new front powertrain adds 250 kW to the 350 kW at the rear, resulting in energy recovery with an output of up to 600 kW – more than double the regenerative capability of the Gen2 vehicles. Additional fraction brake controlled by a brake-by-wire unit.

Efficiency: The electric motor achieves about 95 percent power efficiency compared to around 40 percent for an internal combustion engine. Over 40 percent of the energy used is recuperated via regenerative braking.

Charging capability: The new ultra-high-speed charging capacity of the Gen3 vehicles should add around 600kW of energy during the race. This means that the chargers of the new Formula E generation would be almost twice as powerful as the world's most advanced commercial chargers. Moreover, the fast-charge technology should guarantee a consistently high battery performance.

Sustainability: According to the component manufacturer, the battery cells in the new Gen3 cars are made from sustainably sourced minerals. After every race season, the battery cells should be reused or recycled. For the construction of the carbon fibre bodywork, the manufacturer states that recycled carbon fibre is used from retired Gen2 vehicles. This should reduce the carbon footprint of production by more than ten percent. To determine measures that can help reduce environmental impact, the carbon footprint of new Formula E vehicles is measured from the very start of the design phase. All unavoidable emissions will be offset as part of Formula E's net zero carbon commitment.

Team partners

The TAG Heuer Porsche Formula E Team heads into its fourth season supported by 15 partners and is delighted to welcome two new on-car partners at the world premiere of the Porsche 99X Electric Gen3. Cato Networks, the provider of the world's leading SASE cloud platform, and the Swiss wealth management group Julius Bär are represented on the Porsche 99X Electric Gen3 as official partners. Continuing its support of the team, the Swiss manufacturer of luxury watches, TAG Heuer, which has been the team's title and timing partner right from the start, as well as the Swiss energy and automation technology group ABB and simulation software specialist ANSYS. Also completing the highly valued circle of nine on-car partners is: ExxonMobil with its Mobil brand as a technology partner, together with the global brand and technology enterprise Henkel with its brand LOCTITE, the fashion company Hugo Boss and the sports lifestyle company Puma.

ANTÓNIO FÉLIX DA COSTA NEUER PORSCHE-WERKSFAHRER IN DER FORMEL E

ANTÓNIO FÉLIX DA COSTA BECOMES NEW PORSCHE WORKS DRIVER IN FORMULA E

Prominenter Neuzugang für Porsche in der Formel E: António Félix da Costa verstärkt als neuer Werksfahrer das TAG Heuer Porsche Formel-E-Team und bildet zusammen mit Pascal Wehrlein das Fahrerduo für die Saison 9 der ABB FIA Formel-E-Weltmeisterschaft. Sein erstes Rennen für Porsche wird der 30-jährige Portugiese am 14. Januar 2023 beim Mexico City E-Prix bestreiten, bei dem für die Formel E eine neue Ära mit den Rennautos der Gen3 beginnt.

António Félix da Costa ist ein Mann der ersten Stunde in der Formel E. Seit die erste Elektrorennserie der Welt 2014 ein neues Kapitel in der Motorsport-Geschichte aufschlug, ist er mit dabei. In der Saison 2019/2020 sicherte er sich den Meistertitel. Bei insgesamt 96 Starts hat er bisher sieben Rennen gewonnen, stand 16 Mal auf dem Podium und holte acht Pole-Positions. Auch in anderen Rennserien feierte der begeisterte Surfer, der im Lissaboner Vorort Cascais nur einen Steinwurf vom Strand entfernt wohnt, zahlreiche Erfolge. Beim legendären Macau Grand Prix siegte er 2012, sowie 2016 und 2022 holte der ehemalige Formel-1-Testfahrer von Red Bull Racing einen Klassensieg bei den 24 Stunden von Le Mans.

„Ich freue mich riesig, dass António zu uns an Bord kommt. Er verfügt über herausragende Fähigkeiten als Rennfahrer und hat schon mehrfach gezeigt, dass er nicht nur in der Formel E Siege einfahren kann", sagt Thomas Laudenbach, Leiter Porsche Motorsport. „Wir schätzen ihn als Fahrer, aber auch als Mensch. Er ist ein positiver Typ, der sehr gut zu uns und in die Porsche-Motorsportfamilie passt. Ich bin zuversichtlich, dass wir in den kommenden Jahren gemeinsam um Siege und Titel kämpfen werden."

„Für mich geht ein Traum in Erfüllung. Ich freue mich sehr darauf, endlich loszulegen und mit dieser Mannschaft Rennen zu gewinnen", sagt António Félix da Costa, der fünf Sprachen spricht und sich selbst als „Motorsport-Junkie" bezeichnet. „Ich wurde in meiner Karriere so oft von einem Porsche geschlagen, nicht nur in der Formel E, deshalb weiß ich: Porsche tut alles, um zu gewinnen. Das ist die DNA von Porsche. Ich teile diese Ambitionen und kann es kaum erwarten, alle im Team kennenzulernen und mit ihnen dafür zu arbeiten, dass wir erfolgreich in die Gen3-Ära starten."

„Die Vorfreude auf die Zusammenarbeit mit António ist groß", sagt Florian Modlinger, Gesamtprojektleiter Formel E. „Ich kenne ihn aus den verschiedensten Rennserien und schätze ihn menschlich sehr. Unglaublich, was er in der Formel E schon geleistet hat. Wir werden alles tun, um ihm für die Gen3 ein konkurrenzfähiges Auto an die Hand zu geben, mit dem er um Siege und Titel fahren kann. Das ganze Team freut sich auf ihn."

A prominent new team member joins Porsche in Formula E: António Félix da Costa reinforces the TAG Heuer Porsche Formula E Team as the new works driver and joins forces with Pascal Wehrlein as the driver pairing for season 9 of the ABB FIA Formula E World Championship. The 30-year-old from Portugal contests his first race for Porsche on 14 January 2023 at the Mexico City E-Prix, where the Gen3 racing cars will herald a new era for Formula E.

António Félix da Costa has been involved in Formula E since day one, when the world's first electric racing series wrote a new chapter in motor racing history in 2014. In the 2019/2020 season, he took home the championship title. So far in his Formula E career, he has contested 96 races with seven victories, 16 podium finishes and eight pole positions. The passionate surfer, who lives close to the ocean in Cascais near Lisbon, has also secured many accolades in other racing series. He won the legendary Macau Grand Prix in 2012 and 2016, and in 2022, the ex-Formula 1 test driver for Red Bull Racing clinched a class win at the 24 Hours of Le Mans.

"I'm delighted that António is coming on board. He has an incredible skill set as a racing driver and has demonstrated many times that he's a winner, not only in Formula E," says Thomas Laudenbach, Vice President Porsche Motorsport. "We hold him in high regard as a driver and on his own merits as a person. He's a positive guy who is a great fit for us and the Porsche Motorsport family. I'm confident that we'll fight for victories and titles together for years to come."

"It's like a dream come true. I'm really looking forward to cracking on and winning races for this team," says António Félix da Costa, who speaks five languages and is a self-proclaimed "motorsport junkie". "I've been beaten by a Porsche many times in my career, and not only in Formula E, so I know that Porsche does everything to win. It's in the brand's DNA. I share the same ambition and can hardly wait to bond with the team and work together to ensure a successful start to the Gen3 era."

"We're very much looking forward to working with António," says Florian Modlinger, Director Factory Motorsport Formula E. "I know him from various racing series and I have a lot of respect for him on a personal level. It's incredible what he has already achieved in Formula E. We'll do our utmost to give him a competitive Gen3 car so that he can fight for wins and titles. The team is very much looking forward to welcoming him."

HUGO BOSS AG PHONE +49 7123 940 BOSS.COM
BE YOUR OWN
BOSS

PORSCHE
KCMG
2
MOTUL
GTD PRO
9
HAGERTY
PFAFF
MOTUL

driveway
MOTUL
driveway
MOTUL
driveway
MOTUL

GT RACING

DAYTONA
PORSCHE
WeatherTech
WeatherTech
IMSA
MICHELIN

WEC

IMSA WEATHERTECH SPORTSCAR CHAMPIONSHIP

27.01.–30.01.2022	Daytona International Speedway, USA
17.03.–19.03.2022	Sebring International Raceway, USA
08.04.- 09.04.2022	Long Beach, USA
30.04.–01.05.2022	Laguna Seca Raceway, USA
14.05.–15.05.2022	Mid-Ohio Sports Car Course, USA
03.06.–04.06.2022	Detroit, USA
24.06.–26.06.2022	Watkins Glen, USA
02.07.–03.07.2022	Canadian Tire Motorsports Park, Canada
15.07.–16.06.2022	Lime Rock Park, USA
06.08.–07.08.2022	Road America, USA
27.08.–28.08.2022	Virginia International Raceway, USA
28.09.–01.10.2022	Road Atlanta, USA

(l.-r.): Matt Campbell, Mathieu Jaminet, Felipe Nasr

Titelgewinn in der GTD-Pro-Klasse mit Matt Campbell und Mathieu Jaminet, knapp verpasster Titel mit Ryan Hardwick und Jan Heylen in der GTD-Klasse.

In der IMSA WeatherTech SportsCar Championship waren Porsche-Fahrzeuge in den Klassen GTD-Pro und GTD beteiligt; insgesamt gingen 2022 sechs Teams mit einem Porsche 911 GT3 R an den Start. Pfaff Motorsports absolvierte die komplette GTD-Pro-Saison, während KCMG beim Rolex 24 At Daytona antrat. Dabei war der Start des Porsche mit der Nummer zwei beim längsten Rennen der Saison mit Laurens Vanthoor aus Belgien, Patrick Pilet aus Frankreich, dem Norweger Dennis Olsen und Alexandre Imperatori aus der Schweiz ein einmaliger Einsatz. Das Quartett lieferte sich während des gesamten 24-Stunden-Rennens – selbst bei eisigen Temperaturen in den Nachtstunden – einen harten Kampf mit dem Pfaff-Auto, zu dessen üblicher Fahrerbesetzung Mathieu Jaminet und Matt Campbell sich für die Langstreckenrennen noch der Brasilianer Felipe Nasr gesellte. Erst in den letzten Minuten entschied sich das Duell zugunsten von Jaminet im Pfaff-Porsche, nachdem Vanthoor sich beim Versuch, die Führung zu übernehmen, gedreht hatte. Vanthoor / Pilet / Olsen / Imperatori fielen noch bis auf den dritten Rang der Klasse GTD-Pro zurück. Und auch während der Saison lief es gut für Pfaff: Dank fünf Klassensiegen, davon drei in den letzten fünf Saisonrennen, ging das Team mit den beiden Fahrern Campbell und Jaminet mit einem nahezu uneinholbaren Vorsprung im Fahrer- und im Teamklassement der Kategorie GTD-Pro in das Finale in Road Atlanta. Für die Truppe von Chris Pfaff wäre der Titel schon in trockenen Tüchern gewesen, sobald das erste Auto die Startlinie überquert hätte. Und obwohl die in Kanada beheimatete Mannschaft keine einzige Runde hätte abschließen müssen, hätte sie den Lauf beinahe noch gewonnen. Als die karierte Flagge das 25. Petit Le Mans beendete, wurde sie letztendlich jedoch auf dem dritten Platz notiert. Aber das spielte keine Rolle, der

Ryan Hardwick, Jan Heylen, Zacharie Robichon

Title win in the GTD Pro class with Matt Campbell and Mathieu Jaminet, narrowly missed title with Ryan Hardwick and Jan Heylen in the GTD class.

By virtue of five victories, including three from the last five races of the 2022 IMSA WeatherTech SportsCar Championship season, Pfaff Motorsports entered the finale at Michelin Raceway Road Atlanta with a nearly unassailable lead in the GTD Pro Driver and Team championships. Simply by rolling off the starting grid, the Chris Pfaff-owned team clinched the GTD Pro championship as soon as the first car crossed the starting line after the completion of the scheduled formation lap. The Pfaff Porsche 911 GT3 R didn't even have to cross under the green flag to be awarded the title. This was also true for drivers Matt Campbell (Australia) and Mathieu Jaminet (France). It was the first IMSA championship for either driver, the second for the team. Despite not having to even finish a single green flag lap, the Canada-based programme nearly bookended the year with wins, falling just short with a third-place finish at the 25th Annual Petit Le Mans in the red, black and white "Plaid Porsche".

In total, six teams raced the Porsche 911 GT3 R in the IMSA WeatherTech SportsCar Championship in 2022. One team, Pfaff, focused on the full GTD Pro season while KCMG joined the all-pro category at the Rolex 24 At Daytona. That was a one-off entry in the season's first, and its longest, race with drivers Laurens Vanthoor (Belgium), Patrick Pilet (France), Dennis Olsen (Norway) and Alexandre Imperatori (Switzerland). It waged a full-race battle with the Pfaff car, which was shared with Felipe Nasr (Brazil) for the endurance races, throughout the twice-around the clock competition even in the freezing temperatures of the nighttime hours. It was not until the closing minutes, after a bumper-to-bumper, fender-to-fender, doorhandle-to-doorhandle skirmish, that Jaminet took the chequered flag ahead of Vanthoor. The result was only decided after Vanthoor spun the KCMG entry while attempting to overtake for the lead.

Wright Motorsports carried the Porsche banner in the GTD class throughout the year with 2021 Porsche Cup recipient Jan Heylen (native of Belgium now living in the USA) and Ryan Hardwick (USA). With 2021 class champion Zacharie Robichon (Canada), they created a strong trio in the endurance rounds. Hardpoint drivers Rob Ferriol (USA) and Katherine Legge (UK) raced the majority of the events – joined by Stefan Wilson (UK) and Nick Boulle (USA) for the long races. At select early races GMG Racing entered the a car for American drivers Kyle Washington and James Sofronas while Jeroen Bleekemolen (Netherlands) and Klaus Bachler (Austria) shared the seat for the enduros. Michelin Pilot Challenge regulars Team TGM with owner/driver Ted Giovanis (USA), brothers Hugh and Matt Plumb (USA) and Owen Trinkler (USA) raced at Daytona. WeatherTech Racing entered a Porsche in the first two events of the season for Cooper MacNeil (USA), Julien Andlauer (France), Matteo Cairoli (Italy) and Alessio Picariello (Belgium).

Matt Campbell, Mathieu Jaminet, Felipe Nasr

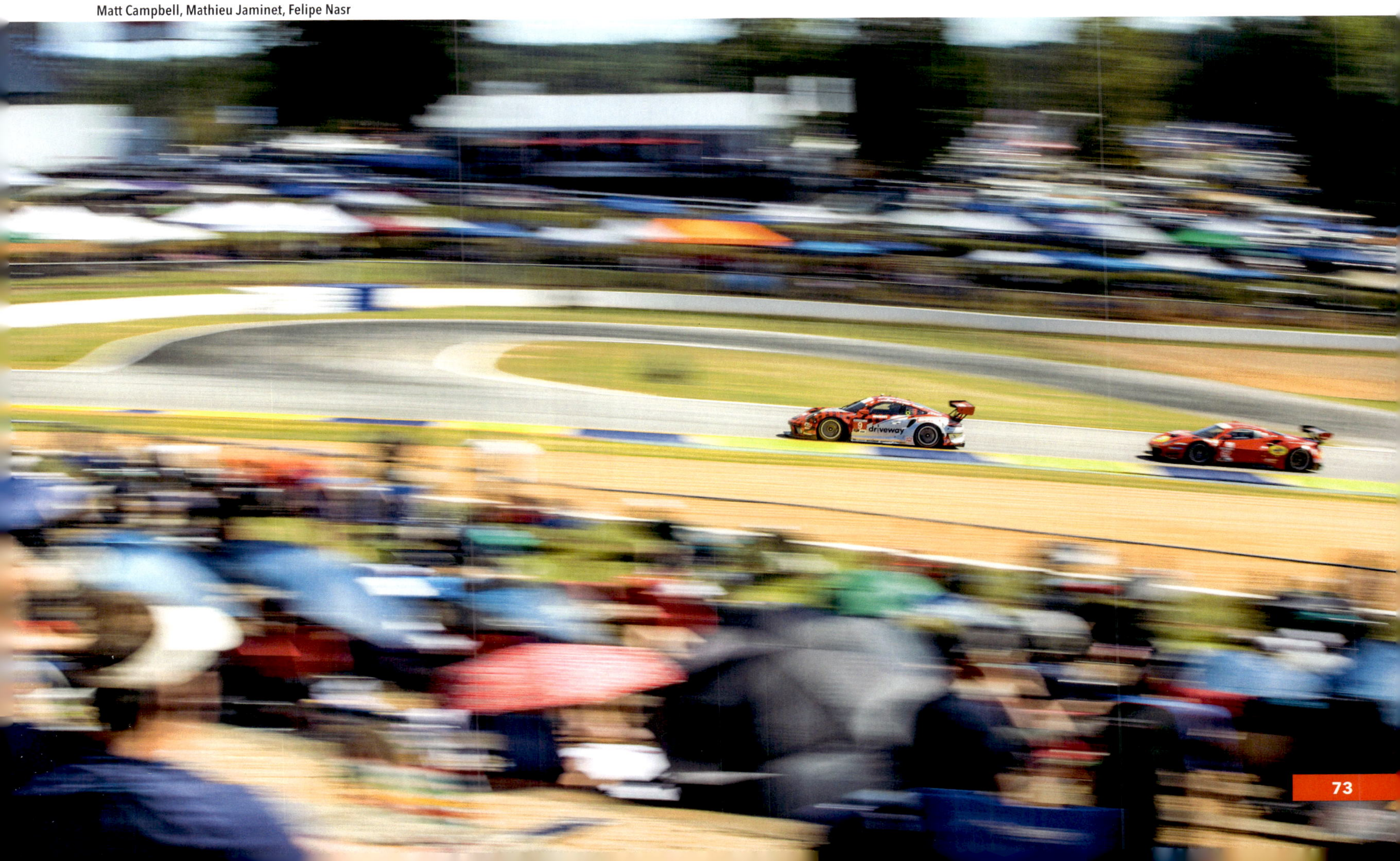

Ryan Hardwick, Jan Heylen, Zacharie Robichon

Australier Campbell und der Franzose Jaminet feierten ihren ersten Titelgewinn in der IMSA WeatherTech Meisterschaft dennoch ausgelassen. „Es war ein unglaubliches Jahr für uns, ich könnte nicht stolzer auf jedes einzelne Teammitglied von Pfaff Motorsports sein. Wir haben in den vergangenen zwei Saisons unglaubliche Erfolge erzielt", strahlte Teammanager Steve Bortolotti nach dem Triumph.
In 2022 gewann Pfaff in der GTD-Pro-Klasse das Rolex 24 At Daytona, die Läufe auf dem WeatherTech Raceway Laguna Seca, sowie im Canadian Tire Motorsport Park und feierte Gesamtsiege im Lime Rock Park und auf dem VIRginia International Raceway. Zudem erreichte die Truppe drei weitere Podiumsplätze: je eine dritte Position beim Finale in Road Atlanta, sowie bei den Six Hours of the Glen und einen zweiten Rang in Road America. Mit dem Gesamtsieg in der GTD-Pro-Klasse bejubelte Pfaff Motorsports zum zweiten Mal in Folge einen IMSA-Titel, im Jahr 2021 gewann das Unternehmen mit dem Porsche 911 GT3 R die GTD-Klasse.
Die Kanadier debütierten 2019 in der GTD der IMSA WeatherTech SportsCar Championship. Seit jenem ersten Auftritt setzt das Team denselben Porsche 911 GT3 R ein. In den vier Saisons, in denen exakt dieses Fahrzeug in der GTD- und später auch in der GTD-Pro-Klasse lief, hat es elf Siege und fünf Pole Positions errungen, bevor es am Saisonende 2022 in Rente geschickt wurde. Es wird beim Saisonauftakt 2023 im Januar des kommenden Jahres durch den neuen Porsche 911 GT3 R vom Typ 992 ersetzt.
Während Pfaff Motorsports in der Klasse GTD-Pro erfolgreich war, hielt Wright Motorsports das gesamte Jahr über die Porsche-Fahne in der GTD-Klasse hoch; sie meldeten den nunmehr in den USA lebenden Belgier Jan Heylen, den US-Amerikaner Ryan Hardwick und den Kanadier Zacharie Robichon für ihren Porsche mit der Nummer 16. Die Hardpoint-Piloten Rob Ferriol aus den USA und Katherine Legge aus Großbritannien teilten sich für den Großteil der GTD-Rennen den Wagen mit der Nummer 99, für den sie bei den langen Läufen Unterstützung durch den Briten Stefan Wilson und den US-Amerikaner Nick Boulle bekamen. Bei ausgewählten Auftritten zu Beginn der Saison setzte GMG Racing die Nummer 34 für die amerikanischen Fahrer Kyle Washington und James Sofronas ein, während sich der Niederländer Jeroen Bleekemolen und der Österreicher Klaus Bachler bei den Endurance-Läufen als dritter Pilot abwechselten. Das Michelin-Pilot-Challenge-Team TGM mit Besitzer und Fahrer Ted Giovanis aus den USA, den US-amerikanischen Brüdern Hugh und Matt Plumb, sowie dessen Landsmann Owen Trinkler ließ den Porsche mit der Startnummer 64 in Daytona von der GTD-Leine. Und schließlich schrieb WeatherTech Racing für die ersten beiden Veranstaltungen der Saison noch einen in der GTD-Klasse genannten Porsche für Cooper MacNeil aus den USA, den Franzosen Julien Andlauer, den Italiener Matteo Cairoli und den Belgier Alessio Picariello ein.
Wright Motorsports mit Hardwick und Heylen verpasste den GTD-Titel äußerst knapp, gerade einmal 23 Zähler lagen am Ende zwischen dem belgisch-amerikanischen Duo und dem neuen Champion Roman de Angelis. Die Fahrzeuge der Klasse GTD sind identisch mit denen der GTD-Pro-Klasse, allerdings werden die Renner in der GTD-Klasse mit Pro-Am-ähnlichen Fahrerpaarungen besetzt anstelle der ausschließlich professionellen Piloten, die in den GTD-Pro-Autos zum Einsatz kommen.
Das Porsche-Kundenteam Wright Motorsports wollte die GTD-Saison beim Finale auf dem Michelin Raceway Road Atlanta eigentlich so abschließen, wie sie es beim Rolex

Cooper MacNeil, Julien Andlauer, Alessio Picariello

Matt Campbell

24 At Daytona begonnen hatte: mit einem Sieg. Letztendlich belegten sie jedoch nur den vierten Platz und verpassten damit die für den Titelgewinn in der Klasse GTD erforderlichen Punkte. Hardwick / Heylen feierten 2022 zwei Rennsiege und dürfen sich nun Vize-Champions der GTD-Klasse in der IMSA WeatherTech SportsCar Championship nennen. Im Jahr 2021 gewannen Heylen und Trent Hindman, zu denen sich damals in seinem letzten Profirennen noch Patrick Long gesellte, auf den letzten Metern des Zehn-Stunden-Rennens die Endurance-Wertung.

„Dass wir den Titel nur knapp verpasst haben, bricht mir zwar das Herz, aber es macht mich auch stolz, dass wir bis zum Schluss im Titelkampf dabei waren. Ryan und Jan sind eine unglaubliche Saison gefahren und haben in einem so starken Feld echten Kampfgeist bewiesen. Die Crew hat in der Boxengasse immer wieder Positionen gutmachen können und die Leistung und Standfestigkeit des Porsche sucht in dieser Serie ihresgleichen. Wir haben fehlerfrei gearbeitet und ich bin stolz auf jeden Einzelnen", so John Wright, Teambesitzer von Wright Motorsports.

Insgesamt war 2022 für Porsche im nordamerikanischen Automobilsport eine Saison, in der neben dem Sieg in der Fahrer-, Team- und Herstellerwertung auch die eigenen Rekorde weiter ausgebaut werden konnten. Bei einer Teilnahme an ausnahmslos jedem IMSA-Rennen, das jemals ausgetragen wurde, hat Porsche Stand Ende 2022 insgesamt 593 IMSA-Siegertrophäen in seinem Regal stehen. Das sind 243 Pokale mehr als der nächste Konkurrent Chevrolet bis zu diesem Zeitpunkt gesammelt hat. Darüber hinaus hat der deutsche Sportwagenhersteller 472 IMSA-Pole-Positions erobert, was ebenfalls einen Rekord darstellt und 111 erste Startplätze in der Klasse mehr sind als die Bilanz von Chevrolet aufweist. Der Porsche 911 GT3 R, der 2023 durch die neueste Generation auf der Plattform des Typs 992 abgelöst wird, hat seit seinem Debüt beim Rolex 24 At Daytona 2019 14 Siege und zehn Titel in den IMSA-Klassen GTD und GTD Pro zu dieser Bilanz beigetragen.

Rob Ferriol, Katherine Legge, Stefan Wilson

Matt Campbell, Mathieu Jaminet

(l.-r.): Matt Campbell, Mathieu Jaminet, Felipe Nasr

Kyle Washington, James Sofronas

(l.-r.): Volker Holzmeyer, Jan Heylen, Thomas Laudenbach, Alwin Springer

Rob Ferriol, Katherine Legge, Stefan Wilson

The 2022 season was record-setting for the team, drivers and Porsche in North American auto racing. It marked a celebration not only for the Team and Drivers' title but also for Porsche which took top honors among manufacturers. Having been involved in every IMSA race ever held, Porsche has 593 race winning trophies (combined chassis/engine) on its shelf through to the end of 2022. The record is 243 more than nearest rival, Chevrolet. Additionally, the German sports car maker has 472 IMSA pole positions, which is also a record. It has started first in its class a phenomenal 111 more times than Chevy.

Pfaff Motorsports debuted in the GTD class of the IMSA WeatherTech SportsCar Championship in 2019. The team has used the same Porsche 911 GT3 R to compete every year since. Over the four seasons they have been eligible to race in the GTD and now GTD Pro classes, the "Plaid Porsche" has earned 11 career wins and five pole positions before it was finally retired at year's end. It will be replaced by the new type 992 Porsche 911 GT3 R racer at the season-opening Rolex 24 in January of 2023.

Pfaff Motorsports' race victories this season include the Rolex 24 At Daytona, WeatherTech Raceway Laguna Seca, Canadian Tire Motorsport Park and overall victories at both Lime Rock Park and at VIRginia International Raceway. The Steve Bortolotti-managed program had three other podium finishes including third place at the Road Atlanta finale as well as the Six Hours of the Glen and a second-place at Road America during the season.

The 2022 GTD Pro class marked back-to-back titles for Pfaff. In 2021, with the same Porsche 911 GT3 R race car, the operation won the GTD class title.

"It's been an incredible year, and I couldn't be more proud of every member of the Pfaff Motorsports team,' said Steve Bortolotti, Team Manager of Pfaff Motorsports. "We've achieved incredible success over the past two seasons, but it's not every year you're fortunate enough to have the opportunity to chase records with minimal risk."

Wright Motorsports and its drivers Ryan Hardwick and Jan Heylen fell just shy of the GTD championship finishing the year in second-place only 23 points behind the winners. The class is identical to the GTD Pro class but with a Pro-Am style driver line-up . Full-season Porsche privateer Wright entered each race of the season. The stalwart Porsche customer team arrived at the Michelin Raceway Road Atlanta eager to finish the year as started, with a major endurance race victory. Having won the Daytona 24 Hours in January, they were optimistic of their chances in the Petit Le Mans. However, they finished the race in fourth place, short of the needed points tally for their second successive title. Hardwick/Heylen closed 2022 with two race wins, the second coming at WeatherTech Raceway Laguna Seca. .

"While it's heartbreaking, it makes me so proud that each year, we're right there in the fight to the very end," says John Wright, team owner of Wright Motorsports. "Ryan and Jan drove an incredible season, and really showed some true grit against such a competitive field. The crew consistently gained positions in pit lane, and the Porsche's power and stability have no match in this series. We executed flawlessly and I'm proud of everyone."

The Porsche 911 GT3 R race car, which will be replaced in 2023 with the newest iteration based on the type 992 platform, has proven an impressive racing machine since its 2019 Rolex 24 At Daytona debut. In that time, Porsche customer teams compiled 14 victories and ten championships in the IMSA GTD and GTD Pro classes – seven of those wins coming in 2022. Five of the victories have come from Pfaff Motorsports (Rolex 24 At Daytona, WeatherTech Raceway Laguna Seca, Canadian Tire Motorsport Park, Lime Rock Park, VIRginia International Raceway) and two from Wright Motorsports (Rolex 24 At Daytona and WeatherTech Raceway Laguna Seca).

Matt Campbell, Mathieu Jaminet, Felipe Nasr

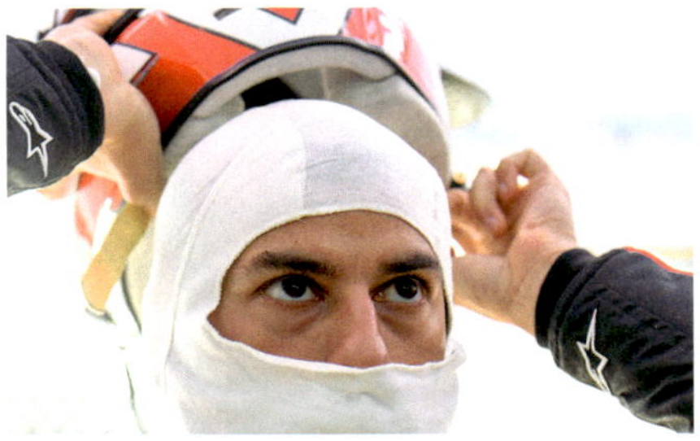

MOTUL
POLE AWARD

VICTORY LANE
Welcome home.
VICTORY LANE
MOTUL

CHAMPIONS

driveway
MOTUL

driveway
driveway
MOTUL

Matt Campbell, Mathieu Jaminet, Felipe Nasr

(l.-r.): Ryan Hardwick, Jan Heylen, Zacharie Robichon

Cooper MacNeil, Julien Andlauer, Alessio Picariello

DRIVER STANDINGS **GTD PRO**

POS	NO	DRIVERS	CAR	TEAM	POINTS
1	**9**	**Mathieu Jaminet, Matt Campbell**	**Porsche 911 GT3 R II**	**Pfaff Motorsport**	**3497**
2	14	Ben Barnicoat	Lexus RC F GT3	Vasser Sullivan	3277
3	3	Antonio Garcia, Jordan Taylor	Chevrolet Corvette C8.R GTD	Corvette Racing	3194
7	**79, 97**	**Cooper MacNeil**	**Porsche 911 GT3 R II**	**WeatherTech Racing**	**1701**
10	**9**	**Felipe Nasr**	**Porsche 911 GT3 R II**	**Pfaff Motorsport**	**992**
21	**79**	**Alessio Picariello, Julien Andlauer**	**Porsche 911 GT3 R II**	**WeatherTech Racing**	**524**
24	**2**	**Alexandre Imperatori, Dennis Olsen, Laurens Vanthoor, Patrick Pilet**	**Porsche 911 GT3 R II**	**KCMG**	**321**
32	**79**	**Matteo Cairoli**	**Porsche 911 GT3 R II**	**WeatherTech Racing**	**253**

DRIVER STANDINGS **GTD**

POS	NO	DRIVERS	CAR	TEAM	POINTS
1	27	Roman DeAngelis	Aston Martin Vantage GT3	Heart of Racing Team	2898
2	**16**	**Jan Heylen, Ryan Hardwick**	**Porsche 911 GT3 R II**	**Wright Motorsports**	**2875**
3	32	Steven McAleer	Mercedes-AMG GT3 Evo	Team Korthoff Motorsports	2860
16	**99**	**Rob Ferriol, Katherine Legge**	**Porsche 911 GT3 R II**	**Team Hardpoint**	**1292**
19	**16**	**Zacharie Robichon**	**Porsche 911 GT3 R II**	**Wright Motorsports**	**1191**
35	**99**	**Stefan Wilson**	**Porsche 911 GT3 R II**	**Team Hardpoint**	**627**
42	**99**	**Nick Boulle**	**Porsche 911 GT3 R II**	**Allied Racing**	**435**
52	**34**	**James Sofronas, Kyle Washington**	**Porsche 911 GT3 R II**	**GMG Racing**	**323**
56	**64**	**Hugh Plumb, Matt Plumb, Owen Trinkler, Ted Giovanis**	**Porsche 911 GT3 R II**	**TeamTGM**	**252**
71	**34**	**Jeroen Bleekemolen, Klaus Bachler**	**Porsche 911 GT3 R II**	**GMG Racing**	**106**

DRIVER STANDINGS **MICHELIN ENDURANCE CUP GTD PRO**

POS	NO	DRIVERS	CAR	TEAM	POINTS
1	62	Daniel Serra, Davide Rigon	Ferrari F488 GT3 Evo	Risi Competizione	35
2	**9**	**Mathieu Jaminet, Matt Campbell**	**Porsche 911 GT3 R II**	**Pfaff Motorsport**	**33**
3	3	Antonio Garcia, Jordan Taylor	Chevrolet Corvette C8.R GTD	Corvette Racing	33
8	**9**	**Felipe Nasr**	**Porsche 911 GT3 R II**	**Pfaff Motorsport**	**28**
14	**79, 97**	**Cooper MacNeil**	**Porsche 911 GT3 R II**	**WeatherTech Racing**	**18**
18	**2**	**Alexandre Imperatori, Dennis Olsen, Laurens Vanthoor, Patrick Pilet**	**Porsche 911 GT3 R II**	**KCMG**	**17**
20	**79**	**Alessio Picariello, Julien Andlauer**	**Porsche 911 GT3 R II**	**WeatherTech Racing**	**14**
29	**79**	**Matteo Cairoli**	**Porsche 911 GT3 R II**	**WeatherTech Racing**	**8**

TEAM STANDINGS **GTD**

POS	NO	TEAM	CAR	POINTS
1	27	Heart of Racing Team	Aston Martin Vantage GT3	2898
2	**16**	**Wright Motorsports**	**Porsche 911 GT3 R II**	**2875**
3	32	Team Korthoff Motorsports	Mercedes-AMG GT3 Evo	2860
12	**99**	**Team Hardpoint**	**Porsche 911 GT3 R II**	**1292**
21	**34**	**GMG Racing**	**Porsche 911 GT3 R II**	**373**
22	**64**	**TeamTGM**	**Porsche 911 GT3 R II**	**252**

TEAM STANDINGS **GTD PRO**

POS	NO	TEAM	CAR	POINTS
1	**9**	**Pfaff Motorsports**	**Porsche 911 GT3 R II**	**3497**
2	14	Vasser Sullivan	Lexus RC F GT3	3277
3	3	Corvette Racing	Chevrolet Corvette C8.R GTD	3194

TEAM STANDINGS **MICHELIN ENDURANCE CUP GTD PRO**

POS	NO	TEAM	CAR	POINTS
1	62	Risi Competizione	Ferrari F488 GT3 Evo	35
2	**9**	**Pfaff Motorsports**	**Porsche 911 GT3 R II**	**33**
3	3	Corvette Racing	Chevrolet Corvette C8.R GTD	33
7	**79**	**WeatherTech Racing**	**Porsche 911 GT3 R II**	**18**
11	**2**	**KCMG**	**Porsche 911 GT3 R II**	**17**

MANUFACTURER STANDINGS **GTD**

POS	MANUFACTURER	CAR	POINTS
1	BMW	BMW M4 GT3	3307
2	Mercedes-AMG	Mercedes-AMG GT3 Evo	3235
3	Aston Martin	Chevrolet Corvette C8.R GTD	3193
4	**Porsche**	**Porsche 911 GT3 R II**	**3004**

MANUFACTURER STANDINGS **GTD PRO**

POS	MANUFACTURER	CAR	POINTS
1	**Porsche**	**Porsche 911 GT3 R II**	**3497**
2	Lexus	Lexus RC F GT3	3307
3	Chevrolet	Chevrolet Corvette C8.R GTD	3204

MANUFACTURER STANDINGS **MICHELIN ENDURANCE GTD PRO**

POS	TEAM	CAR	POINTS
1	**Porsche**	**Porsche 911 GT3 R II**	**39**
2	Ferrari	Ferrari F488 GT3 Evo	36
3	Lexus	Lexus RC F GT3	34

EUROPEAN LE MANS SERIES

15.04.–17.04.2022 Paul Ricard, France
13.05.–15.05.2022 Imola, Italy
01.07.–02.07.2022 Monza, Italy
26.08.–28.08.2022 Barcelona, Spain
23.09.–25.09.2022 Spa-Francorchamps, Belgium
14.10.–16.10.2022 Portimão, Portugal

Christian Ried, Lorenzo Ferrari, Gianmaria Bruni

Erfolgreiche Saison für Porsche in der European Le Mans Series – Proton Competition sichert sich den Meistertitel in der hartumkämpften LMGTE-Klasse

Drei Porsche 911 RSR gingen 2022 in der stark besetzten LMGTE-Klasse der European Le Mans Series (ELMS) an den Start. Sechs vierstündige Rennen standen im Kalender der Meisterschaft – und das Jahr hätte nicht spannender sein können: In jedem Lauf durften die Fans einen anderen Sieger bejubeln. In einem packenden Titelkampf, der bis zum Saisonfinale in Portimão offen war, setzte sich letztlich Proton Competition durch. Für Porsche und das Team war es der erste Titelgewinn in der kontinentalen Langstreckenserie des ACO seit 2020. Zum Erfolgstrio im 911 RSR mit der Startnummer 77 gehörten Porsche-Werksfahrer Gianmaria Bruni, sein italienischer Landsmann Lorenzo Ferrari sowie Christian Ried, der zugleich Teamchef der Mannschaft ist. Mit einem zweiten Rang auf dem Circuit Paul Ricard in Le Castellet starteten die Piloten bereits erfolgreich in die Saison. Beim zweiten Lauf im italienischen Imola erlitt das Team jedoch einen Rückschlag: Aufgrund eines mechanischen Problems musste die Mannschaft aus Ummendorf in Baden-Württemberg das Fahrzeug bereits in der Anfangsphase abstellen. Beim folgenden Lauf auf dem norditalienischen Highspeed-Kurs in Monza meldeten sich Bruni, Ferrari und Ried mit einem zweiten Rang in der Klasse erfolgreich zurück. Noch mehr Grund zur Freude hatte das Team dann beim vierten Saisonrennen auf dem Circuit de Barcelona-Catalunya. Auf dem spanischen Formel-1-Kurs fuhr das treue Porsche-Kundenteam den ersten und einzigen Klassensieg in der Saison ein. Vom dritten Startplatz hatte sich das Trio im Verlauf bis an die Spitze gekämpft und gab diese nicht wieder ab. Mit rund 14 Sekunden Vorsprung überquerte Bruni die Ziellinie souverän als Sieger. Nach einem neunten Rang auf der Ardennenachterbahn von Spa-Francorchamps reichte den drei Piloten beim Saisonfinale im portugiesischen Portimão Rang fünf zum Titelgewinn in

(93): Michael Fassbender, Zacharie Robichon, Richard Lietz
(18): Andrew Haryanto, Alessio Picariello, Martin Rump
(77): Christian Ried, Lorenzo Ferrari, Gianmaria Bruni

Successful season for Porsche in European Le Mans Series – Proton Competition secures the title in the hard-fought LMGTE class

Three Porsche 911 RSRs raced in the highly contested LMGTE class of the European Le Mans Series. Each of the six four-hour races produced a different winner. Eventually, it was Porsche's Proton Competition that came out on top in the battle for the title that went down to the wire at Portimão. For Porsche and the team, it was the first title win in the continental ACO endurance series since 2020. The successful trio in the #77 911 RSR consisted of Porsche works driver Gianmaria Bruni, his Italian compatriot Lorenzo Ferrari and team principal Christian Ried. They started the season with second place at Paul Ricard, but retired early from the second race at Imola due to a technical issue. At Monza, they finished second again and went on to score their only win of the season at Barcelona. After a ninth-place finish at Spa-Francorchamps, fifth in the finale at Portimão was enough to seal the LMGTE crown. Proton Competition ran another 911 RSR for Hollywood star Michael Fassbender. Born in Heidelberg, the German-Irish actor enjoyed his third ELMS season with the Porsche team in 2022. Together with works driver Richard Lietz and Zacharie Robichon, he raced the #93 car. The trio got its season off to a successful start with third at Paul Ricard, but it was the only podium result of the season. The driving team ended up eleventh in the final standings. Absolute Racing ran another 911 RSR for its second season in ELMS. The team led by Ingo Matter and Fabien Fior received technical support from Proton Competition. Its drivers Andrew Haryanto, Alessio Picariello and Martin Rump finished third in class at Spa, which was their best season result. The team was sixth in the final standings.

Christian Ried and Andrew Haryanto

Christian Ried

(77): Christian Ried, Lorenzo Ferrari, Gianmaria Bruni - (18): Andrew Haryanto, Alessio Picariello, Martin Rump

17 APRIL
GOODYEAR

4 HOURS OF LE CASTELLET
17 APRIL
GOODYEAR

Proton Competition
PORSCHE

M. Fassbender
Robichon
R. Lietz

CHRIS

ABSOLUTE RACING
HARYANTO

Michael Fassbender, Zacharie Robichon, Richard Lietz

Michael Fassbender

Andrew Haryanto, Alessio Picariello, Martin Rump

der LMGTE-Klasse. Das Team erhielt damit auch eine Einladung für die legendären 24 Stunden von Le Mans im Jahr 2023. Einen zweiten Porsche 911 RSR setzte Proton Competition für Hollywood-Star Michael Fassbender ein. Der, in Heidelberg geborene, deutsch-irische Schauspieler bestritt 2022 bereits seine dritte ELMS-Saison mit dem Porsche-Team. Gemeinsam mit dem österreichischen Porsche-Werksfahrer Richard Lietz und Zacharie Robichon teilte er sich das Cockpit der Startnummer 93. Mit einem dritten Klassenrang in Le Castellet begann die Saison für das Fahrertrio ähnlich erfolgreich wie für das Schwesterfahrzeug. Doch am Ende sollte es der einzige Podestrang für das Fahreraufgebot sein. Was folgte, waren zwei siebte Ränge in Imola und Spa-Francorchamps sowie ein Ausfall in Monza. Nach zwei achten Positionen in Barcelona und Portimão schloss das Team die Saison auf Platz elf der Gesamtwertung ab. Einen weiteren Porsche 911 RSR setzte Absolute Racing ein. Für die Mannschaft aus Hong Kong war es die zweite Saison in der ELMS. Technische Unterstützung erhielt das Team von Ingo Matter und Fabien Fior dabei von Proton Competition. Der Porsche 911 RSR mit der Startnummer 18 ging erneut im beliebten Gummienten-Design, welches sich gegen Diskriminierung ausspricht und das Motto „OneWorldOneRace" trägt, an den Start. Am Steuer des Porsche wechselten sich Andrew Haryanto, Alessio Picariello und Martin Rump ab. Ihr bestes Saisonergebnis holten sie als Dritte in Spa-Francorchamps. Die Saison beendete die Mannschaft auf der sechsten Position in der Gesamtwertung der LMGTE-Klasse.

Team Proton Competition

Andrew Haryanto, Alessio Picariello, Martin Rump

(l.-r): Lorenzo Ferrari, Gianmaria Bruni, Richard Lietz, Zacharie Robichon, Michael Fassbender, Christian Ried

(l.-r.): Gianmaria Bruni, Christian Ried, Lorenzo Ferrari

(93): Michael Fassbender, Zacharie Robichon, Richard Lietz - (77): Christian Ried, Lorenzo Ferrari, Gianmaria Bruni - (18): Andrew Haryanto, Alessio Picariello, Martin Rump

DRIVER STANDINGS **GTE**

POS	NO	DRIVERS	CAR	TEAM	POINTS
1	77	**Christian Ried, Gianmaria Bruni, Lorenzo Ferrari**	**Porsche 911 RSR II**	**Proton Competition**	**82**
2	57	Frederik Schandorff, Mikkel Jensen	Ferrari F488 GTE Evo	Kessel Racing	78
3	83	Michelle Gatting, Sarah Bovy	Ferrari F488 GTE Evo	Iron Lynx	70
7	**18**	**Andrew Haryanto, Martin Rump, Alessio Picariello**	**Porsche 911 RSR II**	**Absolute Racing**	**57**
14	93	**Michael Fassbender, Richard Lietz, Zacharie Robichon**	**Porsche 911 RSR II**	**Proton Competition**	35

TEAM STANDINGS **GTE**

POS	NO	TEAM	CAR	POINTS
1	77	**Proton Competition**	**Porsche 911 RSR II**	**82**
2	57	Kessel Racing	Ferrari F488 GT3 Evo	78
3	83	Iron Lynx	Ferrari F488 GT3 Evo	70
6	**18**	**Absolute Racing**	**Porsche 911 RSR II**	**49**
11	93	**Proton Competition**	**Porsche 911 RSR II**	35

FIA WORLD ENDURANCE CHAMPIONSHIP

FIA WORLD ENDURANCE CHAMPIONSHIP

16.03.–18.03.2022	Sebring 1000 Miles, Florida, USA
05.05.–07.05.2022	Spa-Francorchamps 6 Hours, Belgium
08.06.–12.06.2022	Le Mans 24 Hours, France
08.07.–10.07.2022	Monza 6 Hours, Italy
09.10.–11.09.2022	Fuji 6 Hours, Japan
10.11.–12.11.2022	Bahrain 8 Hours, Bahrain

Porsche erhoffte sich beim werksseitigen Abschied des 911 RSR einen Titel. Die Kundenteams Dempsey Proton Racing und Project 1 siegten unterdessen dreimal in der Klasse.

(88): Fred Poordad, Patrick Lindsey, Jan Heylen - (56): - Brendan Iribe, Ollie Millroy, Ben Barnicoat
(86): Michael Wainwright, Ben Barker, Riccardo Pera

In der Langstrecken-Weltmeisterschaft ist seit der Premierensaison 2012 immer wieder die Rede von „Übergangsjahren". Die Organisatoren versuchen alles, die Meisterschaft fit für die Zukunft zu machen. 2022 war da keine wirkliche Ausnahme: Es war das letzte Jahr, in dem in der LMGTE Pro-Kategorie um den WM-Titel gekämpft wurde. Die Klasse, in der sich Porsche mit Ferrari bis zum Schluss ein Duell um den Titel lieferte, gehört der Geschichte an. Damit ist auch die Ära des Porsche 911 RSR zu Ende – werksseitig zumindest. In der LMGTE Am-Klasse dürfen die Fahrzeuge 2023 noch von Privatteams eingesetzt werden, ehe ab 2024 mit GT3-Autos gefahren wird.

Unter diesen Umständen hätte sich das Porsche GT Team natürlich nichts sehnlicher gewünscht, als das Kapitel mit einem Titel abzuschließen. Doch aus den Hoffnungen wurde nichts und die Enttäuschung stand Kévin Estre und Michael Christensen nach dem letzten Rennen ins Gesicht geschrieben. Rund zwei Stunden vor Rennende beim Finale in Bahrain traten Getriebeprobleme am Ferrari der Tabellenführer Alessandro Pier Guidi und James Calado auf. Die beiden Porsche-Werksfahrer Estre und Christensen witterten ihre Chance, in der Tabelle doch noch vorbeizuziehen und die Weltmeisterschaft nach Weissach zu holen. Doch zur großen Überraschung aller Beteiligten fiel der AF Corse-Ferrari nicht aus, sondern hielt bis zum Fallen der Zielflagge. „So hatten wir uns das nicht vorgestellt. Wir sind angetreten, um beide Titel zu holen – nun stehen wir mit leeren Händen da", fasste es Kévin Estre zusammen. „Wir hatten im finalen Rennen einfach nicht den notwendigen Speed. Wir haben dann versucht, strategisch noch etwas zu erreichen, aber dabei fehlte uns das nötige Glück. In der zweiten Saisonhälfte war Ferrari leider immer schneller als wir."

Kévin Estre, Michael Christensen

Porsche hoped to crown the farewell season of its factory-911 RSRs with a title, but remained empty-handed. Meanwhile, customer teams Dempsey Proton Racing and Project 1 scored three class wins.

Since 2012, the inaugural year of the World Endurance Championship, many a season was called a "transition year". The organisers try everything to make the championship fit for the future. 2022 was no real exception: it was the final year in which a world championship title was at stake in the LMGTE Pro category. The class in which Porsche staged a duel for the title with Ferrari that went down to the wire is now a thing of the past. And as a result, the era of the 911 RSR has come to an end as well, at least as a factory car. In the LMGTE Am class, privateer teams are still allowed to run the cars in 2023 before GT3 cars will be used from 2024 onwards. In these conditions, the Porsche GT Team wanted nothing more eagerly than crowning this chapter with a title win. However, hopes were blown and after the final race, Kévin Estre and Michael Christensen were visibly disappointed. With around two hours remaining in the finale at Bahrain, gearbox issues occurred on the Ferrari with points leaders Alessandro Pier Guidi and James Calado. Porsche works driver Estre and Christensen saw their chances of still moving ahead in the standings and bring the world championship to Weissach. However, to the big surprise of everyone involved, the AF Corse Ferrari didn't retire, but held on until the chequered flag was waved. "This is not how we imagined it. We came here to win both titles and now we stand here empty-handed," Kévin Estre summed up. "We just didn't have the speed in the final race. We then tried to do something strategic, but luck wasn't on our side. Unfortunately, Ferrari was always faster than us in the second half of the season."

Richard Lietz and Gianmaria Bruni

Michael Wainwright, Ben Barker, Riccardo Pera

Matteo Cairoli, Mikkel Pedersen, Nicolas Leutwiler

Julien Andlauer, Fred Poordad, Patrick Lindsey

Was von der Saison 2022 bleibt, sind Einzelerfolge bei den „großen" Rennen im Kalender. So setzten sich Gianmaria Bruni, Richard Lietz und Frédéric Makowiecki bei den 24 Stunden von Le Mans durch. Außerdem ging der Sieg beim Auftakt in Sebring aufs Konto des Porsche-Werksteams.
Ähnlich verlief das Jahr aus Porsche-Sicht in der LMGTE Am-Klasse. Zwar schaffte es keines der Kundenteams, einen Titel einzufahren – gejubelt werden durfte dennoch mehrmals. Allen voran das Team Project 1 hatte Grund zur Freude. Nach einer holprigen Saison gelang beim Finale in Bahrain endlich der Befreiungsschlag in Form eines Doppelsiegs. Niki Leutwiler, Mikkel O. Pedersen und Matteo Cairoli setzten sich im achtstündigen Rennen gegen die Konkurrenz durch und überquerten die Ziellinie als Erste. PJ Hyett, Gunnar Jeanette und Ben Barnicoat machten im Schwesterfahrzeug als Zweitplatzierte den Erfolg perfekt. „Mich hat das so unfassbar stolz gemacht, die Jungs da oben auf dem Treppchen zu sehe , so wollen wir weitermachen!", sagte Axel Funke dazu. Der Teammanager von Project 1 war zu Recht stolz, da es zugleich der erste Doppelsieg eines Porsche-Teams in der LMGTE Am-Klasse war.

Matteo Cairoli, Mikkel Pedersen, Nicolas Leutwiler

Ben Barnicoat, Gunnar Jeannette, PJ Hyett

(l.-r.): Richard Lietz, Gianmaria Bruni, Kévin Estre, Michael Christensen

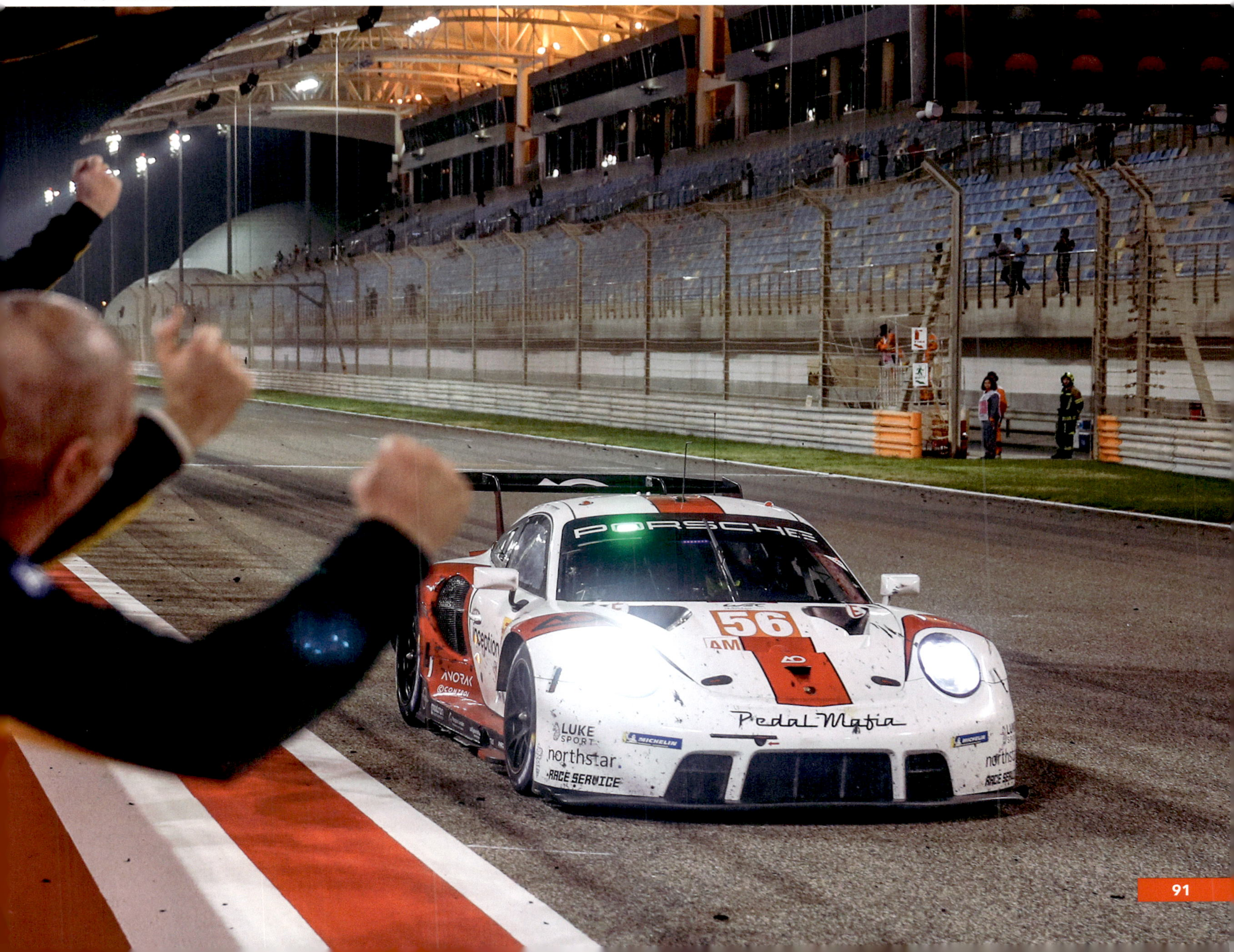

Dass zwei weitere Porsche-Siege eingefahren wurden, ist der Mannschaft von Dempsey Proton Racing zu verdanken. „Dazu hat das ganze Team mit großem Engagement und sehr viel Herzblut beigetragen", so Teamchef Michael Ried. „Wir können damit sehr zufrieden sein. Was uns gefehlt hat, ist eine gewisse Konstanz über die gesamte Saison, um mit weiteren Topergebnissen auf diesen Siegen aufbauen zu können. Wir hätten uns damit im Titelrennen eine noch bessere Position sichern können."
Sowohl im belgischen Spa-Francorchamps als auch im italienischen Monza triumphierte das Proton-Team. Beide Male saßen Christian Ried und seine britischen Teamkollegen Sebastian Priaulx und Harry Tincknell am Steuer. Außerdem setzte der Rennstall rund um die beiden Ried-Brüder einen Porsche 911 RSR für Fred Poordad, Patrick Lindsey und Jan Heylen ein. Hinzu kam der Einsatz eines Fahrzeugs, das bei den 24 Stunden von Le Mans unter WeatherTech-Flagge am Start war. Cooper MacNeil, Julien Andlauer und Thomas Merrill belegten hierbei Rang drei. Das Trio landete vor Ben Barker, Michael Wainwright und Riccardo Pera von GR Racing.

Kévin Estre, Michael Christensen

Gianmaria Bruni, Richard Lietz

(l.-r.): Ollie Millroy, Brendan Iribe, Ben Barnicoat

Christian Ried, Harry Tincknell, Sebastian Priaulx

(46): Matteo Cairoli, Mikkel Pedersen, Nicolas Leutwiler · (56): Brendan Iribe, Ollie Millroy, Ben Barnicoat

What remains from the 2022 season are one-off achievements in the "major" races on the calendar. For instance, Gianmaria Bruni, Richard Lietz and Frédéric Makowiecki came out on top in the Le Mans 24 Hours. Moreover, victory in the season opener at Sebring went to the Porsche works team.

From a Porsche perspective, the year in the LMGTE Am class was a similar affair. None of the customer teams managed to win a title, but there was reason to celebrate on multiple occasions. The Project 1 team first and foremost could be happy. After a patchy season, the team finally came good with a 1-2 in the finale at Bahrain. Niki Leutwiler, Mikkel O. Pedersen and Matteo Cairoli had the better of their opponents in the eight-hour race and crossed the finish line in first place. PJ Hyett, Gunnar Jeanette and Ben Barnicoat completed the success by finishing second with the sister car. "Seeing the guys up there on the podium made me so incredibly proud," Axel Funke commented. The Project 1 teammanager had every right to be proud as it was

Nicolas Leutwiler

Fred Poordad

Fred Poordad, Patrick Lindsey, Jan Heylen

Brendan Iribe, Ollie Millroy, Ben Barnicoat

Fred Poordad, Patrick Lindsey, Jan Heylen

(l.-r.): Harry Tincknell, Sebastian Priaulx, Christian Ried

also the first-ever 1-2 by a Porsche team in the LMGTE Am class.
It was thanks to the Dempsey Proton Racing team that two further Porsche race wins were achieved. "The entire team has contributed to that with massive commitment and a lot of passion," team principal Michael Ried said. "We can be very happy with this. What we lacked is a certain consistency throughout the season to build on these victories with further top results. Like that, we could have achieved a better position in the battle for the title."
The Proton team was victorious both at Spa-Francorchamps in Belgium and at Monza in Italy. On both occasions, Christian Ried and his British teammates Sebastian Priaulx and Harry Tincknell were the drivers. On top of that, the team led by the two Ried brothers ran a Porsche 911 RSR for Fred Poordad, Patrick Lindsey and Jan Heylen. Yet another car ran under the WeatherTech banner in the Le Mans 24 Hours. Here, Cooper MacNeil, Julien Andlauer and Thomas Merrill ended up in third place ahead of GR Racing's Ben Barker, Michael Wainwright and Riccardo Pera.

Tubbs Wanigasekera and Michael Christensen

Matteo Cairoli, Mikkel Pedersen, Nicolas Leutwiler

Pedal Mafia
BTR Logistics
WeCare

BOSS

stilo

CHRIS

HRX

HRX
inception

BOSS
WEC

8 Hours Bahrain

PORSCHE
MANTHEY

MICHELIN
HOPKINS
WEC

HOPKINS
P. Poordad
sparco

(l.-r.): Ben Barnicoat, Gunnar Jeanette, P.J. Hyett, Matteo Cairoli, Mikkel Pedersen, Nicolas Leutwiler

DRIVER STANDINGS **LMGTE**

POS	NO	DRIVERS	CAR	TEAM	POINTS
1	51	Alessandro Pier Guidi, James Calado	Ferrari 488 GT3 Evo	AF Corse	135
2	92	Kévin Estre, Michael Christensen	Porsche 911 RSR II	Porsche GT Team	132
3	52	Antonio Fuoco, Miguel Molina	Ferrari 488 GT3 Evo	AF Corse	131
4	91	Gianmaria Bruni	Porsche 911 RSR II	Porsche GT Team	125
5	91	Richard Lietz	Porsche 911 RSR II	Porsche GT Team	115
7	91	Frédéric Makowiecki	Porsche 911 RSR II	Porsche GT Team	60
13	92	Laurens Vanthoor	Porsche 911 RSR II	Porsche GT Team	24
15	77	Christian Ried, Harry Tincknell, Sebastian Priaulx	Porsche 911 RSR II	Dempsey-Proton Racing	19
16	46	Matteo Cairoli, Mikkel Pedersen, Nicolas Leutwiler	Porsche 911 RSR II	Team Project 1	17
17	56	Ben Barnicoat	Porsche 911 RSR II	Team Project 1	15
18	86	Benjamin Barker, Michael Wainwright, Riccardo Pera	Porsche 911 RSR II	GR Racing	12
20	56	Gunnar Jeannette, P. J. Hyett	Porsche 911 RSR II	Team Project 1	9
21	88	Fred Poordad, Jan Heylen, Maxwell Root	Porsche 911 RSR II	Dempsey-Proton Racing	8
22	56	Oliver Millroy, Brendan Iribe	Porsche 911 RSR II	Team Project 1	6

Christian Ried

DRIVER STANDINGS **LMGTE AM**

POS	NO	DRIVERS	CAR	TEAM	POINTS
1	33	Ben Keating, Marco Sørensen	Aston Martin Vantage AMR GTE	TF Sport	141
2	98	Paul Dalla Lana, David Pittard, Nicki Thiim	Aston Martin Vantage AMR GTE	Northwest AMR	118
3	33	Henrique Chaves	Aston Martin Vantage AMR GTE	TF Sport	113
6	77	Christian Ried, Harry Tincknell, Sebastian Priaulx	Porsche 911 RSR II	Dempsey-Proton Racing	83
7	46	Matteo Cairoli, Mikkel Pedersen, Nicolas Leutwiler	Porsche 911 RSR II	Team Project 1	71
9	56	Ben Barnicoat	Porsche 911 RSR II	Team Project 1	55
10	86	Benjamin Barker, Michael Wainwright, Riccardo Pera	Porsche 911 RSR II	GR Racing	50
12	88	Fred Poordad	Porsche 911 RSR II	Dempsey-Proton Racing	38
13	88	Jan Heylen	Porsche 911 RSR II	Dempsey-Proton Racing	36
16	56	Oliver Millroy	Porsche 911 RSR II	Team Project 1	28
18	56	Gunnar Jeannette, P. J. Hyett	Porsche 911 RSR II	Team Project 1	27
21	56	Brendan Iribe	Porsche 911 RSR II	Team Project 1	24
22	88	Maxwell Root	Porsche 911 RSR II	Dempsey-Proton Racing	24
24	88	Patrick Lindsey	Porsche 911 RSR II	Dempsey-Proton Racing	14
26	56	Takeshi Kimura	Porsche 911 RSR II	Team Project 1	4
27	88	Julien Andlauer	Porsche 911 RSR II	Dempsey-Proton Racing	2

MANUFACTURER STANDINGS **LMGTE PRO**

POS	NO	MANUFACTURER	CAR	POINTS
1	51,52	Ferrari	Ferrari 488 GTE Evo	269
2	91,92	Porsche	Porsche 911 RSR II	257
3	64	Chevrolet	Chevrolet Corvette C.8 R	102

TEAM STANDINGS **LMGTE AM**

POS	NO	TEAM	CAR	POINTS
1	33	TF Sport	Aston Martin Vantage AMR GTE	141
2	98	Northwest AMR	Aston Martin Vantage AMR GTE	118
3	85	Iron Dames	Ferrari 488 GTE Evo	93
4	77	Dempsey - Proton Racing	Porsche 911 RSR II	83
5	46	Team Project 1	Porsche 911 RSR II	71
7	56	Team Project 1	Porsche 911 RSR II	55
8	86	GR Racing	Porsche 911 RSR II	50
9	88	Dempsey - Proton Racing	Porsche 911 RSR II	38

MICHELIN LE MANS CUP

15.04.–16.04.2022	Paul Ricard, France
13.05.–14.05.2022	Imola, Italy
07.06.–11.06.2022	Le Mans, France
01.07.–02.07.2022	Monza, Italy
23.09.–24.09.2022	Spa-Francorchamps, Belgium
15.10.–16.10.2022	Portimão, Portugal

Ebimotors gewann mit Emanuele Busnelli und Fabio Babini die GT3-Wertung beim Highlight des Michelin Le Mans Cup im Rahmen der 24 Stunden von Le Mans.

Mit Ebimotors und Parker Racing nahmen zwei Porsche-Mannschaften am Michelin Le Mans Cup teil. Während Ebimotors die letzten beiden Saisonrennen in Belgien und Portugal ausließ, stieß Parker Racing erst beim Finale in Portimão zum Starterfeld hinzu.

Ebimotors startete mit Emanuele Busnelli und Fabio Babini am Steuer mit einem siebten Platz in Le Castellet in die Saison, beim Heimrennen im italienischen Imola eroberte die Truppe Rang drei. Noch besser lief es im ersten Lauf von Le Mans. Babini und WRT-Mann Arnold Robin gingen im Kampf um die Führung in der GT3-Klasse Tür an Tür in die finale Runde mit dem besseren Ende für den Porsche-Piloten. Auf den letzten Kilometern verteidigte er sich erfolgreich gegen einen drückenden Audi und durfte sich im Ziel über den ersten Saisonsieg freuen. Im zweiten Heat in Frankreich zog Ebimotors gegen Bullitt Racing im Duell um Position drei den Kürzeren, auch hier fiel die Entscheidung erst im letzten Umlauf. Als Vierter wurden Busnelli / Babini auch in Monza abgewinkt, am Ende reichte es für das Duo zum sechsten Platz in der GT3-Abschlusstabelle.

Erst beim letzten Rennen in Portimão gab Parker Racing sein Debüt im Michelin Le Mans Cup 2022; Nick Jones und Scott Malvern sahen die Zielflagge als Fünfter. Ebenfalls nur ein Rennwochenende absolvierte der zweite Ebimotors-Porsche mit der Fahrerpaarung Paolo Venerosi und Max Busnelli, die sich in Le Mans die GT3-Positionen sechs und fünf sicherten.

Nick Jones, Scott Malvern

Team Ebimotors

Ebimotors, and its drivers Emanuele Busnelli and Fabio Babini, won the GT3 class of the the Michelin Le Mans Cup on the support bill of the Le Mans 24 Hours

Two Porsche teams, Ebimotors and Parker Racing, took part in the Michelin Le Mans Cup. While Ebimotors opted to miss the last two rounds of the season in Belgium and Portugal, Parker Racing only joined the field for the finale at Portimão. Ebimotors, and its drivers Emanuele Busnelli and Fabio Babini, got their campaign underway with seventh place at Le Castellet, and then the team finished third in its home round at Imola in Italy. In the first race at Le Mans, things improved for the team. Babini and WRT driver Arnold Robin were door-to-door going into the final lap in the battle for the lead, and it was the Porsche driver who came out ahead. It wasn't easy; in the final few kilometres, he had to defend against the charging Audi but he eventually brought home the team's first win of the season. In the second race in France, Ebimotors lost out to Bullitt Racing in the duel for third place. Busnelli / Babini also finished fourth at Monza and the duo ended up sixth in the end-of-season GT3 standings.

In the final race at Portimão, Parker Racing made its debut in the 2022 Michelin Le Mans Cup. Nick Jones and Scott Malvern took the chequered flag in fifth place. The second Ebimotors Porsche also ran at Le Mans for Paolo Venerosi and Max Busnelli.

Fabio Babini and Emanuele Busnelli

Emanuele Busnelli, Fabio Babini

Fabio Babini, Emanuele Busnelli

Fabio Babini,
Emanuele Busnelli

DRIVER STANDINGS **GT3**

POS	NO	DRIVERS	CAR	TEAM	POINTS
1	55	Kasper J. Jensen, Kristian Poulsen	Honda NSX GTO Evo 22	GMB Motorsport	109
2	88	Lars Engelbreckt Pedersen	Honda NSX GTO Evo 22	GMB Motorsport	93
3	44	Gustav Birch, Jens Reno Moller	Honda NSX GTO Evo 22	GMB Motorsport	76
6	46	Emanuele Busnelli, Fabio Babini	Porsche 911 GT3 R	Ebimotors	57

TEAM STANDINGS **GT3**

POS	NO	TEAM	CAR	POINTS
1	22	GMB Motorsport	Honda NSX GT3 Evo 22	109
2	88	GMB Motorsport	Honda NSX GT3 Evo 22	93
3	44	GMB Motorsport	Honda NSX GT3 Evo 22	76
5	46	Ebimotors	Porsche 911 GT3 R	46

ASIAN LE MANS SERIES

ASIAN LE MANS SERIES

12.02.2022	*Dubai, United Arab Emirates*
13.02.2022	*Dubai, United Arab Emirates*
19.02.2022	*Abu Dhabi, United Arab Emirates*
20.02.2022	*Abu Dhabi, United Arab Emirates*

Herberth Motorsport gewinnt die Hälfte aller GT-Rennen in der Asian Le Mans Series, wird aber trotzdem nur Gesamt-Zweiter der GT-Klasse.

Die Asian Le Mans Series bestand aus vier Läufen, die im Februar 2022 an zwei aufeinanderfolgenden Wochenenden in Dubai und Abu Dhabi ausgetragen wurden. Neben LMP-Klassen waren auch GT-Fahrzeuge zugelassen. Bester Porsche-Vertreter war das Trio Alfred Renauer / Robert Renauer / Ralf Bohn unter der Flagge von Herberth Motorsport, das trotz der meisten GT-Siege aller Teilnehmer Platz zwei in der GT-Abschlusstabelle belegte. Renauer / Renauer / Bohn konnten die beiden Läufe in Abu Dhabi für sich entscheiden, wurden in den ersten beiden Heats der Saison, die in Dubai ausgetragen wurden, aber nur auf den Positionen acht und sechs notiert – unter anderem, weil es in Saisonrennen zwei nach einer Kollision mit dem Mercedes vom Haupt Racing Team eine Durchfahrtsstrafe gab. Am Ende fehlten acht Zähler auf die neuen Champions.

Beim letzten der vier 4-Stunden-Rennen durfte Herberth Motorsport sogar einen Doppelsieg bejubeln, denn hinter Triumphator Renauer / Renauer / Bohn kreuzte das Schwesterauto mit Antares Au / Klaus Bachler / Yifei Ye den Zielstrich. Au, Bachler und Ye konnte dabei nicht einmal eine Zehn-Sekunden-Strafe aufhalten, die sie wegen eines Fehlers beim Boxenstopp bekommen hatten. Der Abstand der beiden Porsche 911 GT3 R betrug im Ziel gerade einmal 0,616 Sekunden.

In der Abschlusswertung der Klasse GT Am reihte sich die Mannschaft Herberth Motorsport mit Jürgen Häring und Marco Seefried am Steuer eines Porsche 911 GT3 R ebenfalls auf Rang zwei ein.

Finn Gehrsitz, Jürgen Häring, Marco Seefried

Antares Au, Klaus Bachler, Yifei Ye

Herberth Motorsport takes half of the GT class wins in Asian Le Mans Series, but still only ends up second in the final GT class standings

Alfred Renauer, Ralf Bohn, Robert Renauer

Antares Au and Yifei Ye

The Asian Le Mans Series consisted of four races, held on two back-to-back weekends in Dubai and Abu Dhabi in February 2022. Alongside the prototype classes, GT cars also competed. Under the Herberth Motorsport banner, Alfred Renauer, Robert Renauer and Ralf Bohn were the best Porsche representatives. They scored the most GT class wins, but even that record was still not enough to claim the title. They finished second in the final GT class standings. Renauer, Renauer and Bohn won both races at Abu Dhabi, but only finished eighth and sixth in the first two races of the season that were held in Dubai after they were penalised with a drive-through penalty following a collision with the Haupt Racing Team's Mercedes. Eventually, they ended the season eight points down on the new champions.

In the final four-hour race of the year, Herberth Motorsport scored a 1-2 as the sister car of Antares Au / Klaus Bachler / Yifei Ye finished second behind the winning Renauer / Renauer / Bohn entry. Not even a ten-second time penalty for a pit stop infringement prevented Au, Bachler and Ye from claiming the second spot on the podium. At the finish, the gap between the two Porsche 911 GT3 Rs was only 0.616 seconds.

In the final GT Am class standings, the Herberth Motorsport pairing of Jürgen Häring and Marco Seefried also ended up second in a Porsche 911 GT3 R.

Antares Au, Klaus Bachler, Yifei Ye

DRIVER STANDINGS **GT**

POS	NO	DRIVERS	CAR	TEAM	POINTS
1	7	Ben Barnicoat, Brendan Iribe, Ollie Millroy	McLaren 720S GT3	Inception Racing	70
2	91	**Alfred Renauer, Ralf Bohn, Robert Renauer**	**Porsche 911 GT3 R**	**Herberth Motorsport**	**62**
3	44	David Perel, Davide Rigon, Rino Mastronardi	Ferrari F488 GT3 Evo	Rinaldi Racing	55
8	33	**Antares Au, Klaus Bachler, Yifei Ye**	**Porsche 911 GT3 R**	**Herberth Motorsport**	**20**
13	12	**Benjamin Barker, Giorgio Roda, Philipp Sager**	**Porsche 911 GT3 R II**	**Dinamic Motorsport**	**5,5**
15	99	**Finn Gehrsitz, Jürgen Häring, Marco Seefried**	**Porsche 911 GT3 R**	**Herberth Motorsport**	**2**
16	48	**Nico Pronk, Peter Kox, Stéphane Kox**	**Porsche 911 GT3 R**	**Saalocin by Kox Racing**	**1,5**

TEAM STANDINGS **GT**

POS	NO	TEAM	CAR	POINTS
1	7	Inception Racing	McLaren 720S GT3	70
2	91	**Herberth Motorsport**	**Porsche 911 GT3 R**	**62**
3	44	Rinaldi Racing	Ferrari F488 GT3 Evo	55
8	33	**Herberth Motorsport**	**Porsche 911 GT3 R**	**20**
13	12	**Dinamic Motorsport**	**Porsche 911 GT3 R II**	**5,5**
15	99	**Herberth Motorsport**	**Porsche 911 GT3 R**	**2**
16	48	**Saalocin by Kox Racing**	**Porsche 911 GT3 R**	**1,5**

DRIVER STANDINGS **AM**

POS	NO	DRIVERS	CAR	TEAM	POINTS
1	20	John Loggie, Mikael Grenier, Valentin Pierburg	Mercedes-AMG GT3	SPS Automotive Performance	86
2	57	Axcil Jefferies, Francesco Zollo, Roman Zieman	Ferrari F488 GT3 Evo	Kessel Racing	86
3	99	**Finn Gehrsitz, Jürgen Häring, Marco Seefried**	**Porsche 911 GT3 R**	**Herberth Motorsport**	**60**

TEAM STANDINGS **AM**

POS	NO	TEAM	CAR	POINTS
1	20	SPS Automotive Performance	Mercedes-AMG GT3	86
2	57	Kessel Racing	Ferrari F488 GT3 Evo	86
3	99	**Herberth Motorsport**	**Porsche 911 GT3 R**	**60**

DTM

29.04.–01.05.2022	Portimão, Portugal
20.05.–22.05.2022	Lausitzring, Germany
17.06.–19.06.2022	Imola, Italy
01.07.–03.07.2022	Norisring, Germany
26.08.–28.08.2022	Nürburgring, Germany
09.09.–11.09.2022	Spa-Francorchamps, Belgium
23.09.–25.09.2022	Red Bull Ring, Austria
07.10.–09.10.2022	Hockenheim, Germany

(l.-r.): Timo Bernhard, Gerhard Berger, Thomas Preining, Robert Lechner

Starke Premierensaison für SSR Performance und KÜS Team Bernhard in der DTM – Olsen siegt in Belgien, Preining mit zwei Siegen bis zum Finale mit Titelchancen

Nach einem Gaststart von SSR Performance im Vorjahr bestritten 2022 erstmals zwei Porsche-Teams mit insgesamt drei Fahrzeugen die gesamte Saison in der DTM. Neben SSR Performance, die mit Dennis Olsen und Laurens Vanthoor antraten, gehörte auch das KÜS Team Bernhard mit Thomas Preining zum hochkarätigen Teilnehmerfeld. Zum Saisonstart war es Vanthoor, der an den ersten beiden Wochenenden in Portimão und am Lausitzring dreimal Punkte für Porsche sammelte. Insgesamt taten sich die Piloten im Porsche 911 GT3 R gegen die Konkurrenz aber oftmals schwer. Ab dem zweiten Auslandsgastspiel in Imola zeigte die Leistungskurve, besonders bei Thomas Preining, deutlich nach oben. Rang vier im ersten Rennen für den Österreicher, sowie Platz neun für Olsen brachten den beiden Piloten die ersten Zähler der Saison ein. Aufgrund eines Unfalls schaffte es Preining jedoch nicht, diesen Trend auch im zweiten Rennen auf dem Traditionskurs fortzusetzen. Der große Befreiungsschlag für Porsche gelang auf dem Stadtkurs von Nürnberg. Im ersten Qualifying sicherte sich Preining einen Platz in der ersten Startreihe. Olsen und Vanthoor mussten das Rennen aus dem Mittelfeld aufnehmen. In dem von zahlreichen Safety-Car-Phasen geprägten Lauf behielten die Porsche-Piloten einen kühlen Kopf und fuhren ein nahezu perfektes Ergebnis ein: Preining sicherte sich den Sieg und Olsen machte als Zweiter den Doppelerfolg für Porsche perfekt. Vanthoor rundete das starke Resultat als Vierter ab und fuhr außerdem sein bestes Saisonergebnis ein.

KÜS Team Bernhard

Christian Engelhart

Strong debut season in DTM for SSR Performance and KÜS Team Bernhard – Olsen wins in Belgium, Preining in contention for the title until the finale after winning twice

The 2022 DTM season saw two Porsche teams embark on a full-season campaign for the first time. SSR Performance, which made a guest appearance in 2021, ran two cars, for Dennis Olsen and Laurens Vanthoor, while KÜS Team Bernhard ran one car for Thomas Preining. After a promising start in the first two events of the season at Portimão and Lausitz, where Vanthoor scored points three times, in general the Porsche drivers struggled.

From Imola onward, however, the trend was upward, especially for Preining. In the first race on the Italian circuit near Bologna the Austrian finished fourth for his first points of the season, while Olsen took ninth to open his account. At the Norisring street circuit, Porsche finally came good. In first qualifying, Preining secured a front row grid slot and in the race, which was marked by numerous safety car interventions, the Porsche drivers scored a near-perfect result with victory for Preining, second for Olsen and fourth for Vanthoor.

(92): Laurens Vanthoor - (94): Dennis Olsen

AMG

DTM
#94
EDAG

#94

#94

26
DEKRA

DTM

SCHAEFFLER
EDAG

PAUL
DEKRA
DTM
24
HYLO
REMUS

92

DTM
KÜS

THOMAS
PREINING
24
KÜS Team Bernhard

KÜS
PAUL

#94
SSR

DTM
KÜS
HYLO
PAUL
MAHLE
Porsche Zentrum Mannheim

DEKRA
DEKRA

START
your

REMUS
PAUL
KÜS

Dennis Olsen

Laurens Vanthoor

Nach der Sommerpause startete die DTM auf der Kurzanbindung des Nürburgrings in die zweite Saisonhälfte. Auf einen Dreifachausfall am Samstag folgte mit Rang zwei für den Norweger Olsen am Sonntag ein erneuter Podiumserfolg für die Zuffenhausener. Das insgesamt erfolgreichste Wochenende erlebten die Porsche-Teams auf dem Circuit Spa-Francorchamps. In den verregneten Ardennen erwischten Olsen und Preining ein perfektes Qualifying und sicherten sich die Plätze in der ersten Startreihe. Olsen münzte die erste Pole Position für Porsche in der DTM auch direkt in seinen ersten Sieg um. Preining komplettierte das Podium auf dem dritten Rang. Am Sonntag wiederholte der KÜS Team Bernhard-Pilot von Startplatz acht kommend den Podiumserfolg des Vortages und überquerte erneut als Dritter die Ziellinie.
Zwei Wochen später setzte der Österreicher beim Heimspiel auf dem Red Bull Ring dann nochmal einen drauf. Nach aussichtsreichen freien Trainings, die er jeweils auf Rang zwei beendete, folgte jedoch ein ernüchterndes erstes Qualifying. Von Startplatz 13 ging der Lokalmatador ins Rennen und kämpfte sich bis auf die fünfte Position nach vorn. Auch im zweiten Qualifying tat sich Preining gegen die starke Konkurrenz schwer und beendete das Zeittraining als Achter. Wie am Vortag überzeugte er auch im zweiten Lauf mit einer starken Performance. Beim Fallen der Zielflagge ließ er alle Konkurrenten hinter sich und sicherte sich mit seinem zweiten Saisonerfolg den Heimsieg in Spielberg. Insgesamt war Preining in den Monaten Juli bis September der Pilot, den es zu schlagen galt. Mit zwei Siegen und zwei weiteren Podiumsplätzen sammelte der Porsche-Werksfahrer zwischen den Events auf dem Norisring und Red Bull Ring mehr Punkte als jeder andere Fahrer im Feld. Vor dem Finale in Hockenheim hatte Preining als Fünfter der Meisterschaft und damit bester Porsche-Pilot noch theoretische Chancen auf den Titel. Doch mehrere schwere Unfälle im ersten Rennen beendeten die Saison von Preining und Olsen frühzeitig. Und auch für Ersatzmann Christian Engelhart, der anstelle von Vanthoor ins Steuer des Porsche 911 GT3 R griff, lief es nicht rund: Nach Rang 14 am Samstag schied der Deutsche im letzten Saisonrennen vorzeitig aus. Insgesamt kann Porsche dennoch positiv auf die erste DTM-Saison zurückblicken. Rang fünf für Thomas Preining in der Gesamtwertung, dazu drei Siege und dank Dennis Olsen auch die erste Pole Position in dieser hart umkämpften Serie zeigen das Potential von Teams, Fahrern und Fahrzeug.

(24): Thomas Preining - (92): Laurens Vanthoor

Thomas Preining

After the summer break, the second half of the season started at the Nürburgring with another podium success for Porsche as Olsen finished second during Sunday's race. At Circuit de Spa-Francorchamps, the Porsche teams had their most successful weekend. In the Ardennes, Olsen and Preining locked out the front row of the grid and the Norwegian converted Porsche's first pole position in DTM into his own maiden win. Preining took the final podium slot in third and repeated this result the following day from eighth on the grid.
A fortnight later, the Austrian did even better in his home round at the Red Bull Ring. Fifth in the Saturday race from 13th on the grid, he was the star on Sunday, moving up from eighth on the grid to become the first Austrian to win a DTM race on home soil. Going into the finale at Hockenheim, he was fifth in the standings and still had a chance at the title, but multiple accidents in the Saturday race ended the season early for Preining and for Olsen. Stepping in for Vanthoor, Christian Engelhart also had a hard time, 14th on Saturday and he retired from Sunday's race. Still, Porsche had a positive maiden season in DTM with three wins, the first pole position and fifth in the final standings for Preining.

Laurens Vanthoor

DRIVER STANDINGS

POS	NO	DRIVERS	CAR	TEAM	POINTS
1	31	Sheldon van der Linde	BMW M4 GT3	Schubert Motorsport	164
2	22	Lucas Auer	Mercedes-AMG GT3 Evo	Mercedes-AMG Team Winward	153
3	33	René Rast	Audi R8 LMS GT3 Evo II	ABT Sportsline	149
5	24	**Thomas Preining**	**Porsche 991 GT3 R II**	**KÜS Team Bernhard**	**116**
10	94	**Dennis Olsen**	**Porsche 991 GT3 R II**	**SSR Performance**	**89**
18	92	**Laurens Vanthoor**	**Porsche 991 GT3 R II**	**SSR Performance**	**30**

TEAM STANDINGS

POS	TEAM	CAR	POINTS
1	Schubert Motorsport	BMW M4 GT3	226
2	Mercedes-AMG Team Winward	Mercedes-AMG GT3 Evo	152
3	ABT Sportsline	Audi R8 LMS GT3 Evo II	152
8	**SSR Performance**	**Porsche 991 GT3 R II**	**119**
10	**KÜS Team Bernhard**	**Porsche 991 GT3 R II**	**115**

MANUFACTURER STANDINGS

POS	MANUFACTURER	POINTS
1	Audi	441
2	Mercedes-AMG	413
3	BMW	327
4	**Porsche**	**234**

ADAC GT MASTERS

22.04.–24.04.2022	*Oschersleben, Germany*
20.05.–22.05.2022	*Red Bull Ring, Austria*
24.06.–26.06.2022	*Zandvoort, Netherlands*
05.08.–07.08.2022	*Nürburgring, Germany*
19.08.–21.08.2022	*Lausitzring, Germany*
23.09.–25.09.2022	*Sachsenring, Germany*
21.10.–23.10.2022	*Hockenheim, Germany*

Bis zum Finale hält Joos Sportwagentechnik den Titelkampf offen. Es ist nicht das einzige Porsche-Team, das im ADAC GT Masters Höhen und Tiefen erlebt

Porsche-Fans brauchten im ADAC GT Masters 2022 starke Nerven. Denn obwohl der Porsche 911 GT3 R zu den schnellsten Fahrzeugen im Feld gehörte, fehlte häufig das nötige Glück. Nicht selten platzten die Hoffnungen auf eine Podestplatzierung erst kurz vor Rennende – oder einmal auch erst danach.

Sven Müller und Joel Sturm wurden bei der Auftaktveranstaltung in Oschersleben zu den tragischen Helden. Nachdem sich das Duo von Allied-Racing den dritten Platz erkämpft hatte, folgte wenige Tage später die Disqualifikation. Weil bei einer Benzinprobe der falsche Sprit festgestellt wurde, flogen die Beiden aus der Wertung. Glücklicherweise gab es für die Newcomer von Allied-Racing dann aber doch einige Highlights – so ging es für sie am Nürburgring beide Male aufs Podest. Stärkstes Porsche-Team im ADAC GT Masters 2022 war unterdessen Joos Sportwagentechnik. Die Mannschaft rund um Michael Joos hatte sich mit Routinier Christian Engelhart und Youngster Ayhancan Güven ein schlagkräftiges Aufgebot zusammengestellt. Doch auch das deutsch-türkische Duo erlebte bittere Enttäuschungen im Titelkampf: Beim Rennen im niederländischen Zandvoort rollte Engelhart wenige Meter vor der Ziellinie aus und büßte somit die mögliche Tabellenführung ein. Auf dem Sachsenring wurde der 911 GT3 R des Teams unverschuldet aus dem Rennen gerissen. Dass sich die Joos-Truppe davon nicht unterkriegen ließ, bewies sie beim Finale eindrucksvoll mit dem zweiten Saisonsieg und dem Vizetitel in der Gesamtwertung.

Als Randerscheinung der Saison 2022 dürfte der Auftritt von ID Racing gewertet werden. Denn das neu formierte Team rund um Iris Dorr startete nur bei den ersten Läufen. Der ursprünglich mit Herberth Motorsport geplante Einsatz eines Porsche 911 GT3 R trug nur wenig Früchte. Da half auch der überraschende fünfte Platz von Robert Renauer und Klaus Bachler beim Auftakt in Oschersleben nicht viel. Bachler war auch mit von der Partie, als mit Dinamic Motorsport ein weiteres Porsche-Team einen Gaststart absolvierte.

Klaus Bachler,
Robert Renauer

Christian Engelhart, Ayhancan Güven

Joel Sturm, Sven Müller

Joel Sturm and Sven Müller

DRIVER STANDINGS

POS	NO	DRIVERS	CAR	TEAM	POINTS
1	48	Raffaele Marciello	Mercedes-AMG GT3 Evo	Mann Filter Team Landgraf	193
2	**91**	**Christian Engelhart, Ayhancan Güven**	**Porsche 911 GT3 R II**	**Team Joos Sportwagentechnik**	**178**
3	4	Jules Gounon, Fabian Schiller	Mercedes-AMG GT3 Evo	Drago Racing Team ZVO	153
10	**22**	**Sven Müller, Joel Sturm**	**Porsche 911 GT3 R II**	**Allied Racing**	**106**
29	**44**	**Jaxon Evans**	**Porsche 911 GT3 R II**	**ID Racing**	**18**
31	**44**	**Jannes Fittje**	**Porsche 911 GT3 R II**	**ID Racing**	**15**
32	**44**	**Klaus Bachler, Robert Renauer**	**Porsche 911 GT3 R II**	**ID Racing**	**13**

DRIVER STANDINGS **JUNIOR**

POS	NO	DRIVERS	CAR	TEAM	POINTS
1	18	Ben Green	BMW M4 GT3	Schubert Motorsport	253
2	18	Niklas Krütten	BMW M4 GT3	Schubert Motorsport	231
3	14	Konsta Lappalainen	Lamborghini Huracán GT3 Evo	Emil Frey Racing	208,5
7	**22**	**Joel Sturm**	**Porsche 911 GT3 R II**	**Allied Racing**	**176**
8	**44**	**Jannes Fittje**	**Porsche 911 GT3 R II**	**ID Racing**	**47,5**

TEAM STANDINGS

POS	NO	TEAM	POINTS
1	Emil Frey Racing	Lamborghini Huracán GT3 Evo	212
2	Mann Filter Team Landgraf	Mercedes-AMG GT3 Evo	194
3	Montaplast by Land Motorsport	Audi R8 LMS GT3 Evo II	190
4	**Team Joos Sportwagentechnik**	**Porsche 911 GT3 R II**	**178**
8	**Allied Racing**	**Porsche 911 GT3 R II**	**133**
14	**ID Racing**	**Porsche 911 GT3 R II**	**39**

Joos Sportwagentechnik keep the title fight open till the final and aren't the only Porsche team to be experiencing highs and lows in the ADAC GT Masters

Porsche fans needed steel nerves in the 2022 ADAC GT Masters. Although the Porsche 911 GT3 R was one of the field's fastest cars, it often lacked the necessary good luck. Podium hopes were frequently dashed shortly before finishing – or once afterwards.

Allied-Racing duo Sven Müller and Joel Sturm became two tragic heroes in the Oschersleben season opener. After clinching third place, disqualification soon followed. A fuel control had detected the wrong type, and both flew out of the rating. Luckily, the newcomers still saw some highlights and climbed the Nürburgring rostrum twice.

The strongest 2022 ADAC GT Masters Porsche team was Joos Sportwagentechnik. The team assembled a competitive line-up with stalwart Christian Engelhart and youngster Ayhancan Güven, but the German-Turkish duo faced bitter disappointments in the title fight. Engelhart rolled out some metres before the Zandvoort finish line and forfeited the possible standings lead. The team's 911 GT3 R was undeservedly torn from the Sachsenring race. However, the Joos squad persevered, and the finale's second seasonal win and overall standings vice-championship demonstrated this impressively.

ID Racing's 2022 appearance was marginal – Iris Dorr's newly formed team only participated in initial races. Originally planned use of a Porsche 911 GT3 R together with Herbert Motorsport was unsuccessful, Robert Renauer and Klaus Bachler's surprising Oschersleben fifth made little difference. Bachler was also part of Porsche team Dinamic Motorsport's guest appearance.

Klaus Bachler and Robert Renauer

Adrien De Leener, Klaus Bachler

GT WORLD CHALLENGE EUROPE ENDURANCE CUP

01.04.–03.04.2022	Imola, Italy
03.06.–05.06.2022	Paul Ricard, France
27.07.–31.07.2022	Spa-Francorchamps, Belgium
02.09.–04.09.2022	Hockenheim, Germany
30.09.–02.10.2022	Barcelona, Spain

Dritter in der Meisterschaft: Herberth Motorsport kämpfte bis zu dramatischem Finale im spanischen Barcelona um den Titelgewinn im neuen Gold Cup

Auch 2022 gehörten vier Porsche 911 GT3 R fest zum Starterfeld des GT World Challenge Endurance Cup. Wie im Vorjahr setzte Dinamic Motorsport zwei (#56 Pro-Kategorie, #54 Silver Cup) und Allied Racing einen Boliden ein. Herberth Motorsport komplettierte das Aufgebot mit einem für die komplette Saison eingeschriebenen Fahrzeug.

Und der bayrische Rennstall durfte im italienischen Imola den perfekten Einstand feiern: Zusammen mit Ralf Bohn sicherten sich Alfred und Robert Renauer im neu ausgeschriebenen Gold Cup den ersten Saisonsieg. Die Klasse ersetzt die Am-Kategorie. Pro Fahrzeug muss jeweils ein Bronze-, Silber- und Gold-Fahrer zum Aufgebot gehören. Auf dem Circuit Paul Ricard bekam der Porsche 911 GT3 R #911 Unterstützung von einem zweiten Fahrzeug (#24). In der Pro-Am-Wertung traten Niki Leutwiler, Ivan Jacoma, sowie Alessio Picariello an und schrammten – genau wie das Schwesterfahrzeug – als Vierte knapp am Klassenpodium vorbei. Was folgte, waren zwei enttäuschende Auftritte: Bei den 24 Stunden von Spa fielen alle drei von Herberth Motorsport eingesetzten Porsche aus, in Hockenheim verhinderte ein Reifenschaden kurz vor dem Ziel den sicher geglaubten Sieg der #911. Über 100 Runden hatten Ralf Bohn, Alfred und Robert Renauer das Feld im Gold Cup zuvor angeführt. Wiedergutmachung sollte beim Finale in Barcelona folgen – in Form des Titels im Gold Cup. Und spannender hätte der Kampf um die Meisterschaft nicht sein können: Im ersten Renndrittel verteidigte das Team die dritte Position und verlor dabei einen Teil der Frontschürze, was aber kein allzu großer Nachteil für den Porsche war. Der Kampf spitzte sich zu, als die direkten Konkurrenten zum einen ausfielen und zum anderen einen Reifenschaden erlitten. Durch die Übernahme der Führung rückte das Team bis auf einen einzigen Zähler an die Tabellenführung heran. In der letzten halben Stunde wurde Robert Renauer jedoch in einen Unfall verwickelt, der das Team auf die dritte Position zurückwarf. Am Ende blieben ein Podiumsrang und Platz drei in der Meisterschaft.

Auch in der Pro-Wertung war Porsche dank des Einsatzes von Dinamic Motorsport vertreten. Ihren ersten Podestplatz feierte die Mannschaft mit Rang drei in Hockenheim. Mit dem Sieg im spanischen Barcelona rundeten Klaus Bachler, Matteo Cairoli und Alessio Picariello die Saison erfolgreich ab.

Alfred Renauer, Ralf Bohn, Robert Renauer

Up to the dramatic finale at Barcelona in Spain, Herberth Motorsport battled for title honours in the new Gold Cup but had to settle for third in the championship

The 2022 GT World Challenge Endurance Cup once again included four Porsche 911 GT3 Rs as full season entries. As it was in 2021, Dinamic Motorsport ran two cars, the #56 in the Pro category, the #54 in the Silver Cup, while Allied Racing and Herberth Motorsport rounded out the Porsche contingent with one car each.
The Bavarian Herberth Motorsport team got its campaign off to a perfect start at Imola where Alfred and Robert Renauer, together with Ralf Bohn, won the new-for-2022 Gold Cup. At Circuit Paul Ricard, their #911 received support from a second entry. Niki Leutwiler, Ivan Jacoma and Alessio Picariello raced in the Pro-Am class and just missed out on a podium as they finished fourth in class. The #911 also finished fourth, in the Gold Cup. Next up were two rather disappointing rounds: all three Herberth Motorsport Porsches retired in the Spa 24 Hours while a puncture just before the end at Hockenheim prevented an almost certain victory for the #911 car, Bohn and the Renauers having led the Gold Cup for over 100 laps. In the finale at Barcelona, the team moved up as rivals hit trouble, but Robert Renauer became involved in an accident in the final 30 minutes, dropping back to third. Eventually, the team ended up third in the championship.
In the Pro category, Dinamic Motorsport scored its first podium of the season by finishing third at Hockenheim. With victory at Barcelona, Klaus Bachler, Matteo Cairoli and Alessio Picariello successfully concluded their season.

Matteo Cairoli, Alessio Picariello, Klaus Bachler

Nicolas Leutwiler, Ivan Jacoma, Alessio Picariello

(l.-r.): Alfred Renauer, Ralf Bohn, Robert Renauer

(l.-r.): Matteo Cairoli, Alessio Picariello, Klaus Bachler

DRIVER STANDINGS

POS	NO	DRIVERS	CAR	TEAM	POINTS
1	88	Raffaele Marciello, Jules Gounon, Daniel Juncadella	Mercedes-AMG GT3 Evo	Akkodis ASP Team	89
2	71	Antonio Fuoco	Ferrari F488 GT3 Evo	Iron Lynx	87
3	71	Davide Rigon, Daniel Serra	Ferrari F488 GT3 Evo	Iron Lynx	68
4	54	Klaus Bachler	Porsche 911 GT3 R II	Dinamic Motorsport	54
6	54	Matteo Cairoli	Porsche 911 GT3 R II	Dinamic Motorsport	48
8	24, 56	Alessio Picariello	Porsche 911 GT3 R II	Dinamic Motorsport	40
22	54	Come Ledogar	Porsche 911 GT3 R II	Dinamic Motorsport	14
25	47	Thomas Preining	Porsche 911 GT3 R II	KCMG	12
28	54	Richard Lietz, Kévin Estre, Michael Christensen	Porsche 911 GT3 R II	Dinamic Motorsport	6
29	221	Laurens Vanthoor, Dennis Olsen, Nick Tandy	Porsche 911 GT3 R II	GPX Racing	6
33	74	Matt Campbell, Mathieu Jaminet, Felipe Nasr	Porsche 911 GT3 R II	EMA Motorsport	2

TEAM STANDINGS **PRO-AM**

POS	NO	TEAM	CAR	POINTS
1	20	SPS Automotive Performance	Mercedes-AMG GT3 Evo	129
2	52	AF Corse	Ferrari F488 GT3 Evo	118
3	188	Garage 59	McLaren 720S GT3	99
4	24	Herberth Motorsport	Porsche 911 GT3 R II	49
6	91	Allied Racing	Porsche 911 GT3 R II	18

TEAM STANDINGS

POS	NO	TEAM	CAR	POINTS
1	88	Akkodis ASP	Mercedes-AMG GT3 Evo	97
2	71	Iron Lynx	Ferrari F488GT3 Evo	90
2	32	Team WRT	Audi R8 LMS GT3 Evo II	73
6	54	Dinamic Motorsport	Porsche 911 GT3 R II	56

Super Taikyu®
JapaneseEnduranceRace

SUPER TAIKYU

19.03.–20.03.2022	*Suzuka, Japan*
02.06.–05.06.2022	*Fuji 24 Hours, Japan*
08.07.–10.07.2022	*Sugo, Japan*
30.07.–31.07.2022	*Autopolis, Japan*
03.09.–04.09.2022	*Motegi, Japan*
14.10.–16.10.2022	*Okayama, Japan*
26.11.–27.11.2022	*Suzuka, Japan*

Die japanische Langstrecken-Rennserie Super Taikyu gibt es seit 1991 und wird unter anderem mit GT3- sowie GT4-Fahrzeugen ausgetragen.

Porsche Center Okazaki

In der GT3-Klasse setzte das Porsche-Zentrum Okazaki den einzigen Porsche GT3 R ein. Mit der Fahrerkombination Hiroaki Nagai, Yuta Kamimura und Daisuke Ito holte das Team fünf Pole Positions aus sieben Rennen. Außerdem gab es Siege in Okayama und in Suzuka, Platz zwei in Sugo sowie Rang drei in Autopolis und Motegi zu feiern. Das bedeutete schließlich Position drei in der Abschlusstabelle.

In der GT4-Kategorie ging Birth Racing Project mit einem Cayman GT4 CS MR in seine zweite Saison in der Super Taikyu. Kenji Suzuka, Takeshi, Kohei Fukuda, Kouichi Okumura und Tatsuya Tanigawa bejubelten ihren größten Erfolg mit Rang zwei in Autopolis.

Das Porsche Team Ebi Waimarama, das von den Porsche-Zentren in Tokio eingesetzt wird, wechselte 2022 vom Cayman GT4 CS MR auf einen RS. Die Mannschaft hatte insbesondere bei den 24 Stunden von Fuji Pech, als ausgerechnet zu dem Zeitpunkt ein Motorproblem aufkam, als sie die GT4-Klasse anführte. Das Jahr beendeten sie letztendlich mit einem Triumph in Suzuka und einem zweiten Platz in Sugo. Dabei bildeten Naoya Yamano, Kizuna, Katsumasa Chiyo und Riki Okusa die Stammbesetzung, die für die 24-Stunden-Rennen von Giuliano Alesi und Lee Jung Woo unterstützt wurde.

Super Taikyu, Japan's top tier of endurance racing, has been running for over 30 years, and in 2022 it produced another season of excellent competition and success for Porsche.

Since first entering with the Porsche 911 GT3 R in 2019, Porsche Center Okazaki continued to compete at the sharp end of the GT3 field this season. GT World Challenge Asia teammates Hiroaki Nagai and Yuta Kamimura were joined by Daisuke Ito for the seven-round campaign. The trio took five pole positions across the season and scored victories at both Okayama and Suzuka. Podium finishes at Sportsland Sugo, Autopolis and Mobility Resort Motegi helped the crew to third place in the final standings.

In the GT4 class, Porsche Team EBI WAIMARAMA, run by Porsche Centers in Tokyo, entered a new Porsche 718 Cayman GT4 RS Clubsport. The team were leading the Fuji 24 Hours before engine trouble, but the crew of Naoya Yamano, KIZUNA, Katsumasa Chiyo and Riki Okusa bounced back to take victory in the final round at Suzuka.

Birth Racing Project returned for a second Super Taikyu season in 2022 in their Porsche Cayman GT4 CS MR. The line-up of Kenji Suzuki, TAKESHI, Kohei Fukuda, Kouichi Okumura and Tatsuya Tanigawa picked up a maiden podium in the series at Autopolis and went on to finish an impressive fourth in category. For 2023, the team will make the switch to the Porsche 718 Cayman GT4 RS Clubsport.

(l.-r.): Tatsuya Tanigawa, Kouhei Fukuda, TAKESHI, Kenji Suzuki

(l.-r.): Naoya Yamano, Katsumasa Chiyo, KIZUNA, Riki Okusa, Giuliano Alesi, Lee Jung Woo

Hiroaki Nagai

Birth Racing Project

TEAM STANDINGS **ST-X**

POS	NO	SEASON DRIVERS	TEAM	CAR	POINTS
1	62	Yuya Hiraki, Reiji Hraki, Yutaka Toriba, Shaun Thong	Helm Motorsports	Nissan GT-R GT3	134,5
2	888	Haurki Kurosawa, Shinichi Takagi, Daisuke Yamawaki, Martin Berry, Shaun Thong	Grid Motorsports	Mercedes-AMG GT3 Evo	127
3	**16**	**Hiroaki Nagai, Yuta Kamimura, Daisuke Ito**	**Porsche Center Okazaki**	**Porsche 911 GT3 R**	**111**

TEAM STANDINGS **ST-Z**

POS	NO	SEASON DRIVERS	TEAM	CAR	POINTS
1	500	Ryuichiro Otsuka, Toshihiro Kaneishi, Kakunoshin Ota, Tori Kimura	Team 5Zigen	Mercedes-AMG GT4	131,5
2	885	Hiro Hayashi, Katsuyuki Hiranaka, Eijiro Shimizu, Morio Nitta	Shade Racing	Toyota GR Supra GT4	115,5
3	310	Manabu Yamazaki, Seita Nonaka, Sho Tsuboi, Shinya Hosokawa, Takumi Sanada, Yuya Sakamoto	My Cars CSI Racing	Toyota GR Supra GT4	107
4	**19**	**Kenji Suzuki, Takeshi Matsumoto. Kohei Fukuda, "Hirobon", Takashi Ohno, Tatsuya Tanigawa, Kouchi Okumura**	**Birth Racing Project**	**Porsche 718 Cayman GT4 MR**	**88,5**
5	**22**	**Naoya Yamano, Katsumasa Chiyo, Riki Okusa, "Kizuna"**	**Porsche Team EBI Waimarama**	**Porsche 718 Cayman GT4 RS**	**80**

GT WORLD CHALLENGE ASIA

20.05.–22.05.2022 Sepang, Malaysia
15.07.–17.07.2022 Suzuka, Japan
22.07.–24.07.2022 Fuji, Japan
19.08.–21.08.2022 Sugo, Japan
23.09.–25.09.2022 Okayama, Japan

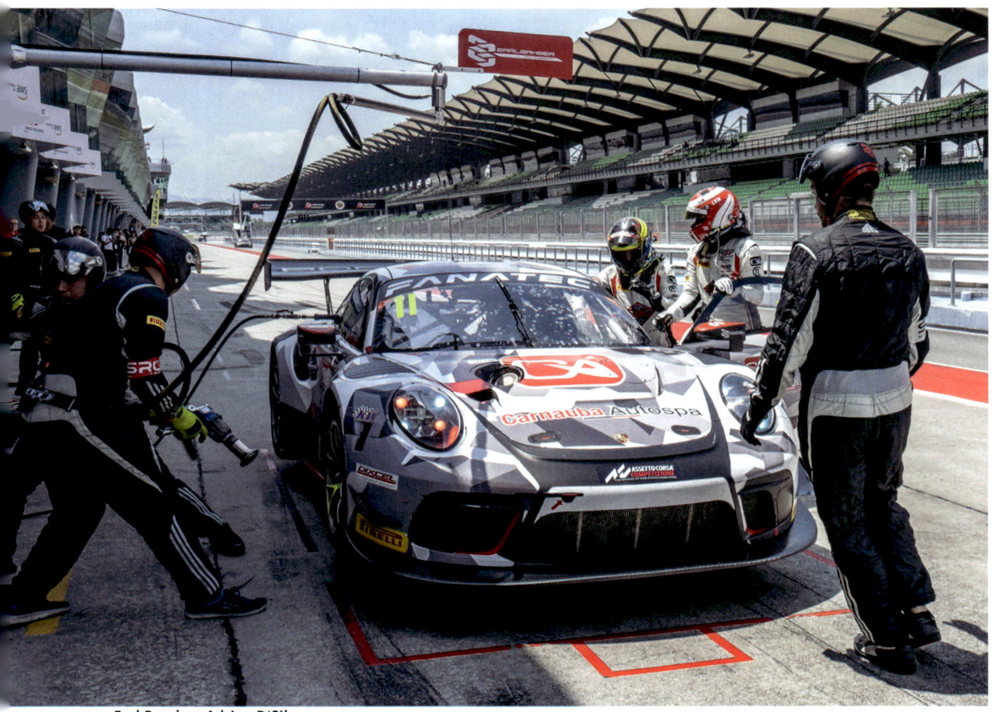

Earl Bamber, Adrian D'Silva

Porsche startete erneut erfolgreich in der Fanatec GT World Challenge Asia powered by aws und verteidigte mit dem Team AMAC Motorsport den Titel in der GT3-Am-Klasse.

Die GT World Challenge Asia 2022 bestand aus fünf Rennwochenenden und begann Ende Mai auf dem Sepang International Circuit. Das Porsche-Team EBM Giga Racing startete mit einem Doppelpodium im ersten Lauf in das Jahr, bevor das in Heat eins noch zweitplatzierte Duo Earl Bamber und Adrian D'Silva im zweiten Rennen des Wochenendes den Sieg an sich reißen konnte.
Tanart Sathienthirakul und Kantadhee Kusiri von AAS Motorsport, die wie Bamber / D'Silva auf einen Porsche 911 GT3 R vertrauten, holten im Laufe der Saison eine Reihe von Podiumsplätzen sowie die Pole Position im Sportsland SUGO; am Ende sicherte sich die thailändische Fahrerpaarung den zweiten Platz in der Klassenwertung GT3 Silver.
Hiroaki Nagai und Yuta Kamimura vom Porsche-Zentrum Okazaki eroberten in ihrem Porsche 911 GT3 R mit der Startnummer 30 insgesamt drei Podestplätze.
Die australische Mannschaft AMAC Motorsport konnte ihren GT3-Am-Titel mit Andrew Macpherson und Ben Porter am Steuer eines 911 GT3 R erfolgreich verteidigen. Die Truppe von EBM Giga Racing, die auf das gleiche Fahrzeugmodell setzte, belegte nach einer soliden Leistung der beiden Piloten Setiawan Santoso und Reid Harker den zweiten Rang in der GT3-Teamwertung.

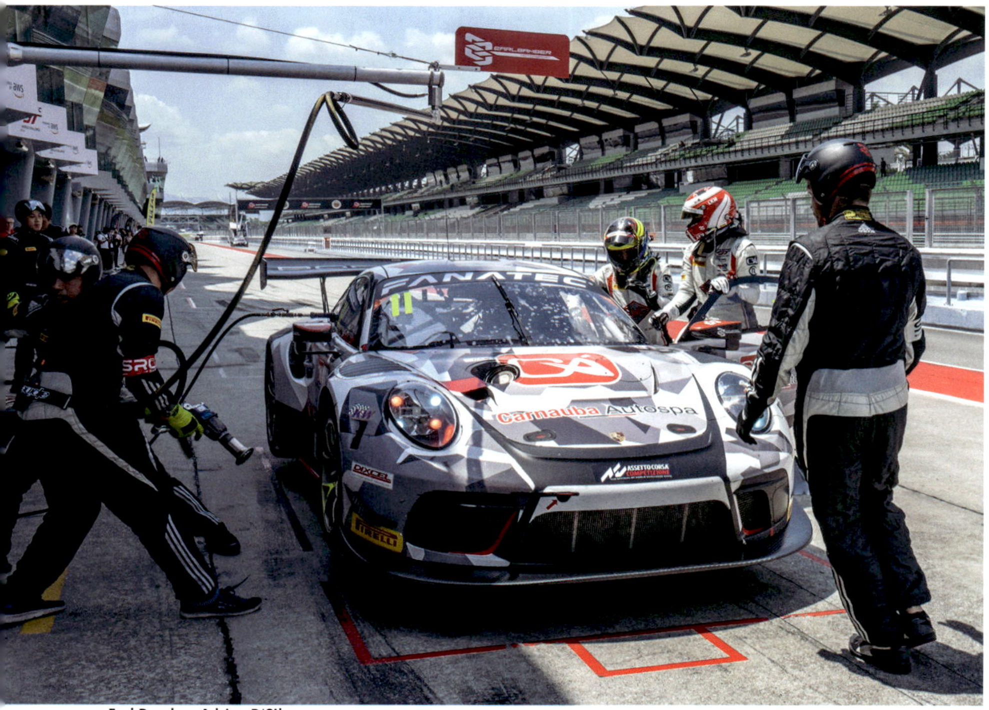

Porsche enjoys another successful Fanatec GT World Challenge Asia powered by aws campaign

GT World Challenge Asia returned with a five-round season in 2022, opening the campaign at Sepang International Circuit. EBM Giga Racing kicked off its year with a double podium in the first of the weekend's races, before Earl Bamber and Adrian D'Silva took victory in the second.

AAS Motorsport's Tanart Sathienthirakul and Kantadhee Kusiri picked up a number of podium finishes throughout the season, as well as pole position at Sportsland SUGO as the Thai pair secured second in the GT3 Silver class. Porsche Center Okazaki's Hiroaki Nagai and Yuta Kamimura also enjoyed a return to the series, taking three podium finishes in their Porsche 911 GT3 R.

Australian team AMAC Motorsport successfully defended their GT3-Am title in 2022, with Andrew Macpherson and Ben Porter securing the championship with a round to spare, at the Okayama International Circuit. EBM Giga Racing finished second overall in the GT3 Teams' Championship after a solid effort by Setiawan Santoso and Reid Harker, with the pair scoring points on multiple occasions in 2022.

Earl Bamber and Adrian D'Silva

„Bankcy", Shinji Takei

Yuta, Kamimura, Hiroaki Nagai

Tanart Sathienthirakul, Kantadhee Kusiri

Andrew Macpherson, Ben Porter

DRIVER STANDINGS **GT3**

POS	NO	DRIVERS	CAR	TEAM	POINTS
1	777	Takeshi Kimura, Kei Cozzolino	Ferrari F488 GT3 Evo	CarGuy Racing	126
2	99	Jefri Ibrahim, Nick Foster	Mercedes-AMG GT3 Evo	Triple Eight JMR	123
3	27	Naoki Yokomizo	Ferrari F488 GT3 Evo	Yogibo Racing	112
7	18	Kantadhee Kusiri, Tanart Sathienthirakul	Porsche 911 GT3 R	EBM Giga Racing	68
8	**30**	**Hiroaki Nagai, Yuta Kamimura**	**Porsche 911 GT3 R**	**Porsche Center Okazaki**	**67**
10	8	Setiawan Santoso, Reid Harker	Porsche 911 GT3 R	EBM Giga Racing	53
11	**11**	**Adrian D'Silva, Earl Bamber**	**Porsche 911 GT3 R**	**EBM Giga Racing**	**43**
16	51	Andrew MacPherson, Ben Porter	Porsche 911 GT3 R	AMAC Motorsport	25

DRIVER STANDINGS **GT3 JAPAN CUP**

POS	NO	DRIVERS	CAR	TEAM	POINTS
1	777	Takeshi Kimura, Kei Cozzolino	Ferrari F488 GT3 Evo	CarGuy Racing	151
2	47	Satoshi Hoshino, Tomonobu Fuji	Aston Martin Vantage GT3	D'Station Racing	121
3	**30**	**Hiroaki Nagai, Yuta Kamimura**	**Porsche 911 GT3 R**	**Porsche Center Okazaki**	**91**

DRIVER STANDINGS **GT3 PRO-AM**

POS	NO	DRIVERS	CAR	TEAM	POINTS
1	99	Jefri Ibrahim, Nick Foster	Mercedes-AMG GT3 Evo	Triple Eight JMR	158
2	777	Takeshi Kimura, Kei Cozzolino	Ferrari F488 GT3 Evo	CarGuy Racing	153
3	47	Satoshi Hoshino, Tomonobu Fuji	Aston Martin Vantage GT3	D'Station Racing	104
7	8	Setiawan Santoso, Reid Harker	Porsche 911 GT3 R	EBM Giga Racing	73
11	**11**	**Adrian D'Silva, Earl Bamber**	**Porsche 911 GT3 R**	**EBM Giga Racing**	**43**

DRIVER STANDINGS **GT3 JAPAN CUP PRO-AM**

POS	NO	DRIVERS	CAR	TEAM	POINTS
1	777	Takeshi Kimura, Kei Cozzolino	Ferrari F488 GT3 Evo	CarGuy Racing	163
2	47	Satoshi Hoshino, Tomonobu Fuji	Aston Martin Vantage GT3	D'Station Racing	127
3	5	Tomohide Yamaguchi, Seiji Ara	BMW M4 GT3	Plus Racing	104
5	30	Hiroaki Nagai, Yuta Kamimura	Porsche 911 GT3 R	Porsche Center Okazaki	91

DRIVER STANDINGS **GT3 SILVER**

POS	NO	DRIVERS	CAR	TEAM	POINTS
1	27	Naoki Yokomizo	Ferrari F488 GT3 Evo	Yogibo Racing	204
2	18	Kantadhee Kusiri, Tanart Sathienthirakul	Porsche 911 GT3 R	EBM Giga Racing	172
3	27	Kiyoto Fujinami	Ferrari F488 GT3 Evo	Yogibo Racing	154

DRIVER STANDINGS **GT3 AM**

POS	NO	DRIVERS	CAR	TEAM	POINTS
1	**51**	**Andrew MacPherson, Ben Porter**	**Porsche 911 GT3 R**	**AMAC Motorsport**	**174**
2	2	Tadao Uematsu, Yudai Uchida	McLaren 720S GT3	Team Uematsu	141
3	7	Yusuke Yamazaki, Yorikatsu Tsujiko	Honda NSX GT3	Comet Racing	130

TEAM STANDINGS **GT3**

POS	TEAM	CAR	POINTS
1	Triple Eight JMR	Mercedes-AMG GT3 Evo	185
2	EBM Giga Racing	Porsche 911 GT3 R	164
3	CarGuy Racing	Ferrari F488 GT3 Evo	126
7	Porsche Center Okazaki	Porsche 911 GT3 R	67
12	AMAC Motorsport	Porsche 911 GT3 R	25

GT SUPER SPRINT CHALLENGE

16.07.–17.07.2022 *Ningbo, China*
05.08.–06.08.2022 *Ningbo, China*
03.09.–04.09.2022 *Zhuhai, China*

Bian Ye

Wang Yi

Eric Zang

In der GT Super Sprint Challenge 2022 feierte Porsche den ersten chinesischen Triumph des Porsche 718 Cayman GT4 RS Clubsport.

Nach einer guten Premierensaison im Jahr 2021 wurde die GT Super Sprint Challenge in 2022 zum zweiten Mal ausgeschrieben. Die Rennserie, die sich an Piloten mit Bronze-Status richtet, ist 2022 bisher zweimal in Ningbo und einmal in Zhuhai gefahren; für die letzten beiden Rennwochenenden im Dezember (nach Redaktionsschluss) wird sie noch Shanghai und Zhuhai ansteuern.

Das Eröffnungswochenende im Juli fand auf dem Ningbo International Circuit statt, wo Wang Yi mit seinem Doppelsieg in der GT4-Kategorie den ersten chinesischen Erfolg für den Porsche 718 Cayman GT4 RS Clubsport eroberte. Du Yu und Jack Pang fuhren in dieser Klasse ebenfalls auf das Podium. Bian Ye sicherte Porsche einen Podestrang in der GT3-Kategorie, während Li Lichao mit zwei Top-Fünf-Platzierungen in die Saison startete. In den folgenden Meetings konnte er sich steigern und stand so beim zweiten Gastspiel in Ningbo sowie in Zhuhai jeweils auf dem Treppchen.

Wang Xiang stieg erst am zweiten Rennwochenende Anfang August in die Super Sprint Challenge ein und holte auf Anhieb die zweite Position, bevor er in Zhuhai mit seinem Porsche 718 Cayman GT4 Clubsport MR noch zweimal das Podium erreichte.

Porsche on the podium trail in GTSSC

The GT Super Sprint Challenge (GTSSC) returned for a second season this year, after a strong debut in 2021. The series, which is aimed at bronze-rated drivers, has raced at Ningbo and Zhuhai so far in 2022, and is set to return to Shanghai and Zhuhai for its final rounds in December.

Ningbo International Circuit hosted the opening weekend in July. There, Silver Rocket's Wang Yi secured the first Chinese win for the Porsche 718 Cayman GT4 RS Clubsport with a strong effort to take victory in both GT4 category races. RSR GT Racing's Du Yu and Jack Pang of Blackjack Racing also picked up podium finishes in the class. Absolute Racing's Bian Ye secured a podium for Porsche in the GT3 category, while Climax Racing's Li Lichao got his campaign underway with a pair of top-five finishes. Lichao built on his solid start to the season in the following races, taking podiums in both the second and third rounds.

Climax Racing's Wang Xiang joined the championship from the second round, picking up second-place in Ningbo before a double podium at Zhuhai in his Porsche 718 Cayman GT4 Clubsport MR.

Zeng Jian Feng

Li Lichao

Wang Yi

Jack Pang

DRIVER STANDINGS **GT3**

POS	NO	DRIVERS	CAR	TEAM	POINTS
1	71	"Rio"	Audi R8 LMS GT3 Evo II	Uno Racing Team	143
2	833	Hu Yuqi	Mercedes-AMG GT3 Evo	Climax Racing	105
3	**2**	**Li Lichao**	**Porsche 911 GT3 R**	**Climax Racing**	**75**
6	3	Bian Ye	Porsche 911 GT3 R	Absolute Racing	27

DRIVER STANDINGS **GT3 AM PLUS**

POS	NO	DRIVERS	CAR	TEAM	POINTS
1	71	"Rio"	Audi R8 LMS GT3 Evo II	Uno Racing Team	143
2	833	Hu Yuqi	Mercedes-AMG GT3 Evo	Climax Racing	105
3	**7**	**Eric Zang**	**Porsche 911 GT3 R**	**Toro Racing**	**30**

DRIVER STANDINGS **GT3 AM**

POS	NO	DRIVERS	CAR	TEAM	POINTS
1	**2**	**Li Lichao**	**Porsche 911 GT3 R**	**Climax Racing**	**140**
2	55	Ray Wu	Audi R8 LMS GT3 Evo	YC Racing	64
3	6	Ye Sichao	Lamborghini Huracán GT3 Evo	Climax Racing	60

DRIVER STANDINGS **GT3 AM MASTERS**

POS	NO	DRIVERS	CAR	TEAM	POINTS
1	**51**	**Xiao Min**	**Porsche 991 GT3 R**	**YC Racing**	**86**
2	68	Xing Yanbin	Audi R8 LMS GT3 Evo	YC Racing	83
3	25	Song Bo	Audi R8 LMS GT3 Evo	Climax Racing	58

DRIVER STANDINGS **GT4**

POS	NO	DRIVERS	CAR	TEAM	POINTS
1	5	Vincent Lin	Audi R8 LMS GT4	Absolute Racing	126
2	**28**	**Wang Xiang**	**Porsche 718 Cayman GT4 RS CS**	**Climax Racing**	**61**
3	**168**	**Wang Yi**	**Porsche 718 Cayman GT4 RS CS**	**Silver Rocket Racing**	**50**
4	**868**	**Zeng Jian Feng**	**Porsche 718 Cayman GT4 RS CS**	**RSR GT Racing**	**47**
6	**969**	**Du Yu**	**Porsche 718 Cayman GT4 RS CS**	**RSR GT Racing**	**42**
8	**911**	**Jack Pang**	**Porsche 718 Cayman GT4 RS CS**	**Blackjack Racing**	**27**

TEAM STANDINGS

POS	TEAM	CAR	POINTS
1	**Climax Racing**	**Porsche 911 GT3 R, Porsche 718 Cayman GT4 RS CS, Audi R8 LMS GT3 Evo II, Lamborghini Huracán GT3 Evo, Mercedes-AMG GT3 Evo**	**203**
2	Absolute Racing	Porsche 911 GT3 R, Audi R8 LMS GT4	153
3	Uno Racing Team	Audi R8 LMS GT3 Evo II	143
4	YC Racing	Porsche 911 GT3 R, Audi R8 LMS GT3 Evo II, Lamborghini Huracán Super Trofeo, Mercedes-AMG GT4	102
5	**RSR GT Racing**	**Porsche 718 Cayman GT4 RS CS**	**89**
6	**Silver Rocket Racing**	**Porsche 718 Cayman GT4 RS CS**	**50**
7	**Blackjack Racing**	**Porsche 718 Cayman GT4 RS CS**	**27**

INTERNATIONAL GT OPEN

29.04.–01.05.2022	*Estoril, Portugal*
20.05.–22.05.2022	*Paul Ricard, France*
17.06.–19.06.2022	*Spa-Francorchamps, Belgium*
08.07.–10.07.2022	*Hungaroring, Hungary*
09.09.–11.09.2022	*Red Bull Ring, Austria*
23.09.–25.09.2022	*Monza, Italy*
14.10.–16.10.2022	*Barcelona, Spain*

Ralf Bohn, Robert Renauer

Klaus Bachler und Riccardo Cazzaniga bescherten Porsche einen Sieg, einen zweiten und einen dritten Platz in der International GT Open.

In der International GT Open 2022 waren Porsche-Teams nur sporadisch vertreten und dennoch durften sie Erfolge feiern. Für den größten Triumph sorgten Klaus Bachler / Riccardo Cazzaniga, die Lauf eins von Monza gewinnen konnten. Cazzaniga startete von der vierten Position, arbeitete sich in einem von vier Safety-Car-Phasen geprägten Regenrennen zusammen mit Bachler aber immer weiter nach vorne; beide hatten beim Abbruch kurz vor der geplanten Zielankunft die Nase vorne. In Heat zwei reichte es für das Porsche-Duo auch aufgrund von fünf Strafsekunden wegen eines von Bachler verschuldeten Unfalls zum fünften Platz.

Zum Finale in Barcelona fanden sich drei Porsche ein. Bachler / Cazzaniga erkämpften sich einmal Rang zwei und einmal die dritte Position. Ralf Bohn und Robert Renauer brachten erstmals in der Saison einen Porsche unter der Bewerbung von Herberth Motorsport an den Start. In Heat eins verhinderte ein Ausrutscher ins Kiesbett, den Bohn aufgrund eines Schubsers eines Rivalen nicht verhindern konnte, eine bessere Platzierung als P23. Im zweiten Lauf sahen sie die Zielflagge als Siebte und waren damit bestes Pro-Am-Paar. Einen Podestplatz in der Am-Klasse eroberten Philipp Sager / Bashar Mardini im zweiten Dinamic-Porsche, die im ersten Rennen Klassenrang drei und Gesamtposition 17 belegten.

Und schließlich nahmen Earl Bamber / Piti Bhirombhakdi mit einem vom Singha Racing Team TP12 vorbereiteten Porsche am Endurance-Rennen von Spa-Francorchamps teil, einem Lauf, der doppelt so lang war wie ein normaler GT-Open-Durchgang. Sie beendeten den über 2:20 Stunden langen Auftritt auf Rang 15.

Riccardo Cazzaniga, Klaus Bachler

Piti Bhirombhakdi, Earl Bamber

Robert Renauer

Klaus Bachler and Riccardo Cazzaniga delivered a win, a second and a third place for Porsche in the International GT Open.

Porsche teams only sporadically raced in the 2022 International GT Open season, but they were nevertheless successful. Winning the first race at Monza, Klaus Bachler / Riccardo Cazzaniga secured the biggest success. Cazzaniga started fourth but, together with Bachler, gradually worked his way up in the race that included four safety car interventions in rainy conditions. The two were in front as the race was stopped a little earlier than planned. In the second race, they finished fifth, also due to a five-second time penalty for Bachler following an accident.

Three Porsches were on the grid for the finale in Barcelona. There, Bachler and Cazzaniga scored one second and one third place in the two races. Herberth Motorsport had its first season outing with Ralf Bohn and Robert Renauer. In the first race, a rival pushed Bohn into the gravel bed and the team finished outside the top 20. In the second race, Bohn and Renauer were the best-placed Pro-Am pairing in seventh overall. Philipp Sager / Bashar Mardini scored a pair of Am class podium results with the second Dinamic Porsche.

And finally, Earl Bamber / Piti Bhirombhakdi participated in the Spa-Francorchamps endurance race with a Porsche prepared by Singha Racing Team TP12. Double the length of a regular GT Open race at 2h 20m, the race saw the duo end up 15th overall.

Ralf Bohn

DRIVER STANDINGS

POS	NO	DRIVERS	CAR	TEAM	POINTS
1	63	Benjamin Hites, Leonardo Pulicini	Lamborghini Huracán GT3 Evo	Oregon Team	118
2	72	Joe Osborne, Nick Moss	McLaren 720S GT3	Optimum Motorsport	125
3	19	Kevin Gilardoni, Glenn van Berlo	Lamborghini Huracán GT3 Evo	Oregon Team	119
9	24	Riccardo Cazzaniga, Klaus Bachler	Porsche 911 GT3 R II	Dinamic Motorsport	46

TEAM STANDINGS

POS	NO	TEAM	CAR	POINTS
1	63	Oregon Team	Lamborghini Huracán GT3 Evo	127
2	72	Optimum Motorsport	McLaren 720S GT3	78
3	9,77,786,911	GetSpeed Performance	Mercedes-AMG GT3 Evo	47
4	24	Dinamic Motorsport	Porsche 911 GT3 R II	29

Philipp Sager, Bashar Mardini

GT AMERICA

POWERED BY AWS

24.02.–26.02.2022	*St. Petersburg, Florida, USA*
15.04.–17.04.2022	*Sonoma Raceway, California, USA*
17.06.–19.06.2022	*Virginia International Raceway, Virginia, USA*
22.07.–24.07.2022	*Watkins Glen International, New York, USA*
05.08.–07.08.2022	*Nashville, Tennessee, USA*
19.08.–21.08.2022	*Road America, Wisconsin, USA*
23.09.–25.09.2022	*Sebring International Raceway, Florida, USA*
07.10.–09.10.2022	*Indianapolis Motor Speedway, Indiana, USA*

Adam Adelson

Ein Unfall beim Finale nahm Porsche-Pilot Adam Adelson die Chancen auf den Titel in der GT America; am Ende belegte er den dritten Platz der Abschlusstabelle.

Wie in fast allen nordamerikanischen Rennserien, an denen Porsche 2022 teilgenommen hat, wurde der Titelkampf auch in der GT4-Klasse der GT America bis zum Schluss geführt. Drei Fahrer hatten beim Finale auf dem Indianapolis Motor Speedway noch Chancen, den Fahrertitel zu gewinnen. Auch die Entscheidung, wer das beste Team des Jahres wird, war noch offen. Adam Adelson in seinem Porsche 718 Cayman CS MR von Premier Racing war das heiße Porsche-Eisen im Titelrennen. Doch die Startnummer 120 hatte mit den beiden Aston-Martin-Piloten Jason Bell und Ross Chouest starke Konkurrenz vor der Brust. Der US-Amerikaner ging das Finalwochenende dennoch konzentriert an und tat, was er tun musste, um sein Auto an der Spitze des Feldes zu halten.

In der Schlussphase kam es dann zu einer Berührung zwischen Adelson und Chouest, die Adelsons Kühler nicht unbeschadet überstand. Er musste seinen Cayman vorzeitig abstellen, was die Titelambitionen von Premier Racing und Porsche schlagartig beendete. Für den doppelten Saisonsieger Adelson blieb letztendlich der dritte Platz in der Fahrerwertung, während Premier Racing die gleiche Position in der Teamwertung belegte. Porsche, die mit Robb Holland von Rotek Racing den einzigen Piloten in ihren Reihen hatten, der in dieser Saison mehr als zwei Rennen gewinnen konnte – er siegte insgesamt dreimal – wurde am Ende Zweiter der Herstellerwertung.

Last lap battles highlighted Porsche teams' performance in SRO GT America

Like nearly all of the 2022 Porsche Motorsport championships in North America, the GT America GT4 class battle came down to the wire. Three drivers entered the finale at the Indianapolis Motor Speedway with an opportunity to take the Driver and Team titles. Adam Adelson was the only Porsche capable of winning the GT4 class championship in the #120 Premier Racing entry. He was up against formidable competition from the Aston Martins of Jason Bell and Ross Chouest. Adelson did all that he could, making up an amazing ten positions at the start of the last race of the season, and keeping his car at the front of the field. Behind, the two Aston's monitored points and positions. Every foot on the track mattered as each position had an effect on the championship order in real time.
In the closing stages however, Adelson and Chouest made contact, which broke Adelson's radiator and ended Premier's, and Porsche's, championship aspirations. Despite parking the car, Adelson had done enough to hold third place in the Drivers' championship having scored two wins during the year, while Premier Racing held the same spot in the Teams' title chase. Porsche earned second in the Manufacturer Championship. Highlight of the year for Porsche was Rotek Racing's Robb Holland who, with three wins, was the only driver to earn more than two victories in the series.

Adam Adelson

Kyle Washington

Robb Holland

DRIVER STANDINGS **SRO3**

POS	NO	DRIVERS	CAR	TEAM	POINTS
1	04	George Kurtz	Mercedes-AMG GT3 Evo	Crowd Strike Racing by Riley Motorsports	333
2	27	Jason Daskalos	Audi R8 LMS GT3	Daskalos Motorsports	182
3	70	Mirco Schultis	Chevrolet Corvette C7 GT3	Mishumotors	172
9	**032**	**Kyle Washington**	**Porsche 911 GT3 R II**	**GMG Racing**	**48**
13	**00**	**P. J. Hyett**	**Porsche 911 GT3 R II**	**Team Hardpoint**	**15**

DRIVER STANDINGS **GT4**

POS	NO	DRIVERS	CAR	TEAM	POINTS
1	50	Ross Chouest	Aston Martin Vantage GT4	Choest Povoledo Racing	182
2	2	Jason Bell	Aston Martin Vantage GT4	GMG Racing	176
3	**120**	**Adam Adelson**	**Porsche 718 Cayman GT4 RS CS**	**Premier Racing**	**150**
5	**99**	**Robb Holland**	**Porsche 718 Cayman GT4 RS CS**	**Rotek Racing**	**132**
13	**30**	**Hutton McKenna**	**Porsche 718 Cayman GT4 RS CS**	**Premier Racing**	**35**
19	**71**	**Jay Logan**	**Porsche 718 Cayman GT4 RS CS**	**GMG Racing**	**22**
22	**66**	**Derek DeBoer**	**Porsche 718 Cayman GT4 RS CS**	**The Racer's Group**	**18**

Hutton McKenna

Derek DeBoer

TEAM STANDINGS **GT4**

POS	TEAM	CAR	POINTS
1	Choest Povoledo Racing	Aston Martin Vantage GT4	185
2	GMG Racing	Aston Martin Vantage GT4	181
3	**Premier Racing**	**Porsche 718 Cayman GT4 RS CS**	**156**
4	**Rotek Racing**	**Porsche 718 Cayman GT4 RS CS**	**137**
24	**NOLASPORT**	**Porsche 718 Cayman GT4 RS CS**	**1**

TEAM STANDINGS **SRO3**

POS	TEAM	CAR	POINTS
1	Crowd Strike Racing by Riley Motorsports	Mercedes-AMG GT3 Evo	341
2	Daskalos Motorsports	Audi R8 LMS GT3	191
3	Zelus Motorsports	Lamborghini Huracán GT3 Evo	178
8	**GMG Racing**	**Porsche 911 GT3 R II**	**60**
10	**Team Hardpoint**	**Porsche 911 GT3 R II**	**15**

MANUFACTURER STANDINGS **GT4**

POS	MANUFACTURER	POINTS
1	Aston Martin	315
2	**Porsche**	**304**
3	Toyota	254

MANUFACTURER STANDINGS **GT3**

POS	MANUFACTURER	POINTS
1	Mercedes-AMG	369
2	Lamborghini	256
3	Ferrari	222
4	**Porsche**	**108**

P. J. Hyett

Gran Turismo Campionato Italiano

CAMPIONATO ITALIANO GRAN TURISMO

21.04.–23.04.2022 Monza, Italy
03.06.–05.06.2022 Misano, Italy
02.09.–04.09.2022 Imola, Italy
21.10.–23.10.2022 Mugello, Italy

Vor allem in der Sprint-Klasse GT Cup waren Porsche-Piloten in der italienischen GT-Meisterschaft erfolgreich; in der AM-Wertung gab es sogar einen Titelgewinn.

In der italienischen GT-Meisterschaft eroberten Porsche-Fahrer im Klassement Sprint GT Cup AM die besten Resultate. „Poppy" und Enrico di Leo holten sich den Titel dieser Klasse vor ihren Markenkollegen Tazio Pieri und Emanuele Tabacchi. Die meisten Rennsiege dieser Kategorie sammelte dabei Pieri, der zweimal triumphierte; das Duo „Poppy" / di Leo gewann ein Rennen. Auch in der Wertung Sprint GT Cup Pro-Am feierten Porsche-Piloten Erfolge. Mit Gianluigi Piccioli belegte ein Ebimotors-Pilot den zweiten Rang der Pro-Am-Abschlusswertung und auch seine Teamkollegen Vito Postiglione und Riccardo Pera schafften den Sprung in die Top 6 des Schlussrankings. An jedem Rennwochenende gab es mindestens einen Porsche-Klassensieg: In Monza gewannen Alessandro Mainetti / Stefano Gattuso von Krypton Motorsport. Rennen zwei, in Misano entschied Piccioli zusammen mit Postiglione Heat zwei für sich. In Imola holte sich Piccioli mit Pera den ersten Platz und auch in Mugello war Ebimotors mit Piccioli / Pera wieder ganz vorne zu finden.

Robert Renauer, Alfred Renauer, Ralf Bohn

Manuel Lauck, Jörg Dreisow

Porsche drivers were particularly successful in the Italian GT championship GT Cup sprint class, and won a title in the AM category.

Porsche drivers fared particularly well in the Sprint GT Cup Am category of the Italian GT championship. In this class, "Poppy" and Enrico di Leo sealed the title ahead of their fellow Porsche drivers, Tazio Pieri and Emanuele Tabacchi. Pieri scored the most race wins in this category, having won twice, while "Poppy" and di Leo won once.

In the Sprint GT Cup Pro-Am standings, Porsche drivers were also successful. Ebimotors driver Gianluigi Piccioli finished the season second in the final Pro-Am standings while his teammates Vito Postiglione and Riccardo Pera also made it into the top six of the end-of-season standings. There was at least one Porsche class win during each race weekend: at Monza, Krypton Motorsport drivers Alessandro Mainett / Stefano Gattuso won race two, Piccioli and Postiglione came out on top in the second race at Misano. At Imola, Piccioli won together with Pera and Ebimotors was on top again at Mugello, once more with Piccioli and Pera.

(l.-r.): Robert Renauer, Alfred Renauer, Ralf Bohn

Giovanni Berton, Alessandro Mainetti, Giacomo Riva

Daniele Cazzaniga, Davide Di Benedetto, Giuseppe Nicolosi

(371): Gianluigi Piccioli, Riccardo Pera - (311): Davide Amaduzzi, Jeffrey Nelson

DRIVER STANDINGS **SPRINT CUP PORSCHE PRO-AM**

POS	NO	DRIVERS	CAR	TEAM	POINTS
1	371	Gianluigi Piccioli	Porsche 991 GT3 Cup	Ebimotors	94
2	301	Vittoria Piria	Porsche 991 GT3 Cup	Tsunami Racing Team	79
3	322	Alessandro Mainetti	Porsche 991 GT3 Cup	Krypton Motorsports	62
4	399	Giovanni Berton	Porsche 991 GT3 Cup	Tsunami Racing Team	50
5	311	Davide Amaduzzi, Jeffrey Nelson	Porsche 991 GT3 Cup	Ebimotors	46

DRIVER STANDINGS **SPRINT CUP PORSCHE AM**

POS	NO	DRIVERS	CAR	TEAM	POINTS
1	302	Enrico Di Leo, "Poppy"	Porsche 991 GT3 Cup	AB Motorsport	98
2	397	Emanuele Maria Tabacchi	Porsche 991 GT3 Cup	EF Racing	74
3	389	Tazio Pieri	Porsche 991 GT3 Cup	Krypton Motorsport	62
4	396	Dario Baruchelli	Porsche 991 GT3 Cup	EF Racing	39
5	398	Thomas Pichler	Porsche 991 GT3 Cup	Autorlando Sport	36

TEAM STANDINGS **GT CUP SPRINT**

POS	TEAM	CAR	POINTS
1	**Ebimotors**	**Porsche 991 GT3 Cup**	**77**
2	Easy Race	Ferrari F488 Challenge Evo	70
3	**Krypton Motorsport**	**Porsche 991 GT3 Cup**	**62**
7	**AB Motorsport**	**Porsche 991 GT3 Cup**	**30**
11	**EF Racing**	**Porsche 991 GT3 Cup**	**17**
14	**Autorlando Sport**	**Porsche 991 GT3 Cup**	**8**

DRIVER STANDINGS **SPRINT CUP PRO-AM**

POS	NO	DRIVERS	CAR	TEAM	POINTS
1	323	Luigi Coluccio, Rocco Mazzola	Ferrari F488 Challenge Evo	Easy Race	88
2	**371**	**Gianluigi Piccioli**	**Porsche 991 GT3 Cup**	**Ebimotors**	**87**
3	306	Giacomo Barri, Eric Scalvini	Lamborghini Huracán GT3 Evo	Eric Scalvini	78
4	**322**	**Alessandro Mainetti**	**Porsche 991 GT3 Cup**	**Krypton Motorsport**	**64**
5	**301**	**Vito Postiglione**	**Porsche 991 GT3 Cup**	**Ebimotors**	**66**

DRIVER STANDINGS **SPRINT CUP AM**

POS	NO	DRIVERS	CAR	TEAM	POINTS
1	**302**	**Enrico Di Leo, "Poppy"**	**Porsche 991 GT3 Cup**	**AB Motorsport**	**91**
2	389	Tazio Pieri	Porsche 991 GT3 Cup	Krypton Motorsport	78
3	**397**	**Emanuele Tabacchi**	**Porsche 991 GT3 Cup**	**EF Racing**	**70**
5	397	Gianfranco Bronzini	Porsche 991 GT3 Cup	EF Racing	51

DRIVER STANDINGS **GT CUP SPRINT**

POS	NO	DRIVERS	CAR	TEAM	POINTS
1	389	Daniele Cazzanga, Davide Di Benedetto, Giuseppe Nicolosi	Porsche 991 GT3 Cup	Krypton Motorsport	55
2	322	Alessandro Mainetti, Giovanni Berton	Porsche 991 GT3 Cup	Krypton Motorsport	35

FANATEC GT WORLD CHALLENGE AMERICA POWERED BY aws

GT WORLD CHALLENGE AMERICA

15.04.–17.04.2022	*Sonoma Raceway, USA*
20.05.–22.05.2022	*New Orleans, USA*
17.06.–19.06.2022	*Virginia International Raceway, USA*
22.07.–24.07.2022	*Watkins Glen International, USA*
19.08.–21.08.2022	*Road America, USA*
23.09.–25.09.2022	*Sebring International Raceway, USA*
07.10.–09.10.2022	*Indianapolis Motor Speedway, USA*

Langjähriges Porsche-Kundenteam Wright Motorsports verpasst den Titel in der GT World Challenge America nur knapp.

Wie die anderen US-amerikanischen SRO-Serien, so endete auch die Saison der Fanatec GT World Challenge America powered by AWS Anfang Oktober auf dem Indianapolis Motor Speedway. Die Porsche-Mannschaft Wright Motorsports ging mit Chancen auf den Fahrer- und den Teamtitel in der Kategorie Pro-Am in das längste Rennen des Jahres, dem 8-Stunden-Lauf von Indianapolis. Obwohl sie vor dem Finale den Vorteil der Tabellenführung genoss und damit als leichter Favorit nach Indianapolis reiste, verpasste sie den Titel knapp. Letztendlich wurde die von John Wright geführte Truppe mit den Fahrern Jan Heylen und Charlie Luck, die beim Finale noch von Elia Erhart unterstützt wurden, Vize-Champion. Auf dem Weg zur zweiten Position des Pro-Am-Abschlussrankings eroberte das Vater-Schwiegersohn-Gespann Luck / Heylen im Porsche 911 GT3 R mit der Startnummer 45 vier Siege, sieben Podiumsplätze sowie zehn Top-Fünf-Platzierungen und hatten am Schluss einen Rückstand von gerade einmal fünf Punkten auf die neuen Pro-Am-Champions Mario Farnbacher / Ashton Harrison. „Die Konkurrenz war in diesem Jahr stark wie eh und je und es war eine Ehre, in einem so hochklassigen Feld dabei zu sein. Jeder einzelne im Team und auch die Fahrer haben diese Saison eine tadellose Leistung erbracht. Dass Charlie Luck in seinem Rookie-Jahr in der Pro-Am-Klasse bis zum letzten Rennen um den Titel kämpft, ist etwas, worauf wir wirklich stolz sein können", so ein glücklicher John Wright.

Jan Heylen, Charlie Luck

Kyle Washington, James Sofronas

Jan Heylen and Charlie Luck

Jan Heylen, Charlie Luck

Porsche customer team narrowly misses SRO GT World Challenge America title

Like other national SRO championships, the 2022 season of the Fanatec GT World Challenge America powered by AWS had its glittering finale at the Indianapolis Motor Speedway. This was the longest race of the year, an eight hour race, and it was fitting that this was the championship decider for the entrants of the US series. Longstanding Porsche customer team Wright Motorsports charged into the finale leading the championship for drivers and team. However, fortune was not with them and they narrowly missed out on the title. Ultimately, the John Wright-owned operation, with drivers Jan Heylen and Charlie Luck (joined by Elia Erhart at Indy), finished the season as runner-up in the standings.

Wright, which had entered the father and son-in-law pairing of Luck and Heylen, ended 2022 with four wins, seven podiums and 10 top-five finishes.

"The competition in this year's battle was as strong as ever, and it was an honour to be amongst such a tight field. This crew and these drivers performed flawlessly again and again, and it really shows. For Charlie Luck to be fighting in the championship in the final race, in his rookie season in the Pro-Am class, is really something to be proud of."

Kyle Washington, James Sofronas

Jan Heylen, Charlie Luck

TEAM STANDINGS **PRO-AM**

POS	TEAM	CAR	POINTS
1	Racers Edge Motorsports	Acura NSX GT3 Evo	216
2	**Wright Motorsports**	**Porsche 911 GT3 R II**	**207**
3	BimmerWorld	BMW M4 GT3	197
13	**Team Hardpoint**	**Porsche 911 GT3 R II**	**6**

DRIVER STANDINGS **PRO-AM**

POS	NO	DRIVERS	CAR	TEAM	POINTS
1	93	Mario Farnbacher, Ashton Harrison	Acura NSX GT3 Evo	Racers Edge Motorsports	212
2	**45**	**Jan Heylen, Charlie Luck**	**Porsche 911 GT3 R II**	**Wright Motorsports**	**207**
3	94	Bill Auberlen, Chandler Hull	BMW M4 GT3	BimmerWorld	195
17	**00**	**P. J. Hyett, Gunnar Jeannette**	**Porsche 911 GT3 R II**	**Team Hardpoint**	**4**

DRIVER STANDINGS **AM**

POS	NO	DRIVERS	CAR	TEAM	POINTS
1	23	Charlie Scardina, Onofrio Triarsi	Ferrari F488 GT3 Evo	Triarsi Competizione	286
2	61	Conrad Grunewald, Jean-Claude Saada	Ferrari F488 GT3 Evo	AF Corse	86
3	88	Jason Harward	Lamborghini Huracán GT3 Evo	Zelus Motorsports	50
5	**032**	**Kyle Washington, James Sofronas**	**Porsche 911 GT3 R II**	**GMG Racing**	**36**

FIA MOTORSPORT GAMES

27.10.–30.10.2022 Paul Ricard, France

Ayhancan Güven

Matt Campbell

Matt Campbell sichert Porsche überlegenen Sieg: Im GT Sprint setzt sich der Australier am Steuer eines Porsche 911 GT3 R souverän gegen die Konkurrenz durch

Auf dem Circuit Paul Ricard fand die zweite Ausgabe der FIA Motorsport Games statt – eine Art olympische Spiele des Motorsports. Porsche war in Frankreich mit dem 911 GT3 R sowohl im GT Cup als auch im GT Sprint vertreten. Im einstündigen GT Sprint setzte sich IMSA-Meister und Porsche-Werksfahrer Matt Campbell gegen die Konkurrenz aus Belgien und Italien durch und fuhr damit für Australien eine Goldmedaille ein. Campbell pilotierte das von Earl Bamber Motorsports und Grove Racing eingesetzte Fahrzeug mit der Startnummer 4. Dank eines starken Starts ging es für den Australier von der zweiten Position direkt an die Spitze. Die Führung behielt er dann ungefährdet bis zum Rennende. Toksport WRT setzte einen weiteren Porsche 911 GT3 R im GT Sprint ein. Für die Türkei ging Ayhancan Güven an den Start. Der ADAC GT Masters-Vizemeister eroberte zu Beginn die zweite Position und setzte sich in der ersten Rennhälfte in der Spitzengruppe fest. Im Verlauf fiel Güven aber einige Positionen zurück und beendete den Lauf letztlich auf Rang fünf. Auch im GT Cup stand ein Porsche 911 GT3 R unter australischer Flagge am Start. Das Fahrzeug mit der Startnummer 4 wurde vom Vater-Sohn-Gespann Stephen und Brenton Grove pilotiert. Ihrem Landsmann konnten es die Beiden aber nicht gleichtun. Das Duo erlebte zwei schwierige Qualifikationsrennen mit einem Ausfall im zweiten Qualifikationslauf. Doch im Rennen kämpften sich die beiden Australier nach vorn und beendeten den Lauf als Siebte.

Matt Campbell

Stephen Grove

Ayhancan Güven

Ayhancan Güven

Stephen Grove, Brenton Grove

GT CUP

OVERALL POS	NO	DRIVERS	NATION	CAR	TEAM	LAPS
Gold	81	Simon Gachet, Eric Debard	France	Mercedes-AMG GT3 Evo	Akkodis SP Team	28
Silver	20	Valentin Pierburg, Fabian Schiller	Germany	Mercedes-AMG GT3 Evo	SPS Automotive Peformance	28
Bronze	93	Ian Loggie, Sam Neary	Great Britain	Mercedes-AMG GT3 Evo	Sky Tempesta Racing	28
7	4	**Stephen Grove, Brenton Grove**	**Australia**	**Porsche 911 GT3 R II**	**Grove Motorsport**	**28**

GT SPRINT

OVERALL POS	NO	DRIVERS	NATION	CAR	TEAM	LAPS
Gold	**1**	**Matt Campbell**	**Australia**	**Porsche 911 GT3 R II**	**Grove Motorsport**	**30**
Silver	63	Mirko Bortolotti	Italy	Lamborghini Huracán GT3 Evo	GRT Grasser Racing Team	30
Bronze	32	Dries Vanthoor	Belgium	Audi R8 LMS GT3 Evo	RACB National Team	30
5	53	**Ayhancan Guven**	**Turkey**	**Porsche 911 GT3 R II**	**Team Turkiye**	**30**

Matt Campbell secures a commanding win for Porsche: in GT Sprint, the Australian has the upper hand against the competition in the Porsche 911 GT3 R

Circuit Paul Ricard served as the venue for the second running of the FIA Motorsport Games, motorsport's equivalent of the Olympics. Porsche was present with the 911 GT3 R in both the GT Cup and GT Sprint. In the one-hour GT Sprint race, IMSA champion and Porsche works driver Matt Campbell had the upper hand against competition from Belgium and Italy, and secured a gold medal for Australia. Campbell drove the #4 Porsche that was jointly run by Earl Bamber Motorsports and Grove Racing. Having made a good start, the Australian immediately shot into the lead from second on the grid and his lead was unchallenged until the end. Toksport WRT ran another Porsche 911 GT3 R in GT Sprint, raced by Ayhancan Güven who was driving for Turkey. Initially, the ADAC GT Masters runner-up was second, but lost positions in the second half of the race and eventually finished fifth. The GT Cup field also included a Porsche 911 GT R running under the Australian flag. Father-and-son pairing Stephen and Brenton Grove shared car number 4. However, they were unable to emulate the performance of their compatriot. The duo had two difficult qualifying races, and retired from the second race. In the feature race, however, the two Australians worked their way up to finish seventh.

MACAU GT GRAND PRIX

17.11.–20.11.2022 Ghia Circuit, Macau

Alexandre Imperatori

Alexandre Imperatori sichert Porsche beim prestigeträchtigen Macau Grand Prix 2022 einen Podestplatz im Macau GT Cup.

Porsche erlebte beim 69. Macau Grand Prix auf dem berüchtigten Guia Circuit ein erfolgreiches Wochenende.

Eine starke Leistung von Alexandre Imperatori im Porsche 911 GT3 R mit der Startnummer elf brachte den Schweizer im Galaxy Entertainment Macau GT Cup auf das Podium. Nachdem er das erste Rennen des Wochenendes noch als Fünfter beendet hatte, konnte er sich in Lauf zwei um zwei Plätze verbessern und mit dem von TORO Racing eingesetzten Porsche in die Top-3 fahren.

RSR GT Racing belegte mit beiden Autos im Samstagrennen des Melco Greater Bay Area Macau GT Cup eine Position unter den ersten Fünf in der GT4-Kategorie. Jiang Ruxi steuerte seinen Porsche 718 Cayman GT4 RS Clubsport mit der Startnummer 30 auf den vierten GT4-Rang, gefolgt von Xia Yu im baugleichen Cayman mit der Startnummer eins. Ruxi setzte seine starke Performance auch im Sonntagrennen fort und schloss das Macau-Wochenende auf dem vierten Platz der GT4-Konkurrenz ab.

Alexandre Imperatori and Alexandre Gibot

Imperatori secures Porsche podium in Macau

Porsche enjoyed a strong weekend at the Guia Circuit during the 69th running of the Macau Grand Prix, as several international drivers and entries returned to compete in the prestigious race.

A brilliant performance from Alexandre Imperatori in the TORO Racing Porsche 911 GT3 R saw him on the podium in the Galaxy Entertainment Macau GT Cup. Finishing the first race of the weekend in fifth, it set him up nicely for the second race and a quick getaway allowed the Swiss racer to move up two places and finish in the top three.

RSR GT Racing got off to a strong start after taking a top-five finish in the GT4 category with both of its entries in Saturday's Melco Greater Bay Area Macau GT Cup race. Jiang Ruxi moved through the field to secure fourth place in the Porsche 718 Cayman GT4 RS Clubsport, followed by Xia Yu in his Porsche 718 Cayman GT4 Clubsport. Ruxi continued his strong pace in Sunday's race to hold position and end his weekend in fourth.

Jiang Ruxi and Xia Yu

Min Heng

Alexandre Imperatori

Alexandre Imperatori

MAIN RACE CLASSIFICATION

POS	NO	DRIVERS	CAR	TEAM	LAPS
1	77	Maro Engel	Mercedes-AMG GT3 Evo	Mercedes-AMG Team Craft-Bamboo Racing	8
2	10	Edoardo Mortara	Audi R8 LMS GT3 Evo II	Audi Sport Team Asia Absolute	8
3	**11**	**Alexandre Imperatori**	**Porsche 911 GT3 R II**	**Toro Racing**	**8**

RACE 1 CLASSIFICATION

POS	NO	DRIVERS	CAR	TEAM	LAPS
1	77	Maro Engel	Mercedes-AMG GT3 Evo	Mercedes-AMG Team Craft-Bamboo Racing	6
2	99	Raffaele Marciello	Mercedes-AMG GT3 Evo	Toro Racing	6
3	4	Ling Kang	Lamborghini Huracán GT3 Evo	Phantom Pro Racing	6
5	**53**	**Alexandre Imperatori**	**Porsche 911 GT3 R II**	**Toro Racing**	**6**
DNF	**66**	**Min Heng**	**Porsche 911 GT3 R II**	**Toro Racing**	**0**

INTERCONTINENTAL GT CHALLENGE

13.05.–15.05.2022 Bathurst, Australia
28.07.–31.07.2022 Spa-Francorchamps, Belgium
06.10.–08.10.2022 Indianapolis, Indiana, USA
09.12.–11.12.2022 Abu Dhabi, United Arab Emirates

Vier international renommierte Rennstrecken, fünf Hersteller: Auch 2022 begeisterte die Intercontinental GT Challenge wieder mit spannender Rennaction

Standen 2021 aufgrund der Pandemie nur zwei Veranstaltungen im Kalender der Intercontinental GT Challenge, kamen ein Jahr später zwei weitere Events dazu. Sehr zur Freude von Fahrern und Fans war der beliebte Mount Panorama Circuit im australischen Bathurst erneut Teil der internationalen Meisterschaft. Darüber hinaus standen die 24 Stunden von Spa, das Indianapolis 8 Hour sowie das 12-Stunden-Rennen auf dem Yas Marina Circuit für Hersteller Porsche auf dem Programm. Beim Auftaktrennen Mitte Mai in Australien starteten insgesamt drei Porsche-Mannschaften. Das Aufgebot der Prostate Cancer Foundation of Australia holte als Zehnter das beste Porsche-Resultat. Weder die Lokalmatadoren von Grove Racing noch das Team Our Kloud- UpTo11 Motorsport sahen nach zwölf Stunden Renndistanz die Zielflagge beim Heimrennen. Im belgischen Spa gehörten vier Porsche 911 GT3 R im Rahmen der Intercontinental GT Challenge zum Starterfeld. Mit Gesamtrang sieben waren es Dennis Olsen, Nick Tandy und Laurens Vanthoor, die im KCMG-Porsche das beste Ergebnis für den Hersteller aus Zuffenhausen einfuhren. Auf dem Indianapolis Motor Speedway im US-Bundesstaat Indiana stellte GMG Racing das erfolgreichste Porsche-Aufgebot: James Sofronas, Kyle Washington und Klaus Bachler kamen auf Gesamtrang neun ins Ziel und sicherten sich damit als Dritte der Pro-Am-Wertung einen Podestplatz. Knapp dahinter sah die Wright Motorsports-Mannschaft als Elfte die Zielflagge.

Ben Barker, Brenton Grove, Stephen Grove

Four internationally renowned race tracks, five manufacturers: the Intercontinental GT Challenge thrilled again with exciting race action in 2022

The Intercontinental GT Challenge calendar comprised only two races in 2021 due to the pandemic, but a year later two further events were once again added. Much to the delight of drivers and fans, the popular Mount Panorama Circuit at Bathurst in Australia was part of the international championship again. Porsche was also represented in the remaining round of the series that included the Spa 24 Hours, the Indianapolis 8 Hour and the 12-hour race at Yas Marina Circuit. A total of three Porsche teams were on the grid for the opening round in Australia in mid-May. Classified tenth, and best-placed Porsche, was the Prostate Cancer Foundation of Australia team. Neither of the local heroes, Grove Racing and the Our Kloud- UpTo11 Motorsport team, made it to the finish after twelve hours of racing in their home event. At Spa in Belgium, four Porsche 911 GT3 Rs competed for International GT Challenge points. Seventh overall was the best result for Porsche, achieved by Dennis Olsen, Nick Tandy and Laurens Vanthoor in the KCMG Porsche. At Indianapolis Motor Speedway in the American state of Indiana, GMG Racing emerged as the most successful Porsche team. James Sofronas, Kyle Washington and Klaus Bachler finished ninth overall and secured a class podium as they ended up third in the Pro-Am classification. Just a little further down, the Wright Motorsports team crossed the finish line in eleventh place.

Klaus Bachler, James Sofronas, Kyle Washington

Elia Erhart, Jan Heylen, Charlie Luck

(l.-r.): Piti Bhirombhakdi, Tanart Sathienthirakul, Christophe Hamon, Earl Bamber

Nick Tandy, Laurens Vanthoor, Dennis Olsen

Scott Taylor, Alex Davison, Craig Lowndes, Geoff Emery

DRIVER STANDINGS

POS	NO	DRIVERS	CAR	TEAM	POINTS
1	77,88,91	Daniel Juncadella	Mercedes-AMG GT3 Evo	Craft-Bamboo Racing, Akkodis ASP Team	68
2	33,75,88	Jules Gounon	Mercedes-AMG GT3 Evo	Triple Eight Engineering, Akkodis ASP Team, Winward Racing	65
3	77,88	Raffaele Marciello	Mercedes-AMG GT3 Evo	Craft-Bamboo Racing, Akkodis ASP Team	50
14	**47**	**Dennis Olsen, Nick Tandy, Laurens Vanthoor**	**Porsche 911 GT3 R II**	**KCMG**	**10**
16	**32**	**James Sofronas, Kyle Washington, Klaus Bachler**	**Porsche 911 GT3 R II**	**GMG**	**6**
17	45	Elia Erhart, Charlie Luck, Jan Heylen	Porsche 911 GT3 R II	Wright Motorsports	4

after round 3 of 4

MANUFACTURER STANDINGS

POS	MANUFACTURER	POINTS
1	Mercedes-AMG	126
2	Ferrari	55
3	Lamborghini	40
5	**Porsche**	**23**

after round 3 of 4

MOBIL 1 SUPERCUP

SCHLBERG
PHILIS

TAGHeuer

Heineken
Heineken
0.0
M. Schuring
D. Pereira
H. King
M. Klein
J. van Lagen
BWT

PORSCHE
MOBIL 1
SUPERCUP

PORSCHE MOBIL 1 SUPERCUP

22.04.–24.04.2022	*Autodromo Enzo e Dino Ferrari, Imola, Italy*
27.05.–29.06.2022	*Circuit de Monaco, Monaco*
01.07.–03.07.2022	*Silverstone, United Kingdom*
08.07.–10.07.2022	*Red Bull Ring, Austria*
22.07.–24.07.2022	*Circuit Paul Ricard, France*
26.08.–28.08.2022	*Spa-Francorchamps, Belgium*
02.09.–04.09.2022	*Zandvoort, Netherlands*
09.09.–11.09.2022	*Monza, Italy*

Jaap van Lagen

Dylan Pereira, der 2015 seinen ersten Auftritt im Porsche Mobil 1 Supercup bestritt, heißt der neue Champion des internationalen Porsche-Markenpokals.

Acht Läufe auf acht verschiedenen Rennstrecken in sieben europäischen Ländern – das waren die Eckdaten des Kalenders des Porsche Mobil 1 Supercup 2022. Einzig in Italien machte der Markenpokal mit identischen Porsche 911 GT3 Cup zweimal Station. Beim Saisonstart in Imola, wo 1993 auch die Premiere der Rennserie erfolgte, empfing die Protagonisten rechtzeitig zum Rennstart strömender Regen. Aus Sicherheitsgründen wurde das Feld hinter dem Safety Car ins erste Rennen des Jahres geschickt, das mit Dylan Pereira den ersten Spitzenreiter verzeichnete. Der Luxemburger konnte sich direkt vom Feld absetzen und fuhr einem sicheren Sieg entgegen. Wesentlich mehr Arbeit hatte Larry ten Voorde, der den zweiten Platz innehatte. Den musste er zunächst gegen Bastian Buus und später gegen Harry King verteidigen, was ihm auch erfolgreich gelang. King sah die Zielflagge als Dritter vor Porsche-Junior Laurin Heinrich.
Fünf Wochen später stoppte der Cup in Monaco, wo Titelverteidiger Ten Voorde seinen ersten Saisontriumph feiern konnte. Der Niederländer sicherte sich mit einem knappen Vorteil von 0,057 Sekunden vor King zunächst die erste Startposition und setzte sich im Rennen dann mit einem Vorsprung von über 4,5 Sekunden gegen Dorian Boccolacci durch. Der Franzose spürte den Atem seines Verfolgers Heinrich deutlich mehr als Ten Voorde den von Boccolacci, doch abgesehen von einer kleinen Chance am Start hatte der Deutsche keine Möglichkeit, einen erfolgreichen Überholversuch gegen seinen fehlerfrei agierenden Vordermann vom Team Martinet by Alméras zu lancieren. Pereira erreichte die Ziellinie als Vierter vor King und musste seine Tabellenführung an Ten Voorde abgeben.

(l.-r.): Larry ten Voorde, Laurin Heinrich, Harry King

Gianmarco Quaresmini

Dylan Pereira, who raced in the Porsche Mobil 1 Supercup for the first time in 2015, became the new champion in the international Porsche one-make series.

The 2022 Porsche Mobil1 Supercup raced in seven European countries, and featured eight rounds at as many circuits. The season got underway in Imola, which had hosted the first-ever race of the series back in 1993. A downpour saw the race start under safety car conditions. Once the field was released, however, Dylan Pereira pulled clear of the pack and went on to claim his first win of the season. Larry ten Voorde had to work hard to defend second from Bastian Buus and then from Harry King. King finished third behind the Dutchman and ahead of Porsche junior driver Laurin Heinrich.

Next up was Monaco where defending champion Ten Voorde converted his pole position into his first win of the season, followed home by Dorian Boccolacci and Heinrich. Pereira finished fourth ahead of King, but that meant he lost the points' lead to Ten Voorde.

At Silverstone, Ten Voorde had a poor start from pole, and that allowed Heinrich, who had started alongside the Dutchman on the front row, to take the lead. Ten Voorde had actually dropped to third behind King, but soon recovered second place. Heinrich, meanwhile, was by that time beyond reach and scored his second win of the year, ahead of Ten Voorde and King, with Pereira fourth and Buus fifth.

At Red Bull Ring, BWT Lechner Racing's Pereira was unfazed by two safety car interventions. He held his nerve to score victory ahead of Heinrich, who had taken advantage of misfortune for Ten Voorde to take second. The Dutchman posted his first non-finish of the year. The SSR Huber Racing driver was the only one to break the stronghold of the BWT Lechner Racing team on the top positions as Lechner

(l.-r.): Oliver Schwab, Bernd Mayländer, Michael Dreiser, Dr. Wolfgang Porsche, Altfrid Heger

(6): Harry King - (7): Bastian Buus

Michael Ammermüller

Anfang Juli ging es im britischen Silverstone um Punkte und Platzierungen. Ten Voorde angelte sich die Pole Position, reagierte am Start jedoch zu spät und kam nicht optimal vom Fleck. Sein Reihennachbar Heinrich ließ sich nicht zweimal bitten und entscheid den Sprint zur ersten Kurve für sich. Ten Voorde lag kurzzeitig sogar noch hinter dem Briten King, doch diesen Makel machte er schon im ersten Umlauf wieder wett und überholte den Mann aus dem Team BWT Lechner Racing. Heinrich jedoch konnte er auf dem Weg zu dessen zweiten Sieg im Supercup nicht mehr bremsen. Als Dritter hinter Heinrich und Ten Voorde klassierte sich King, der sich bei seinem Heimrennen im Duell gegen Pereira behaupten konnte. Buus belegte den fünften Platz, den er sich gegen Lorcan Hanafin hart erkämpfen musste.

Auf dem Red Bull Ring holte Pereira sich die Spitze in der Fahrerwertung des Porsche Mobil 1 Supercup wieder, die er am zweiten Rennwochenende verloren hatte. Der Schützling der österreichischen Mannschaft BWT Lechner Racing konnte auch von zwei Safety-Car-Einsätzen nicht gestoppt werde: Er gewann deutlich vor Heinrich, der von einem Ausfall des zweitplatzierten Ten Voorde profitierte. Der Pilot von SSR Huber Racing sprengte damit auch die Phalanx der Lechner-Fahrer an der Spitze des Feldes. Hinter ihm reihte sich mit Buus nämlich direkt der nächste Lechner-Mann ein und auch auf Position vier fand sich mit King ein Elfer aus dem Hause BWT Lechner Racing wieder. Der Däne Buus konnte in der Steiermark sechs Plätze gutmachen und sich so vom neunten Startplatz bis auf einen Podestrang vorarbeiten.

Zwei Wochen nach dem Österreich-Gastspiel erfolgte im südfranzösischen Le Castellet der Startschuss für die zweite Saisonhälfte und Buus zeigte sich auf dem Circuit Paul Ricard bestens eingestellt. Der 19-Jährige eroberte nicht nur seine erste Pole Position im internationalen Markenpokal, sondern konnte diese auch in seinen Premierensieg ummünzen. Dabei agierte er am Start sowie beim Re-Start nach einer

Organisation of Porsche Mobil 1 Supercup

drivers Buus and King finished third and fourth respectively. Buus had worked his way up from ninth on the grid. With his victory, Pereira claimed back the points' lead he had lost in round two.
The second half of the season started at Le Castellet in the south of France. Buus, just 19 years old, had a great weekend, not only scoring his maiden pole position, but also his first-ever win in the internationally acclaimed one-make series. He remained in control at the start, and the restart after a safety car intervention. Teammate King made it a 1-2 for BWT Lechner Racing while Ten Voorde finished third. Heinrich was fourth on the road but was given a five-second time penalty for track limit infringements that dropped him back to fifth behind Pereira.
At the end of August, a streak of three rounds in three weekends started at the Spa-Francorchamps circuit in Belgium. Having already won twice at the demanding track in the Ardennes, Pereira was keen to add his third victory there. He claimed pole position and scored a commanding lights-to-flag win, finishing almost seven seconds ahead of Team GP Elite's Larry Ten Voorde, who had passed Heinrich for second on the final lap. Sixth overall, Buus made it a record of six rookie class wins from as many races.
From Spa, it was just a brief journey to Zandvoort. The best-placed Dutchman in the standings, Ten Voorde was keen to shine in front of his home crowd and to reduce the gap to Pereira to keep his chances of a successful title defence alive. However, sixth place was all there was in store for him in qualifying while Marvin Klein secured pole position. The French CLRT driver benefited from a penalty for Pereira, who dropped three places as a penalty for a collision with Iaquinta while warming up his tyres. In the race, Klein made good use of his grid position to score his maiden Supercup win. Morris Schuring was second on the road but was given a five-second penalty for an incorrect starting grid position and ended up ninth. Pereira was therefore classified second after a strong recovery drive from eighth on the opening lap. Ten Voorde took the final podium slot ahead of Buus, who celebrated an early rookie title win. BWT Lechner Racing also sealed the teams' crown on the Dutch North Sea coast.
At Monza, it was a déjà vu in qualifying for Klein as he was again promoted to pole position following a penalty for the fastest driver. This time, it was King who was dropped three places, as a penalty for taking off Jaap van Lagen at Zandvoort. This time, however, Klein failed to make the most of his position; instead it was Buus who blasted into the lead and he never looked back, taking the win from King and Pereira. However, the latter two were handed post-race time penalties and dropped back to third for King and fifth for Pereira. That promoted Ten Voorde and Heinrich to second and third. Still, fifth place was enough for Dylan Pereira to secure his maiden Porsche Mobil 1 Supercup title. Larry ten Voorde finished the season as runner-up from Laurin Heinrich and Bastiaan Buus. Norwegian Roar Lindland won the Pro-Am title.

(12): Marvin Klein
(7): Bastian Buus

Team BWT Lechner Racing

Safety-Car-Phase souverän und verteidigte jeweils seine Führung. Hinter ihm kreuzte sein Teamkollege King den Zielstrich, Ten Voorde meldete sich mit Rang drei auf dem Treppchen zurück. Auf der Strecke belegte Heinrich den vierten Platz, den er jedoch kurz nach Rennende wieder abgeben musste. Aufgrund der Missachtung der Streckenbegrenzung wurden ihm drei Strafsekunden auf seine Fahrzeit aufaddiert, was ihn hinter Pereira auf P5 zurückwarf.

Die als anspruchsvoll geltende Traditionsstrecke von Spa-Francorchamps war Ende August der Beginn eines Saisonendspurts, in dem drei Läufe an drei aufeinanderfolgenden Wochenenden zu absolvieren waren. Pereira triumphierte bereits zweimal auf der belgischen Formel-1-Piste und wollte nun seinen dritten Erfolg in den Ardennen hinzufügen. Optimale Voraussetzungen dafür verschaffte er sich mit der besten Rundenzeit im Qualifying: Ganze 0,364 Sekunden war er auf einem Umlauf schneller als sein erster Verfolger Heinrich. Und ähnlich souverän agierte er auch im Rennen, in dem er sich vom Start weg an die Spitze setzte und seinen Vorsprung immer weiter ausbaute. Fast sieben Sekunden vor Ten Voorde sah der Luxemburger die Zielflagge.

Clement Mateu

Lucas Groeneveld

Jesse van Kuijk

(l.-r.): Robert Lechner, Bastian Buus, Dylan Pereira, Harry King, Michael Schöch

Der Mann aus dem Team GP Elite überholte Heinrich erst in der letzten Runde und holte sich so P2 vor dem Deutschen. Weiterhin begeistern konnte auch Buus, der als Sechstplatzierter seinen sechsten Triumph in der Rookie-Wertung feierte. Damit stellte er einen neuen Sieg-Rekord auf.

Von Spa führte die kurze Reise nach Zandvoort. Ten Voorde, bester Niederländer im Gesamtklassement, wollte bei seinem Heimspiel alles geben, um seinen Rückstand auf den in der Gesamtwertung führenden Pereira zu reduzieren und so seine Chancen auf eine erfolgreiche Titelverteidigung aufrecht zu erhalten. Doch im Qualifying reichte es für ihn nur zum sechsten Platz, ganz vorne leuchtete der Name Marvin Klein auf. Dabei war der Franzose Nutznießer einer Strafe gegen Pereira, weil dieser beim Aufwärmen seiner Reifen mit Simone Iaquinta kollidierte. Der Lechner-Pilot wurde daraufhin auf Rang vier zurückgesetzt. Im Rennen konnte Klein seinen Vorteil nutzen, der Fahrer des Teams CLRT errang seinen ersten Triumph im Porsche Supercup. Morris Schuring fühlte sich nach der Zielankunft schon als Zweiter, doch weil er seinen Renner am Start nicht exakt auf die vorgeschriebene Position gestellt hatte, wurde er mit einer Fünf-Sekunden-Strafe belegt und fiel im Klassement auf Rang neun zurück. Profiteur war Pereira, der nach einer unglücklichen ersten Runde nur als Achter notiert wurde, sich dann aber auf den Weg nach vorne machte. Ten Voorde komplettierte das Podest als Dritter, Buus brachte P4 nach Hause. Damit durfte sich der Teenager über den vorzeitigen Gewinn der Rookie-Wertung im Supercup freuen. Und auch die Team-Wertung wurde an der niederländischen Nordseeküste entschieden, der Pokal ging an die Mannschaft BWT Lechner Racing.

In Monza erlebte Klein im Zeittraining zunächst ein Déjà-vu: Wie schon in Zandvoort rückte er auch beim Finale aufgrund einer Strafe gegen den Trainings-Schnellsten auf die Pole Position vor. Vor den Toren von Mailand traf es King, der wegen einer bereits in Zandvoort ausgesprochenen Bestrafung drei Plätze nach hinten versetzt wurde. Im Gegensatz zu Zandvoort konnte Klein seine Pole Position aber nicht in die Führung im Rennen umwandeln, er musste Buus auf den ersten Metern ziehen lassen. In den folgenden Runden bis zum Rennende ließ sich der Däne weder von Klein, noch von King von Rang eins verdrängen und durfte sich über seinen zweiten Supercup-Triumph freuen. King reihte sich als Zweiter ein, als Dritter erreichte Pereira den Zielstrich. Aber beide bekamen wenig später Zeitstrafen, die sie an die dritte (King) und fünfte (Pereira) Stelle nach hinten schoben. Doch auch P5 reichte Dylan Pereira für seinen ersten Titelgewinn im Porsche Mobil 1 Supercup. Larry ten Voorde und Laurin Heinrich fanden sich im Schlussklassement auf den Rängen zwei und drei wieder, Bastian Buus wurde Gesamt-Vierter. Und schließlich ging der Sieg in der Pro-Am-Wertung an den Norweger Roar Lindland.

(19) Dorian Boccolacci - (8): Alexander Fach

Roar Lindland and Team Martinet by Alméras

Lorcan Hanafin

Morris Schuring

uniserver
WARMTESERVICE
FERRARI

HARTL
motorsport

BOSS

2022
Mobil 1
30

2007

GP
Mobil 1
uniserver
WARMTESERVICE
TRADERS
D. van Kuijk

BWT

BWT
uniserver

2014
2016
2018

BOSS

ROLEX

PORSCHE
BWT
PORSCHE

PIRELLI

Laurin Heinrich

Daan van Kuijk

Laurin Heinrich

Max van Splunteren

Rudy van Buren

Robert and Walter Lechner

Team GP Elite

(5): Dylan Pereira · (3): Laurin Heinrich · (6): Harry King · (25): Larry ten Voorde

Leonardo Caglioni

Bastian Buus

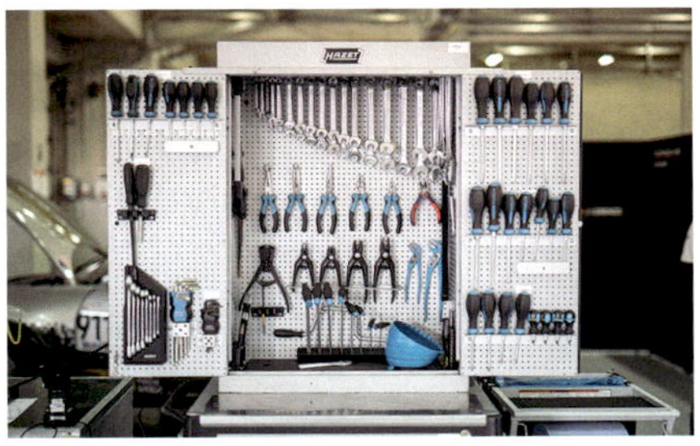

Harry King

Ariel Levi

Roar Lindland

Daan van Kuijk

(l.-r.): Harry King, Bastian Buus, Larry ten Voorde

(3): Laurin Heinrich - (25): Larry ten Voorde - (2): Rudy van Buren - (6): Harry King

(16): Simone Iaquinta · (17): Loek Hartog

Loek Hartog

(10): Jukka Honkavuori · (26): Jesse van Kuijk

Champion Dylan Pereira and Team BWT Lechner Racing

DRIVER STANDINGS **OVERALL**

POS	NO	DRIVERS	TEAM	POINTS
1	5	Dylan Pereira	BWT Lechner Racing	149
2	25	Larry ten Voorde	Team GP Elite	139
3	3	Laurin Heinrich	SSR Huber Racing	123
4	7	Bastian Buus	BWT Lechner Racing	122
5	6	Harry King	BWT Lechner Racing	109
6	12	Marvin Klein	CLRT	78
7	19	Dorian Boccolacci	Martinet by Alméras	59
8	17	Loek Hartog	Ombra Racing	43
9	9	Lorcan Hanafin	Fach Auto Tech	40
10	16	Simone Iaquinta	Dinamic Motorsport	39
11	20	Jaap van Lagen	Martinet by Alméras	35
12	2	Rudy van Buren	Huber Racing	35
13	1	Morris Schuring	Huber Racing	33
14	10	Jukka Honkavuori	Fach Auto Tech	33
15	24	Max van Splunteren	Team GP Elite	26
16	4	Michael Ammermüller	SSR Huber Racing	19
17	18	Gianmarco Quaresmini	Ombra Racing	14
18	26	Jesse van Kuijk	Team GP Elite	14
19	28	Lucas Groeneveld	GP Elite	13
20	8	Alexander Fach	Fach Auto Tech	12
21	27	Daan van Kuijk	GP Elite	9

DRIVER STANDINGS **PRO-AM**

POS	NO	DRIVERS	TEAM	POINTS
1	21	Roar Lindland	Pierre Martinet by Alméras	163
2	11	Clément Mateu	CLRT	145
3	15	Philipp Sager	Dinamic Motorsport	133
4	23	Aaron Mason	Pierre Martinet by Alméras	126
5	22	Stéphane Denoual	Pierre Martinet by Alméras	87

DRIVER STANDINGS **ROOKIES**

POS	NO	DRIVERS	TEAM	POINTS
1	7	Bastian Buus	BWT Lechner Racing	122
2	17	Loek Hartog	Ombra Racing	43
3	9	Lorcan Hanafin	Fach Auto Tech	40
4	1	Morris Schuring	Huber Racing	33
5	8	Alexander Fach	Fach Auto Tech	12

Dorian Boccolacci

TEAM STAND NGS

POS	TEAM	POINTS
1	BWT Lechner Racing	288
2	Team GP Elite	164
3	SSR Huber Racing	140
4	CLRT	95
5	Martinet by Alméras	92
6	Huber Racing	65
7	Ombra Racing	56
8	Fach Auto Tech	47
9	Dinamic Motorsport	39
10	GP Elite	20

(l.-r.): Lorcan Hanafin, Bastian Buus, Loek Hartog

Mobil 1
ROLEX

CARRERA CUP

SYSCOIN
PORSCHE
uniserver
CAREER
REBELS
anecars
TAG Heuer
TIMQ

CAYMAN ISLANDS
Heinrich
MICHELIN

PORSCHE
CARRERA CUP

A. Mathieu
53
Pierre Martinet
TAGHeuer
L. Perrot
29

PORSCHE
CARRERA CUP
DEUTSCHLAND

CARRERA CUP DEUTSCHLAND

05.05.–07.05.2022	*Spa-Francorchamps, Belgium*
20.05.–22.05.2022	*Red Bull Ring, Austria*
17.06.–19.06.2022	*Imola, Italy*
24.06.–26.06.2022	*Zandvoort, Netherlands*
05.08.–07.08.2022	*Nürburgring, Germany*
19.08.–21.08.2022	*Lausitzring, Germany*
23.09.–25.09.2022	*Sachsenring, Germany*
21.10.–23.10.2022	*Hockenheim, Germany*

(43): Willem Meijer - (69): Holger Harmsen

Die Fahrer Laurin Heinrich, Lorcan Hanafin und Carlos Rivas sowie das Team SSR Huber Racing sind die Titelträger des Porsche Carrera Cup Deutschland 2022.

Die 33. Saison des Porsche Carrera Cup Deutschland wartete mit acht Veranstaltungen auf, bei denen jeweils zwei Rennen à 30 Minuten ausgefahren wurden. Sechsmal gastierten die 911er-Piloten im Rahmen des ADAC GT Masters, einmal zusammen mit der DTM und zum Auftakt absolvierten sie im belgischen Spa-Francorchamps zwei Läufe im Rahmen der FIA Langstrecken-Weltmeisterschaft WEC. Der Anfang der Saison gelang insbesondere Laurin Heinrich perfekt, der von der Pole Position einen Start-Ziel-Sieg feiern konnte. Hinter ihm machte Dylan Pereira auf sich aufmerksam, als er vom fünften Startplatz innerhalb von nur zwei Runden bis auf Rang zwei vorfahren konnte. Ein Rivale, den er überholen konnte, war dabei Titelverteidiger Larry ten Voorde, der sich mit der dritten Stelle zufriedengeben musste.

Auch Lauf zwei einen Tag später wurde zur Beute von Heinrich: Er siegte vor dem 17-jährigen Morris Schuring. Der Teenager kassierte in der ersten Kurve nach dem Start Ten Voorde und freute sich über sein bis zu diesem Zeitpunkt bestes Resultat im Porsche Carrera Cup Deutschland. Das Podium wurde von Bastian Buus vervollständigt. Mitte Mai folgte auf dem Red Bull Ring das erste Gastspiel im Rahmen des ADAC GT Masters, bei dem Pereira die Nase vorne hatte. Der Luxemburger musste sich zunächst hinter dem erstmals von der Pole Position gestarteten Loek Hartog einreihen, doch nach zwei Runden drehte er die Reihenfolge an der Spitze um. Der junge Niederländer fiel wenig später noch auf den dritten Platz hinter Heinrich zurück, den er auch ins Ziel brachte.

Ein Rennen später feierte Tabellenführer Heinrich seinen dritten Saisonsieg und baute seine Führung in der Gesamtwertung des Porsche Carrera Cup Deutschland weiter aus. Talent Schuring sowie Routinier Michael Ammermüller komplettierten mit ihren

Drivers of Porsche Carrera Cup Deutschland

Drivers Laurin Heinrich, Lorcan Hanafin and Carlos Rivas and the SSR Huber Racing team were the title winners in the 2022 Porsche Carrera Cup Deutschland.

The 33rd season of the Porsche Carrera Cup Deutschland included eight double-header events, six of them held alongside ADAC GT Masters, one with DTM and one with FIA WEC. Laurin Heinrich started his title-winning season from pole position at the opening race at Spa-Francorchamps, and he converted that into a win ahead of Dylan Pereira and Larry ten Voorde. Heinrich also won on the next day, this time finishing ahead of 17-year-old Morris Schuring, and Bastian Buus.
At Red Bull Ring in mid-May, Loek Hartog scored his maiden pole position, but it was Pereira who won the race, having claimed the lead after two laps. The young Dutchman dropped to third behind Heinrich before the flag. One race later, Heinrich extended his points' lead by taking his third win of the season while Schuring, who had started from pole for the first time, and Michael Ammermüller rounded out the podium, completing the clean sweep of the podium for the SSR Huber Racing team.
At Imola, Buus celebrated his maiden win after erstwhile leader Hartog locked up with three laps remaining. Heinrich and Ten Voorde joined Buus on the podium, the latter after a great recovery drive from 15th place following a collision in the early stages. Hartog only finished fourth. The second race at Imola saw Ten Voorde become the fourth different race winner of the year, finishing ahead of Hartog and Pereira with Heinrich fourth, finishing outside the top three for the first time in the season.

Laurin Heinrich and Christoph Huber

(94): Dylan Pereira - (96): Jan-Erik Slooten - (95): Richard Wagner

(l.-r.): Jan-Erik Slooten, Carlos Rivas, Georgi Donchev

(28): Lucas Groeneveld - (84): Dylan Pereira

(4): Loek Hartog - (94): Dylan Pereira

Rängen zwei und drei den Dreifach-Erfolg des Teams SSR Huber Racing. Schuring, der erstmals von der ersten Startposition ins Rennen ging, begann zwar schwach und fiel im ersten Umlauf bis auf P5 zurück. In der Folge arbeitete sich aber wieder bis auf die zweite Stelle nach vorne. Ammermüller hinter ihm feierte seinen ersten Podestplatz in der Saison 2022.

In Imola durfte Mitte Juni dann Buus zum ersten Mal von der obersten Stufe des Podests jubeln. Im fünften Saisonrennen – dieses Mal im Rahmen der DTM – wurde es gegen Ende noch einmal spannend, als das Treiben nach einer zweiten Safety-Car-Phase wieder freigegeben wurde. Drei Umläufe vor dem Fallen der Zielflagge verbremste sich Spitzenreiter Hartog und Verfolger Buus zog vorbei. Seitdem ist der Däne mit seinen 18 Jahren und 363 Tagen zweitjüngster Rennsieger in der Geschichte des PCC Deutschland – einzig Thomas Preining war bei seinem ersten Erfolg minimal jünger. Für Hartog sollte es indes noch schlimmer kommen, denn auch Heinrich und Ten Voorde überholten ihn und kickten ihn so vom Podium. Letzterer glänzte dabei mit einer tollen Aufholjagd, nachdem er in der Anfangsphase nach einer Kollision bis auf Rang 15 zurückgefallen war.

Auftritt zwei auf der italienischen Rennstrecke sah mit Ten Voorde dann den vierten Rennsieger des Jahres; Hartog und Pereira begleiteten den amtierenden Champion des PCC Deutschland zur Siegerehrung. Heinrich kreuzte die Ziellinie als Vierter und verpasste erstmals in 2022 die Top 3.

Rudy van Buren

Champion Laurin Heinrich and SSR Huber Racing Team

Heinrich then came good again at Zandvoort at the end of June, winning the first race from Ten Voorde and Buus. The race started with a multi-car pile-up in the first corner and a safety car intervention. At the re-start, Heinrich overtook Ten Voorde for the lead and brought victory home.

The following race saw Ten Voorde remain in control, and he won from Allied-Racing's Buus. Heinrich finished third to retain his position as leader in the points standings at the halfway mark of the season.

The second half of the season started at the Nürburgring in early August. Pole sitter Pereira was unable to make the best of his grid position and had to let Heinrich pull away. The latter didn't lead for long either as he lost his position to Ten Voorde. After a duel on the final lap, Buus secured second place from Pereira.

Driving for the locally based IronForce Racing by Phoenix team, Pereira took the spoils on Sunday. Having started from pole position, he also defended his lead after a safety car intervention and went on to score his second win of the year, finishing ahead of Heinrich and Hartog.

Pereira was also unstoppable at Lausitzring in mid-August. On a wet track, Heinrich first overtook Pereira and Ten Voorde with two laps remaining, but then spun after contact with Ten Voorde, handing victory to Pereira. Ten Voorde was second on the road, but incurred a 30-second time penalty and ended up 23rd. Two other Dutchmen, meanwhile, took the other podium slots: Rudy van Buren scored his best result in second, Hartog came third.

Max van Splunteren

(31): Sebastian Freymuth - (14): Morris Schuring

Ende Juni zeigte sich der 20-Jährige in Zandvoort gut erholt von seinem bisher schwächsten Saisonresultat und gewann Lauf eins vor Ten Voorde und Buus. Der Durchgang begann mit einem Unfall mehrerer Fahrzeuge in der ersten Kurve. Als das Rennen wieder freigegeben wurde, ließ Heinrich nach einer erfolgreichen Attacke gegen Leader Ten Voorde nichts mehr anbrennen.
Jener 25-Jährige sollte es einen Heat später besser machen. Abermals an der Spitze fahrend, wehrte er dieses Mal einen Angriff von Buus erfolgreich ab und brachte bei seinem Heimspiel den ersten Platz nach Hause. Der Däne von Allied-Racing war aber auch mit seinem zweiten Rang, dem dritten Podest-Besuch in den vergangenen vier Rennen, zufrieden. Sogar seine siebte Siegerehrung erlebte Heinrich, der als Dritter ins Ziel kam und sich Halbzeit-Champion nennen durfte.
Der Auftakt zur zweiten Saisonhälfte erfolgte Anfang August auf dem Nürburgring. Pole-Mann Pereira konnte seinen Vorteil nicht nutzen und musste Heinrich ziehen lassen. Doch auch der wurde nicht lange vorne notiert, dann übernahm Ten Voorde den Platz an der Sonne. Heinrich verlor unterdessen nach einer Kollision einige Positionen, was Buus auf Rang drei spülte. In der Schlussrunde griff er noch mit Erfolg seinen Vordermann Pereira an und wurde als Zweiter hinter Ten Voorde abgewinkt. Schon am Samstag gab Pereira zu Protokoll, optimistisch für den Sonntag zu sein. Und das stellte der Schützling des Teams IronForce Racing by Phoenix dann auch eindrucksvoll unter Beweis. Zunächst setzte er sich von der ersten Startposition aus in Führung, dann konnte er auch nach Beendigung einer Safety-Car-Phase die Spitze erfolgreich verteidigen. Lohn der Mühen: Der zweite Saisontriumph für den 25-Jährigen. Heinrich reihte sich als Zweiter ein, Hartog klassierte sich als Dritter.
Auch Mitte August auf dem Lausitzring war Pereira nicht zu bremsen. Zwei Runden vor dem Fallen der Zielflagge überholte Heinrich auf regennasser Piste zunächst Pereira und Ten Voorde, bevor das Trio im engen Abstand zueinander in die erste Kurve einbog. Und dort passierte es: Heinrich drehte sich nach einer Berührung mit Ten Voorde, wodurch sich Pereira den Sieg vor den Niederländer sichern konnte. Doch den zweiten Platz durfte der Fahrer des Teams GP Elite nicht lange behalten: Wegen des Verursachens der Kollision mit Heinrich bekam er nachträglich 30 Strafsekunden und fiel auf Position 23 zurück. So war es an Rudy van Buren, mit Rang zwei vor Hartog sein bis dahin bestes Saisonresultat zu feiern.
Einen Tag später war Pereira wiederum nicht zu bezwingen, dieses Mal allerdings mit deutlich weniger Nervenkitzel: P2 ging auf das Konto von Ten Voorde, Heinrich beendete seine Aufholjagd von Startplatz sieben auf Position drei.
Auf dem Sachsenring Ende September ging es dann wieder turbulent zu. Heinrich führte vor Ten Voorde, der nur kurzzeitig die Spitze übernehmen konnte, bevor Heinrich erfolgreich konterte. Den Zielstrich erreichten sie in der Reihung Ten Voorde vor Heinrich und Buus. Doch kurz nach Rennende attestierten die Sportkommissare Ten Voorde, dass er sich zu Unrecht einen Vorteil gegenüber Hartog verschafft habe

Michael Ammermüller

Flynt and Morris Schuring

Christoph Huber - Huber Racing's 100th race

Porsche Carrera Cup Deutschland
ADAC GT Masters Zandvoort (NLD)
24.06. – 26.06.2022

(l.-r.): Hurui Issak, Christoph Huber, Larry ten Voorde, Laurin Heinrich, Bastian Buus

Jesse van Kuijk

The race on Sunday was less eventful although it was another win for Pereira, second for Ten Voorde and third for Heinrich, who had started seventh.
At Sachsenring at the end of the September, there was again plenty of action. After several lead changes, Ten Voorde finished ahead of Heinrich and Buus, but the stewards decided that Ten Voorde had got himself an advantage against Hartog and imposed a time penalty that dropped the defending champion back to fifth That handed victory to Heinrich and Buus with Schuring in third.
As a result, Heinrich was already in a position to seal the title in the 14th race of the season and he did so in style with yet another win. He drove into the lead within the first few metres of the race, and that was all the invitation that he needed. He brought home the win, and with it the title. Pereira overtook Lorcan Hanafin for second and the two finished second and third in that order. As a result, the British rookie took part in the prize-giving ceremony for the first time.

Huub van Eijndhoven

Ariel Levi

Holger Harmsen

und brummten ihm eine Zeitstrafe auf. Er rutschte auf den fünften Rang, während Schuring den letzten verbliebenen Podestplatz erbte.

Damit konnte Heinrich im folgenden 14. Saisonlauf bereits den Titel in trockene Tücher bringen und er machte es mit einem weiteren Triumph. Schon auf den ersten Metern angelte er sich den ersten Platz und fuhr diesen sicher ins Ziel. Hinter dem neuen Champion überholte Pereira am Start Lorcan Hanafin; auch diese beiden Positionen blieben bis zum Ende des Rennens unverändert. Der britische Rookie durfte somit an seiner ersten Siegerehrung im Carrera Cup Deutschland teilnehmen.

Nachdem mit SSR Huber Racing auch das beste Team bereits am Sachsenring feststand, wurden beim Finale Ende Oktober in Hockenheim noch der beste ProAm-Pilot und der beste Rookie gesucht. Davon unbeeindruckt gewann Ten Voorde Heat eins vor Buus und Heinrich, der sich den Podestplatz erst in der letzten Runde gegen Pereira erkämpfen konnte.

Auch das finale Rennen des Jahres sah Ten Voorde, den zweifachen, aber nun entthronten Champion des PCCD, auf Rang eins vor Buus. Pereira schloss seine Saison mit Position drei ab. Jubel auch bei Carlos Rivas, der vor dem letzten Auftritt des Jahres in der ProAm-Wertung noch einen Rückstand von sechs Zählern auf Jan-Erik Slooten hatte. Doch dank seines Klassensieges konnte er sich im Endspurt noch auf den ersten Platz der ProAm-Piloten schieben. Für den Luxemburger war es der vierte ProAm-Titel in Serie. Bester Rookie des Jahres war nach 16 Saisonrennen der Brite Hanafin vor dem Niederländer Huub van Eijndhoven.

Holger Harmsen

PORSCHE
MOTORSPORT
Maßstäbe setzen.
Weltweit.
Die Porsche Markenpokale.
Als Erfolgsgaranten und Kaderschmieden sind die internationalen Porsche Markenpokale von Kundenteams weltweit hoch geschätzt. Über 700 Fahrer in 30 Ländern machen die Titelentscheidungen in allen Serien spannend bis zur buchstäblich letzten Runde, und das immer ganz in Ihrer Nähe! Gleich mehr erfahren – auf dem Porsche Motorsport Hub.

Georgi Donchev

(57): Rudy van Buren · (14): Morris Schuring

(27): Daan van Kuijk - (3): Laurin Heinrich

Torsten van Haasteren and Larry ten Voorde

Huub van Eijndhoven

Champion SSR Huber Racing Team

IRONFORCE RACING
ELTEN
PCH
CARRERA CUP DEUTSCHLAND
Porsche Zentrum Niederrhein

GP ELITE
uniserver

Talent Pool

3 HEINRICH
CHAMPION

(25): Larry ten Voorde - (14): Morris Schuring - (3): Laurin Heinrich

Laurin Heinrich

(13): Alexander Tauscher - (99): Bastian Buus

DRIVER STANDINGS

POS	NO	DRIVERS	TEAM	POINTS
1	3	Laurin Heinrich	SSR Huber Racing	297
2	25	Larry ten Voorde	Team GP Elite	266
3	94	Dylan Pereira	Iron Force Racing by Phoenix Racing	240
4	99	Bastiaan Buus	Allied Racing	236
5	4	Loek Hartog	Black Falcon	185
6	14	Morris Schuring	SSR Huber Racing	161
7	57	Rudy van Buren	Huber Racing	137
8	24	Max van Splunteren	Team GP Elite	82
9	29	Huub van Eijndhoven	GP Elite	82
10	9	Lorcan Hanafin	Fach Auto Tech	78
11	13	Alexander Tauscher	Allied Racing	70
12	26	Jesse van Kuijk	Team GP Elite	69
13	92	Michael Ammermüller	SSR Huber Racing	66
14	40	Jukka Honkavuori	ID Racing	54
15	8	Alexander Fach	Fach Auto Tech	47
16	28	Lucas Groenveld	GP Elite	41
17	23	Lukas Ertl	CarTech Motorsport by Nigrin	38
18	27	Daan van Kuijk	GP Elite	30
19	75	Ariel Levi	Huber Racing	16
20	96	Jan-Erik Slooten	Iron Force Racing by Phoenix Racing	10
21	31	Sebastian Freymuth	HRT Performance	9
22	6	Carlos Rivas	Black Falcon	8
23	20	Harald Proczyk	HP Racing International	6
24	22	Gislain Cordeel	Team GP Elite	5
25	95	Richard Wagner	Iron Force Racing by Phoenix Racing	4
26	5	Sören Spreng	Black Falcon	2
27	98	Jan Seyffarth	HP Racing International	1

DRIVER STANDINGS **PRO-AM**

POS	NO	DRIVERS	TEAM	POINTS
1	6	Carlos Rivas	Black Falcon	306
2	96	Jan-Erik Slooten	Iron Force Racing by Phoenix Racing	296
3	2	Georgi Donchev	Huber Racing	209
4	5	Sören Spreng	Black Falcon	197
5	84	Ahmad Alshebab	CarTech Motorsport by Nigrin	185
6	7	Christof Langer	Fach Auto Tech	184
7	69	Holger Harmsen	HRT Performance	47
8	77	Kim-André Hauschild	HRT Performance	44
9	65	Kai Pfister	HRT Performance	40
10	10	Matthias Jeserich	HRT Performance	23
11	15	Philipp Sager	HRT Performance	22
12	41	Mark Thomas	ID Racing	17

DRIVER STANDINGS **ROOKIE**

POS	NO	DRIVERS	TEAM	POINTS
1	9	Lorcan Hanafin	Fach Auto Tech	294
2	29	Huub van Eijndoven	GP Elite	287
3	13	Alexander Tauscher	Allied Racing	248
4	8	Alexander Fach	Fach Auto Tech	235
5	75	Ariel Levi	Huber Racing	162
6	31	Sebastian Freymuth	HRT Performance	151
7	44	Jonas Greif	SSR Huber Racing	134
8	98	Jan Seyffarth	HP Racing International	120
9	22	Gislain Cordeel	Team GP Elite	22
10	42	Luke Wömer	ID Racing	19

DRIVER STANDINGS **PRO-AM**

POS	TEAM	POINTS
1	SSR Huber Racing	477
2	Team GP Elite	381
3	Allied Racing	317
4	Iron Force Racing by Phoenix Racing	263
5	Black Falcon	202
6	Huber Racing	168
7	GP Elite	163
8	Fach Auto Tech	140
9	ID Racing	62
10	Car Tech Motorsport by Nigrin	41
11	HP Racing International	14
12	HRT Motorsport	12

PORSCHE
CARRERA CUP
FRANCE

CARRERA CUP FRANCE

05.05.–07.05.2022	*Spa-Francorchamps, Belgium*
12.05.–14.05.2022	*Magny-Cours, France*
17.06.–19.06.2022	*Zandvoort, Netherlands*
16.09.–18.09.2022	*Valencia, Spain*
14.10.–16.10.2022	*Paul Ricard, France*

Nach einem spannenden Zweikampf mit Dorian Boccolacci gewann Marvin Klein zum zweiten Mal in Folge die Krone im Porsche Carrera Cup France.

Der Porsche Carrera Cup France 2022 begann Mitte April in Nogaro. Titelverteidiger Marvin Klein holte sich beide Pole Positions, die er in zwei souveräne Rennsiege ummünzen konnte. Auch Jérôme Boullery erlebte ein perfektes Auftaktwochenende und gewann beide Rennen in der Klasse Pro-Am. Ähnlich erfolgreich war auch Sébastien Dussolliet, der sich mit zwei Am-Triumphen an die Spitze der Am-Gesamtwertung setzte.

In Spa-Francorchamps meldete sich Dorian Boccolacci nach einem teils unglücklichen Nogaro-Wochenende eindrucksvoll zurück. Er eroberte die erste Startposition für beide Durchgänge und legte zwei Siege nach. Damit war der Titelkampf zwischen den beiden Rivalen Klein und Boccolacci bereits frühzeitig entbrannt. Boullery bestätigte seine Titelambitionen mit zwei weiteren Pro-Am-Siegen. Die Am-Klasse wurde vom Team ABM dominiert, das zwei Dreifach-Erfolge feiern konnte: Dussolliet gewann zweimal vor Sébastien Poisson und Stéphane Louard.

Eine Woche später ging es für die Teams und Fahrer des PCCF nach Magny-Cours, wo es an Klein war, Boccolaccis starken Spa-Auftritt zu kontern. Dies gelang ihm mit zwei Pole Positions und zwei Rennsiegen. Boullery holte seinen fünften Triumph in Folge in der Pro-Am-Klasse, bevor Clément Mateu die Siegesserie des Piloten von Racing Technology einen Tag später beendete. Beste Am-Vertreter waren in Magny-Cours Louard und Poisson, letztgenannter bejubelte seinen ersten Am-Triumph.

Auch das vierte Meeting in Zandvoort sah wieder einen dominierenden Piloten und dieses Mal war die Rolle wieder Boccolacci zugedacht. Der Schützling von Martinet by Alméras präsentierte sich sowohl in beiden Qualifyings wie auch in beiden Rennen unschlagbar. Die Schlussphase des ersten Heats in den Niederlanden war auch in der Pro-Am-Klasse ereignisreich, als ein Fahrfehler von Boullery seinem fahrenden Teamchef Sylvain Noël einen Vorteil verschaffte, den er nutzte und als erster Pro-Am-Pilot die Ziellinie überquerte. Einen Lauf später stellte Boullery die von ihm gewünschte Reihenfolge wieder her und siegte vor Noël. Unterdessen sammelte Am-Pilot Dussolliet die Klassenerfolge Nummer fünf und sechs.

Im September feierte der Carrera Cup France auf dem Circuito Ricardo Tormo in Valencia seine Rennpremiere und erstmals wurde ein Wochenende in dieser Saison nicht von einem einzigen Fahrer bestimmt: In Spanien teilten sich die beiden Titelrivalen Klein und Boccolacci die ersten Plätze. Anders in den Kategorien Pro-Am und Am, wo Boullery (Pro-Am) und Dussolliet (Am) jeweils Doppelsiege nach Hause fuhren.

Zum Finale in Le Castellet war somit alles bereit für eine spannende Auseinandersetzung um den Titel. Doch CLRT-Mann Marvin Klein hatte keine Lust auf Nervenkitzel: Mit zwei klaren Triumphen gegen den jeweils zweitplatzierten Boccolacci machte er den Deckel auf eine erfolgreiche Titelverteidigung zu. Bester Pro-Am-Pilot des Jahres war Jérôme Boullery, die Lorbeeren für den Am-Gesamtsieg erntete Sébastien Dussolliet.

Alessandro Ghiretti

Porsche Carrera Cup France, Porsche Carerra Cup Benelux, Porsche Carrera Cup Deustchland

After an intense duel, Marvin Klein won the crown for the second year in a row.

The Nogaro race track played host to the start of the 2022 season of the Porsche Carrera Cup France. Defending champion Marvin Klein (CLRT) took pole position for both races, and he converted them into two dominant race wins. A serious contender for the Pro-Am title, Jérôme Boullery (Racing Technology) had the perfect opening weekend, winning both races in the class. Sébastien Dussolliet (ABM) enjoyed similar success in the AM class, moving top of the standings also with two race wins.

At the iconic Spa-Francorchamps track, Boccolacci responded to Klein's round one dominance by grabbing pole position for both races, and he converted each into a win. The fight between him and Klein for the title was very much on and it would continue throughout the season! Boullery confirmed his Pro-Am title ambitions with another pair of victories. The Am class was similarly dominated by Dussolliet, who led home an ABM one-two-three in both races, joined on the podium by Sébastien Poisson and Stéphane Louard.

A week later, the PCCF headed to Magny-Cours. There, Klein produced another flawless performance, claiming two pole positions and two race wins to extend his championship lead. Meanwhile, Boullery bagged his fifth consecutive win in the Pro-Am class, while Stéphane Louard finished ahead of Patrick Charlaix in the Am class on Friday. In Saturday's race, Clément Mateu (CLRT) took advantage in the Pro-Am class and Sébastien Poisson claimed his first win in the Am class.

Mathieu Martins

Sébastien Dussolliet

Jérôme Boullery

Marvin Klein and Team CLRT

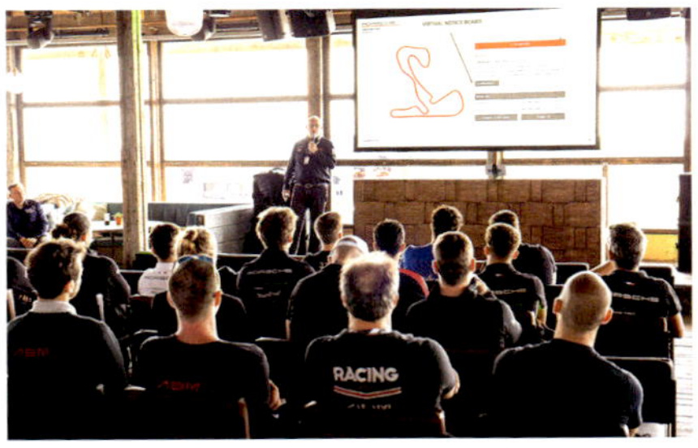

PORSCHE
CARRERA CUP

CIRCUIT PAUL RICARD

M. Klein
99

Pierre Martinet

PORSCHE
CARRERA CUP

M. KLEIN
Champion
2022

CLRT

12:21:23
21.4°C
M. KLEIN
CIRCUIT PAUL RICARD
HEXIS

PORSCHE
CARRERA CUP
FRANCE

Team Champion Martinet by Alméras

(22): Alessandro Ghiretti - (19): Dorian Boccolacci

Round four was held at the Dutch circuit of Zandvoort, and there Boccolacci was in unbeatable form, grabbing pole position for both races and converting his advantage into two race wins. The closing stages of the race were also eventful in the Pro-Am class as an error by Boullery allowed his team manager Sylvain Noël to take advantage, whilst in the Am class Dussolliet returned to winning ways, taking his fifth victory of 2022. Boullery and Dussolliet confirmed their status as favourites in their categories, each claiming a sixth class win in Pro-Am and Am respectively.
In September, PCCF made its first ever trip to the Valencia's Ricardo Tormo racetrack in Spain. Boccolacci took honours in race one before Klein hit back in the rain during Sunday's race. Boullery produced a solid performance in the Pro-Am class to take a double triumph whilst Dussolliet dominated the AM class by winning both races.
With five victories each, Klein and Boccolacci arrived in Le Castellet for the final meeting in a breathtaking finale. Klein took his second consecutive title at the age of 23, having won both races. Boullery and Dussolliet were also among the winners of the year, in Pro-Am and Am respectively.
In 2022, the Porsche Carrera Cup France was once again a thrilling event, fought out to its conclusion, offering its drivers an exciting field of expression and the same kind of sensations.

Aaron Love

Dorian Boccolacci

DRIVER STANDINGS **OVERALL**

POS	NO	DRIVERS	TEAM	POINTS
1	99	Marvin Klein	CLRT	271
2	19	Dorian Boccolacci	Martinet by Alméras	245
3	22	Alessandro Ghiretti	Martinet by Alméras	139
4	999	Bastian Buus	Allied Racing	137
5	23	Aaron Love	Pierre Martinet by Alméras	114
6	24	Mathieu Martins	Pierre Martinet by Alméras	101
7	29	Louis Perrot	TFT Racing	94
8	7	Jérôme Boullery	Racing Technology	87
9	74	Victor Blugeon	ABM	80
10	53	Arthur Mathieu	Martinet by Alméras	79
11	33	Evan Spenle	CLRT	76
12	11	Sylvain Noël	Racing Technology	61
13	12	Alexander Tauscher	Allied Racing	55
14	38	Sébastien Dussolliet	ABM	50
15	44	Clément Mateu	CLRT	38
16	73	Sébastien Poisson	ABM	32
17	59	Maxence Maurice	IMSA Performance	18
18	28	Patrick Charlaix	TFT Racing	15
19	88	Ugo Gazil	CLRT	13
20	911	Christophe Lapierre	Pierre Martinet by Alméras	12
21	74	Karim Ajlani	ABM	9
22	666	Stéphane Louard	ABM	6

DRIVER STANDINGS **PRO-AM**

POS	NO	DRIVERS	TEAM	POINTS
1	7	Jérôme Boullery	Racing Technology	261
2	11	Sylvain Noël	Racing Technology	204
3	44	Clément Mateu	CLRT	168
4	59	Maxence Maurice	IMSA Performance	102
5	911	Christophe Lapierre	Pierre Martinet by Alméras	62
6	74	Karim Aljani	ABM	28

DRIVER STANDINGS **AM**

POS	NO	DRIVERS	TEAM	POINTS
1	38	Sébastien Dussolliet	ABM	268
2	73	Sébastien Poisson	ABM	216
3	28	Patrick Charlaix	TFT Racing	170
4	666	Stéphane Louard	ABM	119

TEAM STANDINGS

POS	TEAM	POINTS
1	Martinet by Alméras	384
2	CLRT	347
3	Pierre Martinet by Alméras	209
4	Allied Racing	192
5	ABM	139
6	TFT Racing	109

Marvin Klein

PORSCHE CARRERA CUP BRASIL | OFFICIAL PARTNER C6 BANK mastercard

C6 BANK MASTERCARD CARRERA CUP BRASIL

02.04.–03.04.2022	*Goiania, Brazil*
23.04.–24.04.2022	*Velocitta, Brazil*
11.06.–12.06.2022	*Interlagos, Brazil*
11.08.–12.08.2022	*Termas de Río Hondo, Brazil*
08.10.–09.10.2022	*Goiania, Brazil*
12.11.–13.11.2022	*Interlagos, Brazil*

João Barbosa

Enzo Elias war zwar der jüngste Teilnehmer im Porsche Carrera Cup Brasil, aber das hielt ihn nicht davon ab, diesen GT3-Markenpokal zu gewinnen.

In der Saison 2022 stand ein brandneues Auto im Scheinwerferlicht des C6 BANK MASTERCARD Porsche Carrera Cup Brasil: Der Porsche 911 GT3 Cup 992, die neuste Generation des GT3-Cup-Fahrzeugs aus dem Hause Porsche, feierte seine Premiere im brasilianischen Cup.

Am besten kam der erst 20 Jahre alte Enzo Elias mit diesem Renner zurecht, das Küken im Starterfeld holte sich den Titel. Und dabei erlebte er mit einem Ausfall einen denkbar ungünstigen Start in die Saison. Dem damit erlittenen Rückstand in der Gesamtwertung musste er fortan nachrennen, denn sein neun Jahre älterer Hauptrivale Marçal Müller präsentierte sich als einer der konstantesten Fahrer. Er erlaubte sich keinen Ausfall, eroberte in jedem Lauf ein Top-Ten-Ergebnis und legte eine beeindruckende Serie von acht Podiumsplätzen in Folge hin. Doch seine Performance hatte auch einen Haken: Müller gewann nur den ersten Heat des Jahres. Und so hatte Elias doch noch eine Chance, die er beim Schopfe packen wollte: In Velocitta gewann er Rennen eins und beendete das zweite auf Platz vier, beim Gastspiel im argentinischen Termas de Rio Hondo erreichte er einen ersten und einen zweiten Rang. In Goiania konnte er dann die Führung in der Fahrerwertung übernehmen. Aber beide Kontrahenten machten es maximal spannend und reisten punktgleich zum Finale nach Interlagos, wo der Carrera Cup Brasil im Rahmen des Formel-1-Rennens antrat. Den jungen Elias schien diese Kulisse zu motivieren, denn er überzeugte auf ganzer Linie und eroberte vor vollen Tribünen und jubelnden Fans den Titel im Porsche Carrera Cup Brasil 2022.

Der neue Champion sammelte fünf von zwölf möglichen Siegen. Der einzige weitere Starter mit mehr als einem Triumph war der siebenfache Champion Miguel

Marçal Muller

Safety Car

Porsche Carrera Cup Brasil sees each of its classes decided at the final race of the year at Interlagos

The 2022 Season of C6 BANK MASTERCARD Porsche Carrera Cup Brasil featured the new Porsche 911 GT3 Cup 992, the next generation of the most iconic racecar. The model arrived in Brasil with a new engine, suspension, and aerodynamics that made it even faster and safer. In other words, the most prestigious and most important single-brand motorsport championship in Latin America got a car to keep up with its high level of competition.

After a hard-fought battle that went to the final round of the year, the Sprint Series title was awarded to the wunderkind Enzo Elias. Despite being just 20 years old and the youngest driver on the grid, this was Enzo's fourth title in Porsche Carrera Cup Brasil. The first came in 2019 in what today is the Sprint Challenge championship. The other two titles came last year with the Endurance Championship title and the Overall title, which adds up the totals from the Endurance and Sprint Series championships.

The opening round turned out to be Elias worst performance of the year. He started the very first race of the year with a retirement and that result set him back all year in the points table. The reason for his chasing of the lead was the spectacular season that was enjoyed by Marçal Müller. The 29-year-old driver had one of the most consistent campaigns, with no retirements, and always finishing in the top ten. That led to an impressive streak of eight consecutive podiums although Müller finished the season with only one win, at the opening race of the season.

(33): Bruno Campos - (9): Edu Guedes

Drivers, Teams and Organisation of C6 BANK MASTERCARD Porsche Carrera Cup Brasil

Start at Termas de Rio Hondo

Werner Neugebauer

Paludo, der zwei Durchgänge gewinnen konnte. In der Endabrechnung hatte Elias acht Punkte mehr auf seinem Konto als der zweitplatzierte Müller. Paludo belegte Position drei, gefolgt von Christian Hahn und Alceu Feldmann.
In der Klasse Carrera Sport fiel die Entscheidung zwischen Franco Giaffone und Lucas Salles erst im letzten Lauf des Jahres. Die Rechnung war dabei einfach: Wer am Ende die Nase vorn hatte, wäre der neue Champion. Am Ende durfte Giaffone jubeln, für Salles blieb Rang zwei der Abschlusstabelle. Eduardo Menossi, Georgios Frangulis und Francisco Horta komplettierten die Top 5. Bei den Carrera Rookies hieß das Duell Lineu Pires gegen Nelson Monteiro mit dem besseren Ende für Pires.

(888): Lineu Pires · (25): Paulo Sousa · (17): Leonardo Sanchez

Elias bounced back at Velocitta, the modern Mogi Guaçu track located a few hundred miles from São Paulo. The youngster won the first race of the weekend and followed that up with fourth place in the second race after the reverse grid format was applied. The series was back to hosting rounds internationally, and so Porsche Carerra Cup Brasil then visited Argentina. The Termas de Rio Hondo Track saw Elias shine brightly with two podium finishes, including second place in the opener, and then a win.
Back to Goiania, Elias still trailed Müller in the points table but he took the lead in the standings having won the first race, and then finished second. That put them level on points, but Elias had won more races. The title went to the final round, held alongside the Brasilian F1 Grand Prix at Interlagos. To keep up with the gala event, Elias did not disappoint. He recorded a Grand Chelem having scored pole position, a win and he led each lap, also setting the fastest lap of the race. Müller finished fourth, and so Elias took the title in front of cheering grandstands.
Elias finished the season with a whopping five wins from a possible 12. The only other driver with more than one win was the 7-time champion Miguel Paludo, who won twice. Elias took the title ahead of Müller, while Paludo finished third, Christian Hahn fourth ahead of Alceu Feldmann.
The fight for the Carrera Sport title also went to the last race of the year and it featured Franco Giaffone and Lucas Salles. They went into the final race virtually tied on points and whoever finished ahead would be the champion. Giaffone had the better luck. After battling with Salles he finished ahead and celebrated his first-ever title in Porsche Carerra Cup Brasil. Eduardo Menossi came in third, followed by Georgios Frangulis. Francisco Horta completed the top five.
The script was no different for the Carrera Rookie. Two drivers went to the final race in São Paulo disputing the title: Lineu Pires and Nelson Monteiro. Starting the final race 12 points ahead of Nelson, Lineu only needed to finish at the top five to be champion and he did so, finishing fourth. Lineu took his first ever title ahead of Monteiro, with Bruno Campos third, followed by Edu Guedes and Sylvio de Barros.

Rouman Ziemkiewicz

Rouman Ziemkiewicz

(26): Christian Hahn · (8): Werner Neugebauer · (544): Marçal Müller

(25): Paulo Sousa - (17): Leonardo Sanchez - (33): Bruno Campos

(184): Enzo Elias - (40): Rodrigo Mello

Edu Guedes

Georgios Frangulis

(7): Miguel Paludo - (73): Enzo Elias - (8): Werner Neugebauer

(88): Georgios Frangulis - (87): Nelson Monteiro

Enzo Elias

(3): Franco Giaffone - (70): Lucas Salles

(l.-r.): Pedro Aguiar, Enzo Elias, Miguel Paludo, Werner Neugebauer, Renan Pizii

scheGT3Cup.com.br

TAG HEUER

montebravo
KILIMA

G.H.MUMM
CHAMPAGNE

bm
ENGENHARIA

Cargill

Mutant

Racing
xperience

STUDIOS
FREMAX

Enzo Elias

Francisco Horta

Marçal Muller

Enzo Elias

DRIVER STANDINGS **CARRERA CUP**

POS	NO	DRIVERS	POINTS
1	73	Enzo Elias	184
2	544	Marçal Muller	176
3	7	Miguel Paludo	171
4	26	Christian Hahn	162
5	1	Alceu Feldmann	138
6	20	Pedro Aguiar	131
7	16	Renan Pizii	121
8	8	Werner Neugebauer	105
9	3	Franco Giaffone	84
10	70	Lucas Salles	81
11	888	Lineu Pires	64
12	87	Nelson Monteiro	58
13	29	Rodrigo Mello	40
14	80	Rouman Ziemkiewicz	36
15	85	Eduardo Menossi	32
16	88	Georgios Frangulis	29
17	77	Francisco Horta	28
18	116	Marcelo Hahn	24
19	33	Bruno Campos	23
20	5	Sylvio de Barros	20
21	9	Edu Guedes	11
22	44	Gustavo Farah	7
23	121	João Barbosa	6
24	17	Leonardo Sanchez	5
25	25	Paulo Sousa	4

DRIVER STANDINGS **CARRERA SPORT**

POS	NO	DRIVERS	POINTS
1	3	Franco Giaffone	102
2	70	Lucas Salles	94
3	85	Eduardo Menossi	67
4	88	Georgios Frangulis	64
5	77	Francisco Horta	58
6	80	Rouman Ziemkiewicz	57
7	116	Marcelo Hahn	40

DRIVER STANDINGS **ROOKIE**

POS	NO	DRIVERS	POINTS
1	888	Lineu Pires	84
2	87	Nelson Monteiro	77
3	33	Bruno Campos	72
4	9	Edu Guedes	72
5	5	Sylvio de Barros	60
6	44	Gustavo Farah	45
7	121	João Barbosa	40
8	25	Paulo Sousa	33
9	17	Leonardo Sanchez	22

CARRERA CUP BENELUX

05.05.–07.05.2022	*Spa-Francorchamps, Belgium*
10.06.–12.06.2022	*Zolder, Belgium*
24.06.–26.06.2022	*Zandvoort, Netherlands*
05.08.–07.08.2022	*Assen, Netherlands*
26.08.–28.08.2022	*Barcelona, Spain*
07.10.–09.10.2022	*Hockenheim, Germany*

Im Carrera Cup Benelux verwies der neue Champion Harry King die beiden belgischen Talente Glenn van Parijs und Ghislain Cordeel auf die Ränge zwei und drei.

Der Porsche Carrera Cup Benelux startete Anfang Mai im Rahmen des belgischen Laufs zur FIA Langstrecken-Weltmeisterschaft in Spa-Francorchamps. In den Ardennen stellte der Brite Harry King seinen Porsche in den Farben von Revs Motorsport zweimal auf die Pole Position und zweimal erklang bei der Siegerehrung die britische Nationalhymne. King verließ Spa mit der maximal möglichen Punktzahl, gefolgt von den jungen Belgiern Glenn van Parijs und Ghislain Cordeel.

Auch Anfang Juni in Zolder war King in den beiden Qualifyings und Rennen unschlagbar, während Van Parijs und Xavier Maassen jeweils einmal Zweite wurden.

Ende Juni in Zandvoort verlängerte der bisher dominierende Pilot seine Siegesserie um einen weiteren Triumph, bevor sie durch Van Parijs' ersten Erfolg des Jahres 2022 beendet wurde. Wenig später zog der Porsche Carrera Cup Benelux nach Assen und dort gelang es Cordeel, nach sechs ersten Startplätzen von King in Folge die Pole-Position-Serie des Tabellenführers zu brechen. Der erstmals Geschlagene sah in den beiden Rennen dann wieder als Erster die Zielflagge.

Das fünfte Wochenende der Saison fand in Barcelona statt und fiel mit dem Belgien-Auftritt des Porsche Mobil 1 Supercup zusammen, weshalb der ebenfalls im Supercup engagierte King auf die Reise nach Spanien verzichten musste. Van Parijs und Maassen nutzten die Chance und entschieden je einen Durchgang für sich.

Zum Finale in Hockenheim kam King dann wieder zurück und zeigte, dass der Weg zum Titel nur über ihn führen würde. Mit zwei Pole Positions, zwei schnellsten Rennrunden und zwei Siegen unterstrich er seine Vormachtstellung eindrucksvoll und darf sich nun Champion im Porsche Carrera Cup Benelux 2022 nennen. Silber ging an Glenn van Parijs, Ghislain Cordeel belegte den dritten Platz des Schlussklassements

(l.-r.): Didier Glorieux, Sören Spreng, Tom Boonen

The 2022 season of the Porsche Carrera Cup Benelux saw the series continue to grow in quality and quantity. With the introduction of the magnificent Porsche 991 GT3 Cup – Type 992, the contenders put on a fantastic show in the high-quality motorsport events. After an exciting final, it was the 21-year-old Briton Harry King who was crowned as the new champion, ahead of two young Belgian talents, Glenn van Parijs and Ghislain Cordeel.

After a test day at the circuit of Spa-Francorchamps, the 2022 Porsche Carrera Cup Benelux was ready for the real work at the beginning of May. The championship was on the same bill as the FIA World Endurance Championship, a triumph of scheduling that has now become a tradition and will be repeated in 2023.
During that first meeting of the season King immediately stamped his authority on the series. The 21-year-old Briton, in the colours of Revs Motorsport, put his Porsche on pole position twice and he converted them both into race wins. King left Spa with the maximum points, followed by van Parijs (NGT Racing) and Cordeel (Team GP Elite).
The pattern was repeated at the beginning of June as the series reconvened at the classic Zolder circuit. King scored maximum points, while van Parijs and Xavier Maassen (#TeamPGZ by RedAnt Racing) finished second in the two races respectively.
At Circuit Zandvoort, the third race held at the end of June, King continued his winning streak in the first race, but van Parijs struck back in the second, and took his first win of the year in the Dutch dunes. A few weeks later, the Porsche 911 GT3 Cup

(l.-r.): Glenn van Parijs, Harry King, Sam Dejonghe

Jan Lauryssen

Start at Zandvoort

(777): Sam Dejonghe - (30): Maxime Soulet

Rik Koen

vor Sam Dejonghe und Xavier Maassen. Für Harry King, der 2020 bereits den Porsche Carrera Cup Great Britain für sich entscheiden konnte, ist es der zweite Titel in einem Porsche-Markenpokal.

In der Pro-Am-Klasse konnte unterdessen Jan Lauryssen begeistern. Der Unternehmer aus Antwerpen war schon 2021 eine der Überraschungen der Saison, als er bei seinem Debüt im Motorsport auf Anhieb den Am-Titel im Porsche Carrera Cup Benelux gewann. Nun stieg er in die Kategorie Pro-Am auf und fügte seiner Vita gleich den zweiten Titel hinzu. Auf dem Weg dorthin sammelte er sieben Klassensiege, stand in Barcelona erstmals auf dem Gesamtpodest und reihte sich in der Gesamtwertung auf einem respektablen achten Rang ein. Didier Glorieux und der ehemalige Straßenradweltmeister Tom Boonen kletterten auf die Plätze zwei und drei der Pro-Am-Abschlusstabelle. In der Am-Wertung war niemand besser als Sébastien Lajoux und Lucas van Eijndhoven eroberte die Rookie-Krone 2022.

Stijn Lowette

moved to Assen and there Cordeel managed to break the streak of pole positions set by King. However, the Briton used that as motivation, and he won both races.
The fifth meeting of the season, in Barcelona, coincided with the Porsche Mobil 1 Supercup. King was therefore busy in Belgium while his fellow contenders for the Porsche Carrera Cup Benelux were racing on the Catalan F1 circuit, competing for victory in the ninth and tenth races of the season. van Parijs and Maassen shared the victories between them in Spain.
Their results, coupled with King missing two races, meant that both van Parijs and Cordeel were in contention for the title at the final in Hockenheim. The still had to find a way to beat the Briton, who returned to the championship to fight for his title. Although the gaps got smaller as the season progressed, King rounded it off in fine style, with two victories to become the 2022 champion of the Porsche Carrera Cup Benelux. Second place went to van Parijs, Cordeel eventually took third place in the championship, ahead of teammates at #TeamPGZ by RedAnt Racing, Sam Dejonghe and Maassen.

(7): Didier Glorieux - (24): Stijn Lowette

Harry King and Olivier Aerts

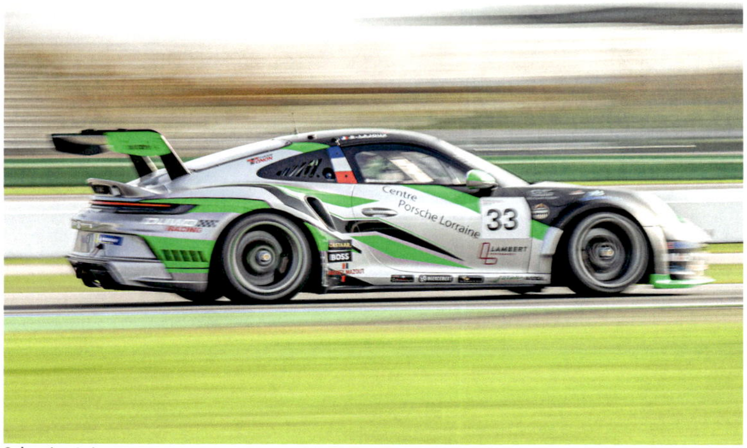

Sebastian Lajoux

Rik Koen

"I have had a very good season in the Porsche Carrera Cup Benelux", said Harry King at the end of the year. "I am also very grateful to the organization of the competition in the Benelux for the professional approach and I look back on the races with pleasure."
For King it was his second title in a Porsche one-make series, having won in the Porsche Carrera Cup GB. "His name really adds value to our beautiful series", says Olivier Aerts, Series Manager of the Porsche Carrera Cup Benelux. "We have seen a very nice competition this season, with fighting to the last metre of the championship on many fronts. I would like to take this opportunity to thank all drivers, teams, employees and partners for a fantastically beautiful championship that has certainly lived up to the expectations. I can already assure everyone that we are working hard on the 2023 season and that season promises to be very nice again."
In 2021 Jan Lauryssen (Q1 Trackracing) surprised many by winning the title in the AM Championship of the Porsche Carrera Cup Benelux on his debut in motorsport. The Antwerp entrepreneur proved in 2022 that that title was no coincidence. After an extremely strong season, with no fewer than seven victories, Lauryssen was crowned champion. In addition, he took his first overall podium in Barcelona and finished in an impressive eighth place in the overall championship. Didier Glorieux (Speedlover) and former road cycling world champion Tom Boonen (#TeamPGZ by RedAnt Racing) took the other podium places.
In the AM Championship, where the competitors always provided a fantastic spectacle, it was the Frenchman Sébastien Lajoux who drove to the title in the colours of DUWO Racing. He finished ahead of Stijn Lowette (NGT Racing) and Sven van Laere (JW Raceservice).
Last but not least, Lucas van Eijndhoven won the Rookie Championship on the final weekend, having scored a double victory to end the season just ahead of Rik Koen (Revs Motorsport).

Jan Lauryssen

(15): Glenn van Parijs · (2): Ghislain Cordeel

Lucas van Eijndhoven
and Team JW Raceservice

MediaMarkt
2
1st
3

PORSCHE
15
TRAFLUX

Sven van Laere

Luc Vanderfeesten

Harry King

DRIVER STANDINGS

POS	NO	DRIVERS	TEAM	POINTS
1	19	Harry King	Revs Motorsport	255
2	15	Glenn van Parijs	NGT Racing	252
3	2	Ghislain Cordeel	Team GP Elite	175
4	777	Sam Dejonghe	Team PGZ by Red Ant Racing	141
5	9	Xavier Maasen	Team PGZ by Red Ant Racing	126
6	9	Rik Koen	Revs Motorsport	95
7	14	Lucas van Eijndhoven	JW Raceservice	91
8	54	Jan Lauryssen	Q1 Trackracing by EMG Motorsport	84
9	30	Maxime Soulet	August Racing by NGT Racing	65
10	7	Didier Glorieux	Speedlover	57
11	33	Sebastian Lajoux	Duwo Racing	54
12	31	Sebastian Freymuth	PG Motorsport	49
13	99	Dylan Derdaele	Speedlover	42
14	13	Jaume Font Casas	Baporo Motorsport	41
15	24	Stijn Lowette	NGT Racing	39
16	21	Tom Boonen	Team PGZ by Red Ant Racing	38
17	13	Joan Vinyes Dabad	Baporo Motorsport	29
18	25	Sven van Laere	JW Raceservice	25
19	97	Koen Wauters	Belgium Racing	21
20	911	Luc Vanderfeesten	Team PGZ by Red Ant Racing	19
21	911	Ad Geerts	Team PGZ by Red Ant Racing	10
22	917	Jeroen Kreeft	Revs Motorsport	8

DRIVER STANDINGS **PRO-AM**

POS	NO	DRIVERS	TEAM	POINTS
1	54	Jan Lauryssen	Q1 Trackracing by EMG Motorsport	247
2	7	Didier Glorieux	Speedlover	213
3	21	Tom Boonen	Team PGZ by Red Ant Racing	173
4	97	Koen Wauters	Belgium Racing	78

DRIVER STANDINGS **AM**

POS	NO	DRIVERS	TEAM	POINTS
1	33	Sebastian Lajoux	Duwo Racing	242
2	24	Stijn Lowette	NGT Racing	167
3	25	Sven van Laere	JW Raceservice	147
4	13	Jaume Font Casas	Baporo Motorsport	137
5	13	Joan Vinyes Dabad	Baporo Motorsport	130
6	917	Jeroen Kreeft	Revs Motorsport	93
7	911	Ad Geerts	Team PGZ by Red Ant Racing	84
8	911	Luc Vanderfeesten	Team PGZ by Red Ant Racing	73
9	17	Willem Meulders	Speedlover	37

DRIVER STANDINGS **ROOKIE**

POS	NO	DRIVERS	TEAM	POINTS
1	14	Lucas van Eijndhoven	JW Raceservice	274
2	9	Rik Koen	Revs Motorsport	270

PORSCHE
CARRERA CUP
ITALIA

CARRERA CUP ITALIA

07.05.–08.05.2022	Imola, Italy
04.06.–05.06.2022	Misano, Italy
16.07.–17.07.2022	Mugello, Italy
17.09.–18.09.2022	Vallelunga, Italy
08.10.–09.10.2022	Monza, Italy
22.10.–23.10.2022	Mugello, Italy

Valentina Albanese and Gianmarco Quaresmini

Porsche Carrera Cup Italia: Gianmarco Quaresmini holt den Titel, aber auch Keagan Masters und der ehemalige MotoGP-Star Jorge Lorenzo glänzen.

Der Champion des Porsche Carrera Cup Italia 2022 heißt Gianmarco Quaresmini. Der Rennfahrer aus Brescia, der seinen nationalen Carrera Cup bereits 2018 gewinnen konnte, feierte seinen zweiten Titel am Ende einer spannenden Saison, in der sich neun verschiedene Piloten auf der obersten Stufe des Treppchens abwechselten und in der der mehrfache MotoGP-Champion Jorge Lorenzo sein Debüt im Automobilsport gab. In seiner ersten Saison in einem Rennauto konnte sich der Spanier immer weiter steigern. So war er in Monza nur zwei Zehntel von der Pole Position entfernt, während er in Mugello nahe daran war, in die Top 5 des Rennens vorzudringen.
Erst im letzten Saisonlauf sicherte sich Quaresmini die Lorbeeren im italienischen PCC und verwies den 22-jährigen Südafrikaner Keagan Masters sowie Diego Bertonelli auf die folgenden Plätze. Der Triumphator sammelte über die Saison hinweg zwei Siege, sieben Podiums-Platzierungen, eine Pole Position sowie eine schnellste Rennrunde. Zusammen mit seinem 19-jährigen Teamkollegen Leonardo Caglioni trug er so auch zum ersten Teamtitel von Ombra Racing bei. Rookie Masters, der für die Mannschaft AB Racing ins Lenkrad griff, kannte vor der Saison keine italienische Strecke, sah die Zielflagge aber dennoch zweimal als Erster und eroberte zudem ein Podium, eine Pole Position sowie fünf schnellste Rennrunden. Bertonelli steuerte mit einem ersten Rang, vier Podestplätzen, einer Pole Position und zwei schnellsten Rennrunden zur erfolgreichen ersten Saison seiner Truppe BeDriver im Carrera Cup Italia bei. Und auch der Gesamt-Vierte Giorgio Amati konnte mit seiner Performance zufrieden sein, hatte er doch seinen Teampartner Alberto Cerqui, keinen Geringeren als den Champion des Vorjahres, hinter sich gelassen.

Quaresmini takes the title while Masters and Lorenzo shine

The 2022 season was another record-breaker for the Porsche Carrera Cup Italia. In the six events scheduled, a total of 12 races, the Italian one-make series saw its highest grid numbers in 15 years. Thirty-seven 911 GT3 Cup cars were registered for the championship representing 17 teams. Of these, 31 were of the new 992 model, which kicked off the new era for the category with new technical regulations. These banned the use of ABS in braking, and thus required an even higher technical ability for the drivers who took part. Gianmarco Quaresmini, the driver from Brescia won his second title having achieved the feat in 2018. It came at the end of a thrilling season that saw as many as nine different drivers take to the top step of the podium, and it also featured the car racing debut of former MotoGP champion Jorge Lorenzo. The two-wheel wizard improved his lap times and qualifying results throughout the season. The Spanish driver, the official standard-bearer of Team Q8 Hi Perform, was only two-tenths from the pole position at Monza, while at Mugello, he came close to getting into the top five during the race.

The Tuscan race circuit saw Quaresmini secure the title, ahead of Keagan Masters, the 22-year-old from South Africa. Masters, who impressed in his rookie season driving for AB Racing, ended the year with two victories, one podium, one pole position and five fastest laps. Diego Bertonelli finished just behind him in the final standings having taken one win, four podiums, one pole position, and two fastest laps in the BeDriver team's first season in the Carrera Cup Italia.

Quaresmini's tally for the season included two wins, one at the opening round in Mugello, the other at Vallelunga, seven podiums, one pole position, and one fastest lap. Thus, together with 19-year-old teammate Leonardo Caglioni (who finished ninth with one win and one podium), he contributed to the first Team title clinched by Ombra Racing. Masters, on the other hand, was also listed as the best of the nine under-23 drivers selected by Porsche Italia for the Scholarship Programme. Giorgio Amati, who was also part of the programme, scored one win, one podium, and one pole position which enabled the 23-year-old Ghinzani Arco Motorsport driver to finish fourth overall, ahead of teammate and 2021 champion Alberto Cerqui. Masters and Amati later participated in the Porsche Junior Shoot Out at the Jerez circuit in Spain.

As the race season progressed, several other drivers had the opportunity to put themselves in the spotlight. Most notably, Lodovico Laurini (sixth overall) earned Dinamic Motorsport a spectacular win at Monza, while 19-year-old Tsunami RT driver Giammarco Levorato scored his first personal success in Race 2 at Vallelunga. In addition, Team Malucelli's experienced GT driver Matteo Malucelli concluded his first season in the Italian one-make series with two victories on his way to eighth

Lodovico Laurini

Alberto Cerqui

Matteo Malucelli

Start at Mugello

(66): Paolo Venerosi - (52): Alberto De Amicis - (25): Simone Riccitelli - (51): Paolo Gnemmi - (54): Luigi Peroni

Jorge Lorenzo

Im Verlauf des Jahres nutzten auch weitere Teilnehmer die Gelegenheit, sich ins Rampenlicht zu stellen: Lodovico Laurini bescherte Dinamic Motorsport einen spektakulären Triumph in Monza, während der 19 Jahre alte Tsunami-RT-Pilot Giammarco Levorato in Rennen zwei von Vallelunga seinen Premierenerfolg verbuchen konnte. Außerdem beendete der erfahrene GT-Mann Matteo Malucelli aus der Mannschaft Malucelli seinen ersten Auftritt im italienischen GT3-Markenpokal mit zwei ersten Positionen.

Auch die Entscheidung um den Titel im Michelin Cup fiel am letzten Rennwochenende in Mugello, die Trophäe ging letztendlich an den Römer Marco Cassarà. Alex De Giacomi erlebte zwar einen besseren Saisonbeginn, doch konnte er seine Tabellenführung im Michelin Cup nicht bis zum Finale verteidigen. Auf dem dritten Platz landete Alberto De Amicis. Davide Scannicchio schließlich sicherte sich den Titel im Silver Cup vor Paolo Venerosi Pesciolini und Luigi Peroni.

Marco Galassi

Giorgio Amati and Massimiliano Cariola

(l.-r.): Marco Cassarà, Gianluca Giorgi, Alex De Giacomi

overall in the final standings. Rounding off the top ten were Enrico Fulgenzi - who managed to lead his EF Racing team to success in Race 2 at Imola at the beginning of the season - and Benedetto Strignano, a promising young driver from Villorba Corse, who ended the season on a high note with two second-place podium finishes at Vallelunga and Monza.

The run-up to the Michelin Cup title was also settled in the last round at Mugello. In his second season with the Raptor Engineering team, Roman driver Marco Cassarà became champion of the category, outperforming Alex De Giacomi, his rival for the title and the leader of the standings in the first part of the season. For Cassarà - who won four races - this was his third title having also won the championship in 2019. De Giacomi, the Brescia-based Tsunami RT driver, finished second with three wins and five podium results. In third place - also fighting for the title until mid-season - was Alberto De Amicis. After his comeback in the Carrera Cup Italia, the Ebimotors driver finished with four wins and one podium. After a win at home in Vallelunga and two podium finishes, Francesco Maria Fenici (AB Racing) achieved a convincing fourth-place finish in his second season in the series, while Paolo Gnemmi (Ebimotors) rounded out the top five.

Lastly, Davide Scannicchio clinched the Silver Cup title. The gentleman driver with ZRS Motorsport claimed the top spot in the category reserved for slightly older 911 GT3 Cup cars (991 gen.II) by scoring five wins and six podiums. The driver from Verona earned his first title, preceding the two Ebimotors' standard bearers Paolo Venerosi Pesciolini and Luigi Peroni.

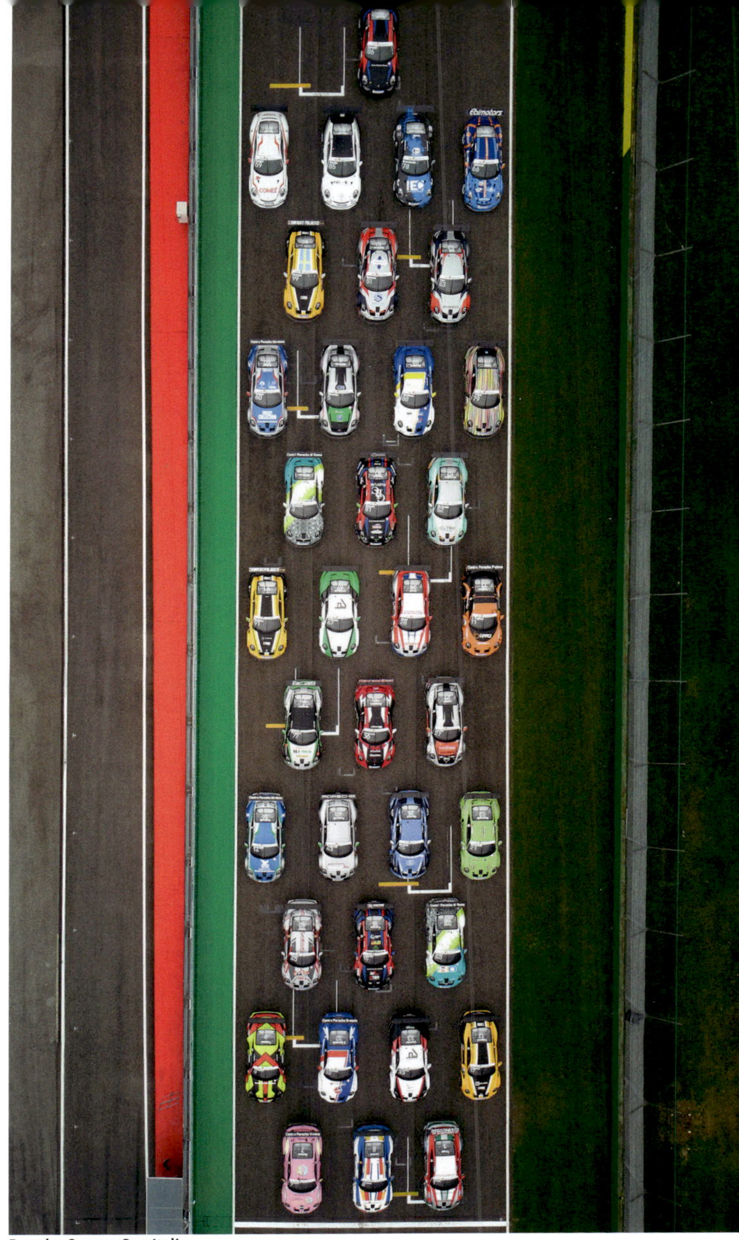

Porsche Carrera Cup Italia

DRIVER STANDINGS **OVERALL**

POS	NO	DRIVERS	TEAM	POINTS
1	32	Gianmarco Quaresmini	Ombra Racing	216
2	3	Keagan Masters	AB Racing	170
3	21	Diego Bertonelli	BeDriver	166
4	28	Giorgio Amati	Ghinzani Arco Motorsport	161
5	1	Alberto Cerqui	Ghinzani Arco Motorsport	147
6	27	Lodovico Laurini	Dinamic Motorsport	143
7	33	Giammarco Levorato	Tsunami RT	141
8	16	Matteo Malucelli	Team Malucelli	126
9	11	Leonardo Caglioni	Ombra Racing	117
10	17	Enrico Fulgenzi	EF Racing	106
11	30	Benedetto Strignano	Scuderia Villorba Corse	106
12	9	Andrea Fontana	Bonaldi Motorsport	60
13	15	Aldo Festante	Raptor Engineering	60
14	8	Jorge Lorenzo	Team Q8 Hi Perform	30
15	25	Simone Riccitelli	Ebimotors	25
16	40	Risto Vukov	GDL Racing	25
17	7	Pietro Delli Guanti	Dinamic Motorsport	24
18	28	Alessandro Giardelli	Ebimotors	23
19	5	Kajus Siksnelis	Dinamic Motorsport	22
20	81	Marco Cassarà	Raptor Engineering	21
21	7	Stefano Monaco	Dinamic Motorsport	17
22	50	Francesco Maria Fenici	AB Racing	11
23	67	Alex De Giacomi	Tsunami RT	9
24	14	Francesco Massimo De Luca	Ebimotors	6
25	52	Alberto De Amicis	Ebimotors	5
26	89	Alexander Schwarzer	BeDriver	2
27	53	Gianluca Giorgi	Ebimotors	1
28	51	Paolo Gnemmi	Ebimotors	1
29	63	Luca Pastorelli	Krypton Motorsport	1
25	71	Gianluigi Piccioli	Ebimotors	1

DRIVER STANDINGS **MICHELIN CUP**

POS	NO	DRIVERS	TEAM	POINTS
1	81	Marco Cassarà	Raptor Engineering	138
2	67	Alex De Giacomi	Tsunami RT	119
3	52	Alberto De Amicis	Ebimotors	105
4	50	Francesco Maria Fenici	AB Racing	68
5	51	Paolo Gnemmi	Ebimotors	66
6	88	Piergiacomo Randazzo	Ombra Racing	45
7	63	Luca Pastorelli	Krypton Motorsport	44
8	53	Gianluca Giorgi	Ebimotors	38
9	60	Marco Galassi	Team Malucelli	37
10	79	Johannes Zelger	Tsunami RT	35
11	89	Alexander Schwarzer	BeDriver	25
12	77	Paolo Biolghini	Racevent	16
13	53	Pietro Negra	Ebimotors	12
14	99	Mike Knutzon	EF Group	10
15	86	Max Montagnese	Raptor Engineering	7
16	77	Carlo Scarpellini	Racevent	3
17	91	Gabriel Rindone	EF Group	3

DRIVER STANDINGS **SILVER CUP**

POS	NO	DRIVERS	TEAM	POINTS
1	78	Davide Scannicchio	ZRS Motorsport	97
2	66	Paolo Venerosi	Ebimotors	77
3	54	Luigi Peroni	Ebimotors	53
4	86	Massimiliano Donzelli	Raptor Engineering	40
5	86	Max Montagnese	Raptor Engineering	38
6	85	Matteo Rovida	BeDriver	37
7	59	Marco Farisini	Team Malucelli	18
8	92	Shintaro Akatsu	EF Racing	8

Diego Bertonelli

TEAM STANDINGS

POS	TEAM	POINTS
1	Ombra Racing	328
2	Ghinzani Arco Motorsport	305
3	Dinamic Motorsport	201
4	AB Racing	176
5	BeDriver	166
6	Tsunami RT	152
7	Team Malucelli	121
8	EF Racing	111
9	Scuderia Villorba Corse	107
10	Raptor Engineering	86
11	Ebimotors	68
12	Bonaldi Motorsport	61
13	GDL Racing	28
14	Krypton Motorsport	2

(l.-r.): Aldo Festante, Leonardo Caglioni, Giammarco Levorato, Giorgio Amati, Benedetto Strignano, Keagan Masters

CARRERA CUP GREAT BRITAIN

23.04.–24.04.2022	*Donington Park, UK*
14.05.–15.05.2022	*Brands Hatch, UK*
11.06.–12.06.2022	*Oulton Park, UK*
30.07.–31.07.2022	*Knockhill, Scotland, UK*
13.08.–14.08.2022	*Snetterton, UK*
27.08.–28.08.2022	*Thruxton, UK*
24.09.–25.09.2022	*Silverstone, UK*
08.10.–09.10.2022	*Brands Hatch, UK*

Will Martin, Josh Malin, Jack Bartholomew and Comline Richardson Racing

Kiern Jewiss sicherte sich in einer spannenden Saison seinen ersten Titel im Porsche Carrera Cup Great Britain.

Im Porsche Carrera Cup Great Britain 2022 wurden 16 Rennen an acht Wochenenden ausgetragen, die Fahrer traten wie üblich in den drei Kategorien Pro, Pro-Am und Am an. Die 2018 eingeführte, teilweise umgekehrte Startaufstellung für das zweite Rennen wurde auch 2022 beibehalten; die Reihenfolge wurde durch die zufällige Umkehrung der Platzierungen der besten vier bis sechs Fahrer aus dem ersten Lauf bestimmt.

An der Spitze der Starterliste stand Kiern Jewiss, Favorit der Pro-Kategorie; der Rookie-Champion von 2021 hatte den Gesamttitel fest im Visier. Will Martin, einer der jüngsten Gewinner in der Geschichte des Cups, wollte seine Erfahrung aus zwei Saisons mit Porsche nutzen und ebenfalls etwas erreichen. Matthew Graham, bester Rookie des Jahres 2020, war ein weiterer Kandidat auf den Gesamtsieg. Zudem gab es mit Adam Smalley, Gus Burton, Jake Giddings und Seb Morris einige hungrige Newcomer. Das Auftaktrennen gewann Smalley, Rookie Theo Edgerton begleitete ihn als Zweiter zur Siegerehrung. Rückkehrer Graham stürmte in Heat zwei an die Spitze und eroberte Platz eins. Nathan Harrison holte zweimal Rang eins in der Pro-Am-Kategorie und Josh Stanton machte gleiches in der Am-Kategorie.

Die zweite Veranstaltung der Saison fand im nassen Brands Hatch statt. Martin meisterte die schwierigen Bedingungen im ersten Heat, was nicht jedem Teilnehmer gelang, und feierte den vierten Triumph seiner Porsche-Karriere. Auch Lokalmatador Jewiss zeigte eine souveräne Leistung und stand nach Rennen vier des Jahres ganz oben auf dem Podium. Will Aspin und Charles Rainford teilten sich die Siege in der Pro-Am-Wertung, während Stanton seine Erfolgsserie in der Amateurwertung fortsetzte.

Die dritte Reise führte nach Oulton Park. Martin überstand zwei Safety-Car-Phasen, um

(27): Nathan Harrison - (52): Angus Whiteside

Kiern Jewiss secured his maiden title in an enthralling season

Porsche Carrera Cup GB, the fastest single-marque GT racing championship in the UK, entered its milestone 20th season in 2022 with a capacity grid packed with racing talent. The season welcomed the latest generation of Porsche 911 racing cars – the 510 hp 'Type 992' 911 GT3 Cup, and signaled the arrival of Porsche Carrera Cup GB 2022 / 2023 Junior Adam Smalley (Duckhams Yuasa Racing with Redline).
The championship retained its traditional position as part of the TOCA package – since its inception in 2003 it has maintained an uninterrupted run supporting the British Touring Car Championship. A full calendar of 16 races took place across eight weekends at circuits up and down the UK, from Thruxton in the south to Knockhill in the north.
With the weekend format, regulations and points structure unchanged from 2021, drivers in three categories – Pro, Pro-Am and Am – competed in a consistent environment, promoting close and exciting racing. The popular partially reversed grid for race two, introduced in 2018, continued for 2022 – the order decided by reversing at random the finishing positions of the top four to six drivers from race one.

Matthew Graham

(10): Will Martin - (16): Matthew Graham - (21): Adam Smalley

(10): Will Martin · (26): Kiern Jewiss

im ersten Rennen als Erster abgewinkt zu werden. Doch es war Pro-Am-Mann Rainford, der mit einer starken Fahrt beeindruckte und bis auf den zweiten Platz vorfuhr; die Zielflagge sah er schließlich als Vierter. Graham verwandelte seine Pole Position im zweiten Heat des Wochenendes dann in den Sieg, gefolgt von einer weiteren beeindruckenden Leistung des in diesem Durchgang zweitplatzierten Rainford.
Ein Zwischenfall an der Startlinie, in den fünf Autos verwickelt waren, machte das folgende Wochenende in Knockhill noch dramatischer. Burton eroberte im ersten Heat seinen ersten Triumph. Martin setzte sich im zweiten Rennen durch, nachdem Smalley, auf der Strecke Erstplatzierter, eine Zeitstrafe erhalten hatte. Rainford und Stanton waren in ihren jeweiligen Klassen auch in Schottland nicht zu bezwingen.
Jewiss stand in Snetterton dann einmal ganz oben auf dem Podium, während Graham den zweiten Lauf gewann. Rainford wurde in seiner Pro-Am-Kategorie erneut zweimal an der Spitze notiert, Stanton musste sich die Am-Erfolge dieses Mal mit Justin Sherwood teilen.
Im elften Saisonrennen, das in Thruxton abgehalten wurde, bejubelte Burton seinen zweiten Triumph, während der amtierende Sprint-Challenge-GB-Champion Edgerton im zwölften Lauf des Jahres einen Sieg einfuhr. Unterdessen rückte Rainford mit zwei weiteren ersten Plätzen näher an den Pro-Am-Titel heran. Stanton fügte seiner Bilanz von 2022 zwei Klassenerfolge hinzu und krönte sich damit vorzeitig zum Champion der Am-Kategorie.
Am Silverstone-Wochenende kreuzte Jewiss die Ziellinie zweimal als Erster. Zwei Klassenerfolge für einen jubelnden Rainford reichten aus, um sich den Pro-Am-Titel zu sichern. Bester Am-Fahrer auf der Formel-1-Strecke war in beiden Heats Stanton.
Beim Finale in Brands Hatch holte Jewiss die letzte Pole Position der Saison und verschaffte sich damit eine gute Ausgangsposition im Titelkampf. Ganz anders war die Stimmungslage bei Martin, einem seiner Rivalen, der nach einem Zwischenfall im vorletzten Rennen des Jahres 2022 ausschied und Jewiss so seinerseits den Weg zum Titelgewinn vereinfachte. Rainford unterstrich seine beeindruckende Saison und sicherte sich im finalen Rennen den vielbeachteten ersten Gesamtsieg eines Pro-Am-Piloten vor dem neuen Champion Jewiss, während Mark Radcliffe seine ersten Erfolge in der Am-Kategorie sammelte.
Nach seiner guten Debütsaison darf sich Gus Burton nun bester Rookie des Jahres 2022 nennen; Comline Richardson Racing wurde erstmals als bestes Team im Carrera Cup GB ausgezeichnet.

Angus Whiteside

Adam Smalley

(57): Gus Burton · (10): Will Martin · (21): Adam Smalley · (54): Theo Edgerton

Alongside awards for the top drivers in each category, the best Rookie, team, and the driver with the highest number of fastest laps would receive a share of the championship's impressive prize package. The Porsche Carrera Cup GB Young Driver Development Programme, an evolution of the Rookie initiative, also continued, allowing eligible drivers to compete for prize money, while receiving insight from Porsche Motorsport GB including media support and tyre training sessions by Michelin.

Team Parker Racing was one of six returning teams hoping to replicate past successes. It faced experienced rivals including Redline Racing, JTR, Comline Richardson Racing, Valluga and CCK Motorsport. New teams, Rosland Gold Racing by Century Motorsport and Toro Verde GT, fielded entries as they sought to establish themselves in the Porsche paddock.

Leading the charge of the returning drivers was Pro category favourite, Kiern Jewiss (Team Parker Racing) – the 2021 Rookie champion returned with the overall title firmly in his sights. Will Martin (Comline Richardson Racing), one of the youngest winners in the history of the championship, was also poised to exploit his experience from two seasons racing with Porsche. 2020 Rookie champion, Matthew Graham (Redline Racing), was another proven race winner with the pace to challenge for outright glory. Smalley was not the only hungry newcomer – the Junior was joined by new faces Gus Burton (Rosland Gold Racing by Century Motorsport), Seb Morris (Team Parker Racing) and Jake Giddings (Toro Verde GT).

Showcasing the Porsche Motorsport Pyramid came Theo Edgerton (JTR), the 2021 Porsche Visit Cayman Islands Sprint Challenge GB champion, who arrived to further his Porsche career at the wheel of the 911 GT3 Cup. Likewise, Jack Bartholomew (Comline Richardson Racing) was another talented Sprint Challenge GB race winner staying within the Porsche family and making the logical step up to Carrera Cup GB.

Reigning Pro-Am category champion Ryan Ratcliffe (Team Parker) returned for 2022, however, he faced challenges from equally skillful returnees Nathan Harrison (Redline Racing) and Charles Rainford (CCK Motorsport). Meanwhile, new names Hugo Ellis (JTR), Will Aspin (Team Parker) Angus Whiteside (Toro Verde GT) and Charles Bateman (Team Parker) hoped to upset the established Pro-Am order.

The first driver to take three back-to-back Am category championships (2019, 2020, 2021), Justin Sherwood (Team Parker Racing), met his biggest threat yet in 2022. Am category champion in 2018, Peter Mangion (Toro Verde GT) was back, joined by the driver with the most victories in Am category history (27), Peter Kyle-Henney (Toro Verde GT). Former Pro-Am ace Nigel Rice (Redline Racing) also returned following two seasons racing in Sprint Challenge GB. Meanwhile, having shown his potential in 2021, came Josh Stanton (JTR), and completing the category were debutants with Valluga, Mark Radcliffe and Michael Clark.

The first race of the opening weekend, the 350th since the championship began, was won by Smalley on his championship debut. The dream start to the Junior's Porsche career saw him joined on the overall podium by an impressive Edgerton. Returnee Graham then stormed to the front of a 25-strong grid to claim victory in round two. Harrison clinched two Pro-Am category wins with Stanton doing the same in Am – both drivers underlining their intentions in 2022.

A wet and wild Brands Hatch was the scene of the season's second meeting. Martin drove to victory in the weekend's dramatic first race. He mastered difficult conditions while others fell by the wayside, taking the fourth win of his Porsche racing career. Local hero, Jewiss, delivered a confident performance to stand on the top step of the podium following round four. Aspin and Rainford shared the spoils in Pro-Am while Stanton maintained his unbroken run of victories in Am.

(l.-r.): Kiern Jewiss, Matthew Graham, Charles Rainford

(36): Karl Leonard - (2): Oliver White - (77): Charles Bateman

(77): Charles Bateman - (33): Ryan Ratcliffe - (9): Will Aspin

Adam Smalley

(15): Nigel Rice - (6): Ian Loggie

(l.-r.): Peter Kyle-Henney, Josh Stanton, Nigel Rice

(26): Kiern Jewiss - (99): Charles Rainford - (90): Josh Malin

Josh Stanton and Team JTR

The third weekend of the season took place at Oulton Park in Cheshire. Martin survived two Safety Car restarts to record victory in the first race, but it was Rainford who impressed as he ran as high as second overall before finishing fourth. Graham turned reverse grid pole position into race two victory, followed to the flag by another impressive Rainford performance. The result made Martin and Graham the season's first repeat winners.

A start line incident involving five cars added drama to the Scottish weekend. Burton took his maiden victory in the first race at Knockhill. Martin emerged ahead in the second encounter after winner on the road – Smalley – received a time penalty. Rainford (Pro-Am) and Stanton (Am) each continued their run of consecutive category wins. Jewiss was back on the top step of the podium at Snetterton, while reverse grid pole-sitter Graham won the afternoon's sprint. Rainford topped his category again, while Stanton took one Am win, Sherwood the other – his first of the season. Burton claimed his second win in round 11 at Thruxton, while reigning Sprint Challenge GB champion, Edgerton, drove to a breakthrough maiden victory in the weekend's second race. Rainford moved closer to Pro-Am championship glory with two more victories. When Stanton added two category wins to his remarkable 2022 tally, it was enough to see him crowned Am category champion.

The Silverstone weekend saw Jewiss snatch two overall victories sending the Pro category title fight down to the wire at the season finalé. Two category wins for a jubilant Rainford was enough to see him take Pro-Am championship honours. Jewiss took the final pole position of the season at the Brands Hatch finalé, while title rival Martin was eliminated following a dramatic incident in the penultimate race of 2022 leaving Jewiss a clear path to the championship. Underlining his impressive journey, Rainford secured a popular maiden overall victory in the final while Radcliffe recorded his first Am category win.

Following his impressive debut season, Burton secured Rookie title honours while Comline Richardson Racing were named Teams Champions for the first time. The 21st season of Porsche Carrera Cup GB in 2023 will see Smalley enter the final year of his Junior programme. As he looks to build on a successful 2022 campaign, which saw him finish second in the overall standings, the 21-year old will target championship glory.

Charles Rainford and Team CCK Motorsport

Kiern Jewiss

Justin Sherwood and Josh Stanton

Kiern Jewiss

Kiern Jewiss

(l.-r.): Will Martin, Gus Burton, Kiern Jewiss

DRIVER STANDINGS **PRO**

POS	NO	DRIVERS	TEAM	POINTS
1	26	Kiern Jewiss	Team Parker Racing	141
2	21	Adam Smalley	Duckhams Yuasa Racing with Redline	103
3	10	Will Martin	Comline Richardson Racing	97
4	57	Gus Burton	Rosland Gold Racing by Century Motorsport	87
5	54	Theo Edgerton	JTR	69
6	16	Matthew Graham	Redline Racing	62
7	41	Jake Giddings	Team Parker Racing	26
8	90	Josh Malin	Comline Richardson Racing	23
9	89	Jack Bartholomew	Comline Richardson Racing	17
10	2	Oliver White	Duckhams Yuasa Racing with Redline	15
11	30	Seb Morris	Team Parker Racing	9
12	5	Micah Stanley	Redline Racing	9
13	59	Ross Wylie	Toro Verde GT	7
14	97	Scott Malvern	Team Parker	0

DRIVER STANDINGS **ROOKIE**

POS	NO	DRIVERS	TEAM	POINTS
1	57	Gus Burton	Rosland Gold Racing by Century Motorsport	186
2	54	Theo Edgerton	JTR	181
3	89	Jack Bartholomew	Comline Richardson Racing	54
4	9	Will Aspin	Team Parker	53
5	8	Hugo Ellis	JTR	41

DRIVER STANDINGS **PRO-AM**

POS	NO	DRIVERS	TEAM	POINTS
1	99	Charles Rainford	CCK Motorsport	156
2	27	Nathan Harrison	Redline Racing	111
3	52	Angus Whiteside	Toro Verde GT	67
4	33	Ryan Ratcliffe	Team Parker	64
5	8	Hugo Ellis	JTR	64
6	9	Will Aspin	Team Parker	60
7	77	Charles Bateman	Team Parker	51
8	36	Karl Leonard	Team Parker Racing	0

DRIVER STANDINGS **AM**

POS	NO	DRIVERS	TEAM	POINTS
1	95	Josh Stanton	JTR	170
2	15	Nigel Rice	Redline Racing	71
3	7	Justin Sherwood	Team Parker Racing	61
4	25	Mark Ratcliffe	Valluga	60
5	22	Peter Kyle-Henney	Toro Verde GT	34
6	44	Peter Mangion	Toro Verde GT	12
7	31	Michael Clark	Valluga	12
8	66	Nick Jones	Team Parker Racing	8
9	34	Dominique Bastien	Team Parker Racing	0
10	6	Ian Loggie	Toro Verde GT	0
11	98	Lee Frost	Toro Verde GT	0
12	14	Finlay Cooper	Team Parker Racing	0

Seb Morris

TEAM STANDINGS

POS	TEAM	POINTS
1	Comline Richardson Racing	320
2	Duckhams Yuasa Racing with Redline	311
3	Team Parker Racing	289
4	JTR	231
5	Redline Racing	199
6	Rosland Gold Racing by Century Motorsport	186
7	CCK Motorsport	146
8	Team Parker	98
9	Toro Verde GT	61
10	Valluga	8

PORSCHE
CARRERA CUP
SCANDINAVIA

CARRERA CUP SCANDINAVIA

13.05.–14.05.2022	Scandinavian Raceway, Sweden
17.06.–18.06.2022	Drivecenter Arena, Sweden
05.08.–06.08.2022	Scandinavian Raceway, Sweden
19.08.–20.08.2022	Gelleråsen Arena, Sweden
16.09.–17.09.2022	Rudskogen Motorsenter, Norway
30.09.–01.10.2022	Mantorp Park, Sweden

Der Schwede Lukas Sundahl hat es wieder geschafft: Er holt sich in einem dramatischen Finale des Porsche Carrera Cup Scandinavia den fünften Titel in Folge.

Andreas Ahlberg and Lukas Sundahl

Lukas Sundahl darf sich nun fünffacher Champion im Porsche Carrera Cup Scandinavia nennen. Doch dieses Mal musste der 26-Jährige aus Växjö besonders hart um den Titel kämpfen, denn er gewann mit nur einem Punkt Vorsprung vor dem zweitplatzierten Ola Nilsson.

Das Saisonfinale in Mantorp Park vor 10.000 Zuschauern war voller Dramatik. Drei Wochen zuvor hatte Nilsson alle drei Rennen in Norwegen gewonnen und sich damit mit Nachdruck in den Titelkampf katapultiert. Und er eröffnete das Finale auf die für ihn bestmögliche Weise. Als Marcus Annervi und Felix Rosenqvist im Kampf um die Führung aneinandergerieten, bekam Nilsson den Sieg auf dem Präsentierteller serviert. Sundahl sah die Zielflagge als Fünfter, was bedeutete, dass er und Nilsson mit jeweils 228 Punkten in den letzten Lauf der Saison gingen.

Beide Kontrahenten begannen den finalen Showdown nebeneinander aus der zweiten Reihe, Sundahl startete von P3 und Nilsson von P4. Sie hielten ihre Positionen bis vier Minuten vor Rennende, dann attackierte Nilsson seinen Rivalen und zwängte sich mit Kontakt an ihm vorbei. Der amtierende Champion wurde dabei von der Strecke gedrängt und verlor Plätze. Nilsson hingegen überquerte die Ziellinie als Dritter und war zu diesem Zeitpunkt der neue Champion, bis ihn die Rennleitung kurze Zeit später für die Kollision mit Sundahl bestrafte, indem sie ihn im Ergebnis hinter seinen Unfallgegner zurücksetzte. Damit konnte Sundahl seinen fünften Titel im Porsche Carrera Cup Scandinavia in Folge feiern, seinen ersten im Porsche 911 GT3 Cup der Generation 992 und seine erste schwedische GT-Meisterschaft. Außerdem gewann er zusammen mit seinen Teamkollegen Andreas Ahlberg und Albin Wärnelöv für seine neue Mannschaft Micke Kågered Racing

Lukas Sundahl claimed fifth straight title in dramatic finale

🇬🇧 Lukas Sundahl won his fifth Porsche Carrera Cup Scandinavia title in a row, but this year the 26-year-old from Växjö had to dig deep to bring home the title. This was the 19th edition of the Porsche Carrera Cup Scandinavia, with 31 drivers taking part, and it was the most hard-fought in the history of the championship. Sundahl won by a single point over the runner-up, Ola Nilsson.

The season finale was held at the classic Mantorp Park circuit, in front of 10,000 spectators and it was full of drama. Three weeks earlier, Ola Nilsson had won the three heats in Norway and had catapulted himself into the fight for the title. Nilsson opened the finale in the best way possible, taking victory after Marcus Annervi and Felix Rosenqvist collided while fighting for the lead. Nilsson had the win handed to him on a plate, while Sundahl managed only fifth place which meant that he and Nilsson were tied on points going into the final race of the season.

Sundahl and Nilsson started alongside each other on the second row of the grid. Sundahl was quicker away and grabbed third place, just ahead of his rival for the title. They ran like that until four minutes from the end of the race, when Nilsson decided that he had to try something. He passed Sundahl but not before hitting him from behind and pushing him off the track, causing Sundahl to lose positions. Nilsson finished third and thought he had done enough to win the title, but the race directors had other ideas and penalized him enough to be classified as finishing behind Sundahl. Thus, Sundahl celebrated his fifth straight title, his first in the Porsche 911 GT3 Cup (992) and his first Swedish GT Championship.

As if that wasn´t enough Sundahl, together with his teammates Andreas Ahlberg and Albin Wärnelöv, also won the team championship for his new team, Micke Kågered Racing. To top it off, Sundahl was also awarded the TAG Heuer Fastest Lap Award for having set the most fastest laps during the season.

(l.-r.): Hannes Morin, Hampus Ericsson, Emil Persson

Ola Nilsson

Cars and Drivers of Porsche Carrera Cup Scandinavia

Drivers of Porsche Carrera Cup Scandinavia

(l.-r.): Marcus Annervi, Ola Nilsson, Hampus Ericsson

den Titel des besten Teams. Und er erhielt auch noch den TAG Heuer Fastest Lap Award für die meisten schnellsten Runden der Saison.

Nilsson, der nach vier Jahren Rennpause sein Comeback gab, akzeptierte die Strafe und war mit seinem zweiten Rang in der Gesamtwertung zufrieden. Der Pilot von Mtech Competition erlebte einen soliden Start in die Saison und hatte sich insbesondere nach seinem Dreifachsieg bei einem denkwürdigen Porsche-Festival im Rudskogen Motorsenter zu einem heißen Titelanwärter gemausert. Am Ende reichte es für den Vize-Titel vor Emil Persson und Hampus Ericsson, dem jüngeren Bruder des Indy500-Siegers Marcus Ericsson. Bemerkenswert: Hampus Ericsson erzielte die meisten Podestränge im PCC Scandinavia 2022, allerdings war kein erster Platz dabei. Als Fünfter der Gesamtwertung schloss Marcus Annervi die Saison ab. Nach fünf fünften Positionen in der ersten Saisonhälfte stand der Rookie in der Gelleråsen Arena, der Heimstrecke seines Teams, zum ersten Mal ganz oben auf dem Podium.

Im Porsche Approved Cup für Porsche 911 GT3 (991 II) lieferten sich Andreas Ahlberg und Hannes Morin einen Kampf um den Titel, der sich über die gesamte Saison erstreckte. Morin hatte die meisten Siege, die meisten Pole Positions und die meisten schnellsten Runden, aber auch zwei Ausfälle in seiner Statistik verbucht. Das half Ahl-

Jan Magnussen

Nilsson, who made his racing comeback after a four-year break, accepted the penalty and was happy with his second place overall. Representing Mtech Competition, he had a solid start to the season and became a true challenger for the title with his triple win at a memorable Porsche Festival at Drivecenter Arena in Norway, just a few days after his 35th birthday.
Behind the top two, Emil Persson finished third in the points standings. Persson took his first wins during the season and lay second in the standings behind Sundahl heading into the race in Norway. After a poor weekend, however, Persson dropped to fourth in the standings, but he made a strong comeback in the finale with two second places. It was a nice ending to the season for the Kristoffersson Motorsport-driver who missed out on a top three finish by a single point last year.
The Guest Driver programme peaked at the Mantorp Park finale. The series had managed to entice the Swedish IndyCar-duo of Marcus Ericsson and Felix Rosenqvist to be part of the grid. Their participation played a big part in attracting the largest crowd of the season. Rosenqvist made his fourth guest appearance in Porsche Carrera Cup Scandinavia, but this was the first time he failed to reach the podium. Ericsson, this year's Indy 500-winner, drove his first race ever in Sweden. He claimed fifth place in the second heat, and he also set the fastest lap of the race.

Jan Magnussen

Marcus Annervi and Race Team Gelleråsen - By AFR

Emil Persson

(9): Thomas Karlsson - (21): Kjelle Lejonkrans

berg, der in jedem Rennen punktete, mit knappem Vorsprung den ersten Titel in seiner Rennsportkarriere zu gewinnen. Durch seinen Erfolg konnte sein Team Micke Kågered Racing alle drei Titel des Jahres 2022 an sich reißen.
Das sehr beliebte Gastfahrerprogramm von Porsche Schweden erreichte beim Finale in Mantorp Park seinen Höhepunkt. Der Serienorganisation war es gelungen, das schwedische IndyCar-Duo Marcus Ericsson und Felix Rosenqvist in die Startaufstellung zu locken. Ihre Teilnahme trug wesentlich dazu bei, dass das Rennwochenende die meisten Zuschauer der gesamten Saison anlockte. Rosenqvist absolvierte sein viertes Gastspiel im Porsche Carrera Cup Scandinavia, stand dabei aber zum ersten Mal nicht auf dem Treppchen. Ericsson hingegen fuhr sein erstes Rennen überhaupt in seiner schwedischen Heimat. Er belegte im zweiten Lauf den fünften Platz und fuhr die schnellste Rennrunde.

(l.-r.): Kjelle Lejonkrans, Pontus Fredricsson, Hampus Hedin

Andreas Ahlberg

Hampus Ericsson

He was beaten in both heats by his younger brother Hampus, who finished the season fourth in the points standings. In fact, Hampus scored the most podium finishes (nine) in the championship. While never scoring a win, his Fragus Motorsport team-mates, Edvin Hellsten and Pontus Fredricsson were credited with one win each. Hellsten finished sixth in the standings and Fredricsson seventh.

A very popular guest driver during the season was the Norwegian F2-star Dennis Hauger who entered the race at Drivecenter Arena in Fällfors, where he took one second place, and the race in Norway. The Dane Jan Magnussen has made guest appearances in Porsche Carrera Cup Scandinavia. This time, with support from Porsche Denmark, the former F1-driver made a more sustained effort by taking part in four out of six races. He claimed his maiden podium finishes by crossing the line as third in both heats at Scandinavian Raceway in Anderstorp.

Marcus Annervi was the Rookie of the Year. The former Porsche Sprint Challenge Scandinavia champion, driving for Race Team Gelleråsen - By AFR, showed consistency at a high level from the start. Having scored five fifth places in the first half of the season, Marcus finally climbed the podium as a winner at Gelleråsen Arena, the home track of his team. It was his first win, and he scored another one, and two more podium finishes, and ended fifth in the points overall.

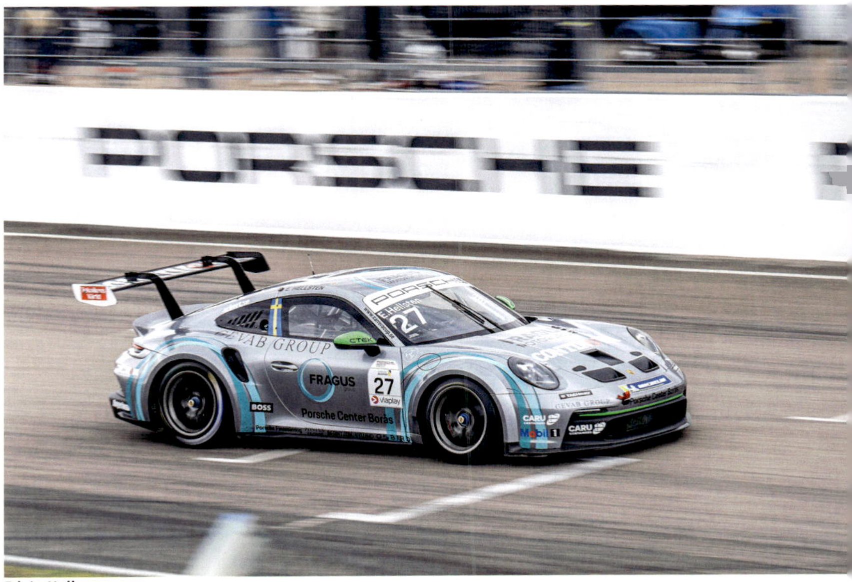
Edvin Hellsten

(25): Hampus Ericsson - (27): Edvin Hellsten - (1): Lukas Sundahl

(l.-r.): Raine Wermelin, Hampus Ericsson, Marcus Ericsson, Carl Philip Bernadotte

Marcus Ericsson

Felix Rosenqvist

Ola Nilsson

Christoffer Bergström

Annervi was one of six winners during the 2022 season. Not since 2017 have so many different drivers won a race over a season. Robin Knutsson also made a strong debut season, coming from STCC, for his team, WestCoast Racing. Robin finished eighth overall. Annervi was one of three newcomers from Porsche Sprint Challenge Scandinavia, and Knutsson was one of five from STCC.

In the Porsche Approved Cup, for Porsche 911 GT3 (991 II), Andreas Ahlberg and Hannes Morin fought for the title all season. Morin finished with the most wins, most pole positions and most fastest laps, but two retirements meant that Ahlberg claimed the title, his first in his racing career. Ahlberg scored points in all races and combined a high level of consistency and performance in every heat. Ahlberg's victory meant that his team, Micke Kågered Racing, could celebrate a unique Grand Slam by winning all three championships.

Third behind Ahlberg and Morin was the Masters Cup winner of 2021, Christoffer Bergström. Behind him, Albin Wärnelöv and Kjelle Lejonkrans finished fourth and fifth. The Porsche Carrera Cup Scandinavia 2022 season consisted of six race weekends and fourteen heats. The second race, at Drivecenter Arena in Skellefteå, had one of its three heats cancelled, something that has never happened before in the history of the championship. Thick fog covered the track and the race director decided to cancel the heat due to safety reasons. The cancelled heat was moved to the next race, at Scandinavian Raceway in Anderstorp.

Christoffer Bergström and Team Pampas

Oscar Löfquist

Lukas Sundahl and Andreas Ahlberg with Team Micke Kågered Racing

100 000 SEK

Lukas Sundahl

DRIVER STANDINGS

POS	NO	DRIVERS	TEAM	POINTS
1	1	Lukas Sundahl	Micke Kågered Racing	237
2	20	Ola Nilsson	Mtech Competition	236
3	45	Emil Persson	Kristoffersson Motorsport	220
4	25	Hampus Ericsson	Fragus Motorsport	214
5	61	Marcus Annervi	Race Team Gelleråsen - By AFR	179
6	27	Edvin Hellsten	Fragus Motorsport	161
7	11	Pontus Fredricsson	Fragus Motorsport	121
8	32	Robin Knutsson	WestCoast Racing	91
9	23	Jan Magnussen	Porsche Experience Racing	89
10	36	Andreas Ahlberg	Micke Kågered Racing	65
11	15	Hannes Morin	Steber Racing	63
12	911	Dennis Hauger	Porsche Experience Racing	61
13	48	Mikael Karlsson	WestCoast Racing	41
14	91	Oscar Löfquist	Kjellin Motorsports	40
15	42	Christoffer Bergstrom	Team Pampas	35
16	21	Kjelle Lejonkrans	Fragus Motorsport	25
17	17	Gustav Bergström	Kristoffersson Motorsport	23
18	8	Marcus Ericsson	Porsche Experience Racing	21
19	9	Thomas Karlsson	Mtech Competition	21
20	44	Hampus Hedin	Fragus Motorsport	15
21	92	Anton Marklund	Porsche Experience Racing	14
22	3	Erlend Juan Olsen	Jaffa Racing	12
23	51	Ole William Nærsnes	Jaffa Racing	11
24	14	Robin Hansson	Fragus Motorsport	8
25	911	Felix Rosenqvist	Porsche Experience Racing	8
26	22	Albin Wärnelöv	Micke Kågered Racing	6
27	28	Patrick Rundquist	Fragus Motorsport	5
28	60	Franck Århage	Arhage Motorsport	5
29	62	Lars-Bertil Rantzow	Mtech Competition	3
30	71	Markus Lönnroth	Steber Racing	0
31	66	Nermin Sipkar	Sipkar Motorsport	0

DRIVER STANDINGS **PORSCHE APPROVED CUP**

POS	NO	DRIVERS	TEAM	POINTS
1	36	Andreas Ahlberg	Micke Kågered Racing	283
2	15	Hannes Morin	Steber Racing	274
3	42	Christoffer Bergström	Team Pampas	198
4	22	Albin Wärnelöv	Micke Kågered Racing	159
5	21	Kjelle Lejonkrans	Fragus Motorsport	149
6	3	Erlend Juan Olsen	Jaffa Racing	145
7	71	Markus Lönnroth	Steber Racing	109
8	51	Ole William Nærsnes	Jaffa Racing	104
9	60	Franck Århage	Arhage Motorsport	99
10	66	Nermin Sipkar	Sipkar Motorsport	69
11	14	Robin Hansson	Fragus Motorsport	28
12	62	Lars-Bertil Rantzow	Mtech Competition	21
13	28	Patrick Rundquist	Fragus Motorsport	14

TEAM STANDINGS

POS	TEAM	POINTS
1	Micke Kågered Racing	532
2	Fragus Motorsport	483
3	Steber Racing	364
4	Mtech Competition	273
5	Jaffa Racing	247
6	Kristoffersson Motorsport	240
7	Team Pampas	197
8	Porsche Experience Racing	189
9	Race Team Gelleråsen - By AFR	176
10	WestCoast Racing	132
11	Arhage Motorsport	99
12	Sipkar Motorsport	69
13	Kjellin Motorsports	40

Dennis Hauger

PORSCHE
CARRERA CUP
ASIA

CARRERA CUP ASIA

29.07.–31.07.2022 Zhuzhou International Circuit, China
26.08.–28.08.2022 V1 Tianjin International Circuit, China
23.09.–25.09.2022 Zhuzhou International Circuit, China
28.10.–30.10.2022 Zhuzhou International Circuit, China

(l.-r.): Ling Kang, Leo Ye, Luo Kailuo

Ein neuer Champion in jeder Klasse des Porsche Carrera Cup Asia: Pro-Pilot Leo Ye, Pro-Am-Mann Lu Wei und Am-Vertreter Henry Kwong waren nicht zu schlagen.

Der Porsche Carrera Cup Asia fuhr 2022 seine 19. Saison, die aufgrund der Corona-Pandemie aus vier Rennwochenenden in China bestand. 22 Piloten nahmen am GT3-Markenpokal teil, darunter sieben Fahrer, die ihr Debüt im Cup gaben. Das Starterfeld bestand aus neun Pro-, acht Pro-Am- und fünf Am-Kandidaten.

Die Saison begann im Juli auf dem Zhuzhou International Circuit. Leo Ye übernahm von der Pole Position kommend die Führung und baute seinen Vorsprung auf rund sechs Sekunden aus, ehe das Safety Car das Treiben neutralisierte. Doch auch dadurch konnte er nicht gestoppt werden und überquerte die Ziellinie letztendlich als Erster. Ling Kang bejubelte den zweiten Platz, den er sich gegen Cup-Debütant Luo Kailuo hart erkämpfen musste. Beide Kontrahenten wechselten mehrfach die Positionen, bis Ling Kang schließlich die Oberhand behielt.

Im zweiten Rennen des Wochenendes feierte Leo Ye erneut einen Start/Ziel-Sieg. Hinter ihm stritten sich Ling Kang, Luo Kailuo und Daniel Lu Wenlong, der zu diesem Zeitpunkt noch amtierende Champion des Carrera Cup Asia, um die Ränge zwei bis vier. Letztgenannter setzte sich durch, während Luo Kailuo die dritte Stelle belegte.

In der Pro-Am-Klasse holte Zhou Bihuang die erste Siegertrophäe der Saison, Lu Wei wurde als Zweiter vor Bao Jinlong abgewinkt. Im zweiten Rennen revanchierte sich Lu Wei und gewann vor Bao Jinlong und Zhou Bihuang. In der Am-Kategorie triumphierte Neuling Tang Ruobin in Heat eins, Titelverteidiger Eric K. dominierte den zweiten Lauf. Der spannende Aufgalopp war wegweisend für das, was danach kommen sollte. Keiner der amtierenden Champions der einzelnen Kategorien lag nach den ersten beiden Durchgängen an der Spitze seiner jeweiligen Klassen-Tabelle; stattdessen wurden sowohl in der Pro-Am- als auch in der Am-Kategorie schnelle Newcomer ganz oben notiert.

Porsche Carrera Cup Asia

A new champion in every Porsche Carrera Cup Asia: Leo Ye in Pro, Lu Wei in Pro-Am and Henry Kwong in Am were unbeatable.

The Porsche Carrera Cup Asia returned for its 19th season in 2022, with a four round, eight race season. As in 2021, the 2022 season was held in the shadow of the pandemic. However, this did not slow down the momentum of Asia's premier one-make series. The team at Porsche Motorsport Asia Pacific Ltd. once more pulled out all the stops and, against all odds, were able to host the most number of races possible given the circumstances.

The series was blessed to have 22 competitors this year, including seven drivers who made their series debut, 15 returning drivers, and 12 Dealer Teams. There was a good spread of drivers across the three categories, nine Pro drivers, eight Pro-Am and five Am, to keep the series competitive throughout the grid. The Porsche Talent Pool returned once again, with four Pro drivers gaining the benefits of Porsche coaching, training on and off track, and much more.

A delayed start saw the 2022 season began in Zhuzhou International Circuit in July, following the Official Test Days at the same circuit. Starting the first race as he meant to go on, JUNJIE Racing's Leo Ye – who finished fourth in the 2021 championship – secured pole position, fastest lap and a race win. Leo had a strong start to the race, developing a six-second lead by the time the safety car came out. On his debut Carrera Cup Asia race, TORO Racing's Luo Kailuo started third and finished in the same position, following a furious on-the-track battle with BD Group's Ling Kang. The two switched positions a number of times before Ling Kang eventually came out ahead. The second race of the weekend saw Ye once again secure pole position, fastest lap, and a lights-to-flag victory, hungrily devouring every available point. With Kang and Kailuo also starting in the same positions as the previous day, reigning Carrera Cup Asia overall champion Daniel Lu Wenlong, this year racing for Meidong Racing, started fourth and joined his fellow Talent Pool drivers for a three-way battle for second. Wenlong eventually took the position, while Kailuo finished third.

Reigning three-time Carrera Cup Asia Pro-Am champion Bao Jinlong, driving for Team Shanghai Yonda, started third in Pro-Am for the first race, potentially a sign that he would be facing some stiff competition this year. Claiming the first Pro-Am pole of the season was series newcomer Lu Wei, driving for R&B Racing, with Porsche Beijing Central & Goldenport's Zhou Bihuang starting second. Wei had a less-than-ideal start to his first race, dropping down four places at the start, with Bihuang shoring up a healthy five-second lead by lap three. Bihuang claimed the first Pro-Am win of the season, with Wei coming in second and Jinlong in third. The second race of the season saw Wei's rise begin in earnest. Taking home points for pole position, fastest lap and Pro-Am victory, Wei was followed over the finish line by Jinlong, with Bihuang coming in third. This sent Wei to the top of the points table, with an on-the-track rivalry already developing between the newcomer and reigning champion Jinlong.

The Am category returned in 2022 following its debut in the 2021 season, with reigning champion Eric K returning once again with KiddyWorld Racing, along with Triple Ace Racing's Henry Kwong and Shanghai Pudong & Waigaoqiao 69 Racing's Jacky Wu who both made their series debuts in 2021. The first race didn't go as

(20): Daniel Lu Wenlong - (99): Luo Kailuo - (777): Leo Ye

Bao Jinlong

Porsche Carrera Cup Asia Talent Pool

Daniel Lu Wenlong

Brian Lee and Jacky Wu

(777): Leo Ye - (22): Ling Kang

Auf dem V1 Tianjin International Circuit schien dann Leo Ye unaufhaltsam, er fügte seiner Bilanz zwei weitere Siege hinzu. Daniel Lu Wenlong belegte in Lauf drei des Jahres Rang zwei und es sah so aus, als würde er Leo Ye Paroli bieten können. Doch in der zweiten Saisonhälfte erlebte er eine Reihe von Enttäuschungen, so dass der Podestplatz von Tianjin sein letzter in 2022 sein sollte.

Zum dritten Rennwochenende kehrte der Cup auf den Zhuzhou International Circuit zurück, wo Leo Ye ein weiteres perfektes Wochenende mit zwei Pole Positions und zwei Siegen hinlegte. Damit stellte er den 2015 von Chris Van der Drift aufgestellten Rekord von sechs aufeinanderfolgenden ersten Plätzen im Carrera Cup Asia ein. Vor der letzten Station, die nach Corona-Ausbrüchen auf anderen Strecken erneut in Zhuzhou stattfand, war Leo Ye bei einem Vorsprung von 54 Punkten und noch maximal 53 zu holenden Zählern bereits Champion. Die letzten beiden Rennen waren dann auch nicht die besten des neuen Titelträgers, er kletterte nur einmal als Zweiter auf das Podium.

Im Gegensatz zum ungefährdeten Durchmarsch von Leo Ye an der Spitze der Fahrerwertung bot der Kampf um den zweiten Tabellenplatz zwischen Ling Kang und Luo Kailuo mehr Spannung. Nach einem eher enttäuschenden zweiten Rennwochenende für beide Rivalen, an dem keiner von ihnen einen Podestrang erobern konnte, melde-

(l.-r.): Bao Jinlong, Lu Wei, Min Heng

planned for the returning drivers however, with all three spinning out at some point during the race, and leaving the field open for newcomers Climax Racing's Tang Ruobin and Team KRC's Zhu Zhiyao, with Tang finishing a respectable two seconds ahead of Zhu, while Jacky Wu finished in third. Having had a disappointing first race, Eric K discovered his mojo in Round two, winning the race a clear 20-seconds ahead of Henry Kwong, with Tang finishing in a respectable third.

The stunning opening of the season set the stage for what was to follow. None of the series reigning champions were at the top of the points table following the first stop, with series newcomers topping both the Pro-Am and Am categories. The second round of the season saw the series make its debut at V1 Tianjin International Circuit, for a joint race weekend alongside the Porsche Sports Cup China. This was the point in the season where Leo Ye began to seem unstoppable. Once again he claimed both pole positions and two lights-to-flag victories over the weekend. Leo earned a point for fastest lap in the first race, yet dropped his first point of the season by failing to claim fastest lap during Round 4 due to the safety car being out for most of the race.

Following up on his first podium of the season in Round 2, Daniel Lu finished second in round three, at this point in the season looking like he was going to be troubling Ye's lead. However the back half of Daniel's season saw a succession of disappointments, and the round would be the final podium the reigning champion saw all season. The big star of the season continued to be Ye.

The third round saw the series return to Zhuzhou International Circuit, where Ye took home another perfect weekend, two pole positions, two victories, and fastest lap. This brought Ye equal with Chris Van der Drift's 2015 record of six consecutive Carrera Cup Asia wins. Going into the final round of the season – once again in Zhuzhou, following COVID outbreaks at other circuits –Ye was already the mathematical champion. The final two races ended up not being Leo's best of the season, taking home a single second-place podium finish. Despite this, Ye had already claimed the 2022 Porsche Carrera Cup Asia Champion, having had the most dominant start in the series' history.

The battle for second place was fiercely fought between Ling Kang and Luo Kailuo. After a relatively disappointing second round for the two rivals – with neither seeing a podium – their battle against each other livened up in the third round, with Kang claiming two second place podiums and Kailuo taking home two third-place finishes. Going into the final round of the season, Kang was ahead of Kailuo by a daunting 19 points. With Ye finally slowing down somewhat at the last round – his championship already secured –Kailuo won the final two races outright, having earned a podium finish at each of the season's six races at Zhuzhou International Circuit. Kang earned a second-place finish in the final race of the season. However it wasn't enough to take his position back from Kailuo. The season ended with Kang in third, just five points behind Kailuo.

As the best performing Talent Pool driver of the class of 2022, Luo Kailuo won the opportunity to join the 2022 Porsche Motorsport Junior Programme Shootout on behalf of the Porsche Carrera Cup Asia.

The Pro-Am category saw a fierce fight for first place. Lu Wei had a fantastic round in Tianjin, taking home every point available but one. Bao Jinlong was on Lu Wei's heels the whole time, finishing second behind Wei in five races throughout the season. With a single DNF result marring his record in Round five, Wei saw a podium in every other race of the season, coming in third in the final race, where Bao Jinlong finished second and TORO Racing's Min Heng came in first. Jinlong finished out a frustrating season without a single first-place finish, eventually coming in second in the championship. Thanks to his last-minute flourish, Min Heng snuck into third place in the Pro-Am championship, having seen a total of four podiums throughout the season. One notable Carrera Cup Asia veteran on the tracks this year was Team BetterLife's Li Chao. With over 100 race starts, Chao celebrated his tenth consecutive year with the series in 2022, a milestone that affirms both Chao's passion for the series and the sense of camaraderie and family that brings so many drivers back year after year.

The Am category was fairly dominated in 2021 by Eric K. Having returned this year, Eric frequently found himself staring at Henry Kwong's brake lights, only managing to score two victories in Rounds two and eight. Henry took home five victories across

NIght of Champions

ten sich beide ein Meeting später wieder auf dem Treppchen zurück. Ling Kang holte zwei zweite Plätze und Luo Kailuo zweimal P3. Vor der Finalstation lag Ling Kang 19 Punkte vor Luo Kailuo, der die letzten beiden Saisonrennen für sich entscheiden konnte. Ling Kang belegte im finalen Durchgang den zweiten Platz, der jedoch nicht ausreichte, um Luo Kailuo Gesamtposition zwei noch streitig zu machen. Somit beendete Ling Kang das Jahr fünf Punkte hinter Luo Kailuo als Dritter der Abschlusstabelle.
In der Pro-Am-Kategorie hatte Lu Wei zu Halbzeit drei Rennsiege auf seiner Habenseite und konnte auch in der zweiten Hälfte weiter gewinnen. Abgesehen von einem Ausfall stand er zudem immer auf dem Podest. Bao Jinlong war Lu Wei die ganze Zeit über auf den Fersen und wurde hinter ihm fünfmal Zweiter – einen Sieg konnte er jedoch nie feiern. Und auch im Schlussklassement der Pro-Am-Gruppe belegte er den zweiten Platz hinter dem neuen Champion Lu Wei. Min Heng triumphierte im letzten Heat und schob sich auf der Zielgeraden des Carrera Cup Asia noch auf den dritten Rang der Gesamtwertung.
In der Am-Kategorie sah Vorjahres-Champion Eric K. häufig nur die Bremslichter des fünffachen Saisonsiegers Henry Kwong; er selbst konnte nur zwei Läufe gewinnen. Und dennoch war das Titelrennen eng, am Ende hatte Henry Kwong ganze zehn Punkte mehr gesammelt als Eric K. Einer der schnellen Neulinge war Tang Ruobin, der während der gesamten Saison mit Eric K. und Henry Kwong mithalten konnte, beim Auftakt siegte und in jedem weiteren Heat auf dem Podium stand. Da er das Finalwochenende auslassen musste, blieb ihm nicht mehr als der dritte Platz der Am-Wertung.

(23): Eric Kwong - (65): Brian Lee

Lu Wei

MICHELIN
R&B RACING
morfuns
CONSPIT
Mobil 1
JUNJIE 骏捷车队
Leo Ye
PORSCHE
CARRERA CUP
ASIA
Leo Ye

V1 天津国际赛车场

2010
2013
传承奖杯
Legacy Trophy

闵衡
MIN Heng
吕威
LU Wei
TORO

亚洲保时捷卡雷拉杯 2022
Porsche Carrera Cup Asia 2022
十年特别奖
Special Award
李超
Li Chao
Team Betterlife

PORSCHE
CARRERA CUP
ASIA
1

the season, securing him the season championship 10 points clear of Eric. One of the most impressive newcomers out on the track this year was Tang Ruobin, who stayed in contention with Eric and Henry throughout the season, claiming a victory in the first race and seeing podiums in every other. Due to unforeseen circumstances, Tang was unable to attend the final round of the season, and eventually finished third.
The final results of the season saw new champions in each category. Leo Ye took home the overall championship, following his fourth-place finish in his 2021 debut season. Lu Wei, racing for the first time ever in the Carrera Cup, took home the Pro-Am championship, ending Bao Jinlong's domination of the Pro-Am category. While Henry Kwong took home the Am trophy, having made his series debut in 2021.
The Porsche Dealer Trophy returned once again, this time with an impressive 12 dealer teams competing for the championship. Thanks to Leo Ye's incredible performance all season, JUNJIE Racing took home the 2022 Dealer Trophy on their first ever season with a 44-point lead. Coming in second was BD Group, and third was TORO Racing thanks to their driver Luo Kailuo. Just a single point separated second and third place finishers this year, promising a showdown between BD Group and TORO next season.
All this leaves the stage set for next year, where the Porsche Carrera Cup Asia celebrates 20-years on the track. Since the first race at Malaysia's Sepang International Circuit in 2003, the series has had 231 races, with almost 200 drivers from 24 countries and regions. The Porsche Carrera Cup Asia is now firmly established as the premier one-make racing series on the continent. In 2023, the series returns to international racing following two years of COVID disruption, visiting South Korea's Yeongam International Circuit, Japan's Suzuka International Circuit, Thailand's Buriram Chang International Circuit, and Malaysia's Sepang International Circuit. The season will also contain two F1 support races, as the season opener in Shanghai, and for the penultimate stop at Singapore's Marina Bay Street Circuit. Two F1 support races and an international roster of the best racing talent in Asia means that the stage is set for a spectacular 20th anniversary celebration.

Night of Champions

DRIVER STANDINGS **OVERALL**

POS	NO	DRIVERS	TEAM	POINTS
1	777	Leo Ye	Junjie Racing	188
2	99	Luo Kailuo	Toro Racing	137
3	22	Ling Kang	BD Group	132
4	233	Zhang Zhendong	Hehehe Racing	87
5	4	Lu Wei	R&B Racing	83
6	718	Yuan Bo	Zheng Tong Auto	74
7	20	Daniel Lu Wenlong	Meidong Racing	72
8	6	Bao Jinlong	Team Shanghai Yonda	70
9	86	Cui Yue	Porsche Holding	52
10	66	Min Heng	Toro Racing	47
11	2	Zhou Bihuang	Porsche Beijing Central & Goldenport	36
12	55	Gao Yujia	Team Jebsen	35
13	3	Bian Ye	Team Shanghai Yonda	35
14	17	Hong Shijie	Team C&D	27
15	91	Henry Kwong	Triple Ace Racing	25
16	23	Eric Kwong	Kiddy World Racing	18
17	9	Li Chao	Team Betterlife	15
18	7	Tang Ruobin	Climax Racing	9
19	21	Francis Tjia	Trans-China Automotive Racing	3
20	69	Jacky Wu	Shanghai Pudong & Waigaoqiao 69 Racing	3
21	12	Wang Zhongwei	Climax Racing	3
22	65	Brian Lee	KRC Racing	3
23	65	Zhu Zhiyao	KRC Racing	1

DRIVER STANDINGS **PRO-AM**

POS	NO	DRIVERS	TEAM	POINTS
1	4	Lu Wei	Junjie Racing	168
2	6	Bao Jinlong	Team Shanghai Yonda	168
3	66	Min Heng	Toro Racing	105
4	17	Hong Shijie	Team C&D	99
5	2	Zhou Bihuang	Porsche Beijing Central & Goldenport	93
6	12	Wang Zhongwei	Climax Racing	61
7	9	Li Chao	Team Betterlife	59
8	21	Francis Tjia	Trans-China Automotive Racing	32

DRIVER STANDINGS **AM**

POS	NO	DRIVERS	TEAM	POINTS
1	91	Henry Kwong	Triple Ace Racing	172
2	23	Eric Kwong	Kiddy World Racing	162
3	7	Tang Ruobin	Climax Racing	117
4	69	Jacky Wu	Shanghai Pudong & Waigaoqiao 69 Racing	116
5	65	Zhu Zhiyao	KRC Racing	70
6	65	Brian Lee	KRC Racing	31

Henry Kwong

TEAM STANDINGS

POS	TEAM	POINTS
1	Junjie Racing	184
2	BD Group	140
3	Toro Racing	139
4	Team Shanghai Yonda	93
5	Zheng Tong Auto	88
6	Meidong Racing	85
7	Team Jebsen	65
8	Porsche Holding	54
9	Team C&D	54
10	Shanghai Pudong & Waigaoqiao 69 Racing	48
11	Porsche Beijing Central & Goldenport	45
12	Team Betterlife	34

Henry Kwong

PORSCHE
CARRERA CUP
JAPAN

CARRERA CUP JAPAN

16.04.–17.04.2022 Okayama International Circuit, Japan
03.05.–04.05.2022 Fuji International Speedway, Japan
28.05.–29.05.2022 Suzuka Curcuit, Japan
06.08.–07.08.2022 Fuji International Speedway, Japan
27.08.–28.08.2022 Suzuka Circuit, Japan
07.10.–09.10.2022 Suzuka Circuit, Japan

In der Pro-Klasse holte Ogawa seinen dritten Titel im PCC Japan, während Ikari und Takami jeweils erstmals Champion in den Klassen Pro-Am und Am wurden.

Tsubasa Kondo and Ryo Ogawa

Der 2001 ins Leben gerufene Porsche Carrera Cup Japan ging im Jahr 2022 in seine 22. Saison, in der elf Rennen auf dem Programm standen: zehn Auftritte, verteilt auf fünf Veranstaltungen in Okayama, Fuji und Suzuka, wurden in Verbindung mit der SUPER GT Serie gefahren, ein Start wurde im Rahmenprogramm des Formel-1-Gastspiels in Suzuka absolviert. Wie im vergangenen Jahr wurde der Cup in drei Klassen ausgeschrieben: Pro, Pro-Am und Am.
In der Pro-Klasse holte sich Kondo beim Auftakt in Okayama die Pole Position. Im Rennen übernahm Ogawa, der von Rang zwei gestartet war, die erste Position und gewann das Duell gegen den Polesitter. Im zweiten Lauf revanchierte sich Kondo mit einem Start/Ziel-Sieg für die Auftaktniederlage. In Heat drei des Jahres, nun in Fuji, triumphierte Kondo abermals. Im vierten Durchgang überholte Ogawa den Führenden Kondo in Runde fünf und feierte schließlich seinen zweiten Sieg. Wenig später in Suzuka erwischte Kondo von Startplatz eins einen schwachen Beginn und Ogawa übernahm die Führung, die er für seinen dritten Saisonerfolg sicher ins Ziel brachte. Im folgenden sechsten Durchgang sicherte Yamada sich seinen ersten PCCJ-Triumph. Nach sechs Rennen gestaltete sich der Kampf um die Tabellenspitze in der Pro-Wertung als ein Duell zwischen den beiden erfahrenen Champions Ogawa und Kondo. Doch letztgenannter verpasste unerwartet die Läufe sieben und acht in Fuji. Yamamoto war bei seinem ersten Auftritt in dieser Saison nah an Ogawa dran, aber Ogawa gewann letztendlich beide Durchgänge. Dadurch vergrößerte er den Abstand in der Punktewertung zwischen sich und Kondo auf 55 Zähler. Für die Heats neun und zehn in Suzuka kehrte Kondo mit zwei Triumphen standesgemäß wieder zurück. Doch diese zwei Erfolge reichten nicht aus, um seine Chancen auf den Titel aufrecht

Drivers and Organisation of Porsche Carrera Cup Japan

In the Pro class, Ogawa claimed his third PCC Japan title while Ikari and Takami each celebrated their maiden title wins in the Pro-Am and Am classes respectively.

The Porsche Carrera Cup Japan, which launched in 2001, celebrated its 22nd season this year with the top class upgrading to the 911 GT3 Cup, Type 992. A total of 11 races were contested over six events. Five of them were double-header weekends, and shared the bill with the SUPER GT series. The final race was a support event for the Japanese Formula One Grand Prix at Suzuka. Ryo Ogawa won the Pro class, securing his third PCCJ title in eight years, and his first since 2014. The veteran driver Ikari was crowned as the Pro-Am Class champion for the first time, while Motoki Takami won the Am Class title during his first ever campaign in the PCCJ series.

The opening two races of the season were held at Okayama in April, followed by Fuji and Suzuka in May. The series then returned to Fuji for another two races, and then headed to Suzuka for the final three races.

The Pro class was extremely hard fought. Tsubasa Kondo, who had won a record fourth title in 2021, returned to the class to take on Ogawa who himself had won two PCCJ titles in 2013 and 2014. Sena Yamamoto, who also competed in the PSCJ as a Porsche Junior driver, entered the class, as well as Ryo Yamada. Returning to the Pro-Am class for the first time in three years was Shinji Takei, who was the first gentleman driver to win the series title in 2017. In the Am class there were five first-time entrants, including Casa Mingo, Ikeda, Takami, KenRyu and Bankcy. They liked up alongside veteran drivers Tomoyuki Takizawa, Tsugio Haruyama and Shigeto Nagashima.

Bingo Racing Team

"Ikari" and Shinji Takei

Ryo Ogawa and Team

Motoki Takami

(98): "Ikari" - (77): Masaru Hamasaki - (10): Motoki Takami

"Ikeda" and Shigeto Nagashima

zu erhalten: Mit einem Vorsprung von 45 Zählern bei noch einem zu fahrenden Rennen durfte Ogawa sich zum ersten Mal seit acht Jahren wieder Champion des PCCJ nennen. Allerdings wurde der neue Gesamtsieger Ogawa in allen acht Qualifyings, in denen sie bis zu diesem Zeitpunkt gegeneinander antraten, hinter Kondo notiert, sodass er darauf brannte, Kondo die Pole Position beim letzten Meeting abzunehmen – was er auch schaffte. Wenig später gewann er auch das Finale.

In der Pro-Am-Klasse tobte ein Kampf zwischen Ikari, Hamasaki und Takei: Nach acht Rennen hatten Ikari und Takei jeweils drei Siege auf ihren Konten, Hamasaki konnte zweimal gewinnen. Alle drei hatten keinen problemfreien Saisonverlauf: Takei musste beim ersten Auftritt in Fuji nach einem Unfall in beiden Läufen zusehen. Beim sechs-

(7): "Ikeda" - (17): "KenRyu"

Kondo opened his account with pole position in Okayama with a new lap record. In the race, however, it was fellow front-row starter Ogawa who took the lead. The two fought the entire race but it was Ogawa who took the first win of the Type 992 Cup in Japan. In the second race, Kondo again started from pole position, and this time converted that into his first win of the year.
Kondo was again the man in form at Fuji, setting pole position with a lap that was nearly a second faster than the previous record. He went on to score his second win of the year, but in race two was forced to settle for second behind his nemesis for the season, Ogawa. Kondo had again started on pole, but Ogawa passed him on the fifth lap and never looked back.
The first visit to Suzuka marked the halfway point of the season, and Kondo continued his blistering qualifying form, again setting a new lap record on his way to pole position. His start was less impressive though, and he was passed by Ogawa who had started third on the grid. The second race of the weekend saw Yamada, who had entered the race as a reserve driver, take his first PCCJ win.
The standings were tight at the top, with Ogawa leading Kondo by 132 points to 127, but Kondo then unexpectedly missed the seventh and eighth races at Fuji. Ogawa took full advantage and won both races from pole position. Kondo returned to action at the next meeting, again at Suzuka, and again he took consecutive pole-to-flag victories, but Ogawa had done enough to secure the title, opening an

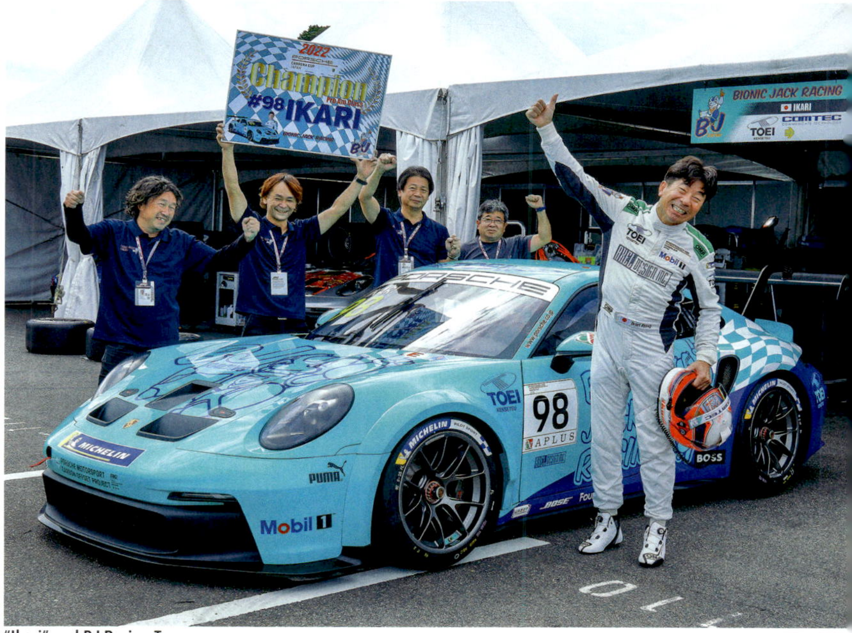

"Ikari" and BJ Racing Team

(60): Ryo Ogawa - (1): Tsubasa Kondo

Ryo Yamada

ten Saisonlauf in Suzuka kollidierten Takei und Ikari im Kampf um die erste Position in der Pro-Am-Klasse und Hamasaki profitierte davon. Letztgenannter musste dann beim zweiten Gastspiel in Suzuka passen, da sein Auto nach einem Unfall noch nicht repariert war. Ikari entschied beide Rennen auf der japanischen Grand-Prix-Piste für sich und gewann mit seinen Triumphen Nummer vier und fünf in seinem achten Jahr den lang ersehnten Titel in der Pro-Am-Kategorie. Solchermaßen motiviert holte er sich dann auch noch den letzten Siegerpokal des Jahres auf der großen Formel-1-Bühne. In der Am-Klasse, in der viele neue Fahrer antraten, waren alle Augen auf Takami gerichtet. Obwohl er kaum Rennerfahrung hatte, stand er bei allen elf Rennen auf der Pole Position der Am-Klasse. Er gewann die ersten vier Läufe des Jahres, doch im fünften Heat in Fuji gelang Nagashima in der letzten Runde ein spektakuläres Überholmanöver und dieser sah die Zielflagge als Erster. Ab dem sechsten Durchgang arbeitete Takami dann an einer weiteren Siegesserie, die erst beim Finale endete. In Suzuka wurde er nach einem Unfall nur Siebter seiner Klasse. Daraufhin lieferten sich Bankcy und Nagashima ein Duell um den ersten Platz, in dem sich Bankcy gegen Rennende absetzte und seinem ersten Triumph entgegenfuhr. Den Am-Titel konnte er Takami nicht mehr entreißen.

(9): Shinji Takei - (98): "Ikari" - (10): Motoki Takami - (77): Masaru Hamasaki
(63): Shigeto Nagashima - (5): "Casa Mingo" - (66): "Bankcy"

(l.-r.): „Ikeda", Shigeto Nagashima, Team KRM

Start at Fuji

insurmountable 45-point lead with only one race remaining. However, while he was the champion, Ogawa had yet to beat Kondo in qualifying and so he set about rectifying that situation in support of the Japanese Grand Prix. He achieved his goal and converted his pole position to victory at the final race.

The Pro-Am Class was a battle between three veteran drivers – Ikari, Hamasaki and Takei. It was Takei who drew first blood, with a lights-to-flag victory and a new lap record in the opening round of the season. Ikari won the second race to put himself into contention. Takei missed the next race at Fuji after an accident in testing. Ikari and Hamasaki shared the wins at Fuji, but Takei returned for the next meeting in Suzuka. Despite scoring pole position, Ikari got ahead of him at the start and went on to win for the third time this season. Ikari and Takei battled for the top spot in the sixth race of the season but collided with eachother, allowing Hamasaki to win for the second time this season.

The series then returned to Fuji, and Takei took lights-to-flag wins in both races but Hamasaki retired after crashing with Yamamoto, who had stalled on the grid and was unable to score. That crash kept Hamasaki out of the next race meeting at Suzuka. There, Ikari won the two races to take the Pro-Am Class title, his first in eight years of trying. He then followed that up with victory at the Japanese Grand Prix support race, bringing his total for the season to six.

In the Am Class, where many new drivers entered the series, all eyes were on Takami. He set a class course record in the qualifying session for the opening race. Despite having almost no racing experience, he set new records at Okayama, Fuji and Suzuka. Furthermore, he scored pole position in the Am Class at each of the 11 races, and started ahead of the Pro-Am Class drivers eight times. He won the first four races, but in the fifth at Fuji, Nagashima made a spectacular comeback on the last lap to take his first win of the year. From the sixth race onwards, Takami returned to his winning ways, but in the final race, he had an accident and finished in seventh in the class. Bankcy scored his first win of the year, ahead of Nagashima after a tough fight. At the season end, Takami had won nine times to take the championship title, with Nagashima second and Bankcy third. Course records were broken at every circuit, and the year showed off the speed of the Cup machines and the excellent driving techniques of all the PCCJ drivers.

Shigeto Nagashima and "Bankcy"

CASA MINGO
5

1ST
BINGO
AGREX

Mobil 1
BOSS
MICHELIN
BOSCH
NISSAN
SUBARU

BOSS

Ogawa
60

Ogawa
60

HONDA

www.porsche.co.jp

9
APLUS
BINGO
Fountain

SUZUKA CIR
47

10 MOTO+
2022
P1

BRIDGESTONE

PORSCHE
CARRERA CUP
JAPAN

adidas

PORSCHE
CARRERA CUP
JAPAN
Mobil 1
MICHELIN

BINGO
ART OF CARS

SUZUKA CIRCUIT
DENSO

Ryo Ogawa and Shinji Takei

Tsugio Haruyama

(51): Tsugio Haruyama - (17): "KenRyu" - (5): "Casa Mingo"

DRIVER STANDINGS PRO

POS	NO	DRIVERS	TEAM	POINTS
1	60	Ryo Ogawa	Showa Auto with Bingo Racing	247
2	1	Tsubasa Kondo	NK Racing	197
3	7	Ryo Yamada	Team KRM	70
4	91	Sena Yamamoto	Porsche Japan Junior Programme	20

DRIVER STANDINGS PRO-AM

POS	NO	DRIVERS	TEAM	POINTS
1	98	"Ikari"	BJR Porsche	241
2	9	Shinji Takei	Bingo Racing	189
3	77	Masaru Hamasaki	Voing with Ventiler	167

DRIVER STANDINGS AM

POS	NO	DRIVERS	TEAM	POINTS
1	10	Motoki Takami	47 Trading with Rn-Sports	254
2	63	Shigeto Nagashima	TUC Group & Team KRM	211
3	66	"Bankcy"	Bingo Racing	149
4	5	"Casa Mingo"	Team Rightway	124
5	23	Tomoyuki Takizawa	Fach Auto Tech	94
6	7	"Ikeda"	Hyper Water Racing Team	92
7	51	Tsugio Haruyama	Bingo Racing	86
8	17	"KenRyu"	Fach Auto Tech	77

(l.-r.): Philipp von Witzendorff, "Ikari", Ryo Ogawa, Motoki Takami, Michael Dreiser

TEAM STANDINGS

POS	TEAM	POINTS
1	Bingo Racing	384
2	Team KRM	250

PORSCHE
PAYNTER DIXON
CARRERA CUP
AUSTRALIA

TITLE PARTNER
paynter dixon

PAYNTER DIXON CARRERA CUP AUSTRALIA

07.04.–10.04.2022	*Melbourne, Victoria, Australia*
21.05.–22.05.2022	*Winton, Victoria, Australia*
17.06.–19.06.2022	*Darwin, Northern Territory, Australia*
08.07.–10.07.2022	*Townsville, Queensland, Australia*
29.07.–31.07.2022	*The Bend, South Australia, Australia*
19.08.–21.08.2022	*Sandown, Victoria, Australia*
06.10.–10.10.2022	*Bathurst, New South Wales, Australia*
28.10.–30.10.2022	*Surfer's Paradise, Queensland, Australia*

(11): Jackson Walls - (17): Callum Hedge

Aaron Loves großartiges Comeback wurde nicht belohnt, er musste sich im Titelrennen des Porsche Carrera Cup Australia hinter Harri Jones anstellen.

Um den Titel im Porsche Paynter Dixon Carrera Cup Australia kämpften im Rekordstarterfeld von 32 Porsche GT3 Cup des Typs 992 zwei Nachwuchspiloten, die beide Absolventen der Porsche Sprint Challenge in Australien sind: Harri Jones und Aaron Love – mit dem besseren Ende für Jones.

Die Saison begann in Melbourne im Rahmen des Formel-1-Gastspiels. Nachdem Love die Pole Position eroberte und die drei ersten Rennen gewann, fiel er im vierten Lauf nach einer Berührung mit einem Konkurrenten weit zurück. Damit ging die Gesamtwertung des Wochenendes an Max Vidau, ohne dass dieser einen einzigen Rennsieg verbuchen konnte. Ex-Champion David Wall wurde Zweiter, Love blieb Rang drei.

Nach diesem Auftritt sollte die PCC-Australia-Saison von Love eigentlich beendet sein, denn für den Rest des Jahres waren für ihn Starts im Carrera Cup France und im Porsche Supercup vorgesehen. Und beim zweiten Rennwochenende fehlte er tatsächlich, was sein Rivale Jones nutzte. Nach den drei Läufen von Winton, von denen er zwei als Erster beendete, übernahm er die Tabellenführung. Ein konstantes Wochenende in Darwin - er wurde Wochenend-Zweiter hinter Sieger Dale Wood - ließ Jones seine Spitzenposition weiter ausbauen, bevor der Cup zum vierten Meeting nach Townsville reiste.

Dort siegte der junge neuseeländische Rookie Callum Hegde, aber das Thema war die Rückkehr von Aaron Love, die zeigte, dass das Titelrennen noch lange nicht entschieden war. Sein starkes Wochenende, gepaart mit einer schwachen Leistung von Jones, der nur Zehnter der Wochenend-Wertung wurde, sorgte für eine erste Trendwende in der Jagd um den Titel.

Sam Shahin

Pre-Start at Gold Coast

Pre-Start at Darwin

(74): David Russell - (17): Callum Hedge

Harri Jones fends off late Aaron Love charge to win the Porsche Paynter Dixon Carrera Cup Australia

THE remarkable story of the 2022 Porsche Paynter Dixon Carrera Cup Australia Championship started in Melbourne, ended on the Gold Coast and in between carried a rollercoaster ride that few could have had predicted. The battle for the title was fought between a pair of Porsche Michelin Junior drivers: both graduates of Porsche Michelin Sprint Challenge in Australia. Queenslander Harri Jones and West Australian star Aaron Love ended up duelling for the crown, though their respective pathways to title contention would prove vastly different.

The season started in Melbourne, supporting the Formula 1 Rolex Australian Grand Prix and though Love claimed pole position and won three of the four races, he could only manage 13th in the finale following contact with another competitor. That turned the round over to Max Vidau, who emerged as the highest point scorer, and therefore round winner, for Tekworkx Motorsport without claiming a single race win. Former champion David Wall was second while Love was third. That was supposed to be the end of Love's campaign. International commitments in Carrera Cup France and Porsche Supercup were expected to fill the remainder of his year.

Harri Jones set about working his way to the front with his customary consistency and smart, thinking race craft. He took the championship lead following Round two at Winton, claiming two of the three races to claim the round win ahead of David Russell and the ever-present Dylan O'Keeffe. A consistent weekend in Darwin – he was second to round winner Dale Wood – saw him further build his lead as the series headed to Townsville for round four.

Harri Jones

Racing at Gold Coast

Auch im The Bend Motorsport Park dominierte Love und weil Jones erneut Probleme hatte, begann es immer spannender zu werden. Außerdem war Love in Sandown erfolgreich und siegte im einzigen Rennen in Bathurst, wo die zwei weiteren Läufe wegen Regens ausfielen.
Mit einem Rückstand von 74 Punkten auf Jones reiste Love zum Finale an die Gold Coast und obwohl seine Titelchancen nicht allzu groß waren, gab er nochmal alles. Im ersten Durchgang wurde er als Vierter abgewinkt, gewann dann die Rennen zwei und drei sowie das gesamte Wochenende, doch sein Comeback reichte nicht aus, um Jones noch vom Platz an der Sonne zu verdrängen. Und so durfte Harri Jones seinen zweiten Titel im Porsche-Markenpokal feiern, der gleichzeitig die dritte Trophäe für sein Team McElrea Racing war. Am Ende betrug sein Vorsprung gerade einmal elf Punkte auf Love, obschon dieser zwei komplette Rennwochenenden verpasste. Auf Rang drei der Abschlusstabelle beendete David Russell die Saison, gefolgt von Dylan O'Keeffe und David Wall.
In der Pro-Am-Wertung war der Titel noch härter umkämpft. Die Führung in der Klasse wechselte an den ersten sechs Rennwochenenden sage und schreibe sechs Mal. Geoff Emery siegte im Rahmen des Grand Prix von Melbourne und übernahm Position eins, die er wenig später jedoch an Stephen Grove abgeben musste, nachdem dieser ein starkes Wochenende in Winton erlebte. Titelverteidiger Sam Shahin

Harri Jones and Team

(100): Dale Wood
(11): Jackson Walls
(12): Harri Jones

Young New Zealand rookie Callum Hegde won in North Queensland, but it was the return of Aaron Love that indicated the championship was far from over. His strong weekend, coupled with a disaster for Jones (he finished 10th overall) saw the first momentum shift in the title race.

Love returned for more at The Bend Motorsport Park a few weeks later, and dismantled the field in the first two races to claim his second round win – the first repeat winner of the season. With Jones struggling again, the title battle was beginning to look interesting. Love won again at Sandown – all three races, this time – and then claimed the lone race at Bathurst (the final two were rained out) to put himself in title calculations by the time the field headed to the Gold Coast.

Trailing jones by 74 points, it was always going to be a tough ask for Aaron Love – but he threw everything he could at the job, despite having to start from 15th after missing a lap in qualifying. He was fourth by the end of race one, won races two and three and the weekend overall, however the largest comeback in Carrera Cup history still wasn't enough to edge out Jones.

The McElrea Racing driver claimed the title, his second in one-make Porsche competition and the third for the team, and earned his ticket to the Porsche Mobil 1 Supercup Shootout at the end of the year. The final margin was just 11 points, but Jones' strong start to the year and a solid rebound from his mid-season struggles was more than enough to make him the deserving winner. Love was second, despite missing two full rounds, with his comeback the stuff of Carrera Cup Australia legend.

The battle for third overall came down to the final round: EMA Motorsport's David Russell pinching the final podium spot from the ever-consistent GWR/RAM driver Dylan O'Keeffe in the final races on the Gold Coast. With O'Keeffe fourth, David Wall was fifth to continue his run of six straight seasons of top five championship finishes. Callum Hedge was top rookie in sixth, Dale Wood was seventh while former Bathurst winner Luke Youlden's full time comeback netted him eighth, just ahead of Christian Pancione and Max Vidau.

Geoff Emery

Mark Webber and Sam Shahin

(27): Liam Talbot - (22): Dean Cook - (7): Tim Miles - (4): Stephen Grove

Geoff Emery

Barry Hay and Dale Wood

(l.-r.): Sam Shahin, David Wall, Max Vidau, Geoff Emery, Stephen Grove, Aaron Love

Harri Jones

führte nach der dritten Runde in Darwin die Tabelle an, Emerys Triumph in Townsville brachte ihn nach Meeting vier wieder an die Spitze. Shahin übernahm nach dem fünften Rennwochenende auf seiner Heimstrecke The Bend wieder P1, während Emery nach seinem ersten Platz in Sandown zum zweiten Mal in dieser Saison an die erste Stelle sprang.
Und so fuhr Emery mit 22 Punkten Vorsprung auf seinen Teamkollegen Dean Cook zum Finale an die Gold Coast. Letzterer sparte sich sein bestes Ergebnis für den Schlussakt auf und gewann das letzte Rennen der Saison. Es war sein erster Triumph in 2022; er wurde damit punktgleich mit Emery an der Spitze des Rankings notiert. Da er aber weniger Rennsiege holte als sein Kontrahent, ging der Pokal für den Champion letztendlich an Emery.

Dylan O'Keeffe

In Morris Pro-Am the title battle was even more competitive, with the Carrera Cup 'race within a race' completing a remarkable year and its most remarkable title finish ever. The series lead changed hands six times in the first six rounds. Geoff Emery won at the Formula 1 Rolex Australian Grand Prix to become the early season leader. However, Stephen Grove rocketed to the top following his strong weekend at Winton in round two.

Defending champion Sam Shahin led Grove in the standings following the third round in Darwin with Emery back to third, though his win in Townsville quickly propelled him back to the top of the standings following round four. Sam Shahin, who had dropped to third following the trip to Queensland, rebounded at his home circuit at The Bend to re-take the lead following the fifth round, while Geoff Emery jumped from third to first for the second time in the season following his win at Sandown.

So, it headed to the Gold Coast with Emery leading his teammate Dean Cook by 22 points. The latter saved his best for last: Cook won the final race of the season in a dramatic conclusion to the championship. It was his first win of the season and remarkably tied the points with his Ashley Seward Motorsport teammate Emery – but the latter claimed the big prize thanks to his multiple race victories, compared to Cook's lone effort.

Liam Talbot finished third in Pro-Am with Sam Shahin dropping to fourth, having led the Championship twice throughout the year.

The 2022 Porsche Paynter Dixon Carrera Cup Australia season was one for the record books; the series biggest ever. With a record grid of 32 Type-992 Porsche 911 GT3 Cup Cars on track, the 2022 season produced a show that will long be remembered.

(17): Callum Hedge - (999): Aaron Love

Simon Fallon

Australia
MELBOURNE

FERRARI

FLACK
YOULDEN

SIMON FALLON

boostmobile

(l.-r.): Harri Jones, Dean Cook, Liam Talbot, Dale Wood, Dylan O'Keeffe, Sam Shahin

DRIVER STANDINGS **PRO**

POS	NO	DRIVERS	TEAM	POINTS
1	12	Harri Jones	Mackellar Group	831
2	999	Aaron Love	Sonic Motor Racing	820
3	74	David Russell	EMA Motorsport	777
4	88	Dylan O'Keeffe	RAM Motorsport	767
5	38	David Wall	Paynter Dixon	737
6	17	Callum Hedge	Earl Bamber Motorsport	678
7	100	Dale Wood	Timken Racing	568
8	53	Luke Youlden	TekworkX Motorsport	529
9	76	Christian Pancione	VCM Performance	522
10	72	Max Vidau	TekworkX Motorsport	512
11	11	Jackson Walls	Objective Racing	502
12	777	Simon Fallon	Sonic Motor Racing	470
13	5	Ryan Suhle	Earl Bamber Motorsport	441
14	333	Brad Shiels	Royal Purple Racing	399
15	45	Duvashen Padayachee	Rentcorp	300
16	6	Angelo Mouzouris	Sonic Motor Racing	298
17	8	Nick McBride	Porsche Centre Melbourne	285
18	25	Michael Almond	The PSA Group	250
19	28	Bayley Hall	Hall Finance and Insurance	230

DRIVER STANDINGS **ENDURANCE CUP PRO**

POS	NO	DRIVERS	TEAM	POINTS
1	998	Aaron Love	Sonic Motor Racing	321
2	74	David Russell	EMA Motorsport	266
3	12	Harri Jones	Mackellar Group	258
4	38	David Wall	Paynter Dixon	227
5	88	Dylan O'Keefe	RAM Motorsport	217
6	17	Callum Hedge	Earl Bamber Motorsport	190
7	777	Simon Fallon	Sonic Motor Racing	175
8	11	Jackson Walls	Objective Racing	171
9	53	Luke Youlden	TekworkX Motorsport	160
10	76	Christian Pancione	VCM Performance	144
11	72	Max Vidau	TekworkX Motorsport	137
12	5	Ryan Suhle	Earl Bamber Motorsport	128
13	333	Brad Shiels	Royal Purple Racing	119
14	100	Dale Wood	Timken Racing	118
15	8	Nick McBride	Porsche Centre Melbourne	108
16	6	Angelo Mouzouris	Sonic Motor Racing	105
17	42	Duvashen Padayachee	Rentcorp	90
18	25	Michael Almond	The PSA Group	66
19	28	Bayley Hall	Hall Finance and Insurance	65

Geoff Emery

DRIVER STANDINGS **MORRIS PRO-AM**

POS	NO	DRIVERS	TEAM	POINTS
1	48	Geoff Emery	Force Accessories	913
2	22	Dean Cook	Zonzo Racing	913
3	27	Liam Talbot	Paynter Dixon	887
4	13	Sam Shahin	The Bend Motorsport Park	803
5	14	Matthew Belford	Porsche Centre Melbourne	689
6	20	Adrian Flack	AGAS National	687
7	77	Rodney Jane	Sonic Motor Racing	683
8	77	Stephen Grove	Sonic Motor Racing	605
9	7	Tim Miles	Miles Advisory Partners	550
10	9	Marc Cini	Hallmarc	503
11	222	Scott Taylor	Scott Taylor Motorsport	404
12	86	Drew Hall	Wall Racing	367
13	101	Tony Quinn	Local Legends	132
14	45	Indiran Padayachee	Rentcorp	75

DRIVER STANDINGS **ENDURANCE CUP PRO-AM**

POS	NO	DRIVERS	TEAM	POINTS
1	27	Liam Talbot	Paynter Dixon	315
2	22	Dean Cook	Zonzo Racing	234
3	20	Adrian Flack	AGAS National	228
4	14	Matthew Belford	Porsche Centre Melbourne	217
5	48	Geoff Emery	Force Accessories	213
6	13	Sam Shahin	The Bend Motorsport Park	206
7	77	Rodney Jane	Sonic Motor Racing	182
8	7	Tim Miles	Miles Advisory Partners	173
9	4	Stephen Grove	Grove Racing	167
10	9	Marc Cini	Hallmarc	146
11	86	Drew Hall	Wall Racing	144
12	222	Scott Taylor	Scott Taylor Motorsport	131
13	101	Tony Quinn	Local Legends	43
14	45	Indiran Padayachee	Rentcorp	23

(l.-r.): David Russell, Harri Jones, Dylan O'Keeffe

DRIVER STANDINGS **MICHELIN JUNIOR**

POS	NO	DRIVERS	TEAM	POINTS
1	12	Harri Jones	Mackellar Group	831
2	17	Callum Hedge	Earl Bamber Motorsport	677
3	76	Christian Pancione	VCM Performance	522
4	72	Max Vidau	TekworkX Motorsport	512
5	11	Jackson Walls	Objective Racing	502
6	777	Simon Fallon	Sonic Motor Racing	470
7	5	Ryan Suhle	Earl Bamber Motorsport	441
8	6	Angelo Mouzouris	Sonic Motor Racing	298
9	26	Bayley Hall	Hall Finance and Insurance	230

(777): Simon Fallon
(12): Harri Jones
(999): Aaron Love

PORSCHE
CARRERA CUP
NORTH AMERICA

CARRERA CUP NORTH AMERICA
PRESENTED BY THE CAYMAN ISLANDS

16.03.–17.03.2022	Sebring International Raceway, USA
08.04.–10.04.2022	Long Beach Street Circuit, USA
29.04.–01.05.2022	Laguna Seca Raceway, USA
23.06.–25.06.2022	Watkins Glen International, USA
15.07.–17.07.2022	Streets of Toronto, Canada
04.08.–07.08.2022	Road America, USA
02.09.–04.09.2022	Indianapolis Motor Speedway, USA
28.09.–30.09.2022	Michelin Raceway Road Atlanta, USA

Parker Thompson, Alan Metni, Mark Kvamme und Kelly-Moss wurden als Champions des Porsche Carrera Cup North America gefeiert.

Der Porsche Carrera Cup North America Presented by the Cayman Islands erlebte eine erfolgreiche zweite Saison. Alle drei Klassen, Pro, Pro Am und Am, wurde im letzten 40-Minuten-Rennen des Jahres auf dem Michelin Raceway Road Atlanta entschieden. An den insgesamt acht Veranstaltungswochenenden starteten 48 Fahrer – unter ihnen NASCAR-Star Jeff Gordon – und 19 Teams in einem Markenpokal, der ausschließlich mit dem Porsche 911 GT3 Cup, Typ 992, bestritten werden konnte. Fünf Siege, drei Pole Positions und drei schnellste Rennrunden brachten Parker Thompson aus Kanada im Fahrzeug von JDX Racing den Pro-Titelgewinn. Nach zwei Erfolgen auf dem WeatherTech Raceway Laguna Seca sowie je einem Triumph in Road America, auf dem Indianapolis Motor Speedway und in Road Atlanta konnte er sich mit Rang drei im finalen Lauf des Jahres den Titel sichern, da sein stärkster Rivale Kay van Berlo nach einer Berührung mit einem Kontrahenten ausschied und so keine Zähler erhielt.
Van Berlo, Vizechampion von 2021, startete mit vier Siegen in Folge grandios in die Saison – er gewann auf dem Sebring International Raceway sowie auf dem Stadtkurs von Long Beach jeweils beide Durchgänge. Mit zwei weiteren ersten Plätzen in Watkins Glen wurde er im Porsche der Mannschaft Kelly-Moss insgesamt sechs Mal als Erster abgewinkt. Zudem erzielte der Niederländer sieben Pole Positions sowie sieben schnellste Rennrunden und dennoch fand er sich am Ende des Jahres mit 16 Punkten weniger als Thompson auf Rang zwei der Abschlusstabelle wieder.
Der US-Amerikaner Riley Dickinson ging als dritter und letzter Kandidat mit Chancen auf den Pro-Titel in das Finale. Doch auch die Punkte für den Sieg im letzten Rennen des Jahres reichten nicht aus, um sich in der Abschlusswertung weiter nach vorne

Efrin Castro

Efrin Castro

Mark Kvamme

Thompson, Metni, Kvamme and Kelly-Moss celebrated as Porsche Carrera Cup North America champions

🇬🇧 Porsche Carrera Cup North America Presented by the Cayman Islands celebrated a successful second season. Each of the three drivers' championships, Pro, Pro-Am and Am, went down to the final 40-minute race of the one-make series, which was held at Michelin Raceway Road Atlanta. Over the course of the eight event weekends, 48 drivers and 19 teams made at least one start in the series, which races only the Porsche 911 GT3 Cup car, type 992. Included in those 48 drivers were regulars along with one-off champions such as NASCAR great Jeff Gordon and Porsche Junior Laurin Heinrich.

The series enjoyed remarkable growth in its second year. The Sebring season-opener had 43 entries, and over the course of the season there was an average car count in the mid-30s each event. With four drivers capable of capturing the Pro class title, two in the Pro-Am and three in the Am class heading into the final weekend, the year was a thriller to the end.

Five wins, three pole positions and three fastest race laps earned the Pro championship for Canadian Parker Thompson, who drove for JDX Racing. The winner of both races at WeatherTech Raceway Laguna Seca (rounds five and six) and single trips to victory lane at Road America (round 12) and Indianapolis Motor Speedway (round 13) drew Thompson into contention. Victory in the first of two races held at Road Atlanta put him into a prime spot for the title and after Dutchman Kay van Berlo had contact in the final race, Thompson secured his first Al Holbert Cup.

Champion Mark Kvamme and Thomas Laudenbach

Michael McCann

(9): Parker Thompson - (6): Trenton Estep - (2): Sean Varwig

(99): Alan Metni - (2): Sean Varwig - (13): Varun Choksey

zu schieben als auf den dritten Rang. Dickinson wurde im 16. Saisonlauf auf der Strecke zwar als Zweiter abgewinkt, doch da Gaststarter Laurin Heinrich nicht punktberechtigt war, bekam der Kelly-Moss-Schützling die volle Punktzahl für Position eins gutgeschrieben.

Sogar einen Sieg mehr als Dickinson durfte Trenton Estep feiern, er war insbesondere in Toronto der dominierende Fahrer. Dort gewann der Mann aus dem Team MDK Motorsports nicht nur beide Durchgänge, sondern begann auch beide Heats von der Pole Position und fuhr einmal die schnellste Rennrunde.

In der Pro-Am-Klasse reisten die beiden Kelly-Moss-Teamkollegen Alan Metni und Efrin Castro als einzige verbliebene Titelanwärter zum Finale; der US-Amerikaner Metni ging als Führender mit leicht besseren Chancen in die letzten beiden Rennen. Doch Castro, der aus der Dominikanischen Republik kommt, ließ sich nicht entmutigen und tat mit zwei Siegen alles in seiner Macht Stehende, um den Titel doch noch an sich zu reißen. Aber es sollte nicht genug sein: Metni eroberte die Pro-Am-Krone mit einem Vorsprung vor genau einem einzigen Punkt. Der Kanadier Marco Cirone belegte im Porsche von Mark Motors Racing den dritten Platz im Pro-Am-Schlussranking vor den US-Amerikanern Curt Swearingin und Matt Halcome. Die Pro-Am-Klasse ist für Fahrer im Alter zwischen 36 und 57 Jahren reserviert.

Laurin Heinrich

Leh Keen

For van Berlo the final race was gut-wrenching. He had driven to a championship-building second-place finish the day before, just behind Thompson. In doing so the 2021 runner-up raised his podium total to five, plus six wins. The early championship favorite swept rounds one and two at the Sebring International Raceway as well as rounds three and four on the Long Beach street course. He added back-to-back victories at Watkins Glen International (rounds seven and eight) for a total of six wins, more than anyone else in the class behind the wheel of the Kelly Moss Porsche. He scored seven pole positions and seven fastest race laps.

Riley Dickinson entered the finale as the last driver with a shot at the Pro title. He secured third-place by winning the final race of the year. It was his second win (round 14 at Indianapolis Motor Speedway being the other). Dickinson had three fastest race laps and three pole positions.

Trenton Estep was also a race winner this year. The American scored three victories, at rounds nine and 10 in Toronto, as well as round 12 at Road America. The also scored three pole positions and two fastest laps in the MDK Motorsports Porsche, and was classified fourth in the final standings.

Echoing the thrilling battle of last season, Kelly Moss teammates Alan Metni and Efrin Castro of the Dominican Republic entered the finale as the only remaining contenders for the Pro-Am title. The balance between Metni and Castro was more consistent in 2022 and it was the former who led going onto the final race weekend. Castro won both races, but even that was not enough and it was Metni who was awarded the Pro-Am trophy by a single point. Castro finished the year on eight wins, Metni three. Canadian Marco Cirone finished third with three wins in the Mark Motors Racing Porsche. Curt Swearingin did not win in 2022 but had four podium finishes in the ACI Motorsports machine. Closing the top five was 2021 Pro-Am 991 class champion Matt Halcome with two podium finishes. The Pro-Am class is for drivers between the ages of 36 and 57.

Midway through the season, American Mark Kvamme was marching away with the Am championship in the MDK Motorsports Porsche. However, the ten-time race winner missed the rounds at Toronto, thereby opening the door to John Goetz and Bill Smith. When Smith missed the meeting at Road America, that flipped the top-

Kay van Berlo

In der ersten Saisonhälfte war Mark Kvamme in der Am-Klasse, die für Piloten ab 57 Jahren ausgeschrieben ist, klar auf dem Weg zum Titel. Doch nach fünf Rennsiegen musste er die Läufe in Toronto auslassen und eröffnete seinen beiden Landsleuten John Goetz und Bill Smith somit unerwartet neue Chancen. Doch die waren nicht von langer Dauer, denn nach vier weiteren ersten Plätzen kam er mit neun Saisonsiegen in der Tasche zum Finale. Und dort machte er mit einem zweiten und einem ersten Platz den Am-Titelgewinn klar. Verfolger Goetz gewann zweimal in 2022, für ihn blieb Rang zwei der Am-Wertung vor Smith, der dreimal von der obersten Stufe des Treppchens jubeln durfte. Als Teilnehmer mit den meisten Triumphen erhielt Kvamme zusätzlich noch den Michelin Race Wins Award.
Kelly-Moss sicherte sich zum zweiten Mal in Folge die Lorbeeren des besten Teams im Porsche Carrera Cup North America. Und Kay van Berlo gewann den Junior-Titel für Fahrer bis 26 Jahre.

Champion Parker Thompson

(12): Laurin Heinrich - (53): Riley Dickinson

three in the class for drivers age 57 and older. Entering the final weekend, Kvamme charged to a second place finish in round 15, and a victory in the last race to lock the title. Goetz, in the Wright Motorsports Porsche, was runner-up having won twice (round three at Long Beach and round 15 at Road Atlanta) and scored ten additional podium finishes. Smith, in the Topp Racing Porsche, was third in the standings having scored three wins (round eight at Watkins Glen and a sweep of Toronto). Grady Willingham in the Goldcrest Porsche and Joseph Lombardo in the Kelly Moss prepared car finished in fourth and fifth. As the driver who scored the most victories, Kvamme received the Michelin Race Wins Award.

For the second year, a trip for two to the five-star Kimpton Seafire Resort + Spa in the Cayman Islands was the champion's award in each class. The four-night stay in the five-star resort includes airfare, transportation, a visit to Stingray City and a culinary experience in one of the esteemed restaurants in the Grand Cayman. Additionally, PMNA provided a full-season entry fee for the champion of each class towards the 2023 Carrera Cup season. TAG Heuer increased its support by celebrating the top-three in each class with a timepiece as well as the top pole winner in each class. In addition to the annual Porsche Night of Champions in Stuttgart, Germany, each title-winner will earned a trip to the Porsche Ice Force Pro Experience in Canada.

With seven overall wins and eight additional overall podiums, Kelly Moss scored their second consecutive Entrants Championship. JDX Racing had five wins. MDK Motorsports had three overall wins. Official points for Entrant are awarded only to the highest placing team car overall, regardless of class.

Kay van Berlo won the Junior Championship for drivers 26-years or younger, earning the opportunity to compete in the Porsche Junior Global Shootout plus $40,000 USD financial support for a test day prior to the Shootout.

(9): Parker Thompson - (53): Riley Dickinson

Thomas Laudenbach at Sebring

Mobil 1

iFLY

Racing for Children
Mobil 1
Medical Properties Trust

MICHELIN

MICHELIN

TITLE PARTNER
VISIT
CAYMAN
ISLANDS
GRAND PRIX
MICHELIN
PORSCHE
deluxe
Mobil 1

84
deluxe
Mobil 1

ROAD AMERICA

FLYNN

Next Level

(l.-r.): Trenton Estep, Parker Thompson, Riley Dickinson

DRIVER STANDINGS **PRO AND PRO-AM**

POS	NO	DRIVERS	TEAM	POINTS
1	9	Parker Thompson	JDX Racing	306
2	3	Kay van Berlo	Kelly-Moss	290
3	53	Riley Dickinson	Kelly-Moss	264
4	6	Trenton Estep	MDK Motorsports	247
5	58	T. J. Fischer	Topp Racing	125
6	7	Michael McCarthy	Kelly-Moss	111
7	13	Varun Choksey	Wright Motorsports	110
8	12	Leh Keen	311RS Motorsport	109
9	11	Dimitri Dimakos	311RS Motorsport	99
10	77	Travis Wiley	Topp Racing	96
11	8	Michael McCann	McCann Racing	86
12	81	Grant Talkie	ACI Motorsports	71
13	99	Alan Metni	Kelly-Moss	67
14	65	Efrin Castro	Kelly-Moss	66
15	2	Sean Varwig	Kelly-Moss	43
16	24	Adam Adelson	Premier Racing	42
17	91	Matty Graham	MDK Motorsports	34
18	84	Marco Cirone	Mark Motors Racing	33
19	17	Curt Swearingen	ACI Motorsports	27
20	88	Hutton McKenna	Wright Motorsports	20
21	43	Jeff Kingsley	MDK Motorsports	17
22	47	Justin Oakes	NOLASport	12
23	69	Thomas Collingwood	BGB Motorsports	10
24	56	Jeff Mosing	Topp Racing	8
25	42	Bill Smith	Topp Racing	7
26	32	Kyle Washington	GMG Racing	7
27	23	P. J. Hyett	Kelly-Moss	7
28	55	Matt Halcone	Goldcrest Motorsports	6
29	16	Pedro Torres	ACI Motorsports	5
30	57	John Goetz	Wright Motorsports	4
31	95	Conor Flynn	Irish Mike's Racing	3
32	43	Mark Kvamme	MDK Motorsports	2
33	44	Moisey Uretsky	Accelerating Performance	1
34	28	Bob Mueller	Goldcrest Motorsports	1

DRIVER STANDINGS **PRO-AM**

POS	NO	DRIVERS	TEAM	POINTS
1	99	Alan Metni	Kelly-Moss	289
2	65	Efrin Castro	Kelly-Moss	288
3	84	Marco Cirone	Mark Motors Racing	210
4	17	Curt Swearingen	ACI Motorsports	200
5	55	Matt Halcone	Goldcrest Motorsports	160
6	69	Thomas Collingwood	BGB Motorsports	138
7	47	Justin Oakes	NOLASport	119
8	56	Jeff Mosing	Topp Racing	106
9	16	Pedro Torres	ACI Motorsports	106
10	18	Richard Edge	ACI Motorsports	101
11	44	Moisey Uretsky	Accelerating Performance	92
12	32	Kyle Washington	GMG Racing	68
13	23	P. J. Hyett	Kelly-Moss	52
14	30	Dominique Lequeux	Goldcrest Motorsports	51
15	97	Craig Conway	Irish Mike's Racing	49
16	26	Peter Atwater	JDX Racing	14
17	22	Carlos De Quesada	Alegra Motorsports	7
18	89	Mike Zoi	Ansa Motorsports	6

DRIVER STANDINGS **AM**

POS	NO	DRIVERS	TEAM	POINTS
1	43	Mark Kvamme	MDK Motorsports	317
2	57	John Goetz	Wright Motorsports	298
3	42	Bill Smith	Topp Racing	245
4	21	Grady Willingham	Goldcrest Motorsports	149
5	92	Joseph Lombardo	Kelly-Moss	108
6	10	Vernon McClure	Kelly-Moss	100
7	4	Robert Hanley	JDX Racing	94
8	29	Jeffrey Majkrzak	Goldcrest Motorsports	79
9	28	Bob Mueller	Goldcrest Motorsports	69
10	19	Tom Balames	Kelly-Moss	24
11	80	Joe Still	Goldcrest Motorsports	14

Champion Alan Metni

TEAM STANDINGS

POS	TEAM	POINTS
1	Kelly-Moss	340
2	JDX Racing	307
3	MDK Motorsports	286
4	Topp Racing	199
5	311RS Motorsport	189
6	Wright Motorsports	163
7	ACI Motorsports	126
8	McCann Racing	121
9	Premier Racing	101
10	Mark Motors Racing	86
11	Goldcrest Motorsports	75
12	BGB Motorsports	59
13	Irish Mike's Racing	52
14	NOLASport	49
15	Accelerating Performance	38
16	GMG Racing	37
17	Octavia Tequila Racing	2

SPRINT CHALLENGE

PORSCHE
SPRINT CHALLENGE
MIDDLE EAST

OFFICIAL PARTNER
LechneRRacing

SPRINT CHALLENGE MIDDLE EAST

04.11.–06.11.2021 Sakhir, Bahrain
03.12.–05.12.2021 Jeddah, Saudi Arabia
21.01.–22.01.2022 Dubai, United Arab Emirates
12.02.–13.02.2022 Abu Dhabi, United Arab Emirates
18.03.–20.03.2022 Sakhir, Bahrain
25.03.–27.03.2022 Jeddah, Saudi Arabia (non-championship)

Team Champion Saudi Racing

Fahad Algosaibi hielt den jungen Niederländer Morris Schuring im Kampf um den Titel in der Porsche Sprint Challenge Middle East in Schach.

Das erste Wochenende der Porsche Sprint Challenge Middle East 2021/2022, das im Rahmen des 8-Stunden-Rennens von Bahrain stattfand, wurde vom niederländischen Teenager Morris Schuring dominiert. Er entschied gleich beide Läufe für sich: den ersten vor seinem Landsmann Daan van Kuijk, während Fahad Algosaibi aus Saudi-Arabien mit einem Rückstand von fast zehn Sekunden als Dritter das Podium komplettierte; den zweiten vor Algosaibi, der fast drei Sekunden hinter dem 16-Jährigen die Ziellinie erreichte. Dritter in Heat zwei wurde der Deutsche Richard Wagner. Über den Gesamtsieg in der GT4 freute sich Khaled Alahmadi aus Saudi Arabien in Rennen 1 und im zweiten Rennen der 15-jährige Österreicher Charlie Wurz, Sohn des ex-Formel-1-Fahrers Alexander Wurz.

Das nächste Gastspiel wurde im Rahmen der Formel-1-Premiere in Saudi-Arabien auf dem Straßenkurs von Jeddah ausgetragen. Insbesondere das erste Nachtrennen sorgte dabei für eine beeindruckende Atmosphäre im Rekordfeld der 25 Teilnehmer. Nicht neu war hingegen der Triumphator, er hörte auch auf dem Jeddah Corniche Circuit auf den Namen Schuring. Die saudischen Lokalmatadore Bandar Alesayi und Algosaibi begleitete ihn zur Siegerehrung. Einen Durchgang später meldete sich Dylan Pereira auf der obersten Stufe des Treppchens. Der Luxemburger begann schon den dritten Saisonlauf von der Pole Position, wurde in der ersten Kurve aber von einem Kontrahenten umgedreht. Nun gewann er das 150. Rennen des PSCME vor Alesayi und James Dorlin.

Am dritten Wochenende der Saison im Dubai Autodrome standen neben dem vielversprechenden Youngster aus den Niederlanden auch einheimische Talente im Rampenlicht. Algosaibi feierte am Freitag seinen insgesamt vierten Sieg in der PSCME, gefolgt vom Niederländer Lucas Groeneveld und von Wagner. Pech hingegen für Pole-Mann

Fahad Algosaibi kept young Dutchman Morris Schuring at bay in the battle for the Porsche Sprint Challenge Middle East title.

The Porsche Sprint Challenge Middle East returned for a landmark 13th season in the winter of 2021/2022, featuring the region's leading drivers, all competing in the powerful and dynamic Porsche 911 GT3 Cup (Type 992) and, for the second time, in Porsche 718 Cayman GT4 Clubsport (Type 982) cars at Bahrain International Circuit, "The Home of Motorsport in the Middle East".

Held as a support event to the WEC 8 hours of Bahrain, the first weekend was dominated by dutch teenager Morris Schuring, who won both races, the first one ahead of fellow countryman Daan van Kuijk, while Fahad Algosaibi from Saudi competed the overall podium-placers 9.259s back in third place. In race two, 16-year-old Schuring completed a fantastic double. This time he finished ahead of Fahad Algosaibi from Saudi Arabia, who was 2.886 seconds behind. Richard Wagner from Germany came third 4.295s back. Victory in the GT4-class, went to Khaled Alahmadi from Saudi-Arabia in race 1, and to till 15-year-old Austrian Charlie Wurz, son of ex-F1-driver Alexander Wurz, in race 2.

Morris Schuring

Podium at Yas Marina Circuit

Lucas Groeneveld

Fahad Algosaibi

van Kuijk und dem bisherigen Dominator Schuring. Letztgenannter startete eine optimistische Aktion, die damit endete, dass er selbst ausschied und van Kuijk nur auf Rang zwölf ins Ziel kam. Am Samstag gelang Schuring dann ein tolles Comeback: Er triumphierte in beeindruckender Manier vor dem erneut starken Algosaibi und vor Thierry Vermeulen, einem weiteren Niederländer im Starterfeld des PSCME.
Der Schauplatz der nächsten beiden Auftritte war nach zwei Jahren Pause der Yas Marina Circuit – und der sah bereits die erste Titelentscheidung. Schon nach dem ersten Durchgang sicherte sich Saudi Racing den Pokal für das beste Team der Saison. Den größten Erfolg im ersten Rennen holte sich Alesayi von eben jener Mannschaft Saudi Racing, der von der Pole Position direkt in Führung ging und diese bis zur Ziellinie nicht mehr abgab. Dabei durfte er sich keinen einzigen Fehler erlauben, denn Schuring war ihm über die gesamte Renndistanz auf den Fersen und kam knapp hinter ihm ins Ziel. Für den zweiten Lauf eroberte Schuring den besten Startplatz, den er auch in einen Sieg ummünzen konnte.
Doch am Ende hat es für den Teenager nicht gereicht, denn es war Algosaibi, der dem letzten Wochenende der Saison 2021/22 seinen Stempel aufdrückte. Im Rahmenprogramm der Formel 1 in Bahrain bejubelte er Rang eins im ersten Lauf vor Vermeulen und Alesayi und setzte sich auch im zweiten Heat im Kampf um P1 durch. Dieses Mal ließ er seinen härtesten Titelrivalen Schuring und Vermeulen hinter sich, den beiden Verfolgern blieben nur die Positionen zwei und drei. Und auch in der Abschlusstabelle musste Schuring sich mit der zweiten Stelle hinter Algosaibi zufriedengeben, Alesayi und der Brite Dorlin folgten auf den Plätzen drei und vier. Der frisch gekrönte Champion: „Natürlich freue ich mich total über diese Saison, vielen Dank an alle die mir das ermöglichten und ganz besonders an Lechner Racing für die Organisation so einer tollen Rennserie über all die Jahre."

Start at Bahrain international circuit

Organisation of Porsche Sprint Challenge Middle East

Jan Dobber

Sören Spreng

(l.-r.): Robert Lechner, Michael Schöch, Walter Lechner

(46): Saud Al Saud
(47): Khaled Alahmadi

Start at Jeddah Corniche Circuit

The second round took place as a support event to the Formula 1 debut in Saudi Arabia on a fascinating new street circuit, extremely fast, but tight and narrow at the same time, with the first night race providing a very impressive atmosphere for the record field of 25 participants. Victory in the two races of the weekend went to youngster Morris Schuring, who had already dominated the first weekend in Bahrain, in the fascinating night race on Saturday – ahead of local Saudi racers Bandar Alesayi and Fahad Algosaibi. Dylan Pereira, Porsche Mobil 1 Supercup champion in 2022, who had been on pole position, but was spun around in the first corner from behind, made up for his bad luck on Sunday, winning the 150th race of the PSCME, with Alesayi and James Dorlin on the podium as well. Both wins in the GT4-class again went to Charlie Wurz. The third weekend of the season at the Dubai Autodrome saw local talent in the limelight as well as the very promising youngster from the Netherlands. Fahad Algosaibi from Saudi Arabia celebrated his fourth victory ever in the PSCME in the first race on Friday, ahead of Dutchman Lucas Groeneveld and German Richard Wagner. Pro-Am class runner Algosaibi already came back as the leader from P4 on the grid at the end of the first lap, while the two front runners in qualifying, pole sitter Daan van Kuijk and his Dutch fellow countryman Morris Schuring were soon out of the race for victory. Schuring started an over-optimistic action, which ended in the two touching and himself having to retire and van Kuijk only finishing in P12. The second race on Saturday saw a great comeback for Dutch youngster Schuring: The 16-year-old won in an impressive way ahead of an again very strong Fahrad Algosaibi and another Dutchman, Thierry Vermeulen. The GT4 class was dominated by Saud Al Saud from Saudi Arabia, who claimed both pole positions and also both victories. For the next round after two years, the Porsche Sprint Challenge Middle East 2021/2022 came back to the Yas Marina Circuit – and already saw the first championship decision: After race one, Saudi Racing secured the team title, proving again that local talent is advancing more and more in this highly competitive series. It was Bandar Alesayi from Saudi Racing who claimed victory in the first race, taking the lead immediately from pole position and never losing it until the finish line. But the Saudi driver had to fight hard for his first win of the season, as Dutch youngster Morris Schuring was very close to him most of the race distance, finally finishing 0.517 seconds behind. In the second race it was Schuring who had claimed pole position and with a good start went to the lead ahead of his Saudi championship rival Algosaibi. GT4-class winners were Saud al Saud and Khaled Alahmadi. Schuring, who was going to celebrate his 17th birthday on the 20th of February, was happy about the victory, which kept him in close contention in the fight for the championship: "I am just 6 points behind before the final races at Bahrain in March, so everything is still possible!"

But in the end, it did not work out for the Dutch teenager. At the final round of the championship, held as a support race to the Bahrain F1 GP in March 2022, it was Fahad Algosaibi, who dominated the whole weekend and finally claimed the title. He won both races, the first one ahead of Thierry Vermeulen from the Netherlands, while Algosaibi's countryman Bandar Alesayi took the last spot on the podium.

In race 2, he was joined on the podium by the Dutch pair of Morris Schuring and Thierry Vermeulen. "Of course it is great to be able to celebrate this success on such a great weekend with two wins at such a great venue", the new champion was ever so happy. "Thank you to everybody who made this possible for me and especially to Lechner Racing for organizing such a great racing series for many years now." The wins in the GT4 class were claimed by Khaled Alahmadi and Saud Al Saud respectively, with Alahmadi also securing the title.

Jaber Al Khalifa, Chief Executive of Bahrain International Circuit (BIC) Sheikh Salman bin Isa Al Khalifa

Ali Al Khalifa

PORSCHE

150TH RACE
2009 - 2021
PORSCHE SPRINT CHALLENGE MIDDLE EAST

S. SPRENG

BWT

حلبة البحرين الدولية
BAHRAIN INTERNATIONAL CIRCUIT

MICHELIN
BOSS

JEDDAH
CORNICHE
CIRCUIT

PORSCHE
SPRINT CHALLENGE
MIDDLE EAST
LechneRacing

PORSCHE
SPRINT CHALLENGE

aramco
stc

Mobil
GP ELITE
BEEK CAPITAL

DORLIN

stc

BWT

Podium at Bahrain International Circuit

Richard Wagner

(l.-r.): Fahad Algosaibi, Morris Schuring, Richard Wagner

Mark J. Thomas

Fahad Algosaibi and HRH Prince Khalid bin Sultan Al Faisal Al Saud

DRIVER STANDINGS **GT3 OVERALL**

POS	NO	DRIVERS	TEAM	POINTS
1	7	Fahad Alogsaibi	Saudi Racing	213,5
2	1	Morris Schuring	BWT Junior Racing	197,5
3	77	Bandar Alesayi	Saudi Racing	188,5
4	8	Daan van Kuijk	Team GP Elite	151,5
5	23	James Dorlin	Team JDA	150,5
6	15	Lucas Groeneveld	Team GP Elite	140,5
7	69	Thierry Vermeulen	Team GP Elite	115
8	32	Alexander Malykhin	Team JDA	107
9	2	Ghislain Cordeel	Team GP Elite	102,5
10	87	Richard Wagner	DHL Team	95
11	4	Sören Spreng	Team GP Elite	93,5
12	72	Steven van Rhee	Team GP Elite	84
13	25	Jan Dobber	Team GP Elite	71
14	9	Andrey Mukovoz	Duwo Racing	53
15	55	Nicolas Misslin	JMB Racing	52
16	10	Ali Al Khalifa	Team Bahrain	50,5
17	3	Dylan Pereira	DHL Team	23,5
18	5	Mark J. Thomas	Team M3L	16
19	60	Fawaz Algosaibi	One Percent	6
20	12	David Grover	Roshn Team	6

DRIVER STANDINGS **GT4**

POS	NO	DRIVERS	TEAM	POINTS
1	47	Khaled Alahmadi	Saudi Racing	221,5
2	46	Saud Al Saud	Saudi Racing	216,5
3	41	Leo Willert	Heizer Monkeys Racing Team	118
4	45	Jaber Al Khalifa	Team Bahrain	92
5	40	Maciej Walenda	Lava Racing	86
6	48	Charlie Wurz	BWT Junior Racing	77,5
7	43	Mashhur Bal Hejaila	Mash Racing	65,5
8	43	"Ollie Jumper"	Drei Bruder Racing	65
9	44	Franz Dziwok	FDRS-FA1 Racing	40
10	17	Faisal bin Laden	Saudi Falcons	26,5
11	49	Saud Al Faisal	Al Faisal Racing	23,5
12	44	Bandar Alireza	Saudi Racing	19,5
13	42	Saud Abdulrahman	Al Saudia Team	19

TEAM STANDINGS

POS	TEAM	POINTS
1	Saudi Racing	428
2	Team Bahrain	142,5

DRIVER STANDINGS **GT4 CENTRAL EUROPE REGION CATEGORY**

POS	NO	DRIVERS	TEAM	POINTS
1	41	Leo Willert	Heizer Monkeys Racing Team	118
2	40	Maciej Walenda	Lava Racing	86
3	48	Charlie Wurz	BWT Junior Racing	77,5
4	43	"Ollie Jumper"	Drei Bruder Racing	65
5	44	Franz Dziwok	FDRS-FA1 Racing	40

Bandar Alesayi

VISIT CAYMAN ISLANDS SPRINT CHALLENGE GREAT BRITAIN

07.05.–08.05.2022	*Silverstone, UK*
28.05.–29.05.2022	*Thruxton, UK*
24.06.–26.06.2022	*Croft, UK*
08.07.–09.07.2022	*Oulton Park, UK*
10.09.–11.09.2022	*Brands Hatch, UK*
15.10.–16.10.2022	*Donington Park, UK*

Pro-Pilot Harry Foster und Am-Fahrer Carl Cavers triumphieren in der bisher längsten Saison der Porsche Sprint Challenge Great Britain.

Die dritte Saison der Porsche Visit Cayman Islands Sprint Challenge GB war die bisher größte; sie umfasste 15 Läufe und damit drei mehr als in den Vorjahren. In zwei Kategorien – Pro und Am – traten an sechs Wochenenden identische Porsche 718 Cayman GT4 Clubsport gegeneinander an.

Das Pro-Fahrerfeld bestand aus bekannten Namen und aufregenden Neulingen. Matthew Armstrong kehrte zusammen mit Charles Clark in die Serie zurück. Harry Foster, der Ende 2021 sein erfolgreiches Debüt gegeben hatte, wollte an diesen Schwung anknüpfen. Gegen die Etablierten kämpften auch die Newcomer Toby Trice, Matt Greenwood und Steve Roberts. Carl Cavers kam mit Ambitionen auf den Gesamtsieg in die Am-Klasse zurück, sah sich jedoch neuen Herausforderungen durch die Debütanten Rupert Laslett, John White, Jason Pelosi, William Tewiah und Timothy Creswick gegenüber, die alle versuchen wollten, dieser Kategorie ihren Stempel aufzudrücken.

Der Saisonauftakt in Silverstone war das erste Wochenende in der Geschichte der Serie, an dem drei Rennen auf dem Programm standen. Armstrong holte sich einen der drei Siegerpokale, Clark angelte sich die anderen beiden Trophäen. Cavers war derweil der Schrittmacher in der Am-Klasse, er konnte drei Erfolge verbuchen. In Thruxton, der schnellsten Rennstrecke Großbritanniens, war Foster drei Wochen später an der Reihe und eroberte den ersten Triumph seiner Porsche-Karriere, bevor er diese Leistung in Heat fünf wiederholte. Cavers und Laslett teilten sich die Am-Siege. Mit zweimal Rang eins kehrte Armstrong in Croft auf die Siegerstraße zurück. Pelosi etablierte sich derweil als neuer heißer Kandidat für Top-Platzierungen in der Am-Klasse, er ließ in beiden Läufen von Croft alle Am-Rivalen hinter sich. Die zweite

Toby Trice

Harry Foster

Stuart Gibson

(23): Jason Pelosi - (5): Rupert Laslett

Ben McLoughlin

Harry Foster in Pro and Carl Cavers in Am triumph in biggest Sprint Challenge GB season yet

The third season of Porsche Visit Cayman Islands Sprint Challenge GB was its biggest yet, taking place across 15 rounds – up from 12 in previous years. Continuing to showcase an important level of the Porsche Motorsport Pyramid, drivers in two categories – Pro and Am – raced identical 718 Cayman GT4 Clubsports across six weekends. The championship featured on the three largest domestic motorsport packages in the UK, racing in support of the British Touring Car Championship (BTCC), British GT Championship and Porsche Club GB Motorsport.

Eight teams, three returning and five new, entered the championship. Returnees – 2021 Teams champions Team Parker Racing, Redline Racing and Valluga – were challenged by newcomers Parr Motorsport, Deranged Motorsport, RaceLab, Raceway Motorsport and SVG Motorsport.

The Pro category driver lineup featured a mixture of familiar names and exciting newcomers. Matthew Armstrong (Team Parker Racing) made his return to the championship alongside fellow podium finisher, Charles Clark (Team Parker Racing). Having made his successful debut at the end of 2021, Harry Foster (Team Parker Racing) arrived looking to build on that momentum. Fighting the established order came new names Toby Trice (SVG Motorsport), Matt Greenwood (RaceLab) and Steve Roberts (Redline Racing).

Carl Cavers

Saisonhälfte begann in Oulton Park, wo sich Clark und Foster den Ruhm in der Pro-Kategorie teilten, während Laslett im Am-Feld dominierte.
Mitte September in Brands Hatch erlebte Foster dann ein perfektes Wochenende: Pole Position und Erster in allen drei Durchgängen, was ihn erstmals an die Spitze der Fahrerwertung katapultierte. Neueinsteiger Callum Davis beeindruckte bei seinem Debüt und fuhr in seinem erst zweiten Rennen in der Am-Klasse auf das Podium. Die beiden Am-Titelanwärter Cavers und Laslett gingen mit nur zwei Punkten Abstand in das finale Wochenende des Jahres und sorgten dafür, dass der Kampf in beiden Kategorien bis zum Schluss spannend blieb.
Donington Park sollte Mitte Oktober dann der Schauplatz für die Entscheidungen sein: Vier Fahrer hatten noch Chancen auf den Gesamtsieg, aber es war Foster, der am Ende die Nase vorn hatte und sich den Pro-Titel sicherte. Cavers zeigte sich unterdessen in der Am-Gruppe unschlagbar und konnte so den Titel in der Kategorie Am erringen. Die Mannschaft Parker Racing holte sich schließlich den Pokal für das beste Team.

Matthew Armstrong

(l.-r.): Jason Pelosi, Rupert Laslett, Carl Cavers

(9): Matthew Armstrong · (77): Charles Clark

Sam Smelt

Carl Cavers (Valluga) returned to the Am category with designs on outright glory, however, he would face fresh challenges from debutants Rupert Laslett (Raceway Motorsport), John White (Team Parker Racing), Jason Pelosi (Deranged Motorsport), William Tewiah (RaceLab) and Timothy Creswick (Parr Motorsport) as they each sought to make their mark on the category battle.

The Silverstone season opener hosted the championship's first ever triple-header weekend. Armstrong took a maiden victory but Clark emerged ahead chalking up two wins. Meanwhile, Cavers was the pacesetting Am, recording three category victories. At the fastest circuit in the UK, Thruxton, it was Foster's turn to take the first win of his Porsche racing career, before repeating the performance in round five. Cavers and newcomer Laslett shared Am category wins, establishing a close rivalry. Armstrong returned to winning ways with two overall victories at Croft, however, the weekend signalled the arrival of Roberts – he took pole position and ran his rivals close. Pelosi was a new winner in Am, recording two category victories. The second half of the season got underway at Oulton Park – Clark and Foster shared Pro glory setting up a four-way championship fight. Meanwhile, Laslett dominated Am, bringing his points tally closer than ever to that of rival Cavers.

The second triple header of the season at Brands Hatch saw Foster execute a perfect weekend – pole position and a hat-trick of wins, propelling him into the lead of the championship for the very first time. Newcomer Callum Davis (Valluga) impressed on his racing debut, achieving an Am category podium result in only his second ever race. Am title hopefuls Cavers and Laslett would arrive for the final three races separated by just two championship points, ensuring both category battles would go down to the wire.

Donington Park was the scene for the championship decider. Four drivers entered the weekend with a chance of claiming overall glory, but it was Foster who emerged ahead, securing the 2022 Pro category title at the penultimate race of the season. Meanwhile, Cavers put together a perfect weekend to take the Am category title in style. Each received their share of a healthy prize pot and a holiday for two to the Cayman Islands. Team Parker Racing took the Team Championship for 2022.

In 2023, as part of a three-year agreement, Sprint Challenge GB will race exclusively on the TOCA package. The championship will race in support of the BTCC on six weekends, four of those also alongside Carrera Cup GB. The 18-race season begins at Donington Park in April and concludes at Brands Hatch in October.

David Stirling

Harry Foster

Start at Oulton Park

(23): Jason Pelosi - (17): John White

Callum Davis

(56): Steve Roberts - (16): Harry Foster

Harry Foster

Matthew Armstrong

Charles Clark

William Tewiah

DRIVER STANDINGS **PRO**

POS	NO	DRIVERS	TEAM	POINTS
1	16	Harry Foster	Team Parker Racing	181
2	77	Charles Clark	Team Parker	165
3	56	Steve Roberts	Redline Racing	160
4	9	Matthew Armstrong	Team Parker Racing	149
5	11	Toby Trice	SVG Motorsport	109
6	25	Matt Greenwood	Race-Lab	93

DRIVER STANDINGS **AM**

POS	NO	DRIVERS	TEAM	POINTS
1	22	Carl Cavers	Valluga	191
2	5	Rupert Laslett	Raceway Motorsport	171
3	23	Jason Pelosi	Redline Racing	132
4	17	John White	Team Parker	118
5	86	Tim Creswick	Parr Motorsport	12
6	55	William Tewiah	Race-Lab	7
7	66	John Westbrook	Rob Boston Racing	0

TEAM STANDINGS

POS	TEAM	POINTS
1	Team Parker Racing	484
2	Team Parker	320
3	Redline Racing	317
4	SVG Motorsport	160
5	Valluga	135
6	Race-Lab	118
7	Raceway Motorsport	113
8	Deranged Motorsport	18
9	Parr Motorsport	15
10	Rob Boston Racing	0

Toby Trice

PORSCHE
SPRINT CHALLENGE
NORTH EUROPEAN ZONE

SPRINT CHALLENGE NORTH EUROPEAN ZONE

29.04.–30.04.2022	*Riga, Latvia*
10.06.–12.06.2022	*Botniaring, Finland*
30.06.–03.07.2022	*Pärnu, Estonia*
12.08.–13.08.2022	*Pärnu, Estonia*
26.08.–27.08.2022	*Alastaro, Finland*

Marius Bartkus

Thomas Padovani war der bestimmende Fahrer in der Porsche Sprint Challenge NEZ, doch auch andere Piloten konnten mit tollen Leistungen überzeugen.

Die Porsche Sprint Challenge NEZ 2022 umfasste fünf Rennwochenenden in drei verschiedenen Ländern. Die Saison begann im April in Bikernieki, wo der erst 17 Jahre alte Litauer Kajus Siksnelis den ersten Lauf für sich entscheiden konnte. Thomas Padovani und Thomas Kangro folgten ihm auf das Siegertreppchen. Einen Tag später war es an Padovani, als Erster vor Kangro und Tommi Haru abgewinkt zu werden. Der Pilot von Est1 Racing verließ Lettland als Tabellenführer.
Für das zweite Meeting ging es zum Botniaring. In Heat eins ließ sich Padovani auch von Safety-Car-Phasen nicht aus der Ruhe bringen und siegte klar vor Pole-Mann Mantas Janavicius sowie Kangro. Und auch Durchgang zwei auf der finnischen Rennstrecke wurde zur Beute von Padovani, der dieses Mal in Emil Westman und Janavicius seine stärksten Verfolger sah. Besonders beeindruckend war dabei die Leistung von Westman, der bei seinem Comeback in einem Porsche GT3 Cup der älteren Generation 991 gleich auf das Treppchen vorstieß.
Das dritte Rennwochenende der Saison wurde Anfang Juli auf dem Porsche Ring in Pärnu ausgetragen und auch dort haben seine Kontrahenten kein Mittel gegen die Dominanz von Padovani gefunden. Er triumphierte zweimal und baute seine Führung in der Gesamtwertung weiter aus. Während im zweiten Heat mit Kangro und Haru zwei bekannte Piloten neben Padovani auf das Podest kletterten, stellte sich im ersten Durchgang mit Newcomer Marius Bartkus ein frisches Gesicht neben den Dauersieger.
Mitte August führte die Reise der Porsche Sprint Challenge NEZ noch einmal zum Porsche Ring nach Estland. Lauf eins wurde bei Dämmerung gestartet, doch nachdem sich schon in der ersten Runde mehrere Fahrzeuge drehten, neutralisierte das

(39): Jani Käkelä - (47): Alex Ivanov - (14): Emil Westmann

Thomas Padovani was dominant in the 2022 Porsche Sprint Challenge NEZ

The 2022 Porsche Sprint Challenge NEZ consisted of five race venues in three different countries. Some of the 12 races, which featured a record number of entries, were organised together with the Batlic Touring Car Championship (BaTCC). It was Thomas Padovani, driving for the Est1 Racing team, who dominated the season and was the deserved champion. Thomas Kangro was second for Porsche Estonia while the rookie Jani Käkelä was third overall in the 39 Racing Team entry.
The most anticipated season ever kicked off in Bikernieki, Latvia, in April. Padovani emerged from the weekend in the lead of the championship having scored consistently in both races. Noteworthy was also the fantastic start to his GT racing career for 17-year-old Lithuanian Kajus Siksnelis.
The Finnish circuit of Botniaring hosted a round for the first time in June, and the event attracted a high number of entries. Mantas Janavicius (Porsche Lithuania) secured pole position in qualifying and two podium finishes, but it was Padovani

Jukka Eerola

(89): Jonne Kurikka - (44): Leo Messenger - (73): Get Jugala - (70): Raivo Tamm - (19): Nikolas Pirttilahti

Thomas Kangro

Jonne Kurikka

Safety Car das Treiben zunächst. Und als es nach dem Restart sofort wieder krachte, folgte der Abbruch mit der roten Flagge. Die folgenden beiden Rennen gewann abermals Padovani, der sich so den Titel schon vor dem Finalwochenende sicherte. Das Finale stieg im finnischen Alastaro, wo drei Läufe eingeplant waren. Und die wurden bei seiner Premiere in der Sprint Challenge alle in dominanter Art und Weise von Henri Tuomaala gewonnen, obwohl er nie zuvor ein GT3-Cup-Fahrzeug bewegt hatte. Alex Ivanov, der wie Tuomaala an diesem Wochenende sein Debüt in der Serie feierte, sah die Zielflagge dreimal als Zweiter und war auch im Qualifying Zweitschnellster hinter Tuomaala. Kangro holte zwei dritte Plätze und darf sich nun Vize-Champion nennen; Westman angelte sich in Alastaro einmal P3.

Team Relaa Racing

Nikolas Pirttilahti

(10): Tommi Haru - (48): Thomas Kangro - (77): Thomas Padovani

who dominated the results with two victories. The local Botniaring-ace Emil Westman made a comeback with great success by scoring a second place finish behind the wheel of a 991 generation car.

The third race weekend of the season was held in Pärnu on the fabulous Porsche Ring hosted by the Porsche Weekend Estonia. Padovani again dominated the weekend with two wins, and extended his championship lead still further. In the first race Marius Bartkus (Porsche Lithuania) drove a brilliant debut race and finished second. Padovani started the second race from pole position, and he was never headed. Kangro stepped up his game and followed closely to claim second, ahead of Tommi Haru in third place after a solid day of racing.

Pärnu hosted the next round in August, and it was a beautiful setting for the first race. In the fading light of day the cars set off, but multiple cars spun heading down the main straight, causing the safety car to bring the pack under control. The restart was no better, as several cars collided at the first corner and the race was red flagged for the night. The incidents on Friday resulted in fewer cars taking part in the racing on Saturday. Padovani capitalised on the opportunity to claim two brilliant victories and enjoyed a commanding lead in the standings, so much so that he was already a champion before the season had finished!

The PSCNEZ season 2022 finale took place in Alastaro at the end of August. The Porsche Club Finland Festival hosted three races and each of them was won by Henri Tuomaala (39 Racing) on his debut. He enjoyed a large margin over Alex Ivanov (Est1 Racing) who finished second in each race. Thomas Kangro completed the podium twice while Westman (JKW Motorsport) used every strategic trick to claim a well deserved third place in the second race. And that's with a 991 car against the 992s!

In 2022, Kangro was the best Junior Programme Driver. Kangro improved from last year's third place overall to an impressive second place this year, even having missed four races during the season.

Tomas Svidinskas

Raivo Tamm

Tommi Haru

PORSCHE

PORSCHE

PORSCHE

PORSCHE

ESTI AUTOSPORDI LIIT
ESTONIAN AUTOSPORT UNION
NANKANG

Marius Bartkus

Jani Käkelä

DRIVER STANDINGS

POS	NO	DRIVERS	TEAM	POINTS
1	77	Thomas Padovani	Est1 Racing	207,5
2	48	Thomas Kangro	Porsche Estonia	163
3	39	Jani Käkelä	39 Racing	87
4	10	Tommi Haru	THR Racing	86
5	89	Jonne Kurikka	39 Racing	84
6	73	Get Jugala	Est1 Racing	79,5
7	14	Emil Westmann	JKW-Motorsport	79
8	39	Henri Tuomaala	39 Racing	75
9	20	Raimo Niemi	Relaa Racing	74
10	18	Jukka Eerola	JPE Racing	71,5
11	11	Olli Kangas	SPP Racing	63,5
12	5	Mantas Janavicius	Team #5	61
13	5	Marius Bartkus	Team #5	60,5
14	47	Alex Ivanov	Est1 Racing	60
15	13	Daniel Skurnik	D-Sports	54,5
16	19	Nikolas Pirttilahti	Relaa Racing	45
17	92	Kajus Siksnelis	Porsche Lithuania	39
18	70	Raivo Tamm	Porsche Estonia	29
19	8	Anssi-Jukka Kasi	Relaa Racing	24
20	44	Leo Messenger	Rode Racing	22
21	46	Oliver Tiirmaa	Est1 Racing	22
22	72	Raimo Kulli	Est1 Racing	16
23	33	Simo P. Kangas	SPP Racing	15
24	92	Tomas Svidinskas	Porsche Lithuania	13,5
25	22	Jaari Ollila	SPP Racing	7,5
26	15	John K. Westmann	JKW-Motorsport	5

(l.-r.): Marius Bartkus, Thomas Padovani, Thomas Kangro

PORSCHE
SPRINT CHALLENGE
FRANCE

SPRINT CHALLENGE FRANCE

22.04.–23.04.2022	*Lédenon, France*
20.05.–21.05.2022	*Dijon, France*
09.06.–10.06.2022	*Le Mans, France*
24.06.–25.06.2022	*Val de Vienne, France*
26.08.–27.08.2022	*Magny-Cours, France*
07.10.–08.10.2022	*Paul Ricard, France*
21.10.–22.10.2022	*Le Mans, France*

Start at Dijon-Prenois

Benjamin Paque und Jean-Charles Carminati holen sich die Titel in der Porsche Sprint Challenge France, über 70 Autos beim Rennen in Le Mans.

Im zweiten Jahr der Porsche Sprint Challenge France klassierten sich insgesamt 92 Fahrer in den Wertungen Cup-Serie oder Sport-Cup-Serie. Doch es waren insbesondere diese zwei Piloten, die die Saison 2022 prägten: Benjamin Paque gewann die Cup-Serie für GT3-Cup-Fahrzeuge und Jean-Charles Carminati triumphierte in der Sport-Cup-Serie für GT4-Sport-Cup-Autos.
Für die Saison 2022 waren 47 Fahrzeuge fest eingeschrieben, weitere 33 Starter nahmen an ausgewählten Läufen der Sprint Challenge teil. Besonders beeindruckend war das Feld aber im Rahmen des 24-Stunden-Rennens von Le Mans, wo die Porsche Sprint Challenge France zudem noch 36 weitere Fahrer begrüßen durfte, die zum Teil von sehr weit her angereist kamen: aus China, Malaysia, Mexiko, Kanada und aus den USA. Den ersten Durchgang gewann Mardin Bashar, während Heat zwei an Jean Glorieux ging, den ehemals besten Gentleman im Porsche Carrera Cup France.
Die Abschlusstabelle der Cup-Serie sah letztendlich den erst 18 Jahre alten Benjamin Paque mit seinem Porsche GT3 Cup 992 auf Platz eins; der erfahrene François Chotard musste sich am Steuer seines GT3 Cup 991 II hinter dem Teenager anstellen.
In der Sport-Cup-Serie bestimmten Porsche 718 GT4 Clubsport das Geschehen. Jean-Charles Cartminati, Dimitri Verza, Bertrand Dumarcet und Charles Didier, die alle dieses Fahrzeugmodell ausgewählt hatten, belegten im Schlussklassement in dieser Reihenfolge die Ränge eins bis vier.

Benjamin Paque and Jean-Charles Carminati clinches tiltes, 71 cars at Le Mans opening races

The second season of the Porsche Sprint Challenge France confirmed the success of the first edition with 92 drivers classified in the championship, which saw two winners mark the season by their consistency and speed: Benjamin Paque in the Cup Series (for GT3 Cup cars) and Jean-Charles Carminati in the Sport Cup Series (for GT4 Sportcup cars).

A total of 47 cars were entered for the 2022 season, with a further 33 cars entered for one or more rounds of the championship, not forgetting the 71 cars that competed in the opening race of the Le Mans 24 Hours.

In Le Mans, the Porsche Sprint Challenge France welcomed 36 foreign drivers some of whom came from very far away: China, Malaysia, Mexico, Canada and the USA. The first race was won by the Emirati driver Mardin Bashar, while the second race went to the Belgian Jean Glorieux, former winner of the Porsche Carrera Cup France in the gentleman category.

In the general classification of the Cup Serie, if it is the very young Benjamin Paque who takes the victory at the top of his 18 years by having quickly taken the measure of the 992 GT3 Cup, he precedes the very experienced François Chotard at the wheel of his 991 GT3 Cup II, Yves Godard, the fastest of the drivers in 991 GT3 Cup I finishing fourth while the 991 GT3 R marked a little bit the gap, Olivier Rabot finishing only ninth of the Cup Series.

Podium at Le Mans

In the Sport Cup Series, it was necessary to drive a 718 GT4 Clubsport to be at the top of the ranking, as the first four drivers, Jean-Charles Cartminati, Dimitri Verza, Bertrand Dumarcet and Charles Didier, drove this model, Lucas Glinche, first of the 981 GT4 Clubsport cars, only finishing sixth, behind Gaétan Dupas who had been the fastest driver of the 996 GT3 Cup.

Organisation of Sprint Challenge France

(99): Benjamin Paque - (33): Marlon Hernandez

DRIVER STANDINGS **CUP**

POS	NO	DRIVERS	TEAM	POINTS
1	99	Benjamin Paque	CLRT	164
2	17	François Chotard	Chotard Team	151
3	21	David Sarny	Berto Moteurs	145
4	52	Yves Godard	Team 52	142
5	3	Franck Belard	DBG Motorsport	132
6	33	Marlon Hernandez	CLRT	131
7	9	Gilles Vannelet	Racing Technology	118
8	18	Roland Chotard	Chotard Team	114
9	4	Olivier Rabot	911 Impact	98
10	22	Emil Caumes	CLRT	88
11	3	Daniel Gerarduzzi	DBG Motorsport	85
12	8	Vincent Isavard	Berto Moteurs	84
13	88	Olivier Baharian	CLRT	80
14	44	Cyril Caillo	Racing Technology	77
15	12	Jean Marc Lesage	Berto Moteurs	74
16	50	Michel Ettouati	IMSA Performance	73
17	11	Jérôme Miloe	Racing Technology	68
18	31	Patrick Pelletier	Fun Circuit	67
19	44	Jean Luc Deblangey	Racing Technology	65
20	26	Yoan Forget	KMI	64
21	11	Jean-Louis Miloe	Racing Technology	62
22	7	Denis Papin	Racing Technology	59
23	9	Jean-Luc Beaubelique	Racing Technology	58
24	88	Franck Leherpeur	CLRT	56
25	19	Laurent Cochard	Berto Moteurs	53

DRIVER STANDINGS **SPORT CUP**

POS	NO	DRIVERS	TEAM	POINTS
1	67	Jean-Charles Carminati	Motorsport	160
2	64	Dimitri Verza	CG Motorsport	150
3	76	Bertrand Dumarcet	CG Motorsport	136
4	67	Charles Didier	Riviera Motorsport	131
5	65	Gaétan Dupas	DG Racing	128
6	72	Lucas Glinche	Glinche Racing	118
7	76	Damien Legrez	CG Motorsport	116
8	72	Hervé Glinche	Glinche Racing	108
9	75	Jérôme Daniel	Riviera Motorsport	108
10	69	Olivier Ornielli	MCG Propulsion	91
11	60	Richard Renault	IMSA Performance	78
12	69	Clément Ghielmini	MCG Propulsion	76
13	70	Rodolphe Gabrion	Rempp Racing	75
14	61	Cédric Toison	NAD Systems	72
15	63	Jean-Pierre Cardia	C6 Développement	70
16	67	Julien Goujat	Riviera Motorsport	55
17	71	Daniel Lamoulie	TLR	54
18	66	Mickael Drougard	DM Racing	53
19	68	Jacques Buche	CG Motorsport	36
20	62	Joannis Plagos	Ad Momentum Racing	35
21	111	Sylvain Noel	Racing Technology	33
22	111	Stéphane Bremard	Racing Technology	33
23	70	Fabian Bouche	Rempp Racing	24
24	64	Margaux Verza	CG Motorsport	24
25	111	Eric Thenier	Racing Technology	22
26	111	Frédéric Perriat	Racing Technology	20
27	111	Antoine Bosc	Racing Technology	12
28	68	Didier Jardin	CG Motorsport	11
25	19	Laurent Cochard	Berto Moteurs	53

TEAM STANDINGS

POS	TEAM	POINTS
1	CLRT	336
2	CG Motorsport	291
3	Riviera Motorsport	288
4	Racing Technology	273
5	Chotard Team	265
6	Berto Moteurs	265
7	IMSA Performance	171
8	DBG Motorsport Motorsport	155
9	911 Impact	153
10	Team 52	142
11	DG Racing	128
12	Glinche Racing	118
13	Rempp Racing	87
14	MCG Propulsion	84
15	NAD Systems	72
16	C6 Développement	70
17	Fun Circuit	67
18	KMI	64
19	Jaws Racing	57
20	TLR	54
21	DM Racing	53
22	JMP Team	48
23	Nourry Experience	39
24	Ad Momentum Racing	35
25	Team Fasse	30

PORSCHE
SPRINT CHALLENGE
BENELUX

SPRINT CHALLENGE BENELUX

20.04.–21.04.2022 Zandvoort, Netherlands
03.07.–04.07.2022 Zandvoort, Netherlands
20.07.–21.07.2022 Zolder, Belgium
11.09.–12.09.2022 Assen, Netherlands
13.10.–14.10.2022 Zandvoort, Netherlands

Niels Troost

Ein attraktives neues Format und ein spannender Wettbewerb machten die Porsche Sprint Challenge Benelux 2022 zu einem echten Erfolgsmodell.

Mit einem völlig neuen Format erlebte die Porsche Sprint Challenge Benelux eine erfolgreiche Saison 2022. Die fünf Veranstaltungen fanden unter der Woche statt, so dass alle Trainings und Rennen an einem Tag abgehalten werden konnten – was die Teilnehmer zu schätzen wussten. Austragungsorte waren Zandvoort und Assen in den Niederlanden sowie Zolder in Belgien. Die Sprint Challenge war 2022 offen für verschiedene Modelle des Porsche 911 GT3 Cup, sowie den Porsche Cayman GT4 Clubsport.

Die Saison begann in Zandvoort mit einem Gesamtsieg von Roger Hodenius. Danach folgte ein Duell zwischen den jungen Talenten Flynt Schuring und Jaxon Verhoeven. Schuring gewann am Steuer eines Elfers von Huber Racing fünf Läufe und wurde Champion in der Division I, die für Porsche 911 GT3 Cup vom Typ 992 reserviert war. Dem Speedlover-Duo Jaxon Verhoeven und seinem Vater Jean-Pierre Verhoeven blieben die Ränge zwei und drei der Divisions-Abschlusstabelle.

Michel Arfman war mit sechs Siegen der dominierende Fahrer in der Division II, die Porsche 911 GT3 Cup vom Typ 991 vorbehalten war. Der neue Champion sammelte fast dreimal so viele Punkte wie der zweitplatzierte Joel Uylenbroeck.

In der Division IV für Porsche Cayman GT4 waren es die jungen Piloten des Teams GP Elite, Sasha Norden, Cedric Chassang und Alexander Goddijn, die die Erfolge unter sich aufteilten und den Titelkampf in genau dieser Reihung auch beendeten. Patrick van den Berg schließlich war der Beste in der Division IV - Klasse 981.

With a completely new format, the Porsche Sprint Challenge Benelux enjoyed a 2022 season that bode well for 2023. Various models of the Porsche 911 GT3 Cup were entered, as were the Porsche Cayman GT4 Clubsport.

🇬🇧 The new format saw each of the five meetings take place on weekdays, and all the action on the same day. This was a feature that was appreciated by the drivers of all ages that were competing in the series.

The season started in Zandvoort with an overall victory for Roger Hodenius (Team GP Elite), but what followed was a battle between two young talents, Flynt Schuring (Huber Racing) and Jaxon Verhoeven (Speedlover). Schuring ended the season with five wins and was crowned champion in Division I for the Porsche 911 GT3 Cup – Type 992. Jaxon Verhoeven and his father Jean-Pierre Verhoeven (Speedlover) followed him in the points' standings.

Michel Arfman recorded six victories in Division II, which was reserved for the Porsche 911 GT3 Cup – Type 991. Arfman, in the colours of Team GP Elite, finished ahead of Joel Uylenbroeck (Xenum Motorsport by Speedlover).

In Division IV, reserved for the Porsche Cayman GT4, it was the young drivers of Team GP Elite who dominated the results. Sasha Norden, Cedric Chassang and Alexander Goddijn shared the successes between them, and they finished the championship in that order. Patrick van den Berg (PG Motorsport) was the best in Division IV – Class 981.

(l.-r.): Sacha Norden and Cedric Chassang

Micheal Arfman

Sacha Norden

Start at Zandvoort

DRIVER STANDINGS **TYPE 992**

POS	NO	DRIVER	TEAM	POINTS
1	16	Flynt Schuring	Huber Racing	170
2	9	Jaxon Verhoeven	Speedlover	144
3	9	Jean-Pierre Verhoeven	Speedlover	94
4	4	Floris Dullart	Team GP Elite	87
5	7	Niels Troost	Team GP Elite	86

DRIVER STANDINGS **TYPE 982**

POS	NO	DRIVERS	TEAM	POINTS
1	21	Sacha Norden	Team GP Elite	213
2	42	Cedric Chassang	Team GP Elite	184
3	71	Alexander Goddijn	Team GP Elite	138
4	14	Koen Munnichs	Team GP Elite	85
5	8	Lin Hodenius	Team GP Elite	83

DRIVER STANDINGS **GT4**

POS	NO	DRIVER	TEAM	POINTS
1	21	Sacha Norden	Team GP Elite	213
2	42	Cedric Chassang	Team GP Elite	184
3	71	Alexander Goddijn	Team GP Elite	136
4	33	Patrick van den Berg	PG Motorsport	91
5	14	Koen Munnichs	Team GP Elite	85

DRIVER STANDINGS **TYPE 981**

POS	NO	DRIVERS	TEAM	POINTS
1	33	Patrick van den Berg	PG Motorsport	269
2	90	Jasper Vlasblom	Team GP Elite	42
3	90	Stefan Boers	Team GP Elite	40
4	978	Frank van Asch	RFF	40
5	47	Jeroen Pronk	Team GP Elite	40

PORSCHE
MICHELIN
SPRINT CHALLENGE
AUSTRALIA

TITLE PARTNER MICHELIN

MICHELIN SPRINT CHALLENGE AUSTRALIA

27.05.–29.05.2022	Sydney Motorsports Park, Australia
05.08.–07.08.2022	Queensland Raceway, Australia
16.09.–18.09.2022	Sandown International Raceway, Australia
21.10.–23.10.2022	The Bend Motorsport Park, Australia
11.10–12.10.2022	Bathurst International, Australia
25.11.–26.11.2022	Phillip Island Grand Prix Circuit, Australia

Nach zwei Jahren Corona-Pause wurde wieder eine Sprint Challenge Australia ausgeschrieben, die in Thomas Sargent und Ryan Wood ihre dominierenden Figuren hatte.

Man sagt, dass es nur zwei Fahrzeuge braucht, um ein Autorennen zu veranstalten. Und obwohl die Porsche Michelin Sprint Challenge Australia 2022 mit einer Rekord-Teilnehmerzahl von 30 ein viel größeres Feld als nur zwei Fahrzeuge aufbieten konnte, waren es am Ende vor allem die Leistungen von zwei jungen Piloten, die der packenden Saison ihren Stempel aufdrücken: Thomas Sargent und der von Porsche Neuseeland geförderte Ryan Wood lieferten sich einen spannenden Titelkampf.
Die beiden Talente teilten sich in den ersten acht Läufen des Jahres jeweils die Plätze eins und zwei und erst ein unglücklicher neunter Rang in Tailem Bend sollte Wood die Chancen auf den Titel nehmen. Obwohl er mehr Rennen gewann als sein Kontrahent und bei jeder Veranstaltung auf der Pole Position stand, fehlten ihm in der Gesamtwertung aufgrund des einen Ausrutschers 19 Punkte, da sein Rivale Sargent frei von solchen Ergebnissen blieb. Hinter dem dominierenden Duo war der Kampf um den dritten Platz der Abschlusstabelle ebenso intensiv und wurde letztendlich von Rookie Aron Shields gewonnen, der Courtney Prince auf Position vier verwies.
In der Kategorie Morris Pro-Am holte sich Brett Boulton seinen ersten Porsche-Titel, nachdem er vor der Pandemie bereits zweimal Vize-Champion wurde. Er siegte vor dem scheidenden Titelverteidiger Sam Shahin, während Andrew Goldie die Saison als Pro-Am-Dritter abschloss.
In der Klasse B setzte sich mit Nathan Harburg schließlich überraschend ein Mann durch, der seine erste Saison im Motorsport absolvierte.

Ryan Wood

Ryan Wood

Two-way battle defines a thrilling, record year

🇬🇧 They say that it only takes two cars to put on a motor race and although the 2022 Porsche Michelin Sprint Challenge Australia Series had a record field of 30 cars, in the end it was the exploits of two special young drivers who put on a gripping season-long showcase at the front of the field. CHE Racing driver, Thomas Sargent, and Earl Bamber Motorsport driver, Ryan Wood put on a great show, finishing first and second in the first eight races of the year before the title was decided in Sargent's favour.

It was only an unfortunate ninth place at the Bend Motorsport Park, well past the series' half-way point, that ultimately ended Ryan Wood's chance to beat Sargent. Despite winning more rounds, more races and scoring pole at every event, Wood fell 19 points short in the final standings, while the consistency of Sargent allowed him to claim a faultless victory. Behind them, the fight for third was just as intense and was ultimately claimed by rookie Aron Shields, while Courtney Prince was fourth outright.

In Morris Pro-Am, Brett Boulton finally claimed his first Porsche title, having twice finished runner-up prior to the two-year pause for the series caused by the Pandemic. His victory came over outgoing champion Sam Shahin, who was second, while Andrew Goldie enjoyed a successful season in third.

In Class B, Nathan Harburg was a surprise winne rclaiming the class title, in his rookie season.

Podium at Queensland Raceway

(l.-r.): Lachlan Bloxsom, Brett Boulton, Tom McLennan, Aron Shields, Richard Cowen

Lachlan Harburg

Emanuel Mezzasalma

(8): Madeline Stewart - (23): Lachlan Bloxsom

(266): Jacob Li - (84): Brett Boulton - (29): Daniel Stutterd - (74): Ben Stack

(47): Thomas Sargent - (40): Ryan Wood - (23): Lachlan Bloxsom

Podium at Phillip Island

Nathan Sticklen

Madeline Stewart

Podium at Sydney Motorsports Park

Brett Boulton

Sam Shahin

Courtney Prince

Jacob Li

Thomas Sargent

DRIVER STANDINGS **PRO**

POS	NO	DRIVERS	TEAM	POINTS
1	47	Thomas Sargent	Targa Australia	852
2	40	Ryan Wood	Team Porsche New Zealand	833
3	116	Aron Shields	McElrea Racing	627
4	32	Courtney Prince	Sonic Motor Racing	585
5	23	Lachlan Bloxsom	Bloxsom Team Navy	573
6	59	Jason Miller	Stoke Skis Australia	476
7	88	Harrison Goodman	Sonic Motor Racing	445
8	8	Madeline Stewart	Earl Bamber Motorsport	365
9	81	Tom McLennan	Tom McLennan	182
10	26	Tom Taplin	Taplin Real Estate	141
11	38	Ollie Shannon	Tigani Motorsport	78

DRIVER STANDINGS **MORRIS PRO-AM**

POS	NO	DRIVERS	TEAM	POINTS
1	84	Brett Boulton	Bold Living	822
2	13	Sam Shahin	The Bend Motorsports Park	699
3	22	Andrew Goldie	Cirrus Aircraft	530
4	87	David Greig	DW Motorsport	485
5	35	Indiran Padayachee	Hyundai Forklifts	385
6	2	Richard Cowen	McElrea Racing	310
7	131	Graham Williams	Sonic Motor Racing	294
8	29	Daniel Stutterd	Tekworkx Motorsport	287
9	99	Ross McGregor	Southern Star Windows	267
10	5	Nathan Murray	Garage 1	214
11	100	Emanuel Mezzasalma	EJM Financial Services	213
12	11	Eric Constantinidis	Up to 11 Motorsport	174
13	29	Rob Woods	Tekworkx Motorsport	159
14	74	Christian Fitzgerald	EMA Motorsport	155
15	12	Matt Slavin	Ares Group	154
16	27	Sam Fillmore	Tekworkx Motorsport	135
17	24	Pan Boyaci	GRPB Racing	127
18	222	Scott Taylor	Scott Taylor Motorsport	126
19	18	Travis Knipe	Favrte Racing	85
20	74	Ben Stack	EMA Motorsport	80
21	20	Adrian Flack	Earl Bamber Motorsport	61
22	68	Terrence Knowles	Ashley Seward Motorsport	61
23	9	Marc Cini	Hallmarc	20

DRIVER STANDINGS **CLASS B**

POS	NO	DRIVERS	TEAM	POINTS
1	91	Lachlan Harburg	Autohouse Racing	578
2	266	Jacob Li	ASM/Mars Performance	553
3	34	Nathan Sticklen	Tekworkx Motorsport	552
4	85	Bradley Carr	Car Mods Australia	386
5	3	Jonathan Gliksten	Porsche Melbourne	300
6	58	Gerard Murphy	Australia Zoo	230

DRIVER STANDINGS **ENDURANCE CUP**

POS	NO	DRIVERS	TEAM	POINTS
1	47	Thomas Sargent	Targa Australia	288
2	40	Ryan Wood	Team Porsche New Zealand	231
3	116	Aron Shields	McElrea Racing	205
4	23	Lachlan Bloxsom	Bloxsom Team Navy	168
5	32	Courtney Prince	Sonic Motor Racing	166
6	59	Jason Miller	Stoke Skis Australia	159
7	88	Harrison Goodman	Sonic Motor Racing	143
8	84	Brett Boulton	Bold Living	101
9	13	Sam Shahin	The Bend Motorsports Park	73
10	8	Madeline Stewart	Earl Bamber Motorsport	95
11	81	Tom McLennan	Tom McLennan	50
12	87	David Greig	DW Motorsport	43
13	26	Tom Taplin	Taplin Real Estate	39
14	35	Indiran Padayachee	Hyundai Forklifts	38
15	74	Christian Fitzgerald	EMA Motorsport	32
16	22	Andrew Goldie	Cirrus Aircraft	31
17	29	Rob Woods	Tekworkx Motorsport	29
18	99	Ross McGregor	Southern Star Windows	29
19	24	Pan Boyaci	GRPB Racing	24
20	266	Jacob Li	ASM/Mars Performance	24
21	29	Daniel Stutterd	Tekworkx Motorsport	22
22	12	Matt Slavin	Ares Group	20
23	222	Scott Taylor	Scott Taylor Motorsport	20
24	9	Marc Cini	Hallmarc	20
25	2	Richard Cowen	McElrea Racing	20
26	68	Terrence Knowles	Ashley Seward Motorsport	17
27	11	Eric Constantinidis	Up to 11 Motorsport	15
28	131	Graham Williams	Sonic Motor Racing	15
29	85	Bradley Carr	Car Mods Australia	14
30	91	Lachlan Harburg	Autohouse Racing	14
31	38	Ollie Shannon	Tigani Motorsport	11
32	34	Nathan Sticklen	Tekworkx Motorsport	10
33	58	Gerard Murphy	Australia Zoo	9
34	3	Jonathan Gliksten	Porsche Melbourne	8
35	18	Travis Knipe	Favrte Racing	3
36	100	Emanuel Mezzasalma	EJM Financial Services	3

DRIVER STANDINGS **MICHELIN JUNIOR**

POS	NO	DRIVERS	TEAM	POINTS
1	47	Thomas Sargent	Targa Australia	744
2	40	Ryan Wood	Team Porsche New Zealand	710
3	116	Aron Shields	McElrea Racing	537
4	23	Lachlan Bloxsom	Bloxsom Team Navy	505
5	32	Courtney Prince	Sonic Motor Racing	501
6	8	Madeline Stewart	Earl Bamber Motorsport	307
7	88	Harrison Goodman	Sonic Motor Racing	292
8	26	Tom Taplin	Taplin Real Estate	81
9	38	Ollie Shannon	Tigani Motorsport	78

Pan Boyaci

Sam Shahin

PORSCHE
SPRINT CHALLENGE
CENTRAL EUROPE

OFFICIAL PARTNER
LechneRacing

SPRINT CHALLENGE CENTRAL EUROPE

13.05.–15.05.2022	*Brno, Czech Republic*
27.05.–28.05.2022	*Red Bull Ring, Austria*
10.06.–11.06.2022	*Slovakiaring, Slovakia*
26.08.–27.08.2022	*Hungaroring, Hungary*
09.09.–10.09.2022	*Most, Czech Republic*

Der junge Deutsche Colin Bönighausen hinterließ in der Porsche Sprint Challenge Central Europe seine ersten erfolgreichen Spuren im Automobilsport.

Nachdem im Vorjahr nur Porsche 718 Cayman GT4 Clubsport und Porsche 911 GT3 Cup in der Startaufstellung der Porsche Sprint Challenge Central Europe vertreten waren, kam 2022 als neues Highlight der Porsche 911 GT3 Cup der achten Generation (Modell 992) hinzu. Geblieben ist jedoch das charakteristische Rennformat der Serie. Bis zum Renntag hatten die Fahrer nach wie vor genügend Zeit, um gemeinsam mit den professionellen Instruktoren von Lechner Racing an ihrem Fahrkönnen zu feilen. Mit Ausnahme des Auftaktwochenendes in Brünn waren beide Qualifyings und alle Rennen auf den Samstag terminiert: Auf die beiden Sprints nach dem Mittagessen folgte am Abend der 100-Meilen-Langstreckenlauf.

Bereits im Qualifying für den ersten Sprint des Jahres tauchte ein neuer Name ganz vorne auf, den man sich fortan merken sollte. Colin Bönighausen holte sich Mitte Mai in Brünn die Pole Position für sein PSCCE-Debüt, behauptetet am Start die Führung, behielt auch beim Restart nach einer Safety-Car-Phase einen kühlen Kopf und sicherte sich seinen ersten Sieg in einem Rennwagen. Auch im zweiten Lauf war der erst 17-Jährige wenig später nicht zu bezwingen.

In der Klasse der GT4 Clubsport waren die Protagonisten des Auftakts der Pole Franz Dziwok und der Tscheche Milan Sitnianski. Dziwok übernahm aus der zweiten Reihe kommend zwar sofort die Führung, wurde in der letzten Runde aber von Sitnianski auf Rang zwei verwiesen. Im zweiten Heat machte Dziwok es besser: Wieder zog er zu Beginn des Laufs an Polesetter Sitnianski vorbei, doch dieses Mal gab er den Platz an der Sonne nicht mehr aus seinen Händen. Zusammen mit Lennart Marioneck konnte er am Abend auch noch den Sieg im Langstreckenrennen feiern.

Nach den Veranstaltungen Ende Mai auf dem Red Bull Ring, Mitte Juni auf dem

Maciej Walenda

Start at Hungaroring

Young German Colin Bönighausen made his first successful mark in car racing in the Porsche Sprint Challenge Central Europe

The Porsche 718 Cayman GT4 Clubsport enjoyed the limelight all by itself during the first two seasons of the Porsche Sprint Challenge Central Europe, in 2019 and 2020. Since 2021, the GT4 class shared the track with Porsche 911 GT3 Cup cars. The 2022 season brought what many participants and fans had been waiting for: The new eighth-generation 911 GT3 Cup (model 992) which took part in the Porsche one-make cup for the first time. The 911 GT3 Cup is the ideal machine for aspiring talent as well as for experienced professionals.

The unique race format of the Porsche Sprint Challenge Central Europe remained as entertaining as ever. There was plenty of time before race day for the drivers to hone their driving skills and find their limits together with professional instructors from Lechner Racing. With the exception of the opening weekend in Brno, both qualifying sessions and all races were scheduled for Saturday. The two sprint races were held after lunch followed in the evening by the popular 100-mile endurance race, which featured a driver change and the subsequent chase start, which is characteristic of the PSCCE.

(l.-r.): Robert Lechner, Maciej Walenda, Walter Lechner

(25): Vincent Höllwarth · (26): Ollie Jumper

Klaus Bönighausen, Colin Bönighausen

Slovakiaring und Ende August auf dem Hungaroring, bei denen vor allem Bönighausen und Dziwok einige weitere Triumphe zu ihrer Saisonbilanz hinzufügen konnten, kehrte die PSCCE für das Finale 2022 in die Tschechische Republik zurück. Mit Bönighausen und Vinzent Höllwarth teilten sich die beiden dominierenden Piloten der Saison die erste Startreihe des ersten Sprints von Most und der Österreicher konnte den jungen Deutschen in der Anfangsphase des Rennens erst einmal gehörig unter Druck setzen. Doch Bönighausen ließ sich nicht beirren und feierte einen weiteren Triumph. Der GT4-Erfolg ging erneut an Dziwok vor Sitnianski. In Durchgang zwei sah ein dominierender Bönighausen das Zieltuch mit elf Sekunden Vorsprung vor Höllwarth; in der GT4-Klasse wurde Dziwok von Tomasz Lach bezwungen. Die 100 Meilen von Most gingen ebenfalls an Bönighausen, während sich das Duo Marioneck / Dziwok den letzten Saisonsieg in der GT4-Klasse sicherte.
Talent Bönighausen gewann den GT3-Gesamttitel der Porsche Sprint Challenge Central Europe und war zusammen mit dem punktgleichen Schweizer Beat Ganz auch bester GT3-Teilnehmer der Langstreckenrennen. GT3-Pro-Am-Champion der Sprintwertung wurde Ganz, während der Am-Sprint-Titel in der GT3 an den Österreicher Franz Lahmer ging. Dziwok holte sich sowohl den Gesamt- als auch den Endurancetitel in der GT4, in der Christian Höllwarth als bester AM-Vertreter der Sprintwertung ausgezeichnet wurde.

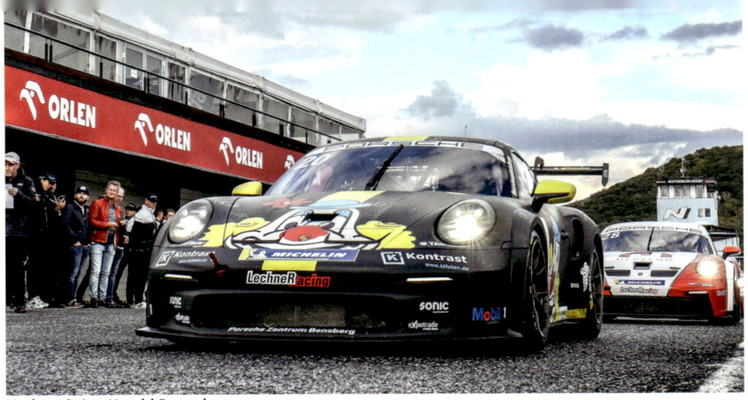

Herbert Geiss, Harald Proczyk

(l.-r.): Robert Lechner, Franz Maier, Walter Lechner

(16): David Assfalg, Ulrich Ziegler - (25): Vincent Höllwarth

Tomasz Lach, Maciej Walenda

Drivers and Team of Porsche Sprint Challenge Central Europe

Start at Slovakiaring

Organisation of Porsche Sprint Challenge Central Europe

Each of the venues on the 2022 schedule had already hosted world championship rounds on two wheels or on four, and so were at the highest of standards. Safety and a well-developed infrastructure are just as much a part of a PSCCE race weekend as the driving challenge. The 5.4-kilometre-long Automotodrom Brno hosted the start of the PSCCE Roadshow. In qualifying for the first sprint race one name emerged as a potential star of the future: 17-year-old Colin Bönighausen did not miss a beat and took pole position on his debut in the PSCCE.

At the start the young German showed incredible confidence to maintain his lead away from the grid. He kept cool at the restart after a Safety Car period and secured his first victory in a race car. Bönighausen was also the fastest driver in the second race and thus was a deserved double winner. The GT4 Clubsport class also took shape early on as Polish driver Franz Dziwok and Milan Sitnianski fought to the final lap. First blood was drawn by Sitnianski who celebrated his first GT4 victory in the PSCCE. Dziwok, last year's ProAM champion, struck back in the second race on Sunday, when again he overtook pole setter Sitnianski at the start, but this time he stayed in front to the chequered flag. Driving with Lennart Marioneck, he was also able to celebrate the victory in the Endurance race.

After events at the Red Bull Ring in Spielberg/Austria, the Slovakia Ring near Bratislava and the Hungaroring near Budapest, the PSCCE returned to the Czech Republic for the final round of 2022, at the Autodrom Most for the final showdown. "It's a very fast and technical track and we always feel very welcome when we come here," said Walter Lechner, Head & Promoter of the series. The final racing day of the season began with the Sprint race. Böninghausen and Vinzent Höllwarth were the two dominant drivers of the season and they shared the front row on the grid. For once the Austrian was able to apply pressure on the young German, but Böninghausen was faultless and scored another victory, finishing 2.6 seconds ahead of his rival, with Beat Ganz seven seconds further back. The GT4 victory again went to Dziwok ahead of Sitnianski. The second race saw Böninghausen finish 11 seconds ahead of Höllwarth, while in the GT4 class Dziwok was beaten by Tomasz Lach. The 100 Miles of Most also went to Böninghausen, while Marioneck/Dziwok secured the last win of the season in the GT4 class. Böninghausen won both the Overall and the Endurance Championship title. The GT3 ProAm champion was Beat Ganz from Switzerland, while the Am title went to Austrian Franz Lahmer. Franz Dziwok claimed both the overall and the endurance title in the GT4 class.

Franz Dziwok

Colin Bönighausen

(25): Vincent Höllwarth · (28): Freddy Kremer, Markus Sedlmaier · (8): Colin Bönighausen, Klaus Bönighausen

Leo Willert

(23): Alexander Hagen Berg, Pal Berg · (93): Zombor Nagy

Klaus Bönighausen and Colin Bönighausen

Pit lane at Autodrom Brno

(8): Colin Böninghausen - (25): Vincent Höllwarth - (26): Ollie Jumper

Ollie Jumper

DRIVER STANDINGS **GT3**

POS	NO	DRIVERS	TEAM	CATEGORY	POINTS
1	8	Colin Böninghausen	Bäderprofis.de	Pro	120
2	25	Vincent Höllwarth	PZ Inntal	Pro	89
3	19	Beat Ganz	Team FMT	Pro-Am	72
4	80	Alex Ellinger	Autopark Wien	Pro-Am	60
5	16	David Assfalg	HP Racing International	Pro-Am	55
6	26	Ollie Jumper	OJ	Pro-Am	51
6	16	Ulrich Ziegler	HP Racing International	Pro-Am	51
8	82	Franz Lahmer	Kogelbauer Motorsport	Am	39
9	63	Leo Willert	Heizer Monkeys Racing	Am	35
10	19	Peter Brunner	Team FMT	Pro	34
11	56	Günter Benninger	Promotech	Am	29
12	28	Freddy Kremer	Kogelbauer Motorsport	Am	28
13	23	Alexander Hagen Berg	Ohana Racing	Pro-Am	26
13	20	Herbert Geiss	HP Racing International	Am	26
15	15	Robert Lukas	Förch Racing	Pro	25
16	23	Pal Berg	Ohana Racing	Am	22
17	20	Harald Proczyk	HP Racing International	Pro	20
18	28	Markus Sedlmaier	Kremer Racing	Am	18
19	38	Stefan Rehkopf	Arkenau Motorsport	Pro-Am	17
20	32	Karol Kret	Förch Racing	Pro	10
21	36	Stefan Fuhrmann	MS Racing	Pro-Am	6
22	48	Volker Sigwarth	Team FMT	Am	4
23	28	Sebastian Daum	Kremer Racing	Pro	3

DRIVER STANDINGS **GT3 ENDURANCE**

POS	NO	DRIVERS	TEAM	CATEGORY	POINTS
1	8	Colin Böninghausen	Bäderprofis.de	Pro	79
1	19	Beat Ganz	Team FMT	Pro-Am	79
3	16	David Assfalg	HP Racing International	Pro-Am	76
4	26	Ollie Jumper	OJ	Pro-Am	62
5	16	Ulrich Ziegler	HP Racing International	Pro-Am	57
6	80	Alex Ellinger	Autopark Wien	Pro-Am	51
7	23	Alexander Hagen Berg	Ohana Racing	Pro	46
8	25	Vincent Höllwarth	PZ Inntal	Pro	40
9	19	Peter Brunner	Team FMT	Pro-Am	39
10	63	Leo Willert	Heizer Monkeys Racing	Pro-Am	34
10	23	Pal Berg	Ohana Racing	Pro-Am	34
12	82	Franz Lahmer	Kogelbauer Motorsport	Am	32
13	56	Günter Benninger	Promotech	Am	31
13	28	Freddy Kremer	Kogelbauer Motorsport	Am	31
15	20	Herbert Geiss	HP Racing International	Am	27
16	28	Markus Sedlmaier	Kremer Racing	Am	22
17	38	Stefan Rehkopf	Arkenau Motorsport	Pro-Am	14
18	8	Klaus Bönighausen	Bäderprofis.de	Pro-Am	13
19	36	Georg Karner	MS Racing	Pro-Am	12
19	36	Stefan Fuhrmann	MS Racing	Pro-Am	12
21	28	Sebastian Daum	Kremer Racing	Pro-Am	10
22	93	Nagy Zombor	Nagy Zombor	Am	7
22	48	Volker Sigwarth	Team FMT	Am	7

DRIVER STANDINGS **GT4 SPRINT**

POS	NO	DRIVERS	TEAM	CATEGORY	POINTS
1	69	Franz Dziwok	FA 1 Racing	Pro-Am	15
2	64	Tomasz Lach	Lava Racing	Pro-Am	96
3	64	Maciej Walenda	Lava Racing	Pro-Am	93
4	21	Milan Sitnianski	Sport Garage	Pro-Am	82
5	9	Christian Höllwarth	PZ Inntal	Am	28
6	9	Manuel Egginger	PZ Inntal	Am	20
7	37	Werner Panhauser	MS Racing	Pro-Am	14
7	47	Stefano Höge	Huber Racing	Pro-Am	14
7	47	Günter Höge	Huber Racing	Am	14
7	48	Peter Brunner	Team FMT	Am	14
7	37	Lena Knötzl	MS Racing	Am	14
7	9	Brendan Hölling	HP Racing International	Am	14
13	6	Reinhold Sampl	Winterfahrtraining.at	Pro-Am	12
13	6	Ronny Weiderer	Winterfahrtraining.at	Am	12
15	48	Volker Sigwarth	Team FMT	Am	10

DRIVER STANDINGS **GT4 ENDURANCE**

POS	NO	DRIVERS	TEAM	CATEGORY	POINTS
1	69	Franz Dziwok	FA 1 Racing	Pro-Am	125
2	64	Maciej Walenda	Lava Racing	Pro-Am	82
3	64	Tomasz Lach	Lava Racing	Pro-Am	82
4	21	Milan Sitnianski	Sport Garage	Pro-Am	90
5	9	Christian Höllwarth	Sport Garage	Pro-Am	31
6	9	Manuel Egginger	PZ Inntal	Pro-Am	17
7	37	Lena Knötzl	MS Racing	Am	17
8	37	Andreas Mayrl	MS Racing	Pro-Am	17
9	48	Peter Brunner	Team FMT	Am	12
10	48	Volker Sigwarth	Team FMT	Am	12
11	6	Reinhold Sampl	Winterfahrtraining.at	Pro-Am	10
12	6	Ronny Weiderer	Winterfahrtraining.at	Pro-Am	10

TEAM STANDINGS

POS	TEAM	POINTS
1	FA 1 Racing	360
2	Bäderprofis.de	320
3	Lava Racing	271
4	Sport Garage	236
5	PZ Inntal GT3	203
6	HP Racing International	192
7	Autopark Wien	159
8	OJ	149
8	Team FMT Brunner	149
10	PZ Inntal GT4	140
11	Heizer Monkeys Racing	115
12	Ohana Racing	106
13	Kogelbauer Motorsport	100
14	Kremer Racing	96
15	Team FMT Sigwarth/Ganz	93
15	HP International - Deiters	93
17	Promotech	84
18	MS Racing Knötzl/Panhauser	69
19	Förch Racing - Lukas	50
20	Arkenau Motorsport	45
21	Winterfahrtraining.at	34
22	Huber Racing	28
23	HP Racing International Hölling	24
23	MS Racing	24
25	Förch Racing - Kret	18
26	Nagy Zombor	14

PORSCHE
SPRINT CHALLENGE
SCANDINAVIA

SPRINT CHALLENGE SCANDINAVIA

13.05.–14.05.2022	*Scandinavian Raceway, Sweden*
17.06.–18.06.2022	*Drivecenter Arena, Sweden*
09.07.–10.07.2022	*Falkenbergs Motorbana, Sweden*
05.08.–06.08.2022	*Scandinavian Raceway, Sweden*
19.08.–20.08.2022	*Gelleråsen Arena, Sweden*
16.09.–17.09.2022	*Rudskogen Motorsenter, Norway*
30.09.–01.10.2022	*Mantorp Park, Sweden*

Carl Philip Bernadotte

Youngster William Siverholm heißt der neue Champion im hochkarätig besetzten Feld der Porsche Sprint Challenge Scandinavia.

Bei der zweiten Auflage der Porsche Sprint Challenge Scandinavia wurde der erst 17 Jahre alte William Siverholm zum Champion gekürt. Das Talent aus Lerum in der Nähe von Göteborg hatte zuvor erst ein Jahr Rennerfahrung gesammelt. In der Porsche Sprint Challenge entwickelte sich Siverholm schnell zu einem Spitzenfahrer, doch sein jugendlicher Überschwang und seine mangelnde Erfahrung standen ihm hin und wieder im Weg. Anfangs mischte er so Podiumsplätze mit dem einen oder anderen Ausfall und der einen oder anderen Strafe. Doch seine Schnelligkeit stand nie in Frage und es war offensichtlich, dass er das Zeug dazu hatte, ganz vorne mitzufahren.

Im Laufe der Saison arbeitete er sich immer weiter Richtung Spitze und nach dem zweiten Gastspiel auf der ehemaligen Formel-1-Strecke von Anderstorp fand er sich dann an erster Stelle der Fahrerwertung wieder, die er bis zum Schluss nicht mehr abgab. Die Titelentscheidung fiel Mitte September im Rudskogen Motorsenter, wo Siverholm beide Läufe von der Pole Position aus gewann.

Kenneth Ahnelöv ging als Tabellenzweiter ins Finale in Mantorp Park, doch nachdem er in einen Zwischenfall am Start verwickelt wurde, humpelte er als enttäuschender Zehnter über die Ziellinie. Janne Gustavssons Aufholjagd brachte ihn noch vor Ahnelöv auf den zweiten Rang der Abschlusswertung. Krister Andero, der nach vier Jahren im Porsche Carrera Cup seine erste Saison in der Porsche Sprint Challenge bestritt, reihte sich als Vierter ein und ließ mit Fredrik Blank, Ludwig Ellhage und Svante Andersson drei von Siverholms Teamkollegen hinter sich.

Der norwegische Skistar Aksel Lund Svindal und der schwedische Prinz Carl Philip, zwei der bekanntesten Gesichter der Sprint Challenge Scandinavia, belegten trotz

Youngster William Siverholm new champion in star-studded field

The Porsche Sprint Challenge Scandinavia, in its second year, saw a new young driver being crowned as the champion. Starting the season in May aged just 16, William Siverholm had only just turned seventeen when he celebrated his first championship title in his racing career.

Siverholm entered the series together with the top team Stenhaga Motorsport after only one year of racing experience behind him. The karting talent from Lerum, in the Gothenburg vicinity, made his racing debut in Formula Nordic in 2021 and finished fourth in the standings.

Siverholm quickly developed into a top driver in Porsche Sprint Challenge, but his youthful exuberance and lack of experience also made the race directors watch him closely. Initially, he mixed podium finishes with the odd retirement and one or two penalties but his speed was never in question and it was obvious that he had what it took to fight for the championship.

He was third in the standings after the second race, second after the third and with the second stop at the former F1-circuit at Anderstorp, he was on top of the points table and he kept his lead all the way to the finish.

Despite his early success in the championship, the first win eluded him until the sixth race of the season. Siverholm dominated at Rudskogen Motorsenter where he won both heats from pole position, a result that secured the championship title.

(l.-r.): Ludwig Ellhage, Kenneth Ahnelöv, Fredric Blank

Jonas Sjöström

(43): Janne Gustavsson - (7): Krister Andero

Aksel Lund Svindal and Ingemar Stenmark

einiger ausgelassener Rennen die Ränge acht und neun des Schlussklassements. Lund Svindal triumphierte beim Auftakt in Anderstorp und ließ in der Drivecenter Arena zwei weitere Podiumsplatzierungen folgen. Wegen Verpflichtungen außerhalb des Motorsports verpasste der ehemalige alpine Skirennläufer, mehrfache Olympiasieger und Weltmeister dann einige Durchgänge und verlor so den Anschluss an die vorderen Positionen der Gesamtwertung.

Prinz Carl Philip, seit vielen Jahren im Porsche Carrera Cup Scandinavia unterwegs, trat 2022 nur zweimal in der Sprint Challenge Scandinavia an. Dies tat er in überzeugender Weise: Er gewann alle vier Läufe, an denen er teilnahm.

Aksel Lund Svindal und Prinz Carl Philip hatten mit der schwedischen Ski-Alpin-Ikone Ingemar Stenmark einen nicht minder bekannten Teamkollegen in der Mannschaft Porsche Experience Racing. Der 66-Jährige, der erst 2021 in den Motorsport einstieg, ließ sich als beste Platzierung einen sechsten Rang gutschreiben.

Wann immer einer des prominenten Trios verhindert war, bot Porsche Schweden die Fahrzeuge anderen Motorsportlern an. So startete unter anderem Mikaela Åhlin-Kotulinsky, die erfolgreichste Motorsportlerin Schwedens, an zwei Rennwochenenden und gewann drei Läufe.

(l.-r.): Krister Andero, Janne Gustavsson, William Siverholm

Thomas Karlsson

Krister Andero

Fredric Blank

William Siverholm

Kenneth Ahnelöv

Another 17-year-old impressed in Norway. Norwegian Isabell Rustad – daughter of the former racing and rallycross star Tommy Rustad – delighted the home crowd by finishing the two races in third and second places.

None of the three title contenders, Janne Gustavsson, Kenneth Ahnelöv or Krister Andero, could match the consistency of Siverholm. Ahnelöv, who was ahead in the standings after three races, held the runner-up position in the championship heading into the final heat. Having been involved in an incident in the start, he limped across the finish line in a disappointing tenth place. Gustavsson's late season charge elevated him to second place in the championship.

Andero, who drove his first Porsche Sprint Challenge season after having spent four years in Porsche Carrera Cup, finished fourth, keeping three of Siverholm's team colleagues, Fredric Blank, Ludwig Ellhage and Svante Andersson, at bay. Two of the more prolific drivers in the championship, the Norwegian alpine star Aksel Lund Svindal and Prince of Sweden, Carl Philip, finished eighth and ninth respectively.

Lund Svindal won the first heat of the season premiere at Scandinavian Raceway in Anderstorp and followed up with two more podium finishes at Drivecenter Arena. Two races into the season he held the lead in the championship. However, due to other engagements outside of racing, he missed two races and lost touch with the lead in the championship. However, the former alpine skiing and multiple Olympic and World Championship gold medalist managed one more podium finish before the season was over.

Prince Carl Philip, who has been a Porsche Carrera Cup Scandinavia driver for many seasons, ran a reduced racing programme for 2022 and made just two appearances. However he made them count and won all four heats in which he took part.

Also racing in the Porsche Experience Racing team was the Swedish alpine skiing icon Ingemar Stenmark. The 66-year-old, who jump-started his racing career in 2021, was not that far off his younger competitors. Stenmark, who still has the most alpine World Cup wins to his credit, 86, had a best finish of sixth.

When the prolific trio was unable to drive, Porsche Sweden offered the Porsche Experience Racing seats to other drivers. Mikaela Åhlin-Kottulinsky, the most successful female driver of Sweden, drove two races and won three heats. On his home track in Falkenberg, the Carrera Cup-driver Thomas Karlsson used the opportunity to finish with a win and a second place.

In total, nineteen drivers took part in the championship that was held over seven races and fourteen heats. Seven drivers were credited with wins, eleven took to the podium.

JULA

WÜRTH WÜRTH

PORSCHE
CARRERA CUP
SCANDINAVIA

William Siverholm

Kenneth Ahnelöv and Race Team Gelleråsen - By AFR

Svante Andersson

Ludwig Ellhage

Isabell Rustad

DRIVER STANDINGS

POS	NO	DRIVERS	TEAM	POINTS
1	5	William Siverholm	Stenhaga Motorsport	227
2	43	Janne Gustavsson	JPG Motorsport	188
3	64	Kenneth Ahnelöv	Race Team Gelleråsen - By AFR	182
4	7	Krister Andero	Prido Racing	167
5	79	Fredric Blank	Stenhaga Motorsport	145
6	96	Ludwig Ellhage	Stenhaga Motorsport	134
7	44	Svante Andersson	Stenhaga Motorsport	129
8	82	Aksel Lund Svindal	Porsche Experience Racing	118
9	13	Carl Philip Bernadotte	Porsche Experience Racing	102
10	19	Mikaela Åhlin-Kottulinsky	Porsche Experience Racing	84
11	56	Ingemar Stenmark	Porsche Experience Racing	78
12	11	Jonas Sjöström	Fragus Motorsport	74
13	10	Pär Englund	Englund Motorsport	63
14	3	Erik Sandell	Pro-Alloy	50
15	9	Thomas Karlsson	Mtech Competition	45
16	24	Isabell Rustad	HTB Racing	37
17	14	Peter Kjellsson	ALT Racing	37
18	16	Thomas Tedenström	Eken Motorsport	26
19	8	Sigurd Wongraven	AutoTech-Sport	13

Carl Philip Ber■adotte and
Aksel L■nd Svindal

C6 BANK MASTERCARD SPRINT CHALLENGE BRASIL

02.04.–03.04.2022	*Goiania, Brazil*
23.04.–24.04.2022	*Velocitta, Brazil*
11.06.–12.06.2022	*Interlagos, Brazil*
11.08.–12.08.2022	*Termas de Río Hondo, Brazil*
08.10.–09.10.2022	*Goiania, Brazil*
12.11.–13.11.2022	*Interlagos, Brazil*

In einem spannenden Finale vor Formel-1-Kulisse gewann Raijan Mascarello beim Debüt des Porsche 911 GT3 Cup 991.2 die Porsche Sprint Challenge Brasil.

(l.-r.): Gustavo Zanon, Guilherme Bottura, Miguel Mariotti, Josimar Jr, Sang Ho Kim

Viel Neues in der Porsche Sprint Challenge Brasil: In dieser Saison wurde erstmals der Porsche 911 GT3 Cup 991 der zweiten Generation eingesetzt, der bis 2021 noch im Carrera Cup verwendet wurde. Außerdem änderte sich der Name der Serie: Aus Porsche GT3 Cup Challenge wurde Porsche Sprint Challenge.

Die gesamte Saison der Sprint Challenge zeichnete sich durch viel Spannung aus, in zwölf Rennen gab es acht verschiedene Sieger. Raijan Mascarello, Cristian Mohr, Marcelo Tomasoni, Nelson Marcondes und Daniel Correa reisten mit Titelchancen zum Formel-1-Grand-Prix nach São Paulo, in dessen Rahmen die Sprint Challenge vor vollem Haus ihr stimmungsvolles Finale austrug.

Doch bevor es zur Entscheidung kam, wurde der Porsche 911 GT3 Cup 991.2 unfreiwillig auf seine Sicherheit geprüft. An Nelson Marcondes' Elfer platzte in Goiania vier Wochen vor dem Finale bei Vollgas ein Reifen, nachdem er über Trümmerteile gefahren ist. Mit einer Geschwindigkeit von 158 km/h schlug er in die Streckenbegrenzung ein, beim Aufprall wurden 4,5 G gemessen. Trotz des heftigen Aufpralls stieg Marcondes allein aus seinem Porsche aus und bewies so, wie sicher dieser ist.

Zurück zum Sportlichen: Jener Marcondes gewann beim Finalwochenende zwar beide Durchgänge, doch das reichte nicht aus, um sich an die Spitze der Gesamtwertung zu setzen. Correa und Tomasoni wurden im ersten Heat in Unfälle verwickelt und schieden ebenso aus dem Titelkampf aus. So hatten im letzten Rennen der Saison nur noch Mascarello und Mohr Chancen auf den großen Wurf.

Und das Finale war voller Dramatik: Mascarello wurde gleich nach dem Start in die Reifenstapel geschoben, nachdem ein gewagtes Manöver von Caio Castro schief ging. Nun musste Mohr nur noch Fünfter werden und er hätte sich zum Champion gekrönt. Und

Daniel Correa

(l.-r.): Ayman Darwich, Marcelo Tomasoni, Raijan Mascarello, Cristian Mohr, Daniel Correa

(55): Ramon Alcaraz - (20): Vina Neves - (14): André Gaidzinski

In a thrilling finale in front of a Formula 1 crowd, Raijan Mascarello won the Porsche Sprint Challenge Brazil in which the Porsche 911 GT3 Cup 991.2 made its debut

There were changes afoot in the Porsche Carrera Cup as the entry level category was renamed as the Sprint Challenge, in keeping with new Porsche strategy around the world, and the class entrants were equipped with the 4-litre 911 GT3 Cup 991 phase 2 cars that were previously used in the Carrera Cup. The phase 1 car was retired, along with the GT3 Cup name, after seven highly successful seasons.
It was a nail-biting Sprint Challenge season throughout as drivers got used to the new car. Through the 12-race season, there were eight different winners, which demonstrated how hard it was to become a two-time winner. It was little surprise, then that at the final round of the year, held in front of the Grand Prix crowd at Interlagos ahead of the Brazilian Grand Prix, an impressive five drivers had the chance to become the champion.

Before that final race, though, the Porsche 911 GT3 Cup 991.2 had its safety record once more put up benefitted to the test, and it passed with flying colors. Nelson Marcondes was the driver who benefited from the latest safety improvements of the car. He was flat out at the Goiania track heading to turn 2 when his tyre burst due to debris on the track. From that point Marcondes was a passenger, crashing through the guard rail having left the track at a speed of 215km/h and with an impact speed against the protection wall of 158km/h. That initial impact recorded 4.5G. The guard rail was split in half and the tyre barrier beyond was the only thing that managed to contain the car. Even with the race being cut short, Marcondes walked away from his car, once more demonstrating how safe the Porsche 911 GT3 Cup is. And the beloved driver not only walked away but handed out the trophies to the winners of the race. Despite the crash, Marcondes was one of the five drivers who were in with a chance of claiming the title at the finale of the season. Raijan Mascarello went to the last race as the points leader, followed by Cristian Mohr, Marcelo Tomasoni, Marcondes, and Daniel Correa. After such an equal season, the driver who had scored more regularly

Urubatan Jr.

(5): Marcelo Tomasoni - (77): Josimar Jr - (1): Urubatan Jr. - (20): Vina Neves

(80): Raijan Mascarello - (22): Caio Castro - (199): Nelson Marcondes

auch wenn er um diese Position kämpfte, hatte er sie im Laufe der 25 Rennminuten nie inne. Im letzten Umlauf versuchte er dann nochmal Alles, um Vordermann Ayman Darwich zu überholen – was in einem Ausfall von Mohr mündete. Somit ging der Titel in die Hände von Mascarello, der schließlich sieben Punkte Vorsprung vor Vize-Champion Marcondes hatte.

In der Sprint Challenge Sport stand der Titelgewinner bereits vor dem Finale fest. Guilherme Bottura dominierte die Saison und lieferte sein Meisterstück im dritten Meeting in Interlagos ab, als er zur Überraschung aller sogar das gesamte Rennen gewann, also auch alle Starter aus der Sprint Challenge hinter sich ließ. Und schließlich ging der Pokal für den besten Teilnehmer der Sprint Challenge Rookie an Gustavo Zanon.

André Gaidzinski

(l.-r.): Urubatan Jr., Marcelo Tomasoni, Daniel Correa, Caio Castro, Miguel Mariotti

was likely to be crowned champion. Although Marcondes won both races in the final round, he couldn't score enough points to become champion due to his retirements from other races earlier in the year. Correa and Tomasoni got caught up in isolated accidents and forfeited their championship hopes. And so there were only two left remaining in contention: Mascarello and Mohr as the season went to the final race.
And the grand finale was filled with drama. Mascarello retired immediately after the race started. Having lined up second on the grid, right before the "S" of Senna turn, Caio Castro made a move, but it didn't pay off and he collided with Raijan. Both ended up at the tyre wall and Raijan took no further part in the race. Instead, he watched the entirety of the race from inside the medical car, rooting for everyone other than Cristian Mohr, who would become champion if he finished fifth or better.
The race went the full distance of 25 minutes + 1 lap, and Mohr was fighting to gain that crucial fifth position but he never achieved it. It was on the last lap that Mohr decided he had nothing left to lose, and made a move to overtake Ayman Darwich at the Lake's Curve. Unfortunately for Mohr, he ended up oversteering into the tyre wall and with that went his hopes of winning the title. The Champion was therefore the capable and deserving Raijan Mascarello, who finished on 156 points, seven ahead of the runner up, Nelson Marcondes. Marcelo Tomasoni was third, followed by Cristian Mohr on 143. Urubatan Junior rounded out the top five.
As for the Sprint Challenge Sport class, the championship arrived at the finale with its title already decided. Guilherme Bottura dominated the 2022 season, and was able to take the fight to more experienced drivers of the Overall category. He even won on the main class, Sprint Challenge, at Interlagos in the third round, much to everyone's surprise. Bottura finished the year on 103 points, a brutal difference compared to the runner-up, Josimar Junior who ended the season an incredible 29 points behind. Miguel Mariotti, Gustavo Zanon and Ramon Alcaraz rounded off the top five places.
For the Sprint Challenge Rookie Class, Gustavo Zanon also won by a comfortable margin. After a dominant season, he arrived at Interlagos for the finale with the title already won. He ended the season 23 points ahead of south Korean driver Sang Ho Kim with Nasser Aboultaif, Piero Cifali, and Junior Dinardi completing the top five.

Raijan Mascarello

Nelson Marcondes

Mobil
Mobil
Mobil

mastercard
C6BANK

Hytera

DRS

(22): Caio Castro - (80): Raijan Mascarello - (199): Nelson Marcondes

Josimar Jr

(78): Rafael Cardoso - (7): Piero Cifali - (71): Sang Ho Kim

Guilherme Bottura

Nelson Marcondes

DRIVER STANDINGS SPRINT CHALLENGE

POS	NO	DRIVERS	POINTS
1	80	Raijan Mascarello	156
2	199	Nelson Marcondes	149
3	5	Marcelo Tomasoni	147
4	3	Cristian Mohr	143
5	1	Urubatan Junior	123
6	117	Guilherme Bottura	114
7	69	Daniel Correa	101
8	555	Ayman Darwich	99
9	77	Josimar Junior	80
10	21	Miguel Mariotti	80
11	22	Caio Castro	78
12	11	Márcio Mauro	73
13	20	Vina Neves	71
14	17	Ricardo Fontanari	70
15	55	Ramon Alcaraz	65
16	33	Gustavo Zanon	55
17	14	André Gaidzinski	49
18	71	SangHo Kim	41
19	99	Nasser Aboultaif	24
20	58	Cláudio Simão	21
21	7	Piero Cifali	21
22	2	Junior Dinardi	18
23	66	Sadak Leite	5
24	83	Marco Billi	2
25	78	Rafael Cardoso	0
26	52	Beto Posses	0

DRIVER STANDINGS ROOKIE

POS	NO	DRIVERS	POINTS
1	33	Gustavo Zanon	105
2	71	SangHo Kim	82
3	99	Nasser Aboultaif	73
4	7	Piero Cifali	72
5	2	Junior Dinardi	50
6	78	Rafael Cardoso	8
7	66	Sadak Leite	8

DRIVER STANDINGS SPRINT SPORT

POS	NO	DRIVERS	POINTS
1	117	Guilherme Bottura	103
2	77	Josimar Junior	74
3	21	Miguel Mariotti	69
4	33	Gustavo Zanon	65
5	55	Ramon Alcaraz	65
6	14	André Gaidzinski	56
7	71	SangHo Kim	41
8	99	Nasser Aboultaif	32
9	58	Cláudio Simão	23
10	2	Junior Dinardi	23
11	7	Piero Cifali	23
12	78	Rafael Cardoso	4
13	66	Sadak Leite	4
14	52	Beto Posses	0

(l.-r.): Claudio Simão, Guilherme Bottura, Miguel Mariotti, Ramon Alcaraz, André Gaidzinski

PORSCHE
SPRINT CHALLENGE
JAPAN

SPRINT CHALLENGE JAPAN

03.04.2022	Fuji International Speedway, Japan
15.05.2022	Sportsland Sugo, Japan
26.06.2022	Fuji International Speedway, Japan
04.09.2022	Suzuka Circuit, Japan

Hideki Ogiwara

Ken Yamamoto heißt der neue Champion der GT3-I in der Porsche Sprint Challenge Japan, während Sena Yamamoto alle acht Läufe der GT4-Kategorie gewann.

Die vierte Ausgabe der Porsche Sprint Challenge Japan erfuhr einige Änderungen. Da im Porsche Carrera Cup Japan ab 2022das neue Cup-Modell des Typ 992 eingesetzt wurde, wurden die GT3-Cup-Porsche der zweiten Generation des Typs 991, die zuvor im Carrera Cup gefahren wurden, ab diesem Jahr in der Klasse GT3-I der Porsche Sprint Challenge Japan genutzt. Gleichzeitig wechselte die GT3-II-Klasse von den 997 zu den Cup-Rennern vom Typ 991 der ersten Generation. Somit waren in beiden GT3-Kategorien der Sprint Challenge Japan ab dieser Saison nur noch Cup-Fahrzeuge vom Typ 991 am Start.

Die Saison 2022 begann Anfang April auf dem Fuji International Speedway und bestand aus insgesamt vier Veranstaltungen à zwei Rennen. Das Finale stand Anfang September in Suzuka auf dem Programm.

In der Klasse GT3-I zeigte Ken Yamamoto, der erstmals in der PSCJ antrat, mit vier Siegen und vier zweiten Plätzen eine meisterliche Leistung und sicherte sich bereits zwei Läufe vor Saisonschluss den Titel.

Die Kategorie GT3-II gewann Hideki Ogiwara, seit der Einführung der PSCJ treuer Teilnehmer der Serie. Er hatte am Ende fünf Punkte mehr auf seinem Konto als Shunsuke Sato, der neue Vize-Champion der GT3-II.

Und schließlich entschied Sena Yamamoto die für Porsche 718 Cayman GT4 reservierte GT4-Klasse in einer Art und Weise für sich, die keine Zweifel an seinem Talent aufkommen ließen. Der vom Porsche Japan Junior Programm unterstützte Rennfahrer triumphierte in allen acht Heats in seiner Klasse.

Ken Yamamoto is the new GT3-I champion in the Porsche Sprint Challenge Japan while Sena Yamamoto managed to win all eight races in the GT4 category.

The Porsche Sprint Challenge Japan (PSCJ) series, now in its fourth year, opened at the Fuji International Speedway on April 3. The series consisted of four events, eight races in total and there was a big overhaul for the competitors as the Porsche Carrera Cup Japan updated to the latest specification cars. The Porsche Carrera Cup Japan switched to the latest Cup car, the Type 992, for this season. That switch meant that the 991 Gen. 2, which was used by the PCCJ from 2018 to last year became the GT3-I class car in the Porsche Sprint Challenge Japan (PSCJ) series this year. At the same time in the PSCJ, the GT3-II Class also upgraded their cars, from the 997 to the 991 Gen 1 Cup specification. The upgrade meant that for the first time the entire PSCJ grid raced 991 generation cars.

The PSCJ was hotly contested throughout the 2022 season. The series started at Fuji in June with a wonderful grid of 27 cars. In the GT3-I class, Ken Yamamoto, who was competing in the PSCJ for the first time, dominated the category by winning four of the eight races, and he finished second in the remaining four. He had secured the title even before the last round and final two races of the season. In the GT3-II class, Hideki Ogiwara, who has competed in the PSCJ series every year since the first season in 2019, took the title by a narrow five-point margin over Shunsuke Sato. Sato had led the class with two races remaining but saw his lead overhauled at the final event of the year.

Meanwhile in the GT4 class, the 718 Cayman GT4 Clubsport was the weapon of choice. Sena Yamamoto, this year's Porsche Japan Junior Programme driver, won each of the eight races and also highlighted his speed as he set a new lap record in the class at Fuji in June and Suzuka in September.

Sena Yamamoto

Masa Taga and „Kuma"

Ken Yamamoto

Ken Yamamoto

„Akiratea"

DRIVER STANDINGS **GT3-I**

POS	NO	DRIVERS	TEAM	POINTS
1	99	Ken Yamamoto	Carshop K with PCJ	140
2	32	"Akiratea"	Good Day Racing	77
3	84	Masa Taga	Girodisc Crefmotorsport	75
4	10	Motoki Takami	47 Trading with RN-Sports	64
5	9	Kenji Kobayashi	KDC 991 Cup	54
6	16	Hiroyuki Kishimoto	Swiftwing Racing	34
7	15	Hikoichiro Kamitori	Grena Racing	33
8	27	Souichiro Mano	Team KRM & NFGT3 Cup	31
9	36	"Sky Chen"	SMJ	25
10	77	"Musashi"	Taro Racing	22
11	92	"Rasset"	927-More than Racing	22
12	38	Aaron May	Team KRM & NFGT3 Cup	20
13	31	"Ooka"	G-Tech More than Racing	17
14	62	"Kuma"	Shirokuma Racing	14
15	6	"Bankcy"	Bingo Racing	14
16	55	Seiya Tanaka	Good Day Racing	12
17	22	Masaya Koyama	Porsche Club Japan	9
18	44	"Hisatea"	Hirix Good Day Racing	6
19	78	Takashi Nanatsuya"	T.N-CO Garage	6
20	7	"Shigeharu"	Team KRM	6
21	36	Tetsuo Ogino	SMJ	2

DRIVER STANDINGS **GT3-II**

POS	NO	DRIVERS	TEAM	POINTS
1	66	Hideki Ogiwara	Team KRM	100
2	26	Shunsuke Sato	Sato Eye Clinic GT3	95
3	25	Takuji Hisaoka	Rokkosan Distillery GT3	74
4	76	Keiichiro Takagi	Toriyoshi Porsche	48
5	88	Hiroshi Yamada	K-1	42
6	33	Yuki Ohta	HC Gallery GT3	28
7	17	"AG"	Imamura KK	27
8	72	Shigeharu Yoshiyama		0

DRIVER STANDINGS **GT4**

POS	NO	DRIVERS	TEAM	POINTS
1	71	Sena Yamamoto	Porsche Japan GT4 Racing	160
2	51	Katsuichiro Yokoi	Navul	30

SPRINT CHALLENGE USA WEST
BY YOKOHAMA

01.04.–03.04.2022	*Laguna Seca Raceway, USA*
15.04.–16.04.2022	*Sonoma Raceway, USA*
22.04.–24.04.2022	*Ozarks International Raceway, USA*
03.06.–05.06.2022	*Virginia International Raceway, USA*
29.07.–31.07.2022	*Road America, USA*
12.08.–14.08.2022	*Utah Motorsports Campus, USA*
02.09.–04.09.2022	*Indianapolis Motor Speedway, USA*
16.09.–18.09.2022	*Circuit of the Americas, USA*

(l.-r.): Paul Nemschoff, Laura Ely, John McInnes

Chris Bellomo, Laura Ely und Michael Gaulke setzen sich in der neu ins Leben gerufenen Porsche Sprint Challenge USA West by Yokohama durch.

Der United States Auto Club USAC, offizieller Veranstalter der Porsche Sprint Challenge North America by Yokohama, hat mit der Porsche Sprint Challenge USA West eine neue Serie für die Westküste eingeführt, die 2022 ihre Premiere feierte.

In der Kategorie GT3 Cup 992 steuerte Chris Bellomo mit einem Fahrzeug von Flying Lizard Motorsports zum sicheren Titelgewinn. Mit dem GT3-Cup-Porsche der neusten Generation zeigte er sich in beeindruckender Form und beendete die Saison mit einem riesigen Vorsprung von 399 Punkten auf den zweitplatzierten Kyle Washington. Auf seinem Weg zum Titel sah Bellomo die Zielflagge in neun Läufen als Erster und einmal als Zweiter.

Deutlich enger verlief die Entscheidung in der Klasse GT3 Cup 991, in der sich Laura Ely und Paul Nemschoff um die Lorbeeren stritten. Die Führung in der Klassenwertung wechselte jedes Wochenende bis zum Finale, bei dem Ely einen Vorsprung von zehn Zählern auf Nemschoff herausfuhr. Die Saisonbilanz der Pilotin von Black Sheep Racing beinhaltet sechs Rennsiege und vier zweite Positionen.

Und schließlich konnte das Team Flying Lizard Motorsports seinen Trophäenschrank mit dem Gewinn der Cayman-Klasse in der Porsche Sprint Challenge USA West noch einmal aufstocken. Der neue Champion Michael Gaulke und sein Teamkollege Paul Bonderson kämpften die ganze Saison hindurch, doch letztlich war es Gaulke, der nach neun Saisonerfolgen und zwei zweiten Rängen die Nase vorne hatte.

Laura Ely

New series in the West brings new champions to the scene

The United States Auto Club (USAC), the official sanctioning body of the Porsche Sprint Challenge North America by Yokohama, added a west coast championship in 2022 to maximize the opportunity for teams and drivers based on the Western side of the United States. The Porsche Sprint Challenge USA West joined the main Sprint Challenge series at several rounds during the season.

In the GT3 Cup 992 Championship, Chris Bellomo drove the Flying Lizard Motorsports entry to the 2022 title. Driving the latest generation GT3 Cup car, Bellomo was in impressive form and finished the season with an incredible 399-point lead over the second placed driver, Kyle Washington. On his way to the title, Bellomo scored nine race victories and a second-place finish.

Laura Ely won the GT3 Cup 991 Championship title after the fiercest of battles. The lead in the standings changed every weekend until the final, where Ely finally established a 10-point gap over Paul Nemschoff. Ely's season total included six race victories and four second place finishes.

The veteran Flying Lizard Motorsports team saw its trophy cabinet added to with the 2022 Porsche Sprint Challenge USA West GT3 Cup Cayman Championship. The title was won largely thanks to the efforts of Michael Gaulke. He, and teammate Paul Bonderson, fought throughout the season, but it was Gaulke who ultimately came out on top having won the first seven races. In total, Gaulke won nine rounds and had two second place finishes.

Stephen Ayers

Kayden Kelly

DRIVER STANDINGS
992 CLASS

POS	NO	DRIVERS	POINTS
1	68	Chris Bellomo	594
2	132	Kyle Washington	195
3	044	Sal Brogna	179
4	63	Richard French	177
5	3	Kay van Berlo	101
6	98	Alan Metni	96
7	042	Raymond Davoudi	92
8	339	Reinhold Krahn	92

DRIVER STANDINGS
991 CLASS

POS	NO	DRIVERS	POINTS
1	09	Laura Ely	583
2	41	Paul Nemschoff	573
3	56	John McInnes	570
4	30	Stephen Ayers	539
5	00	Chris Haunold	484
6	777	Kenton King	270
7	880	Kayden Kelly	94
8	75	Sam Parnagian	91
9	31	William De Leon	86
10	770	Todd Parriott	85

DRIVER STANDINGS
CAYMAN CLASS

POS	NO	DRIVERS	POINTS
1	90	Micahel Gaulke	596
2	42	Paul Bonderson	570
3	157	Sam Parnagian	101
4	154	Derek Harvey	96
5	231	Charles Gordon	94
6	71	Paul Camusi	92
7	57	Philip Parnagian	89

PORSCHE
SPRINT CHALLENGE
NORTH AMERICA
BY YOKOHAMA

SPRINT CHALLENGE NORTH AMERICA
BY YOKOHAMA

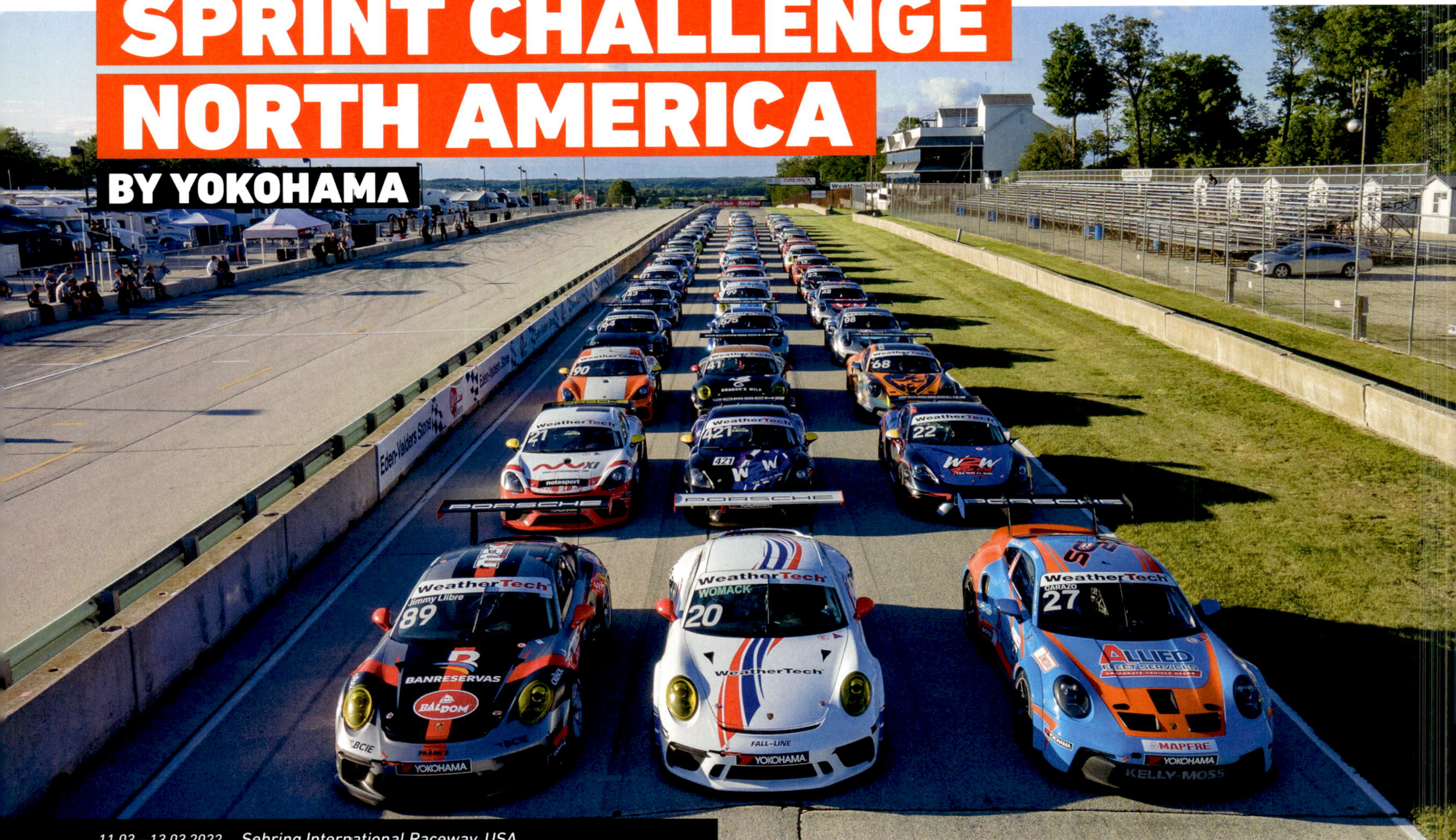

11.03.–13.03.2022	*Sebring International Raceway, USA*
22.04.–24.04.2022	*Ozarks International Raceway, USA*
06.05.–08.05.2022	*Miami International Autodrome, USA*
03.06.–05.06.2022	*Virginia International Raceway, USA*
01.07.–03.07.2022	*Mid-Ohio Sports Car Course, USA*
29.07.–31.07.2022	*Road America, USA*
02.09.–04.09.2022	*Indianapolis Motor Speedway, USA*
16.09.–18.09.2022	*Circuit of the Americas, USA*

(27): Sebastian Carazo · (65): Efrin Castro

Sebastian Carazo, Jimmy Llibre und Aiden Kenny krönen sich in der Porsche Sprint Challenge North America by Yokohama zu den neuen Champions.

Die zweite Saison der Porsche Sprint Challenge North America by Yokohama knüpfte an den Erfolg des Debütjahres an. Zusätzlich wurde ein unabhängiger westlicher Zweig der Serie geschaffen, die Sprint Challenge USA West by Yokohama.

Sebastian Carazo, der die Startnummer 27 des Teams Kelly Moss Road & Race steuerte, gewann in der Porsche Sprint Challenge North America die Klasse GT3 Cup 992. Der neue Champion schloss die Saison mit einem Vorsprung von 63 Punkten auf seinen ersten Verfolger David Williams ab. Carazo erlebte ein dominantes Jahr, in dem er acht Rennen als Erster beendete und zusätzlich drei zweite Plätze verbuchte. Seine bemerkenswertesten Triumphe feierte er beim Großen Preis von Miami auf großer Bühne vor den Augen des Formel-1-Publikums.

Jimmy Llibre, entschied die Klasse GT3 Cup 991 für sich, er bejubelte fünf Siege und wurde in sechs Läufen als Zweiter abgewinkt. In der Endabrechnung hatte er 65 Zähler mehr gesammelt als Vize-Champion Michael Levitas. Llibres Porsche 911 GT3 Cup (Typ 991) mit der Startnummer 89 wurde von der Mannschaft MDK Motorsports eingesetzt.

Und schließlich war Aidan Kenny bester Vertreter der Cayman-Gruppe: Er sah in sechs Heats als Erster die Zielflagge und überquerte die Ziellinie zweimal als Zweiter. Das brachte dem Schützling des Teams W2W Racing 35 Punkte mehr auf seine Habenseite als auf dem Konto seines zweitplatzierten Teamkollegen Mark Smith zu finden waren.

Start at COTA

Carazo, Llibre, Kenny crowned second season champs in Porsche Sprint Challenge.

The second season of Porsche Sprint Challenge North America by Yokohama brought back key races, racers and teams but added in new tracks, fresh champions and even the debut of a western series.

Sebastian Carazo won the 2022 Porsche Sprint Challenge North America GT3 Cup 992 Championship for the Kelly Moss Road & Race team. Carazo finished the season with a 63-point lead over David Williams having had a dominant year, winning a total of eight races and an additional three runner-up finishes. His most notable victories came at the Miami Grand Prix in front of the Formula One paddock and fanbase.

Jimmy Llibre, who drove the MDK Motorsports Porsche 911 GT3 Cup (type 991), took top honors in the GT3 Cup 991 Championship. After an extraordinary campaign, he closed with a 65-point gap to Michael Levitas. Llibre built an impressive resume during the season with five victories and six second place finishes.

Aidan Kenny, driving the W2W Racing, brought home the 2022 Cayman Championship. Kenny started the season winning the first four rounds and went on to win six of the first eight. He finished with a 35-point lead on teammate, Mark Smith. Kenny's 2022 campaign was highlighted by six race wins and a pair of second place finishes.

(43): Mark Kvamme - (24): William Tally

DRIVER STANDINGS
992 CLASS NATIONAL

POS	NO	DRIVERS	POINTS
1	27	Sebastian Carazo	664
2	37	David Williams	601
3	68	Chris Bellomo	560
4	575	Shane Leathers	488
5	042	Raymond Davoudi	487
6	65	Efrin Castro	449
7	17	Dan Sibille	394
8	43	Mark Kvamme	350
9	55	Moisey Uretsky	339
10	98	Alan Metni	320
11	138	Scott Schmidt	315
12	14	Pedro Torres	257
13	48	David Brule	232
14	143	Alex Vogel	208
15	981	Grant Talkie	200
16	132	Kyle Washington	181
17	339	Reinhold Krahn	165
18	52	Robert Todd	94
19	156	Jeff Mosing	92
20	64	P. J. Hyett	86
21	63	Richard French	82
22	69	Thomas Collingwood	80
23	19	Thomas Balames	78
24	87	Matt Halcome	76
25	84	Marco Cirone	45

DRIVER STANDINGS
991 CLASS NATIONAL

POS	NO	DRIVERS	POINTS
1	89	Jimmy Llibre	636
2	39	Michael Levitas	564
3	99	Scott Zdanis	550
4	78	Roberto Turino	549
5	6	Rob Lorndale	496
6	46	Mark Boden	478
7	10	Frank Vitiello	445
8	24	William Tally	407
9	09	Laury Ely	394
10	161	Thomas Herb	390
11	4	Tim Kezman	358
12	20	Patrick Womack	356
13	243	Brent Chambers	306
14	30	Stephen Ayers	293
15	402	Charles Bray	290
16	66	Daniel Bloom	263
17	41	Paul Nemschoff	254
18	81	Geoff Isringhausen	249
19	56	John McInnes	243
20	34	Shawn McKaigue	228
21	722	Philip Martien	201
22	16	Terry Olson	195
23	00	Chris Haunold	163
24	003	Ando Kovacs	162
25	498	Nick Iarossi	155

DRIVER STANDINGS
CAYMAN CLASS NATIONAL

POS	NO	DRIVERS	POINTS
1	22	Aiden Kenny	564
2	421	Mark Smith	529
3	117	Sean McAuliffe	523
4	119	Austin Krainz	500
5	21	Alex Sajady	497
6	5	Mike Martin	442
7	111	Michael Harvey	421
8	90	Michael Gaulke	411
9	33	Michael Clark	410
10	154	Derek Harvey	336
11	42	Paul Bonderson	332
12	520	Tom Kopczynski	331
13	13	Nick Iarossi	321
14	23	Christian Weir	317
15	88	Taylor Maseiro	313
16	619	Roland Krainz	296
17	29	Elias de La Torre	289
18	26	Alain Scalzo	261
19	95	Henry O'Hara	226
20	030	Christian Hodneland	225
21	171	Jorge Madruga	200
22	11	Jean-Francois Formela	190
23	114	Connor Horstmann	189
24	12	Joseph Rizzo	189
25	32	Zoe Barry	181

Start at Indianapolis

ENDURANCE RACING

PORSCHE
99
86
92
PRO
MICHELIN
BTR-Logistics We Care
Pedal Mafia

930

KUS
MANTHEY

92

24 HOURS OF DUBAI

11.01.–15.01.2022 Dubai Autodrome, United Arab Emirates

Niederländische und deutsche Teams feierten Erfolge in den Porsche-Cup-Klassen. Für den Gesamtsieg hat es dieses Jahr für Porsche-Teams nicht gereicht.

Dinamic Motorsport und Herberth Motorsport mit je zwei Porsche 911 GT3 R sowie Joos Sportwagentechnik und DUWO Racing by Herberth Motorsport mit je einem Auto repräsentierten Porsche in der 17. Auflage des 24h-Rennens in Dubai. Im Kampf um den Gesamtsieg spielten sie keine Rolle: In der Pro-Klasse war der Herberth-911 mit den drei Australiern Stephen und Brenton Grove und Anton de Pasquale sowie Sven Müller auf Rang sechs der einzige gewertete Porsche. Das Team Joos Sportwagentechnik hingegen feierte einen tollen Einstand mit Rang zwei in der GT3-Pro-Am-Klasse für Jannes Fittje, Michael Joos, Friedel Bleifuss und Steffen Görig. Der DUWO-Porsche erreichte hier Rang drei.
Das niederländische Team GP Elite bestritt in Dubai sein erstes 24h-Rennen und belegte die ersten beiden Plätze in der neuen 992-Pro-Klasse. Der Klassensieg ging an Lucas Groeneveld, Daan und Jesse van Kuijk und Max van Splunteren. Das Schwesterauto belegte Rang zwei, gefolgt vom Red Camel-Jordans.nl-Porsche, in dem auch Jeroen Bleekemolen zum Einsatz kam. Zur geplanten Teilnahme von Jos Verstappen im GP-Elite-Porsche kam es nicht: Der Ex-F1-Fahrer musste aus persönlichen Gründen abreisen und wurde vom Supercup-Champion Larry ten Voorde ersetzt. Das deutsche Team ID Racing belegte die Plätze vier bis sechs.
In der 992-Am-Klasse sicherte sich das Team HRT Performance die Plätze eins, drei und vier. Die Schweden Henric und Patrick Skoog, Emil Persson und Gustav Bergström gewannen die Klasse. Das belgische Team Red Ant Racing, mit Ex-Rad-Weltmeister Tom Boonen als einem der Fahrer, sicherte sich Rang zwei. NKPP Racing by Bas Koeten Racing, ebenfalls aus den Niederlanden, wiederholte den 991-Klassensieg aus dem Vorjahr, einmal mehr mit Gijs Bessem, Harry Hilders, Bob Herber und Daan Meijer.
Holger Harmsen belegte mit seinen Kollegen J. M. Littman, Nikolaj Gadetskii und Stefan Aust vom HRT Performance Team den vierten Platz in der Klasse und im Gesamtklassement Platz 35.

(933): Larry ten Voorde, Roger Hodenius, Steven van Rhee, Thierry Vermeulen
(934): Max van Splunteren, Lucas Groeneveld, Jesse van Kuijk, Daan van Kuijk

Max van Splunteren, Lucas Groeneveld, Jesse van Kuijk, Daan van Kuijk

Holger Harmsen

(929): Henric Skoog, Gustav Bergstrom, Emil Persson, Patrik Skoog - (923): Laurin Heinrich, Enrico Fulgenzi, Gabriele Rindone, Matthias Hoffsümmer - (934): Max van Splunteren, Lucas Groeneveld, Jesse van Kuijk, Daan van Kuijk

While Porsche teams didn't play a role in the battle for overall honours, Dutch and German teams were successful in the Porsche Cup classes.

Porsche was well represented in the 17th edition of the Dubai 24 Hours. The Dinamic Motorsport and Herberth Motorsport teams each ran two 911 GT3 Rs, while Joos Sportwagentechnik and DUWO Racing by Herberth Motorsport ran one car apiece.

However, the teams didn't play a major role in the battle for overall honours. In the Pro-class, only one Porsche was classified, that of Herberth Motorsport which placed sixth in the hands of Australians Stephen and Brenton Grove, Anton de Pasquale and Sven Müller. Meanwhile, the Joos Sportwagentechnik had a solid debut, finishing second in the GT3 Pro-Am class driven by Jannes Fittje, Michael Joos, Friedel Bleifuss and Steffen Görig. The DUWO Porsche finished third in this class.

Dutch team GP Elite competed in its first 24h race in Dubai and scored a 1-2 in the new 992 Pro class. Lucas Groeneveld, Daan and Jesse van Kuijk and Max van Splunteren drove the class-winning car. The sister car finished second, followed

(l.-r.): Wolfgang Triller, Hendrik Still, Evgeny Kireev, Merabi Mekvabishvili, Christoph Huber, Laurin Heinrich, Matthias Hoffsümmer, Gabriele Rindone, Enrico Fulgenzi

Hendrik Still, Merabi Mekvabishvili, Evgeny Kireev, Wolfgang Triller

24H DUBAI

GP
VolkerWessels

Hankook
S. PEREGUDOV

24H DUBAI
KENSTON GRUPPE
HARTL

PORSCHE

BWT
24H DUBAI
SONAX
BILSTEIN

Hankook
24H DUBAI 2022
DUBAI
24H SERIES

24H DUBAI

PERRIDON
parsiq
PERRIDON HOLDINGS
24H SERIES
24H DUBAI
Eurotrac
KARPACK

GT WORLD CHALLENGE

24H DUBAI

UBAI
24H DUBAI

KENSTON GRUPPE

24H DUBAI

OMP
Hankook
Fastron
ROGER DUBUIS
oppo
24H SERIES
AUTOMOBILI LAMBORGHINI

962

Larry ten Voorde, Roger Hodenius, Steven van Rhee, Thierry Vermeulen

Daniel Alleman, Ralf Bohn, Alfred Renauer, Robert Renauer

(933): Larry ten Voorde, Roger Hodenius, Steven van Rhee, Thierry Vermeulen - (934) Max van Splunteren, Lucas Groeneveld, Jesse van Kuijk, Daan van Kuijk and Team GP Elite

J. M. Littman, Nikolaj Gadetskii, Stefan Aust, Holger Harmsen

by the Red Camel-Jordans.nl-Porsche which featured Jeroen Bleekemolen in the driving line-up. The planned participation by Jos Verstappen in a GP Elite Porsche didn't happen. The ex-F1 driver had to return home for personal reasons, and so he was replaced by Supercup champion Larry ten Voorde. German team ID Racing locked out fourth to sixth place in the final finishing order.

In the 992 Am class, HRT Performance secured first, third and fourth places with Swedes Henric and Patrik Skoog, Emil Persson and Gustav Bergström coming home as the class winners. Belgian team Red Ant Racing, which included former cycling world champion Tom Boonen in its driving roster, finished second. NKPP Racing by Bas Koeten Racing, also from The Netherlands, repeated its 991 class win from the previous year, again with Gijs Bessem, Harry Hilders, Bob Herber and Daan Meijer.

HRT Performance Team

RACE CLASSIFICATION

POS	CLASS	CLASS POS	NO	DRIVERS	CAR	TEAM	LAPS
1	GT3	1	7	Christopher Mies, Mohammed Saud Fahad Al Saud, Axcil Jefferies, Thomas Neubauer, Dries Vanthoor	Audi R8 LMS GT3 Evo	MS7 by WRT	596
2	GT3	2	31	Frédéric Vervisch, Arnold Robin, Maxime Robin, Benjamin Goethe, Jean-Baptiste Simmenauer	Audi R8 LMS GT3 Evo	Team WRT	595
3	GT3	3	75	Mikael Grenier, Kenny Habul, Maro Engel, Jules Gounon	Mercedes-AMG GT3 Evo	SunEnergy1 Racing by SPS Automotive Performance	593
6	GT3	6	92	Sven Müller, Brenton Grove, Stephen Grove, Andton De Pasquale	Porsche 911 GT3 R II	Precote Herberth Motorsport	589
11	GT3 Pro-Am	2	27	Jannes Fittje, Michael Joos, Freidel Bleifuss, Steffen Görig	Porsche 911 GT3 R II	Team Joos Sportwagentechnik	584
12	GT3 Pro-Am	3	93	Andrey Mukovoz, Sergey Peregudov, Stanislav Sidoruk, Dylan Pereira	Porsche 911 GT3 R II	Duwo Racing by Herberth Motorsport	583
14	992 Pro	1	934	Max van Splunteren, Lucas Groeneveld, Jesse van Kuijk, Daan van Kuijk	Porsche 992 GT3 Cup	GP Elite	576
20	992 Pro	2	933	Larry ten Voorde, Roger Hodenius, Steven van Rhee, Thierry Vermeulen	Porsche 992 GT3 Cup	GP Elite	570
22	992 Pro	3	909	Jeroen Bleekemolen, Morris Schuring, Julius Adamovacius, Ivo Breukers	Porsche 992 GT3 Cup	Jordans-Red Camel Racing	566
23	992 Am	1	929	Henric Skoog, Gustav Bergstrom, Emil Persson, Patrik Skoog	Porsche 992 GT3 Cup	HRT Performance	565
26	991	1	991	Gijs Bessem, Daan Meijer, Bob Herber, Harry Hilders	Porsche 991 Cup II	NKPP Racing by Bas Koeten Racing	559
27	992 Am	2	904	Tom Boonen, Luc Vanderfeesten, Kurt Hensen, Philippe Wils	Porsche 992 GT3 Cup	Red Ant Racing	557
28	992 Pro	4	977	Saeed Almheiri, Saif Alameri, Salem Alketbi, Helal Almazarouei, Fahad Alzaabi	Porsche 992 GT3 Cup	Rabdan Motorsport by ID Racing	553
29	992 Am	3	928	Daniel Ros, Erik Behrens, Tommy Graberg, Hans Holmlud	Porsche 992 GT3 Cup	HRT Performance	550
33	992 Pro	5	944	Philipp Sager, Jukka Honkavuori, Alexandr Artemyev, Bashar Mardini, Christopher Zöchling	Porsche 992 GT3 Cup	ID Racing	544
35	992 Am	4	930	J. M. Littman, Nikolaj Gadetskii, Stefan Aust, Holger Harmsen	Porsche 992 GT3 Cup	HRT Performance	542
36	992 Am	5	979	Brent Verheyen, Olivier Dons, Jean-Michel Gerome, Eric Mouez, John De Wilde	Porsche 992 GT3 Cup	Speed Lover	541
42	992 Pro	6	940	Shaun Thong, Audrius Butkevicius, Vincent Piemonte, Adrian Spescha	Porsche 992 GT3 Cup	ID Racing	527
50	992 Am	6	924	Hendrik Still, Merabi Mekvabishvili, Evgeny Kireev, Wolfgang Triller	Porsche 992 GT3 Cup	Huber Racing	510
56	991	2	955	Sabino De Castro, Sergiu Nicolae, Fabrizio Broggi	Porsche 991 Cup II	Willi Motorsport by Ebimotors	495
57	992 Pro	7	962	Eduardo Menossi, Ayman Darwich, Leonardo Sanchez Secundino, Rouman Ziemkiewicz, Atila Roberto de Abreu	Porsche 992 GT3 Cup	Fach Auto Tech	493
65 (DNF)	992 Am	7 (DNF)	931	Michael Blanchemain, Lars Dahmann, Saeed Al Mouri, Cyril Saleilles, Marcel Zalloua	Porsche 992 GT3 Cup	HRT Performance	464
66	991	3	903	Ayrton Redant, Pieter Ooms, Yannick Redant, Glenn van Parijs	Porsche 991 Cup II	Red Ant Racing	457
DNF	992 Am	DNF	961	Alexander Fach, Dominik Fischli, Marcel Wagner, Peter Hegglin, Jan Klingelnberg	Porsche 992 GT3 Cup	Fach Auto Tech	249
DNF	GT3	DNF	67	Matteo Cairoli, Roberto Pampanini, Mauro Calamia, Stefano Monaco	Porsche 911 GT3 R II	Dinamic Motorsport	177
DNF	GT3	DNF	54	Klaus Bachler, Marvin Dienst, Marco Seefried, Murad Sultanov, Stanislav Minsky	Porsche 911 GT3 R II	Dinamic Motorsport	115
DNF	992 Am	DNF	923	Laurin Heinrich, Enrico Fulgenzi, Gabriele Rindone, Matthias Hoffsümmer	Porsche 992 GT3 Cup	Huber Racing	77
DNS	GT3 Pro-Am	DNS	91	Daniel Alleman, Ralf Bohn, Alfred Renauer, Robert Renauer	Porsche 911 GT3 R II	Precote Herberth Motorsport	0

24H SERIES

13.01.–15.01.2022	*Dubai, United Arab Emirates*
25.03.–26.03.2022	*Mugello, Italy*
22.04.–23.04.2022	*Spa-Francorchamps, Belgium*
13.05.–15.05.2022	*Hockenheim, Germany*
08.07.–10.07.2022	*Portimao, Portugal*
09.09.–11.09.2022	*Barcelona, Spain*
01.12.–02.12.2022	*Kuwait Motor Town, Kuwait*

Red Ant Racing gewinnt mit drei Saisonsiegen souverän den Titel in der neuen 992-Klasse – Herberth Motorsport sichert Podien in den GT3-Kategorien

Im Rahmen der 24H Series wurde 2022 die European Championship, zu der fünf Langstreckenrennen zählen, ausgetragen. Neben den Spitzenkategorien für GT3-Fahrzeuge waren besonders Porsche 911 GT3 Cup-Fahrzeuge zahlreich in der Meisterschaft vertreten. Zusätzlich zu den bewährten 991 Cup-Autos der zweiten Generation starteten in dieser Saison auch erstmals die neuen Porsche 911 GT3 Cup 992 in der Serie. In dieser neu formierten Klasse waren es an der Spitze zwei Teams, die um den Meistertitel kämpften. Mit einem Auftaktsieg bei den 12 Stunden von Mugello brachte sich RedCamel-Jordans.nl in eine perfekte Ausgangsposition, doch ab Spa war es Red Ant Racing, die das Geschehen in der Klasse bestimmten. Mit drei Saisonsiegen sowie einem dritten Platz entschied das Team die Meisterschaft letztlich klar für sich. Eine schwierige Saison erlebte Herberth Motorsport. Lediglich ein Podium in der GT3-Pro/Am-Klasse sowie ein Podestplatz in der GT3-AM-Kategorie holte die Mannschaft aus Jedenhofen. Einen spannenden Kampf um die Meisterschaft gab es in der Klasse 991: Nach vier verschiedenen Siegern in vier Rennen setzte sich am Ende E2P Racing dank zwei weiterer Podiumserfolge gegen die Konkurrenz durch. Mit dem 12-Stunden-Rennen in Kuwait fiel Anfang Dezember auch die Entscheidung in der Championship of the Continents. Bei der Premiere fuhr RedCamel-Jordans.nl mit Platz drei überraschend aufs Gesamtpodium und sicherte sich somit den Titel in der 992-Klasse. Bestplatziertes Porsche-Team in Kuwait war derweil die MRS-Mannschaft, die mit einem Porsche 911 GT3 R Platz zwei belegte.

(l.-r.): Ahmad Al Ghanem, Zaid Ashkanani, Mohammad Al-Kazemi

(903): Ayrton Redant, Bert Redant, Yannick Redant, Sam Dejonghe · (909): Fabian Danz, Ivo Breukers, Luc Breukers, Rik Breukers

Red Ant Racing confidently wins title in new 992 category with three victories this season – Herberth Motorsport secures podium finishes in the GT3 categories

The 2022 European Championship, which includes five endurance races, was held within the 24H Series framework. In addition to the top classes for GT3 vehicles, Porsche 911 GT3 Cup race cars were particularly well represented in the championship. Besides the proven second-generation 991 Cup cars, the new Porsche 911 GT3 Cup 992s started for the first time in the series. Two teams fought for the title at the top of the newly-formed category. RedCamel-Jordans.nl's victory at the 12 Hours of Mugello opener put them in the perfect starting position, but after Spa it was Red Ant Racing that shaped events in the category. Three season victories and a third place enabled the team to clearly win the championship. Herberth Motorsport had a problematic season. The Jedenhofen-based squad secured just one GT3 Pro/Am podium and one in the GT3 AM category. There was an exciting battle for the title in the 991 class: after four different winners in four races, E2P Racing finally prevailed over the competition thanks to two further podium finishes. Early December, the 12-hour race in Kuwait finalised the Championship of the Continents decision process. At the race premiere, RedCamel-Jordans.nl surprisingly finished third overall and thus secured the title in the 992 class. Meanwhile, the best-placed Porsche team in Kuwait was Karsten Molitor's MRS squad, which fielded a Porsche 911 GT3 R. Al-Kazemi, Ashkanani and Al Ghanem claimed second position.

Ivo Breukers, Luc Breukers, Rik Breukers

Gabriele Rindone, Matthias Hoffsümmer, Enrico Fulgenzi

Fabrizio Broggi, Sergiu Nicolae, Sabino de Castro

Jörg Dreisow, Alexander Schwarzer, Wolfgang Triller, Marc Basseng, Manuel Lauck

DRIVER STANDINGS
CHAMPIONSHIP OF THE CONTINENTS GT TROPHY

POS	NO	TEAM	CAR	POINTS
1	85	CP Racing	Mercedes-AMG GT3 Evo	74
2	710	Leipert Motorsport	Lamborghini Huracan Super Trofeo Evo	68
3	955	Willi Motorsport by Ebimotors	Porsche 991 Cup II, 992 GT3 Cup	65
4	909	Red Camel-Jordans	Porsche 992 GT3 Cup	64
5	929	QMMF by HRT	Porsche 992 GT3 Cup	63
6	928	HRT Performance	Porsche 992 GT3 Cup	59
7	903	Red Ant Racing	Porsche 992 GT3 Cup	49
10	904	Red Ant Racing	Porsche 992 GT3 Cup	45
21	977	Rabdan Motorsport	Porsche 992 GT3 Cup	28
29	910	E2P Racing	Porsche 991 Cup II	23
32	91	Herberth Motorsport	Porsceh 911 GT3 R II	19
41	912	Porsche L'Orient Racing	Porsche 992 GT3 Cup	14
48	61	EBM	Porsche 911 GT3 R II	6

ROLEX 24 AT DAYTONA

27.01.–30.01.2022 Daytona International Speedway, USA

James Sofronas, Kyle Washington, Jeroen Bleekemolen, Klaus Bachler

Porsche-Kundenteams triumphieren in spannendem Daytona-Finale – Pfaff Motorsports und Wright Motorsports sichern die ersten Porsche-Klassensiege seit fünf Jahren

Bei der 60. Auflage des Langstreckenrennens waren nicht weniger als sieben Kundensportfahrzeuge in den Klassen GTD Pro und GTD am Start. Letztendlich war es die Besatzung des Porsche 911 GT3 R #9 von Pfaff Motorsports, die sich in der GTD-Pro-Klasse durchsetzte. In der GTD-Kategorie siegte Wright Motorsports mit dem Porsche #16.
Um nach fünf Jahren endlich wieder einen Sieg einzufahren, setzte Porsche 2022 alles daran, die Teams bestmöglich zu unterstützen. In der GTD Pro traten daher eine ganze Reihe von Werksfahrern an: Matt Campbell, Mathieu Jaminet und Felipe Nasr für Pfaff Motorsports, Laurens Vanthoor, Patrick Pilet, Dennis Olsen und Alexandre Imperatori für KCMG. WeatherTech Racing setzte auf Matteo Cairoli, Julien Andlauer, Alessio Picariello und Cooper MacNeil.
In der GTD pilotierten Ryan Hardwick, Jan Heylen, Richard Lietz und Zach Robichon den Wright Motorsports-Boliden, während für das Team TGM Ted Giovanis, Hugh Plumb, Matt Plumb und Owen Trinkler ins Steuer griffen. Nick Boulle, Rob Ferriol, Katherine Legge und Stefan Wilson traten im Porsche 911 GT3 R des Teams Hardpoint an. GMG Racing stellte mit Klaus Bachler, Jeroen Bleekemolen, James Sofronas und Kyle Washington ebenfalls eine starke Crew zusammen.
Bei strahlendem Sonnenschein, aber ungewohnt kühlen Temperaturen ging es los. In der GTD-Pro-Klasse dominierten die Porsche-Teams die Anfangsphase des Rennens – sowohl Julien Andlauer für WeatherTech Racing als auch Patrick Pilet im KCMG-Boliden führten zeitweise.
„Meine ersten beiden Stints waren erstklassig", sagte Andlauer. „Von Startplatz 16 ging es kräftig voran. Die niedrigen Außentemperaturen sind nicht schön, aber in der Frühphase hat die Sonne den Asphalt recht gut aufgeheizt. Das hat uns das Anwärmen der Reifen erheblich erleichtert."

Matt Campbell, Mathieu Jaminet, Felipe Nasr and Pfaff Motorsports Team

Porsche customer teams take two class victories in tense final moments at Daytona – Pfaff Motorsports and Wright Motorsports secure first Porsche class wins in five years

🇬🇧 Porsche left an "indelible mark" on the Daytona 24 Hours in 2022, with victory in both the GTD Pro and GTD categories heading to Stuttgart.
The 60th running of the endurance race featured no less than seven customer racing entries spread across the GTD Pro and GTD classes. Ultimately it was the #9 Porsche 911 GT3 R of Pfaff Motorsports that took the spoils in an incredibly close battle with the #2 KCMG entry that went right down to the wire. In GTD, the #16 Wright Motorsports Porsche was victorious after a hard-fought 24 hours.
With its last class victory at Daytona coming back in 2017, Porsche went all out to support its customer teams for the 2022 edition of the 24 Hours of Daytona. Entries from Pfaff Motorsports, KCMG and WeatherTech Racing in GTD Pro featured a whole host of factory drivers. Matt Campbell, Mathieu Jaminet and Felipe Nasr

(l.-r.): Zacharie Robichon, Richard Lietz, Jan Heylen, Ryan Hardwick

Julien Andlauer, Alessio Picariello, Cooper MacNeil, Matteo Cairoli

Julien Andlauer, Alessio Picariello, Cooper MacNeil, Matteo Cairoli

Laurens Vanthoor, Patrick Pilet, Dennis Olsen, Alexandre Imperatori

featured in the Canadian-entered Pfaff Motorsports Porsche. For KCMG, works driver Laurens Vanthoor from Belgium was joined by Patrick Pilet, Dennis Olsen and Alexandre Imperatori. WeatherTech Racing enlisted the help of Matteo Cairoli Julien Andlauer and Alessio Picariello alongside non-professional Cooper MacNeil.
In GTD, which features a mixture of professional and non-professional drivers, Ryan Hardwick, Jan Heylen, Richard Lietz and Zach Robichon partnered up to take on the Wright Motorsports entry, while Team TGM featured Ted Giovanis, Hugh Plumb, Matt Plumb and Owen Trinkler behind the wheel. Nick Boulle, Rob Ferriol, Katherine Legge and Stefan Wilson were charged with piloting the Team Hardpoint Porsche 911 GT3 R. GMG Racing also put together a strong crew, which featured Klaus Bachler, Jeroen Bleekemolen, James Sofronas and Kyle Washington.
The starting grid for the 24-hour race was decided at the qualifying race one week previously. A strong performance by Pfaff Motorsports gave it a front-row grid position, but the Porsche runners struggled from tyre pressure issues. Nevertheless, the

Patrick Pilet, Alexandre Imperatori, Dennis Olsen, Laurens Vanthoor

(l.-r.): Matt Campbell, Mathieu Jaminet, Felipe Nasr

Julien Andlauer, Alessio Picariello, Cooper MacNeil, Matteo Cairoli

ROLEX

HAGERTY

PFAFF
MOTUL

PORSCHE

HAGERTY

PORSCHE
WRIGHT Motorsports

ROLEX
PFAFF
MOTUL

Mathieu Jaminet, Felipe Nasr, Matt Campbell

teams still went into the race in confident mood, as Sebastian Golz, Project Manager Porsche 911 GT3 R, explained: "A total of 35 GT cars will race at Daytona. That's an impressive number. It'll be exciting to see how the new regulations and classes evolve. With our seven customer teams and vehicles, we've been able to establish really strong combinations in the GTD Pro and GTD classes."

The traditional curtain-raiser began in bright sunshine but unseasonably cool temperatures at 13:40. The Porsches were straight out of the blocks in the GTD Pro class, dominating the opening stages of the race. Julien Andlauer led for WeatherTech Racing at points, as did Patrick Pilet in the KCMG entry.

"My first two stints were excellent," said Andlauer. "We ploughed through the field from 16th place. The low air temperatures aren't pleasant, but the sun warmed the asphalt nicely in the early stages. That made it much easier for us to warm the tyres."

As is customary in Daytona, yellow flags were a frequent interruption to the on-track action, especially as darkness – and the temperatures – fell. In total the cars would spend some four hours behind the safety car over a total of 17 full-course yellows. As a result, there was no way for any of the class contenders to establish a strong lead and the pack remained at close quarters.

Sebastian Golz was pleased with Porsche's performance at the halfway stage: "All three teams are consistently running in the top five. Things are also going well in the GTD class. The aim here is to get the amateur drivers safely to the finish and stay in the lead lap."

As Sunday morning progressed, the battle for the lead in both the GTD Pro and GTD classes intensified. The Pfaff Motorsports and KCMG Porsches eked out advantage over their competitors in GTD Pro in the closing stages of the race and, thanks to some smart pit work, emerged for their final stints practically nose to tail in a battle for the lead.

The minutes ticked by, and it appeared that Mathieu Jaminet in the Pfaff Motorsports Porsche had the edge over Laurens Vanthoor for KCMG. However, a slick move by the Belgian edged KCMG into the lead with just a handful of laps remaining.

That wasn't the last of it, though, as Jaminet fought back to retake the lead in the slow infield section of the circuit. Vanthoor never gave up and had one last chance

(l.-r.): Laurens Vanthoor, Patrick Pilet, Alexandre Imperatori, Dennis Olsen,

Ted Giovannis, Hugh Plumb, Matt Plumb, Owen Trinkler

Wie in Daytona üblich wurde das Renngeschehen immer wieder durch gelbe Flaggen unterbrochen. Insgesamt legte das Feld rund vier Stunden hinter dem Safety-Car zurück – bei insgesamt 17 Gelbphasen.
Sebastian Golz, Projektleiter Porsche 911 GT3 R, zeigte sich zur Halbzeit des Rennens zufrieden: „Alle drei Teams sind durchgehend in den Top-5. Auch in der GTD läuft es gut. Ziel ist es dort, die Amateurfahrer zu Beginn gut durch das Rennen zu bekommen und in der Führungsrunde zu bleiben."
Im Laufe des Sonntagmorgens verschärfte sich der Kampf um die Führung in beiden Klassen. Pfaff Motorsports und KCMG konnten sich in der Schlussphase des Rennens einen Vorsprung auf ihre Konkurrenten herausfahren und machten den Sieg dank cleverer Boxenstrategien unter sich aus.
Dabei schien es, als hätte Mathieu Jaminet im Porsche von Pfaff Motorsports einen Vorteil gegenüber Laurens Vanthoor. Ein geschicktes Manöver des Belgiers brachte KCMG jedoch wenige Runden vor Schluss in Führung.
Doch damit nicht genug: Jaminet konterte und übernahm erneut die Führung. Vanthoor gab sich allerdings ebenso wenig geschlagen – in der letzten Runde setzte er in der Schikane zu einem gewagten Manöver an. Es kam zum Kontakt, Vanthoor drehte sich. Jaminet hingegen behielt die Nerven und sicherte den denkwürdigen Sieg für Porsche. Vanthoor überquerte die Ziellinie als Dritter.
„Nicht nur die letzte Runde war ein Spektakel, sondern es war ein unfassbares Duell über zwei Stunden", so Jaminet. „Es war Werbung für den Motorsport und ein perfekter Saisonauftakt für uns."
In der GTD ging der Sieg an Wright Motorsports. Das Quartett war über weite Strecken des Rennens mit den Spitzenreitern auf Augenhöhe und erkämpfte schlussendlich den lang ersehnten Daytona-Sieg für das Team.
„Unser Auto lief über die gesamte Distanz sehr gut, das Team hat perfekt gearbeitet", sagte Richard Lietz. „Unser Porsche 911 GT3 R hat nach Zieldurchfahrt keinen einzigen Kratzer. Genau das war der Schlüssel zu unserem Erfolg."
Damit baute Porsche seine ohnehin schon beeindruckende Bilanz beim Langstreckenklassiker in Florida aus. Der deutsche Hersteller holte seinen 80. Klassensieg, dazu kommen 18 Gesamtsiege als Konstrukteur und vier als Motorenpartner.

Cooper MacNeil

Volker Holzmeyer

Ryan Hardwick, Richard Lietz, Zacharie Robichon, Jan Heylen

(9): Mathieu Jaminet, Felipe Nasr, Matt Campbell - (2): Patrick Pilet, Alexandre Imperatori, Dennis Olsen, Laurens Vanthoor - (16): Ryan Hardwick, Richard Lietz, Zacharie Robichon, Jan Heylen

Ryan Hardwick, Richard Lietz, Zacharie Robichon, Jan Heylen

Julien Andlauer

at glory on what would prove to be the final lap. Flaying the Porsche to an inch of its life, the Porsche factory driver made a highly speculative move at the chicane. The two Porsches made contact – Vanthoor spinning as a result – but Jaminet held his nerve to take a memorable victory for the German manufacturer. Vanthoor recovered to cross the line in third in class.

"The last lap was certainly spectacular, but so was the unbelievable duel over the last two hours," said Mathieu Jaminet. "I drove my heart out every single lap. I really gave it everything I had. That was great promotion for motorsport and a perfect start to the season for us."

In GTD, victory went to the Wright Motorsports crew of Ryan Hardwick, Jan Heylen, Richard Lietz and Zach Robichon. The quartet were up with the front-runners for much of the race and were well in contention for the win as the race drew to a close. Belgian Jan Heylen managed to comfortable hold off a late charge from Aston Martin and Mercedes to record a long-awaited Daytona victory for the team.

"Our car ran really well over the whole distance, the team did a perfect job," said Richard Lietz after the race. "Our Porsche 911 GT3 R crossed the finish line without a single scratch – and that was the secret to our success."

Porsche enhanced its already impressive record at the Floridian endurance classic. The German manufacturer notched up its 80th class win at the race, alongside 18 overall wins as a constructor and four as an engine partner.

(79): Julien Andlauer, Alessio Picariello, Cooper MacNeil, Matteo Cairoli
(9): Mathieu Jaminet, Felipe Nasr, Matt Campbell

RACE CLASSIFICATION

POS	CLASS	CLASS POS	NO	DRIVERS	CAR	TEAM	LAPS
1	DPi	1	60	Tom Blomqvist, Helio Castroneves, Oliver Jarvis, Simon Pagenaud	Acura ARX-05	Meyer-Shank Racing	761
2	DPi	2	10	Filipe Albuquerque, Will Stevens, Ricky Taylor, Alexander Rossi	Acura ARX-05	Konica Minolta-Wayne Taylor Racing	761
3	DPi	3	5	Tristan Vautier, Ben Keating, Richard Westbrook, Loic Duval	Cadillac DPi-V.R	JDC-Miller MotorSports/Mustang Sampling Racing	761
19	GTD Pro	1	9	Mathieu Jaminet, Felipe Nasr, Matt Campbell	Porsche 911 GT3 R II	Pfaff Motorsports	711
21	GTD Pro	3	2	Patrick Pilet, Alexandre Imperatori, Dennis Olsen, Laurens Vanthoor	Porsche 911 GT3 R II	KCMG	711
24	GTD	1	16	Ryan Hardwick, Richard Lietz, Zacharie Robichon, Jan Heylen	Porsche 911 GT3 R II	Wright Motorsports	707
32	GTD	7	64	Ted Giovannis, Hugh Plumb, Matt Plumb, Owen Trinkler	Porsche 911 GT3 R II	TeamTGM	697
20	GTD Pro	8	79	Julien Andlauer, Alessio Picariello, Cooper MacNeil, Matteo Cairoli	Porsche 911 GT3 R II	WeatherTech Racing	673
22	GTD	3	99	Nick Boulle, Stefan Wilson, Rob Ferriol, Katherine Legge	Porsche 911 GT3 R II	Hardpoint	672
DNF	GTD	DNF	34	James Sofronas, Kyle Washington, Jeroen Bleekemolen, Klaus Bachler	Porsche 911 GT3 R II	GMG Racing	88

24 HOURS OF NÜRBURGRING

26.05.–29.05.2022 Nürburging, Germany

(l.-r.): Christian Engelhart, Matteo Cairoli, Alessio Picariello

Falken Motorsports als bestplatzierter Porsche 911 GT3 R in den Top-10 – Siege für KKrämer Racing und Schmickler Performance in der Porsche Endurance Trophy

Die 50. Ausgabe der ADAC TotalEnergies 24h Nürburgring hatte alles zu bieten, was das Motorsportherz begehrt. Nach zweijähriger Abstinenz folgten über 200.000 Menschen dem Ruf der „Grünen Hölle" und fieberten rund um die legendäre Nordschleife mit. Zur Freude der zahlreichen Fans hielt sich auch das berüchtigte Eifelwetter zum Jubiläum zurück, sodass das Rennen erstmals seit 2019 wieder über die volle Distanz ausgetragen werden konnte.

In der Spitzenkategorie SP9 waren acht Porsche 911 GT3 R am Start, doch am Ende sahen nur zwei Fahrzeuge die Zielflagge. Dabei startete das Wochenende für die Porsche-Teams vielversprechend. Von Position 36 ins Rennen gegangen, mischte in der Anfangsphase besonders der Publikumsliebling von Manthey Racing das Feld auf. Kévin Estre steuerte den „Grello" mit der Startnummer 1 innerhalb von 90 Minuten bis auf die führende Position nach vorn. Doch ähnlich wie das Fahrzeug von Toksport WRT schied auch der Titelverteidiger am frühen Samstagabend nach einem Crash aus. Im Laufe der Nacht arbeitete sich Dinamic Motorsport mit der Startnummer 28 durch das Feld und lag auf der fünften Gesamtposition, kollidierte dann aber auf der GP-Strecke unverschuldet mit einem Gegner. Daraufhin musste die Mannschaft den Porsche abstellen. Nach dem Ausfall sah es lange Zeit danach aus, dass KCMG das Rennen als erfolgreichster Porsche beenden würde. Doch eine Stunde vor Rennende schied auch das Team aus Hongkong in Folge eines Unfalls aus. Damit war Falken Motorsports mit Patrick Pilet, Sven Müller, Jaxon Evans und Marco Seefried der bestplatzierte Neunelfer im Feld. Von der 25. Position gestartet, musste Müller nach mehreren Berührungen bereits in der zweiten Runde die Box ansteuern und fiel weit zurück. Das Quartett der

Michael Christensen, Kévin Estre, Frédéric Makowiecki, Laurens Vanthoor

Falken Motorsports as the best-placed Porsche 911 GT3 R in the top 10, victories for KKrämer Racing and Schmickler Performance in Porsche Endurance Trophy

The 50th running of the ADAC TotalEnergies 24h Nürburgring had everything to delight the motorsport fans. After a two-year absence, more than 200,000 spectators came to the "Green Hell" to witness the race. Fine conditions allowed for the race to be run over its scheduled distance for the first time since 2019. Eight Porsche 911 GT3 Rs raced in the SP9 category, but only two of them made it to the finish. They were all exciting to watch, but the Manthey Racing Porsche #1 caused the most excitement, Kévin Estre having moved up from 36th on the grid to the lead within the first 90 minutes. However, the reigning champion car was out following a crash on Saturday afternoon, as was the Toksport WRT car. During the night, the #28 Dinamic

Dennis Olsen, Earl Bamber, Nick Tandy

(l.-r.): Jaxon Evans, Marco Seefried, Sven Müller, Patrick Pilet, Alessio Picariello, Klaus Bachler, Patrick Pilet, Martin Ragginger and Team Falken Motorsports

Jaxon Evans, Sven Müller, Patrick Pilet, Marco Seefried

Startnummer 33 kämpfte sich jedoch im Laufe des Rennens Position um Position nach vorn und überquerte am Ende auf Rang neun die Ziellinie. Knapp dahinter sahen Nico Menzel, Joachim Thyssen, Klaus Rader und Lars Kern die schwarz-weiß-karierte Flagge. Mit Startplatz neun war die Mannschaft von Huber Motorsport das bestplatzierte Porsche-Team im Grid und zeigte über die gesamte Distanz eine fehlerfreie Leistung, die am Ende nicht nur mit einer starken elften Gesamtposition, sondern auch mit Rang drei in der Pro-Am-Wertung belohnt wurde. „Unsere Partnerteams haben großartig gearbeitet und die insgesamt acht Neunelfer in der Topklasse auf dem Weg in Richtung Rennen immer weiter verbessert", sagt Sebastian Golz. Der Projektleiter Porsche 911 GT3 R ergänzt: „Wir wurden am Samstag und am Sonntag regelrecht vom Pech verfolgt. Sechs Fahrzeuge haben wir durch Unfälle verloren, die meisten davon wurden unverschuldet in Kollisionen verwickelt. Wie stark unsere GT3-Kundenteams und unser Auto im Rennen waren, wurde anhand der zwischenzeitlichen Spitzenpositionen von Manthey und Toksport WRT sehr deutlich."

Robin Chrzanowski, Kersten Jodexnis, Peter Scharmach, Max Koch

(l.-r.): Ivan Jacoma, Roberto Pampanini, Mauro Calamia, Kai Riemer and Team

Sven Schnabl

(l.-r.): Thorsten Jung, Nick Salewsky, Michael Rebhan, Marcel Hoppe

Martin Raeder

Motorsport car worked its way up to fifth overall but retired following a collision on the Grand Prix circuit. Then, KCMG looked set to become the most successful Porsche for a long time, but the team from Hong Kong also retired following an accident with just one hour remaining. As a result, Falken Motorsports had the best-placed 911 in the field in the hands of Patrick Pilet, Sven Müller, Jaxon Evans and Marco Seefried which was classified ninth after a strong performance from 25th on the grid. Hubert Motorsport drivers Nico Menzel, Joachim Thyssen, Klaus Rader and Lars Kern, ninth on the grid as the best-placed Porsche team in qualifying, finished 11th overall and third in Pro-Am.

The Porsche Endurance Trophy was part of the endurance racing classic for the first time. Split into two classes, Cup2 for Porsche 911 GT3 Cup cars (992) and the well-known Cup3 class for Porsche 718 Cayman GT4 Clubsport cars, the newly-created trophy attracted 23 entrants. In qualifying, Frikadelli Racing claimed pole position in the Cup2 category. The popular team from Barweiler, which included Klaus Abbelen at the helm, is more commonly known in the SP9 class, but took on the challenge

Peter Ludwig, Noah Nagelsdiek, Reinhold Renger, Maik Rosenberg

Marcel Hoppe, Nick Salewsky, Michael Rebhan, Thorsten Jung

Nico Menzel, Joachim Thyssen, Klaus Rader, Lars Kern

Zum ersten Mal Teil des Langstreckenklassikers war die Porsche Endurance Trophy. Aufgeteilt in zwei Klassen – die Cup2 für Porsche 911 GT3 Cup (992) sowie die bekannte Cup3-Klasse der Porsche 718 Cayman GT4 Clubsport – stellte die neu ausgeschriebene Trophy 23 eingeschriebene Fahrzeuge. Im Qualifying holte sich Frikadelli Racing die Pole-Position in der Cup2-Kategorie. Nachdem das Kult-Team rund um Klaus Abbelen jahrelang in der SP9 am Start war, stellte sich die Mannschaft aus Barweiler erstmals der Herausforderung im Cup-Auto. Direkt dahinter startete die Mannschaft von KKrämer Racing mit Christopher Brück, Moritz Kranz, Alexej Veremenko und Teamchef Karsten Krämer, die sich am Ende den Sieg knapp vor der Black Falcon Mannschaft #123 sicherten. Insgesamt feierten die Sportwagen aus Zuffenhausen beim 24-Stunden-Rennen acht Klassensiege. In der seit Jahren aufstrebenden Klasse der alternativen Treibstoffe belegte Four Motors Bioconcept-Car die ersten beiden Plätze. Außerdem siegte Porsche in der SP4T, SP7 und in drei Produktionswagenklassen. Neben Adrenalin Motorsport Team Alzner Automotive, die im Porsche Cayman 918 die V5 für sich entschieden, und Mathol Racing, die die VT3-Klasse im Porsche Cayman 718S gewannen, ging auch der Sieg in der V6 an Porsche. Huber Motorsport war neben dem Erfolg in der SP9 Pro-Am auch in der SP7 erfolgreich und gewann die Klasse im Porsche 911 GT3 Cup (991).

Klaus Bachler, Alessio Picariello, Patrick Pilet, Martin Ragginger

Klaus Bachler, Alessio Picariello, Patrick Pilet, Martin Ragginger

(l.-r.): Reinhold Renger, Maik Rosenberg, Peter Ludwig, Noah Nagelsdiek, Tobias Müller, Paul Harkema, Tim Scheerbarth, Marco Müller, Martin Meenen, Tobias Wahl, Carsten Palluth, Gabriele Piana, Ben Bünnagel, Mike Stursberg, Mustafa Mehmet Kaya and BLACK FALCON Team

of a Cup car for the first time. Next up on the grid was the KKrämer Racing team of Christopher Brück, Moritz Kranz, Alexej Veremenko and team principal Karsten Krämer, who ended up claiming class victory, just ahead of the #123 Black Falcon entry. In total, sports cars from Zuffenhausen racked up eight class wins in the 24-hour race. In the category for alternative fuels, Four Motors Bioconcept-Car locked out the first two places. Further Porsche class wins were achieved in SP4T, SP7 and three production car classes. Alongside the V5 win for Adrenalin Motorsport Team Alzner Automotive with the Porsche Cayman 918, and Mathol Racing, victorious in VT3 with the Cayman 718S, the V6 class win also went to Porsche. Alongside its SP9 Pro-Am win, Huber Motorsport also came out on top in SP7 with its 911 GT3 Cup (991).

(l.-r.): Laurens Vanthoor, Frédéric Makowiecki, Michael Christensen, Kévin Estre

Michael Christensen, Kévin Estre,
Frédéric Makowiecki, Laurens Vanthoor

(253): Patrik Grütter, Herbert Lösch, Daniel Blickle, Max Kronberg
(70): Rodriguez Menzl, Ulrich Berg, Philip Hamprecht

BMW M POWER

KÖNIGIN DES NÜRBURGRINGS,
KIND DER EIFEL.
AUSSTELLUNG

Christian Engelhart, Matteo Cairoli, Come Ledogar, Thomas Preining

RACE CLASSIFICATION

POS	CLASS	CLASS POS	NO	DRIVERS	CAR	TEAM	LAPS
1	SP9	1	15	Frédéric Vervisch, Kelvin van der Linde, Dries Vanthoor, Robin Frijns	Audi R8 LMS GT3 Evo II	Audi Sport Team Phoenix	159
2	SP9	2	3	Maximilian Götz, Adam Christodoulou, Fabian Schiller	Mercedes-AMG GT3 Evo	Mercedes-AMG Team GetSpeed Performance	159
3	SP9	3	4	Maro Engel, Daniel Juncadella, Jules Gounon	Mercedes-AMG GT3 Evo	Mercedes-AMG Team GetSpeed Performance	159
9	SP9	9	33	Sven Müller, Marco Seefried, Jaxon Evans, Patrick Pilet	Porsche 911 GT3 R II	Falken Motorsports	157
11	SP9	11	25	Nico Menzel, Klaus Rader, Joachim Thyssen, Lars Kern	Porsche 911 GT3 R II	Huber Racing	156
15	CUP2	1	127	Moritz Kranz, Christopher Brück, Alexey Veremenko, Karsten Krämer	Porsche 992 GT3 Cup	KKrämer Racing	151
16	CUP2	2	123	Gabriele Piana, Ben Bünnagel, Mustafa Mehmet Kaya, Mike Stursberg	Porsche 992 GT3 Cup	Black Falcon	151
21	CUP3	1	264	Roberto Pampanini, Mauro Calamia, Ivan Jacoma, Kai Riemer	Porsche 718 Cayman GT4 CS	Schmickler Performance	144
23	CUP2	3	131	Marcel Hoppe, Nick Salewsky, Michael Rebhan, Thorsten Jung	Porsche 992 GT3 Cup	Mühlner Motorsport	143
24	CUP3	2	253	Patrik Grütter, Herbert Lösch, Daniel Blickle, Max Kronberg	Porsche 718 Cayman GT4 CS	G-Tech Competition	143
26	CUP2	4	135	Robin Chrzanowski, Kersten Jodexnis, Peter Scharmach, Maximilian Koch	Porsche 992 GT3 Cup	ClickVers	142
27	CUP3	3	263	Moritz Oberheim, Jens Moetfindt, Florian Naumann, Thorsten Wolter	Porsche 718 Cayman GT4 CS	FK Performance	142
28	CUP3	4	257	Heiko Eichenberg, Fidel Leib, Björn Simon, Stefan Beyer	Porsche 718 Cayman GT4 CS	Sorg Rennsport	142
29	SP7	1	70	Philip Hamprecht, Rodriguez Menzl, Ultrich Berg	Porsche 991 GT3 Cup	Huber Racing	142
30	CUP2	5	132	Timo Scheider, Jan-Erik Slooten, Luca Engstler, Leon Köhler	Porsche 992 GT3 Cup	Iron Force Racing by Phoenix Racing	141
32	CUP3	5	254	Leonard Oehme, Niklas Oehme, Ralf Oehme, Moritz Oehme	Porsche 718 Cayman GT4 CS	9 und 11 Racing	140
36	CUP3	6	262	Daniel Bohr, Heinz Dolfen, Tom Cloet, Oliver Louisoder	Porsche 718 Cayman GT4 CS	Mathol Racing	139
38	CUP3	7	258	Jürgen Vöhringer, Axel Duffner, Rene Höber, Dierk Biermann	Porsche 718 Cayman GT4 CS	W&S Motorsport	139
41	AT	1	320	Thomas Kiefer, Charles Kauffmann, Thomas von Löwis of Menar, Michael Bernd Schmidt	Porsche 991-II GT3 Cup Biofuel	Four Motors Bioconcept Car	136
45	CUP3	8	251	Urs Zünd, Markus Zünd, Viktor Schryba, Benedikt Frei	Porsche 718 Cayman GT4 CS	W&S Motorsport	133
50	CUP2	6	125	Stefan Aust, Christian Bollrath, Jacob Schell, Hans Wehrmann	Porsche 992 GT3 Cup	Huber Racing	132
52	AT	2	633	Karl Pflanz, Nicola Bravetti, Marco Timbal, Ivan Reggiani	Porsche 981 Cayman GT4 CS Biofuel	Four Motors Bioconcept Car	131
55	CUP2	7	129	Bill Cameron, James Cameron, Peter Bonk	Porsche 992 GT3 Cup	PB Per4mance	130
56	SP4T	1	718	Norbert Fischer, Fabian Peitzmeier, Christian Alexander Dannesberger, Ralf Zensen	Porsche 718 Cayman GTS	Nexen Tire Motorsport Team	129
59	V5	1	444	Tobias Korn, Ulrich Korn, Carlos Arimon, Daniel Korn	Porsche 981 Cayman	Adrenalin Motorsport	129
61	CUP3	9	256	Olaf Baunack, Sebastien Carcone, Sabrina Gros, Heiko Gros	Porsche 718 Cayman GT4 CS	Mathol Racing	127
62	V6	1	397	Sebastian Rings, Lukas Pickard, Alain Pier, Alexander Köppen	Porsche 991 Carrera	Köppen Motorsport	127
67	V6	2	228	Rasmus Helmich, Caryl Fitsche, Fabrice Reicher, Xavier Lamadrid, Jr.	Porsche 981 Cayman S	Sorg Rennsport	126
73	V6	3	227	Cesar Mendieta, Alberto Carobbio, Ugo Vicenzi, Reinhard Schmiedel	Porsche 981 Cayman S	Sorg Rennsport	120
84	VT3	1	300	Marcos Adolfo Vazquez, Mattias Trinius, Max Walter von Bär, Thorsten Held	Porsche 718 Cayman S	Mathol Racing	101
85	CUP3	10	255	Tobias Wolf, John Lee Schambony, Alexander Kroker, Simon Eibl	Porsche 718 Cayman GT4 CS	KKrämer Racing	101
DNF	SP9	DNF	18	Dennis Olsen, Nick Tandy, Earl Bamber	Porsche 911 GT3 R II	KCMG	149
DNF	CUP3	DNF	252	Jean-Francois Brunot, Henning Cramer, Jan Jaap van Roon, Andreas Gabler	Porsche 718 Cayman GT4 CS	KKrämer Racing	117
DNC	SP10	NC	85	Dirk-Tobias Wahl, Martin Meenen, Carsten Palluth, Marco Müller	Porsche 718 Cayman GT4 RS CS	Black Falcon Team Textar	99
DNF	CUP2	DNF	122	Noah Nagelsdiek, Reinhold Renger, Peter Ludwig, Maik Rosenberg	Porsche 992 GT3 Cup	Black Falcon	98
DNF	CUP2	DNF	121	Paul Harkema, Tobias Müller, Noah Nagelsdiek, Tim Scheerbarth	Porsche 992 GT3 Cup	Black Falcon Team Identica	97
DNF	SP9	DNF	28	Matteo Cairoli, Thomas Preining, Come Ledogar, Christian Engelhart	Porsche 911 GT3 R II	Dinamic Motorsport	85
DNF	CUP3	DNF	261	Peter Cate, Rüdiger Schicht, Ralf Kesseböhmer, Tony Richards	Porsche 718 Cayman GT4 CS	Mathol Racing	85
DNC	V6	NC	396	Christian Büllesbach, Stefan Kruse, Guido Heinrich, Andreas Schettler	Porsche 981 Cayman S	Adrenalin Motorsport	77
DNF	CUP2	DNF	126	Patrick Huisman, Tracy Krohn, Niclas Jonsson, Mario Farnbacher	Porsche 992 GT3 Cup	RPM Racing	66
DNF	CUP2	DNF	128	Ayhancan Guven, Hendrik von Danwitz, Julian Harrison, Klaus Abbelen	Porsche 992 GT3 Cup	Frikadelli Racing Team	62
DNF	V6	DNF	221	Nils Steinberg, David Drinkwater, Nicolaj Kandborg, Niklas Kry	Porsche 981 Cayman	WS Racing	62
DNF	SP9	DNF	44	Patrick Pilet, Klaus Bachler, Alessio Picariello, Martin Ragginger	Porsche 911 GT3 R II	Falken Motorsports	58
DNF	AT	DNF	420	Matthias Beckwermert, Henrik Bollerslev, Marco van Ramshorst, Christoph Hewer	Porsche 718 Cayman GT4 CS Biofuel	Four Motors Bioconcept Car	44
DNF	SP4T	DNF	181	Andreas Schaflitzl, Jacek Pydys, Alexander Köppen	Porsche 718 Cayman GTS	Köppen Motorsport	39
DNF	SP9	DNF	1	Kévin Estre, Frédérick Makowiecki, Laurens Vanthoor, Michael Christensen	Porsche 911 GT3 R II	Manthey Racing	22
DNF	SP9	DNF	27	Matt Campbell, Julien Andlauer, Mathieu Jaminet	Porsche 911 GT3 R II	Toksport WRT	18
DNF	SP9	DNF	29	Christian Engelhart, Matteo Cairoli, Adrien De Leener, Frederik Schandorff	Porsche 911 GT3 R II	Dinamic Motorsport	11

24 HOURS OF LE MANS

08.06.2022 – 12.06.2022 *Le Mans, France*

Gianmaria Bruni

Porsche siegt beim legendären 24-Stunden-Rennen von Le Mans, WeatherTech Racing sichert sich auf dem Circuit de la Sarthe Podestplatz in der GTE Am

Mit dem Sieg in der GTE Pro-Kategorie erlebte das Porsche GT Team ein ganz besonderes Jubiläumsrennen. Doch die 90. Auflage des berühmten Langstreckenklassikers war kein Selbstläufer für die Porsche-Mannschaft.
Nach einem soliden Saisonstart war die Werksmannschaft mit zwei Fahrzeugen und großen Hoffnungen zum dritten Lauf der FIA Langstrecken-Weltmeisterschaft nach Frankreich gereist.
Das Duo der Startnummer 92, Kévin Estre und Michael Christensen, welches bei den 24 Stunden von Laurens Vanthoor unterstützt wurde, hatte bereits in Sebring gewonnen und in Spa den zweiten Platz belegt und ging somit als Tabellenführer in die dritte Runde. Das Schwesterauto mit der Startnummer 91 wurde von der erfahrenen Crew bestehend aus Gianmaria Bruni, Richard Lietz und Frédéric Makowiecki pilotiert, die 2022 ebenfalls schon auf dem Podium gestanden hatte.
In der Hyperpole-Session am Donnerstagabend zeigte die Werksmannschaft bereits, welche Pace die Porsche 911 RSR haben. Der Franzose Makowiecki fuhr die drittschnellste Zeit in der ereignisreichen Session, Vanthoor folgte knapp dahinter auf Platz vier, womit die Startaufstellung für das Rennen 2022 feststand.
Der verpasste erste Startplatz beendete zwar eine Serie von zehn Pole-Positions in Folge, doch Alexander Stehling, Leiter Werksmotorsport FIA WEC, weiß, dass es in Le Mans auf den Renntag ankommt: „Letztes Jahr standen wir auf Pole, haben das Rennen anschließend aber nicht gewonnen. Also machen wir nun aus der Not eine Tugend und drehen diesen Spieß um. Am Sonntag um 16:00 Uhr fällt die Zielflagge. Erst dann wird abgerechnet. Wir wollen in Le Mans den Klassensieg holen."
Der Samstag brachte strahlenden Sonnenschein und heißes Wetter mit sich, was den

Porsche GT Team: (91): Richard Lietz, Gianmaria Bruni, Frédéric Makowiecki - (92): Michael Christensen, Laurens Vanthoor, Kévin Estre

Porsche returns to winning ways in GTE Pro at the legendary 24 Hours of Le Mans, WeatherTech Racing secure podium in GTE Am at the Circuit de la Sarthe

The Porsche GT Team made a successful return to the 24 Hours of Le Mans in 2022, scoring victory in the GTE Pro category. But it was by no means plain sailing for the Porsche effort, as attrition proved the decisive factor at the Circuit de la Sarthe. The two-car works squad travelled to France for the third round of the FIA World Endurance Championship with high hopes after a solid start to the season. The crew of the number 92 car, Kévin Estre and Michael Christensen, were supported by Laurens Vanthoor for the 24 hours. They had won in Sebring and finished second in Spa, and so led the championship going into round three. The sister 911 RSR was driven by the hugely experienced trio of Gianmaria Bruni, Richard Lietz and Frédéric Makowiecki. The number 91 car crew also had one pre-Le Mans podium finish to their name in 2022.

Cooper MacNeil

Fred Poordad, Max Root, Jan Heylen

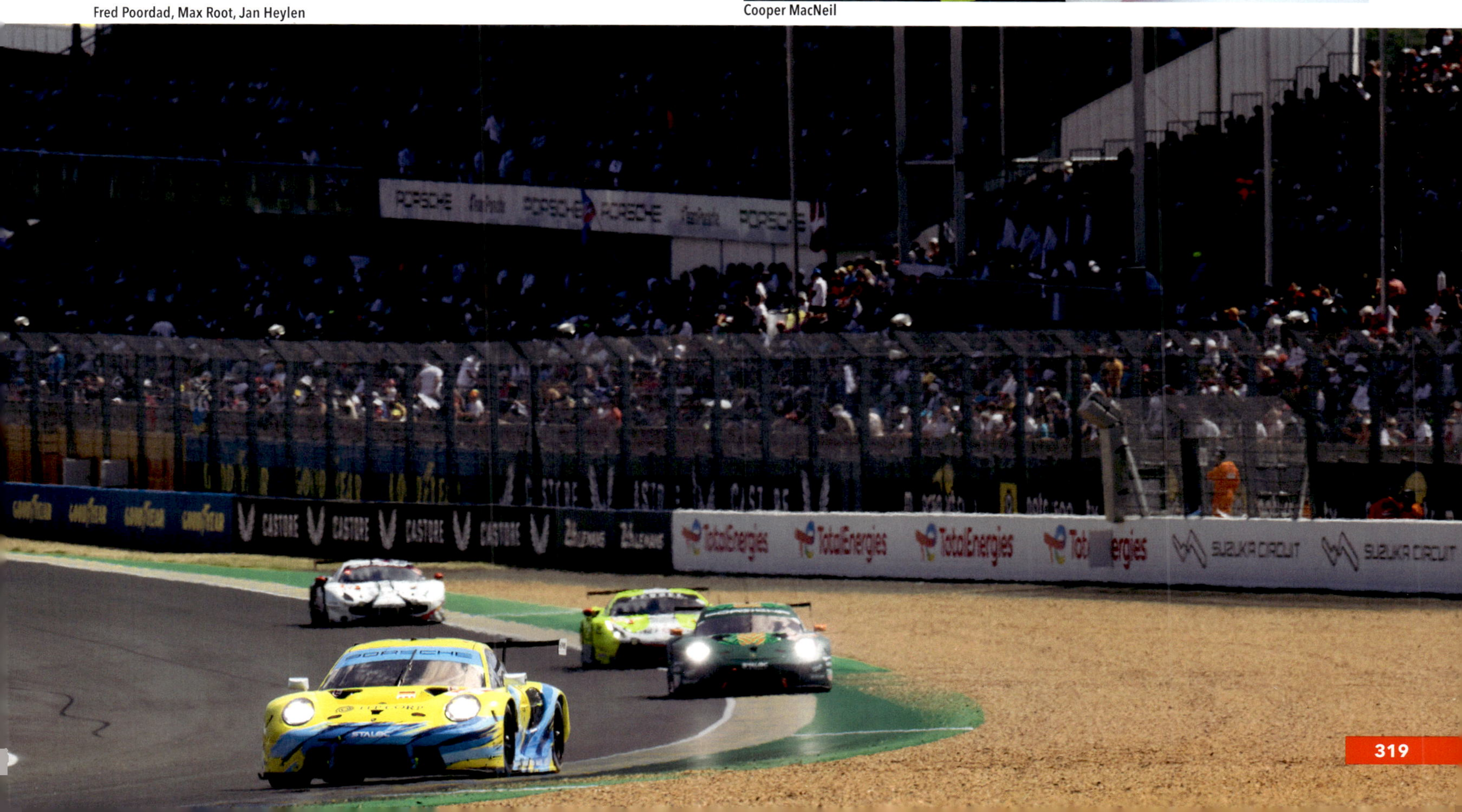

Laurens Vanthoor

ohnehin schon harten Kampf in der GTE-Pro-Klasse noch zusätzlich anheizte. Makowiecki und Estre starteten das Rennen und hielten sich in der Anfangsphase in der Spitzengruppe. Als Lietz und Christensen die Autos für ihre ersten Stints übernahmen, lagen die Porsche auf den Plätzen zwei und drei.

Die führende Corvette gewann zunächst einen deutlichen Vorsprung, da die Rennleitung eine Slow Zone verhängt hatte, aber die Porsche hielten sich auch in der Dämmerung stets in Schlagdistanz zur Spitze. Die Dunkelheit spielte ihnen dann in die Karten, da das Auto bei den kühleren Temperaturen besser funktionierte. Zur Halbzeit des Rennens führte die #92 von Estre, Christensen und Vanthoor mit über einer Minute Vorsprung vor der Corvette, während das Schwesterauto auf Platz vier lag.

„Wir haben zu Beginn zunächst etwas Boden verloren, weil die Autos unserer Konkurrenz bei Sonnenschein und hohen Streckentemperaturen besser funktionierten", sagte Estre nach einem seiner Nachtstints. „In der kühleren Nacht haben wir den Spieß umgedreht und uns an der Spitze einen großen Vorsprung herausgefahren."

So blieb es auch am Sonntagmorgen. Die Crew der #92 schien mit einem Vorsprung von mehr als zwei Minuten alles unter Kontrolle zu haben, doch dann nahm das Unheil seinen Lauf: Christensen erlitt einen Reifenschaden am rechten Vorderreifen, der das Auto erheblich beschädigte. Ein zehnminütiger Reparaturstopp kostete drei Runden und warf die Crew aus dem Kampf um den Klassensieg.

Auch im Laufe des Sonntags gab es weitere Dramen und Unglücksfälle. Das Team mit der Startnummer 91 fuhr jedoch weiterhin ein fehlerfreies Rennen und bahnte sich seinen Weg durch das Feld. Schon bald lagen Bruni, Lietz und Makowiecki an der Spitze und sicherten sich schlussendlich den Sieg in der GTE Pro bei der 90. Auflage des Langstreckenklassikers. „Wir haben ein klassisches Langstreckenrennen erlebt. Derjenige, der am wenigsten Zwischenfälle durchmacht, der steht am Ende auf dem Siegerpodest ganz oben", sagte Thomas Laudenbach, Leiter Porsche Motorsport. „Wir waren mit der Startnummer 91 zur Stelle – weil bei uns niemand aufgegeben hat: die Fahrer nicht und das Team ebenso wenig."

Brendan Iribe, Oliver Millroy, Ben Barnicoat

Team Project 1

Michael Fassbender

The Hyperpole session on Thursday evening gave the factory squad a chance to show what kind of pace the 911 RSRs could offer, and neither of the two cars disappointed. Frenchman Makowiecki was third-fastest in the action-packed session, with Vanthoor just behind in fourth as the grid.

The result ended an unbroken series of ten pole positions, but Director Factory Motorsport FIA WEC Alexander Stehling knows that Le Mans is all about race day. 'Last year we were on pole, but we didn't win the race, so let's turn this game around," he said. "The chequered flag will drop at 16:00 on Sunday. That's the moment of truth. We want to secure the class win at Le Mans."

Saturday brought with it bright sunshine and hot weather, adding extra spice to what would already prove to be a fiercely competitive GTE Pro class battle. Makowiecki and Estre started the race and managed to remain within the leading pack in the opening stages. As Lietz and Christensen took over their respective cars for their first stints, the Porsches were placed second and third.

The lead Corvette gained a significant advantage after the race director imposed a slow zone, but the Porsches were still within striking distance as the daylight faded. The darkness then played right into their hands, with the car performing better in the cooler temperatures. At the halfway stage Estre, Christensen and Vanthoor led by over a minute from the Corvette, with the sister car in fourth.

"We initially lost some ground because our competitors' cars performed better in the sunshine and high track temperatures," said Estre after one of his night-time stints. "In the cooler night temperatures, we turned the tables and established a strong lead."

Kévin Estre, Michael Christensen, Laurens Vanthoor

Christian Ried, Harry Tincknell, Sebastian Priaulx

Cooper MacNeil, Julien Andlauer, Thomas Merrill

Der Italiener Gianmaria Bruni hat sein primäres Ziel nach seinem Wechsel zu Porsche erreicht, während Frédéric Makowiecki beim neunten Anlauf auf die oberste Stufe des Podiums fuhr. Richard Lietz gehörte bereits beim ersten Sieg des RSR im Jahr 2013 zur Siegercrew und wiederholte das Kunststück neun Jahre später.

In der GTE Am hatten fünf Porsche 911 RSR eine Chance auf den Sieg, doch nur ein Team kam ohne Probleme durch das nervenaufreibende Rennen. Die Startnummer 79 von WeatherTech Racing beendete den Langstreckenklassiker auf einem verdienten zweiten Platz.

Dem Team Dempsey-Proton Racing des amerikanischen Schauspielers und Team-Mitbesitzers Patrick Dempsey war das Glück beim Rennen 2022 jedoch nicht hold. Das Auto mit der Startnummer 77, gefahren von Christian Ried, Sebastian Priaulx und Harry Tincknell, war gut unterwegs, verlor aber in der Schlussphase wegen eines gebrochenen Querlenkers Zeit an der Box und beendete das Rennen schließlich auf dem siebten Platz. Das Auto mit der Startnummer 88 von Fred Poordad, Jan Heylen und Maxwell Root überquerte die Ziellinie nach einer Reihe von Problemen als Fünfter. Das Fahrzeug mit der Nummer 93 von Proton Competition, in dem Hollywood-Star Michael Fassbender sein Le-Mans-Debüt feierte, erreichte das Ziel als Achter. Das größte Pech hatte das niedersächsische Team Project 1: Die Fahrzeuge des erfahrenen Kundenteams mussten vorzeitig aufgeben.

Richard Lietz, Gianmaria Bruni, Frédéric Makowiecki

Christian Ried, Harry Tincknell, Sebastian Priaulx

Richard Lietz

Kévin Estre, Michael Christensen, Laurens Vanthoor

Fred Poordad, Max Root, Jan Heylen

Michael Fassbender, Matt Campbell, Zacharie Robichon

Christian Ried, Harry Tincknell, Sebastian Priaulx

That's more or less how things stayed into Sunday morning, with the race being run at a blistering pace offering zero room for error. The crew of the 92 appeared to be in control with a lead of more than two minutes, before disaster struck: Christensen suffered a blowout on the front-right tyre, damaging the car significantly. A ten-minute stop for repairs lost the car three laps and put it out of contention for the class victory.

Drama and misfortune plagued other GTE Pro entries over the course of Sunday. However, the #91 crew continued to race well and without any mistakes, slowly making their way through the field as others fell behind. Bruni, Lietz and Makowiecki led as the race drew to its conclusion and the trio brought the car safely home to wrap up GTE Pro victory at the 90th running of the famous endurance race.

"At the exact moment, we were where we needed to be with our No. 91 car because no one gave up: neither the team nor the drivers," said Thomas Laudenbach, Vice President Porsche Motorsport.

Italian Gianmaria Bruni achieved his primary objective after joining Porsche, while Frédéric Makowiecki finally finished on the top step of the podium at the ninth time of asking. Richard Lietz was part of the winning crew at the RSRs first victory in 2013 and repeated the feat nine years later.

In GTE Am, five Porsche 911 RSRs were in with a shot of victory but only one team managed to get through the gruelling race without any issues. The WeatherTech Racing entry finished the race with a well-deserved second place.

Fortune did not favour the Dempsey-Proton Racing squad of American actor and team co-owner Patrick Dempsey. The number 77 car, driven by Christian Ried, Sebastian Priaulx and Harry Tincknell, had been running well but lost time in the pits in the closing stages due to a broken wishbone and ultimately finished the race in seventh place. The number 88 car of Fred Poordad, Jan Heylen and Maxwell Root crossed the line in fifth after a number of problems during the 24 hours. The number 93 Proton Competition car, in which Hollywood star Michael Fassbender celebrated his Le Mans debut, reached the flag in eighth place. The Project 1 squad from Germany's Lower Saxony experienced the worst luck: The cars fielded by the experienced customer team retired early.

Frédérik Makowiecki, Gianmaria Bruni, Richard Lietz

(l.-r.): Cooper MacNeil, Thomas Merrill, Julien Andlauer

Cooper MacNeil, Julien Andlauer, Thomas Merrill

PORSCHE
Au revoir RSR - LM GTE Pro Winner 22
MICHELIN

LE MANS

(l.-r.): Gianmaria Bruni, Frédéric Makowiecki, Richard Lietz, Bernhard Demmer

RACE CLASSIFICATION **OVERALL**

POS	CLASS	CLASS POS	NO	DRIVERS	CAR	TEAM	LAPS
1	Hypercar	1	8	Sebastien Buemi, Brendon Hartley, Ryo Hirakawa	Toyota GR010	Toyota Gazoo Racing	380
2	Hypercar	2	7	Mike Conway, Jose Maria Lopez, Kamui Kobayashi	Toyota GR010	Toyota Gazoo Racing	380
3	Hypercar	3	709	Franck Mailleux, Richard Westbrook, Ryan Briscoe	Glickenhaus 007 LMH	Glickenhaus Racing	375
28	GTE Pro	1	91	Frédérik Makowiecki, Gianmaria Bruni, Richard Lietz	Porsche 911 RSR	Porsche GT Team	350
31	GTE Pro	4	92	Kévin Estre, Michael Christensen, Laurens Vanthoor	Porsche 911 RSR	Porsche GT Team	348
35	GTE Am	2	79	Julien Andlauer, Thomas Merrill, Cooper MacNeil	Porsche 911 RSR	WeatherTech Racing	343
37	GTE Am	4	86	Ben Barker, Michael Wainwright, Riccardo Pera	Porsche 911 RSR	GR Racing	340
38	GTE Am	5	88	Jan Heylen, Fred Poordad, Maxwell Root	Porsche 911 RSR	Dempsey Racing-Proton Competition	340
44	GTE Am	11	99	Alessio Picariello, Andrew Haryanto, Martin Rump	Porsche 911 RSR	Hardpoint Motorsport/Absolute Racing	338
45	GTE Am	14	77	Harry Tincknell, Seb Priaulx, Christian Ried	Porsche 911 RSR	Proton Competition	336
51	GTE Am	16	93	Matt Campbell, Michael Fassbender, Zacharie Robichon	Porsche 911 RSR	Proton Competition	329
DNF	GTE Am	DNF	56	Ben Barnicoat, Brendan Iribe, Ollie Millroy	Porsche 911 RSR	Team Project 1	241
DNF	GTE Am	DNF	46	Matteo Cairoli, Nicolas Leutwiler, Mikkel Overgaard Pedersen	Porsche 911 RSR	Team Project 1	77

Frédéric Makowiecki

CLASS CLASSIFICATION **LMGTE PRO**

POS	NO	DRIVERS	CAR	TEAM	LAPS
1	91	Gianmaria Bruni, Richard Lietz, Frédéric Makowiecki	Porsche 911 RSR	Porsche GT Team	350
2	51	Alessandro Pier Guidi, James Calado, Daniel Serra	Ferrari 488 GTE	AF Corse-Ferrari	350
3	52	Miguel Molina., Antonio Fuoco, Davide Rigon	Ferrari 488 GTE	AF Corse-Ferrari	349
4	92	Michael Christensen, Kévin Estre, Laurens Vanthoor	Porsche 911 RSR	Porsche GT Team	348

CLASS CLASSIFICATION **LMGTE AM**

POS	NO	DRIVERS	CAR	TEAM	LAPS
1	33	Ben Keating, Henrique Chaves, Marco Sörensen	Aston Martin	TF Sport	343
2	79	Cooper Mac Neil, Julien Andlauer, Thomas Merrill	Porsche 911 RSR	WeatherTech Racing	343
3	98	Paul Dalla Lana, David Pittard, Nicki Thiim	Aston Martin	Northwest AMR	342
4	86	Michael Wainwright, Ricardo Pera, Benjamin Barker	Porsche 911 RSR	GR Racing	340
5	88	Fred Poordad, Maxwell Root, Jan Heylen	Porsche 911 RSR	Dempsey Racing-Proton Competition	340
11	99	Andrew Haryanto, Alessio Picariello, Martin Rump	Porsche 911 RSR	Hardpoint Motorsport/Absolute Racing	338
14	77	Christian Ried, Sebastian Priaulx, Harry Tincknell	Porsche 911 RSR	Dempsey Racing-Proton Competition	336
16	93	Michael Fassbender, Matt Campbell, Zacharie Robichon	Porsche 911 RSR	Proton Competition	329
DNF	56	Brendan Iribe, Oliver Millroy, Ben Barnicoat	Porsche 911 RSR	Team Project 1	241
DNF	46	Matteo Cairoli, Mikkel Pedersen, Nicolas Leutwiler	Porsche 911 RSR	Team Project 1	77

Matteo Cairoli, Mikkel Pedersen, Nicolas Leutwiler

24 HOURS OF SPA-FRANCORCHAMPS

28.07.–31.07.2022 Spa-Francorchamps, Belgium

Piti Bhirombhakdi, Earl Bamber, Tanart Sathienthirakul, Christophe Hamon

Sven Müller, Julien Andlauer, Marvin Dienst

KCMG nach sehenswerter Aufholjagd als bestplatzierter Porsche auf Rang sieben im Ziel – Podiumserfolg im Pro-Am Cup für Singha Racing Team TP 12

Vom letzten Platz gestartet, auf Position sieben als bestplatzierter Porsche die Ziellinie überquert: Diese erfolgreiche Aufholjagd hat die Mannschaft von KCMG rund um Laurens Vanthoor, Dennis Olsen und Nick Tandy bei der 72. Auflage der 24 Stunden von Spa hingelegt. Nach einem Defekt am Fahrzeug war es der Besatzung des Porsche 911 GT3 R #47 nicht möglich, weiter am Qualifying teilzunehmen. Aufgrund dessen musste das Trio vom Ende des Feldes starten. Doch davon ließ sich das Team nicht entmutigen. Die Piloten kämpften sich Schritt für Schritt nach vorn und übernahmen nach rund 14 Stunden zwischenzeitlich sogar die Führung. Lange Zeit war das Fahrzeug im Kampf um die Podestplätze involviert, am Ende reichte es aber nicht, den Platz auf dem Treppchen zu verteidigen. Auch die Mannschaft von EMA Motorsport hatte mit zahlreichen Problemen zu kämpfen: Ein Reifenschaden zu Beginn und ein längerer Reparaturstopp aufgrund einer Kollision kosteten ein mögliches Top-Resultat.

In der Superpole und in der ersten Rennhälfte waren es jedoch zwei andere Porsche-Teams, die auf sich aufmerksam machten. Dank einer grandiosen Runde von Klaus Bachler startete Dinamic Motorsport aus der ersten Startreihe. Und es war auch Bachler, der dem Rennen in der ersten Stunde seinen Stempel aufdrückte. Als die Startampel auf Grün sprang, setzte sich der Österreicher mit einem mutigen Manöver an die Spitze des Feldes und verteidigte diese Position über seinen gesamten Stint. Auch in den folgenden Stunden lag der Porsche des italienischen Rennstalls in aussichtsreicher Position, ehe ein Schaden nach einer Berührung die Mannschaft zur Aufgabe zwang. Ebenfalls lange Zeit in der Spitzengruppe unterwegs war der, im markanten Martini-Design folierte, 911er von GPX Martini Racing. Von Position

Dylan Pereira, Antares Au, Jaxon Evans, Kevin Tse

After exciting catch-up, KCMG finishes seventh as best-placed Porsche at the Spa 24 Hours – podium success for Singha Racing Team TP 12 in Pro-Am Cup

The best-placed Porsche started from last position to finish seventh: KCMG team's Laurens Vanthoor, Dennis Olsen and Nick Tandy delivered a successful chase at the 72nd Spa 24 Hours. After a vehicle fault, the Porsche 911 GT3 R #47 missed qualifying and started from the field's rear, fought forwards undeterred and took the lead intermittently after 14 hours, but couldn't make the podium. EMA Motorsport was also confronted with numerous problems. Tyre damage and a lengthy repair stop dashed hopes of a top result.
Two other Porsche teams initially attracted attention in the Superpole and first race half. Thanks to Klaus Bachler's spectacular lap, Dinamic Motorsport started from a grid first with the Austrian courageously battling to the front, holding the lead for his

Matt Campbell, Felipe Nasr, Mathieu Jaminet

Alfred Renauer, Robert Renauer, Ralf Bohn

Alessio Picariello, Nico Menzel, Stefan Aust, Nicolas Leutwiler

fünf ins Rennen gegangen führten Richard Lietz, Michael Christensen und Kévin Estre das Rennen sogar zeitweise an, ehe ein technischer Defekt in der Nacht das Aus bedeutete.

Herberth Motorsport setzte gleich drei Fahrzeuge beim Langstreckenklassiker ein. Doch nach einem guten Start schieden zwei Fahrzeuge früh durch Unfälle aus. Als einzig verbliebener Porsche des bayrischen Rennstalls lag die #24 lange Zeit gut im Rennen. Bis zum Sonntagvormittag hatten Alessio Picariello, Nico Menzel, Niki Leutwiler und Stefan Aust souverän die Führung im Pro-Am Cup inne, ehe ein Reifenschaden das Rennen des Quartetts beendete. Doch auch wenn es für das Team nicht zum Klassensieg reichte, sorgte eine andere Porsche-Mannschaft für Jubel: Mit Rang drei holte Singha Racing Team TP 12 einen Podesterfolg im Pro-Am Cup. Im Silver Cup beendeten die Porsche 911 GT3 R von Dinamic Motorsport und Allied Racing das Rennen auf den Positionen sechs und sieben.

Michael Christensen, Kévin Estre, Richard Lietz

Nick Tandy, Laurens Vanthoor, Dennis Olsen

Ayhancan Guven, Julien Apotheloz, Alex Malykhin, Florian Latorre

(l.-r.): Sven Müller, Marvin Dienst, Julien Andlauer

entire stint. The Italian squad's Porsche retired after a contact and collision. GPX Martini Racing's distinctively designed 911 was also a frontrunner. Starting from a grid fifth, Richard Lietz, Michael Christensen and Kévin Estre dropped out after a nocturnal technical issue.

From Bavarian Herberth Motorsport's three cars, two retired early after accidents. #24 Porsche with Alessio Picariello, Nico Menzel, Niki Leutwiler and Stefan Aust held a sovereign Pro-Am Cup lead before tyre damage ended the quartet's race. Instead, another Porsche team stepped in – Singha Racing Team TP 12 clinched third place in class. Dinamic Motorsport and Allied Racing's Porsche 911 GT3 Rs finished sixth and seventh in the Silver Cup.

Stephen Grove, Brenton Grove, Adrian Hendry D'Silva, Matthew Payne

Audi Sport

HRX
PORSCHE

MARTINI

PORSCHE
MOTORSPORT
BOSS

(l.-r.): Alfred Renauer, Stefan Aust, Robert Renauer, Ralf Bohn

Joel Sturm, Vincent Andronaco, Patrik Matthiesen, Dominik Fischli

Klaus Bachler

(l.-r.): Piti Bhirombhakdi, Tanart Sathienthirakul, Earl Bamber, Christophe Hamon

(l.-r.): Felipe Nasr, Mathieu Jaminet, Matt Campbell

RACE CLASSIFICATION

POS	CLASS	CLASS POS	NO	DRIVERS	CAR	TEAM	LAPS
1	Pro	1	88	Raffaele Marciello, Daniel Juncadella, Jules Gounon	Mercedes-AMG GT3 Evo	Akkodis ASP	536
2	Pro	2	2	Luca Stolz, Maximilian Götz, Steijn Schothorst	Mercedes-AMG GT3 Evo	Mercedes-AMG Team GetSpeed Performance	536
3	Pro	3	71	Antonio Fuoco, Davide Rigon, Daniel Serra	Ferrari F488 GT3 Evo	Iron Lynx	536
7	Pro	7	47	Nick Tandy, Laurens Vanthoor, Dennis Olsen	Porsche 911 GT3 R II	KCMG	536
22	**Pro**	**16**	**74**	**Matt Campbell, Felipe Nasr, Mathieu Jaminet**	**Porsche 911 GT3 R II**	**EMA Motorsport**	**529**
25	Silver	6	56	Mauro Calamia, Marius Johan Nakken, Giorgio Roda, Mikkel Overgaard Pedersen	Porsche 911 GT3 R II	Dinamic Motorsport	527
29	**Silver**	**7**	**22**	**Joel Sturm, Vincent Andronaco, Patrik Matthiesen, Dominik Fischli**	**Porsche 911 GT3 R II**	**Allied Racing**	**529**
30	Pro-Am	3	39	Piti Bhirombhakdi, Earl Bamber, Tanart Sathienthirakul, Christophe Hamon	Porsche 911 GT3 R II	Singha Motorsport Team Thailand	526
DNF	**Pro-Am**	**DNF**	**24**	**Alessio Picariello, Nico Menzel, Stefan Aust, Nicolas Leutwiler**	**Porsche 911 GT3 R II**	**Herberth Motorsport**	**382**
DNF	Pro	DNF	100	Sven Müller, Julien Andlauer, Marvin Dienst	Porsche 911 GT3 R II	Toksport WRT	374
DNF	**Pro**	**DNF**	**221**	**Michael Christensen, Kévin Estre, Richard Lietz**	**Porsche 911 GT3 R II**	**GPX Racing**	**221**
DNF	Pro-Am	DNF	16	Stephen Grove, Brenton Grove, Adrian Hendry D'Silva, Matthew Payne	Porsche 911 GT3 R II	Earl Bamber Motorsport	206
DNF	**Gold**	**DNF**	**911**	**Alfred Renauer, Robert Renauer, Ralf Bohn**	**Porsche 911 GT3 R II**	**Herberth Motorsport**	**192**
DNF	Pro	DNF	54	Klaus Bachler, Come Ledogar, Thomas Preining	Porsche 911 GT3 R II	Dinamic Motorsport	176
DNF	**Pro-Am**	**DNF**	**9**	**Dylan Pereira, Antares Au, Jaxon Evans, Kevin Tse**	**Porsche 911 GT3 R II**	**Herberth Motorsport**	**100**
DNF	Gold	DNF	91	Ayhancan Guven, Julien Apotheloz, Alex Malykhin, Florian Latorre	Porsche 911 GT3 R II	Allied Racing	57

24 HOURS OF ZOLDER

11.08. – 14.08.2022 Zolder, Belgium

Michiel Haverans, Marc Goossens, Rodrigue Gillion, Nico Verdonck

Q1-Trackracing aus Belgien erkämpft sich Rang zwei bei den 24 Stunden von Zolder – Porsche belegt dank starker Performance die Plätze zwei bis sechs

Das 24-Stunden-Rennen auf dem Circuit Zolder ist jedes Jahr ein Highlight im Kalender der Belcar Endurance Championship. Auch die 44. Ausgabe des Langstreckenrennens bot 2022 wieder eine würdige Herausforderung für die Teams und Fahrer. Insgesamt 13 Fahrzeuge setzten die Porsche-Mannschaften bei heißen Temperaturen in Belgien ein – und durften am Ende feiern: Sie belegten die Plätze zwei bis sechs. Rang zwei sicherte sich das Team Q1-Trackracing mit seinen Fahrern Filip Teunkens, Jan Lauryssen, Tommy Rau und Florian Latorre im Porsche mit der Startnummer #55. Die Belgier lieferten sich bis zum Schluss einen harten Zweikampf mit dem späteren Sieger PK Carsport und sorgten damit für große Begeisterung bei den Fans. Das Podium rundete das Team Belgium Racing im Porsche 911 GT3 Cup #78 auf Rang drei ab. Knapp dahinter überquerte das Team Russel Racing by NGT die Ziellinie. Am Ende fehlten Hans und Frank Thiers, Jeffrey Van Hooydonck, Christoff Corten und Stijn Lowette nur 2,3 Sekunden auf den begehrten Podestplatz. Komplettiert wurde der starke Auftritt der Porsche-Mannschaften von Belgium Racing (#99) und RED ANT Racing (#12) auf den Positionen fünf und sechs.

Toon Hungenaert, Dries Gelade, Frank Geelissen, Fréderic Bouvy

Filip Teunkens, Jan Lauryssen, Tommy Rau, Florian Latorre

Tom Boonen, Luc van der Feesten, Kobe de Breucker, Jimmy de Breucker, Kevin Abbring

Dylan Derdaele, Michael Cool, Kenneth Heyer, Ziad Geris

Belgium's Q1 Trackracing secures second place in the Zolder 24 Hours as Porsche locks out second to sixth place thanks to a strong performance

The 24-hour race at Circuit Zolder is the annual highlight on the Belcar Endurance Championship calendar. In 2022, the 44th running of the endurance race again provided a worthy challenge for teams and drivers. In high temperatures in Belgium, Porsche teams entered a total of 13 cars on the grid and they were able to celebrate at the end: Porsche locked out second to sixth place in the overall classification. The Q1 Trackracing team, with drivers Filip Teunkens, Jan Lauryssen, Tommy Rau and Florian Latorre, finished second with its #55 Porsche. Right up to the end of the race, the Belgian team delighted fans with its hard battle against PK Carsport, the eventual race-winning team. Belgium Racing claimed the final podium slot with its #78 Porsche 911 GT3 Cup. Just behind them was the Russel Racing by NGT team of Hans and Frank Thiers, Jeffrey Van Hooydonck, Christoff Corten and Stijn Lowette. They missed out on the podium by just 2.3 seconds. Belgium Racing (#99) and RED ANT Racing (#12) rounded out the strong performance by the Porsche teams in fifth and sixth places respectively.

Kenneth Heyer

RACE CLASSIFICATION

POS	CLASS	CLASS POS	NO	DRIVERS	CAR	TEAM	LAPS
1	GTA	1	11	Peter Guelinckx, Bert Longin, Stienes Longin, Dries Vanthoor, Nicolas Saelens	Audi R8 LMS GT2	PK Carsport	772
2	GTA	2	55	Filip Teunkens, Jan Lauryssen, Tommy Rau, Florian Latorre	Porsche 992 GT3 Cup	Q1 Trackracing	769
3	GTA	3	78	Michiel Haverans, Marc Goossens, Rodrigue Gillion, Nico Verdonck	Porsche 992 GT3 Cup	Belgium Racing	763
4	GTA	4	2	Hans Thiers, Frank Thiers, Jeffrey Van Hooydonck, Christoff Corten, Stijn Lowette	Porsche 992 GT3 Cup	Russell Racing by NGT	763
5	GTA	5	99	Dylan Derdaele, Michael Cool, Kenneth Heyer, Ziad Geris	Porsche 992 GT3 Cup	Belgium Racing	741
6	GTA	6	12	Bert Redant, Ayrton Redant, Yannick Redant, Sam Dejonghe	Porsche 991 GT3 Cup	Red Ant Racing	714
13	GTB	1	63	Arthur Peters, Benjamin De Cock, Gunther Van den Bergh, Laurent Van Laere, Fernand Lancksweerd	Porsche Cayman GT4	Tip Top Rent	651
19	GTA	8	3	Tom Boonen, Luc van der Feesten, Kobe de Breucker, Jimmy de Breucker, Kevin Abbring	Porsche 991 GT3 Cup	Red Ant Racing	621
20	GTB	4	6	Dirk van Rompuy, Tom van Rompuy, Eric Bruynooghe, Eric Qvick	Porsche Cayman GT4	VR Racing by Red Ant Racing	621
DNF	GTA	DNF	7	Olivier Dons, Jürgen Van Hover, Pieter Ooms, Kurt Hensen, John De Wilde	Porsche 992 GT3 Cup	Speedlover	506
DNF	GTA	DNF	52	Laurent Vandervelde, Stephane Ortelli, Ghislain Cordeel, Sven Van Laere, Benjamin Paque	Porsche 992 GT3 Cup	Q1 Trackracing	322
DNF	GTB	DNF	77	Stephan Beyens, Didier Beyens, Peter Sterken, Davy Suffeleers, Ines Lammens	Porsche Boxster	BE Motorsport	280
DNF	GTA	DNF	17	Toon Hungenaert, Dries Gelade, Frank Geelissen, Frédéric Bouvy	Porsche 991	Rush Competition by Speedlover	190
DNF	GTA	DNF	15	Gregory Stevens, Frank Stevens, Heinrich Lategan, Johan de Bruyn, Glenn Van Parijs	Porsche 992 GT3 Cup	NGT Racing	56

SPORT 2022

WORLD

REALIZUJEME KURZY BEZPEČNÉ JÍZDY -
ŠKOLY SMYKŮ + POVINNÉ ŠKOLENÍ ŘIDIČŮ
TEL.:
www.micanekmotorsport.cz

SPECK X
MICHELIN
MOTUL

232
Mobil 1
BOSS

PORSCHE
22
Porsche Zentrum Regensburg
MICHELIN
PORSCHE
55
STENDER GRUPPE
PORSCHE
68
Stender Group
MICHELIN

PORSCHE
SPORTS CUP
DEUTSCHLAND

PORSCHE SPORTS CUP DEUTSCHLAND

11.06.–12.06.2022 *Nüburgring, Germany*
23.07.–24.07.2022 *Red Bull Ring, Austria*
13.08.–14.08.2022 *Oschersleben, Germany*
17.09.–18.09.2022 *Misano, Italy*
15.10.–16.10.2022 *Hockenheim, Germany*

Sebastian Roth

Im Porsche Sports Cup Deutschland wurde den Fans und Teilnehmern wieder einmal ein abwechslungsreiches Programm aus dem Porsche-Motorsport geboten.

Nach dem abgesagten Auftakt in Hockenheim, der Ende Mai stattfinden sollte, begann der Porsche Sports Cup Deutschland Mitte Juni auf dem Nürburgring und bestand nur noch aus fünf Rennwochenenden.

In der Porsche Sprint Challenge gingen ausschließlich Rennwagen ohne Straßenzulassung an den Start, die auf Michelin-Rennreifen rollten. Bester in dieser Serie war Michael Essmann, der einen Porsche 991 GT3 Cup bewegte. Der Mann aus Rheine konnte zwar kein Rennen gewinnen, doch er durfte dreimal als Zweiter und einmal als Dritter auf das Gesamtpodest klettern. Die meisten Gesamtsiege bejubelte Friedel Bleifuss, der mit seinem Porsche 991 GT3 R vier Läufe für sich entschied. Dessen Klassenrivale Ulrich Becker beendete ebenso wie Lorenz Stegmann und Robert Lukas, beide im Porsche 992 GT3 Cup, zwei Heats auf Rang eins.

In der Rennserie Porsche Sprint GT traten Fahrer auf straßenzugelassenen Porsche mit Straßenreifen von Michelin und einer für den Rennsport geeigneten Sicherheitsausrüstung gegeneinander an. Champion Gian Luca Tüccaroglu sammelte über alle Klassen hinweg nicht nur die meisten Punkte, sondern war mit vier Siegen auch am häufigsten als Erster im Ziel. Christoph Krombach, der für das KÜS Team Bernhard ans Steuer seines Porsche Cayman GT4 CS-MR griff, konnte als bestes Gesamtresultat einen fünften Rang auf dem Nürburgring verbuchen. In der Sprint-GT-Abschlusstabelle fand er sich auf Platz neun wieder, in seiner Klasse 2f wurde er im Schlussklassement auf Position sieben notiert.

Auch in der Porsche Endurance Challenge war Krombach am Start, hier teilte er sich seinen Cayman mit dem jungen Nachwuchstalent Daniel Gregor. Bestes Ergebnis des Duos im 100-minütigen Langstreckenrennen war der dritte Platz am Red Bull Ring. In

(60): Andreas Sczepansky - (68): Tim Stender

Once again, fans and competitors got to enjoy a varied Porsche Motorsport programme in the Porsche Sports Cup Deutschland.

The opening round at Hockenheim was cancelled, which meant that the season only got underway at Nürburgring in mid-June. The cancellation meant that the schedule was reduced to five weekends. In the Porsche Sprint Challenge for Michelin-shod race cars that did not have road-approval, Michael Essmann scored the highest number of points in his 991 GT3 Cup, although he didn't win a race. Friedel Bleifuss scored four outright wins in his 911 GT3 R.
In Porsche Sprint GT competition for road-legal Porsches which ran on Michelin road tyres, Gian Luca Tüccaroglu secured the title and also the most outright victories, four in total. For KÜS Team Bernhard driver Christoph Krombach, fifth place at Nürburgring was his best result. He ended up ninth in the final Sprint GT standings and seventh in his class 2f.

(54): Michael Essmann - (20): Robert Lukas

Christoph Krombach and Daniel Gregor

Christoph Krombach

der Gesamtwertung ihrer Klasse 2f reichte das für die siebte Stelle. Carrie Schreiner teilte sich ihren Porsche 911 GT3 Cup mit Lars Joosten. Tim Stender, Philip Hamprecht landeten in der Gesamtwertung der fünf Meisterschaftsrennen auf Platz drei. Weiter vorne gewann Friedel Bleifuss zusammen mit Jannes Fittje zwei der fünf Saisonläufe, doch der Titel über alle Klassen ging an Dominik Schraml / Steve Caroli. Schließlich wurden im Rahmen des Porsche Sports Cup Deutschland noch Gleichmäßigkeitsprüfungen ausgetragen; die einzige lizenzpflichtige Prüfung war die Porsche Drivers Competition Pro. An der nahm auch Josef Smarda teil; der Kanadier aus Calgary belegte im Endklassement nach zwei Siegen, einem zweiten und einem dritten Rang, Position fünf. Der neue Champion heißt René Klingbeil.

Josef Smarda

Philip Hamprecht and Tim Stender

Carrie Schreiner

Krombach also raced in the Porsche Endurance Challenge, sharing his Cayman with young talent Daniel Gregor. The best result in the 100-minute endurance races was 3rd at Red Bull Ring. They ended up seventh in their class 2f. Further up, Friedel Bleifuss won two of the five races together with Jannes Fittje, but Dominik Schraml / Steve Caroli won the title across all classes. Regularity runs were also part of the events. Josef Smarda from Calgary participated in the Porsche Drivers Competition Pro and ended up fifth in the standings with two wins, one second and one third place. René Klingbeil was crowned champion.

Josef Šmarda and Team Mičánek Motorsport

Daan Magis, Paul Wijtman

Paul Wijtman, Daan Magis

Josef Šmarda

(91): Gian Luca Tüccaroglu - (69): Mariusz Gorecki - (170): Maiko Dufner

„Friedel Bleifuss", Jannes Fittje

Dominik Schraml and Steve Caroli

Michael Essmann and Team CarTech Motorsport by Nigrin

Josef Šmarca

KURT ECKE
MOTORSPORT
ATR

PORSCHE

TEAMWEAR

PORSCHE
SPORTS CUP
DEUTSCHLAND

DEUTSCHLAND
DMSB

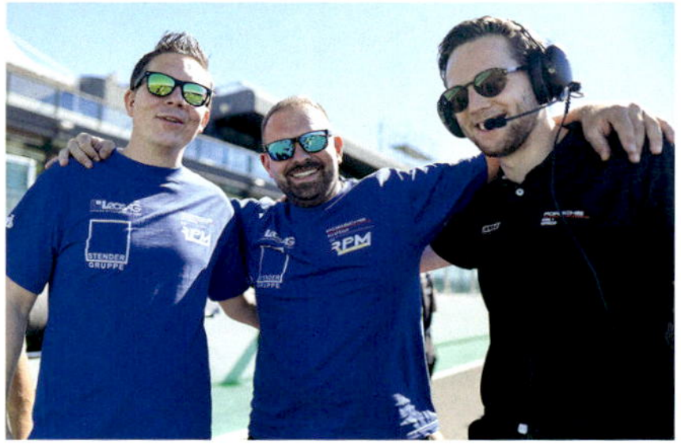

(68): Tim Stender - (165): Philipp Gresek

Carrie Schreiner, Lars Joosten

Paul Wijtman and Daan Magis

ENDURANCE CHALLENGE

POS	NO	DRIVERS	CAR	TEAM	POINTS
1	130	Steve Caroli, Dominik Schraml	Porsche Cayman GT4 CS MR	East Racing Motorsport	91
2	91	Gian Luca Tüccaroglu, Osman Tüccaroglu	Porsche Cayman GT4 CS	Team [a-workx] Motorsport	85
3	68	Tim Stender, Philipp Hamprecht	Porsche 991 GT3 Cup	RPM Racing	75,6
4	138	Michael Joos, Stephan Heim	Porsche 991 GT3 Cup	Joos Sportwagentechnik	63,2
5	166	Philipp Gresek	Porsche 992 GT3 Cup	TM-Racing by Plusline AG	61,2
6	55	Marc Bartels	Porsche 992 GT3 Cup	Porsche Zentrum Mannheim	54,4
7	88	Günther Kraus, Constantin Schöll	Porsche 992 GT3 Cup	Team [a-workx] Motorsport	53,5
8	144	Lars Joosten, Carrie Schreiner	Porsche 992 GT3 Cup	TM-Racing by Plusline AG	50,4
9	52	Carsten Schweizer, Jochen Weiss	Porsche Cayman GT4 CS	Team Speed Monkeys	50,0
10	17	Constantin Berz	Porsche Cayman GT4 CS	Porsche Zentrum Mannheim	50,0

SPRINT GT

POS	NO	DRIVERS	CAR	TEAM	POINTS
1	91	Gian Luca Tüccaroglu	Porsche Cayman GT4 CS	Team [a-workx] Motorsport	168,2
2	69	Mariusz Gorecki	Porsche Cayman GT4 CS	Förch Racing	154,7
3	130	Steve Caroli	Porsche Cayman GT4 CS MR	East Racing Motorsport	140,6
4	92	Sebastian Roth	Porsche Cayman GT4 CS	Seebach Fahrzeugtechnik	95,4
5	52	Carsten Schweitzer	Porsche Cayman GT4 CS	Team Speed Monkeys	95
6	203	Rüdiger Bambach	Porsche 991 GT3	Sportwagen Südwest	80
7	29	Jochen Kilb	Porsche Cayman GT4 CS	Seebach Fahrzeugtechnik	77,2
8	53	Laura Marie Geissler	Porsche Cayman GT4 CS MR	Team Speed Monkeys	73,1
9	175	Christoph Krombach	Porsche Cayman GT4 CS MR	KÜS Team Bernhard	72
10	95	Mihail Mihaylov	Porsche Cayman GT4 RS CS	Overdrive	65

SPRINT CHALLENGE

POS	NO	DRIVERS	CAR	TEAM	POINTS
1	54	Michael Essmann	Porsche 991 GT3 Cup	CarTech Motorsport by Nigrin	185,2
2	145	Stefan Rehkopf	Porsche 991 GT3 Cup		171,8
3	313	Lorenz Stegmann	Porsche 992 GT3 Cup	Stegmann Motorsport	162,2
4	285	Felix Neuhofer	Porsche 992 GT3 Cup	Team Neuhofer Rennsport	156,9
5	20	Robert Lukas	Porsche 992 GT3 Cup	Förch Racing	154,6
6	34	Karol Kret	Porsche 991 GT3 Cup	Förch Racing	145,3
7	165	Philipp Gresek	Porsche 992 GT3 Cup	TM-Racing by Plusline AG	144,2
8	10	Matthias Jeserich	Porsche 992 GT3 Cup	Kurt Ecke Motorsport / ATR	120,2
9	60	Andreas Sczepansky	Porsche 991 GT3 Cup	Kurt Ecke Motorsport	95,4
10	144	Lars Joosten	Porsche 992 GT3 Cup	TM-Racing by Plusline AG	93,2

DRIVERS COMPETITION PRO

POS	NO	DRIVERS	CAR	POINTS
1	49	René Klingbeil	Porsche 991 GT3	226
2	15	"Ehrster"	Porsche Cayman GT4	221
3	202	Tomas Urban	Porsche 997 GTS	216,5
4	71	Jaroslav Mikolas	Porsche 992 GT3	213,5
5	39	Josef Šmarda	Porsche 991 GT3 RS	209
6	184	Horst Wittmann	Porsche Cayman GT4	106
7	123	Jens Heidel	Porsche Cayman GT4	83,5
8	191	Richard Theurer	Porsche 991 GT3	65
9	85	Friedhelm Rieb	Porsche Cayman GT4	57
10	65	Harald Häfner	Porsche Cayman GT4	48,5

PORSCHE
SPORTS CUP
SUISSE

PORSCHE SPORTS CUP SUISSE

28.04.–30.04.2022 Red Bull Ring, Austria
26.05.–28.05.2022 Paul Ricard, France
08.07.–10.07.2022 Franciacorta, Italy
18.08.–20.08.2022 Dijon, France
22.09.–22.09.2022 Mugello, Italy
27.10.–29.10.2022 Misano, Italy

Der Schweizer Porsche-Förderpilot Jasin Ferati gewinnt in einem spannenden Duell gegen Jürg Aeberhard gleich in seinem ersten GT-Jahr den Titel.

Im GT3 Cup der Porsche Sprint Challenge Suisse erlebte Jasin Ferati ein nahezu perfektes Debüt im GT-Sport: Der ehemalige Kart- und Formel-Pilot wurde Anfang Mai beim Saisonauftakt auf dem Red Bull Ring im ersten Lauf zunächst Zweiter und gewann wenig später den zweiten Durchgang. Auch in Heat eins führte er lange, doch ein Fahrfehler gab Verfolger Jürg Aeberhard die Möglichkeit, die Spitze zu übernehmen. Im zweiten Rennen waren die Vorzeichen umgekehrt; hier hatte der Routinier den Platz an der Sonne inne, bis Ferati sich kurz vor dem Zielstrich an ihm vorbeizwängte.

Im Laufe der Saison, die aus insgesamt sechs Rennwochenenden in Österreich, Frankreich und Italien bestand, kristallisierte sich immer mehr heraus, dass das Titelrennen zwischen Ferati und Aeberhard entschieden wird. Beide setzten sich in der Fahrerwertung gemeinsam vom Rest des Feldes ab und reisten Ende Oktober jeweils mit guten Chancen auf den Titelgewinn zum Finale in Misano – mit leichten Vorteilen für Aeberhard. Doch der 19-jährige Jäger Ferati ließ sich nicht verrückt machen und lieferte ein optimales Wochenende ab. Mit der Pole Position, zwei Siegen und zwei schnellsten Rennrunden sammelte der Pilot des Teams Fach Auto Tech die Maximalpunktzahl und schob sich noch an seinem Rivalen aus der Mannschaft ANT Performance vorbei, der in beiden Rennen als Zweiter abgewinkt wurde. Feratis Vorsprung betrug am Ende ganze vier Zähler.

Die GT4-Clubsport-Klasse 10 der Porsche Sprint Challenge Suisse, die für Porsche 718 Cayman GT4 Clubsport mit Manthey-Paket geschaffen wurde, wurde zur klaren Beute von Alexandre Mottet. Der Schützling vom Orchid Racing Team hatte in der Abschlusswertung einen Vorsprung von 84 Punkten auf seinen ersten Verfolger Markus Lietzau aus dem Team Amag First Rennsport – und das, obwohl der neue Champion den Auftakt in der Steiermark ausließ und erst zum zweiten Rennwochenende in Le Castellet in die Serie einstieg. Die Klasse 11, in der Porsche 718 Cayman GT4 Clubsport ohne Manthey-Paket zusammengefasst werden, ging an Andreas Greiling und Jens Richter.

Auch 2022 gab es am Finalwochenende ein zweistündiges Nachtrennen, das als Einzelevent zu keiner Wertung zählte. In einem von Proton Competition vorbereiteten Porsche 991 GT3 R II entschieden Patrick Dinkeldein und Marco Seefried diesen Endurance-Wettbewerb für sich. Rang zwei ging an den vom Porsche Motorsport Club Suisse und der Porsche Schweiz AG geförderten Ferati und Alexander Fach, der vor dem neuen GT3-Champion in den Genuss des Schweizer Porsche-Förderpakets kam. Jörg Dreisow und Manuel Lauck sicherten sich den letzten Podestplatz.

(l.-r.): Michael Kapfinger, Johannes Kapfinger, Dieter Svepes

(119): „Boga" - (181): Valerio Presezzi

Swiss Porsche-backed driver Jasin Ferati crowns maiden year in GT with title win after thrilling duel with Jürg Aeberhard

It was an almost perfect debut in GT racing for Jasin Ferati. Competing in the GT3 Cup of the Porsche Sprint Challenge Suisse, the former karting and single seater driver started with a second place and a win in the season opener at Red Bull Ring. Throughout the season, which featured six race weekends in Austria, France and Italy, Ferati and Jürg Aeberhard were embroiled in a fierce battle that went down to the wire in the finale at Misano. Aeberhard was leading the standings prior to the final round, but 19-year-old Ferati had an amazing weekend in Italy. With pole position, a pair of wins and two fastest race laps, the Fach Auto Tech driver scored the maximum number of points and clinched the title, four points clear of ANT Performance's Aeberard who finished second in both races.
Orchid Racing's Alexandre Mottet was the clear champion in the GT4 Clubsport class. Andreas Greiling and Jens Richter won class 11.
A two-hour non-championship night race at Misano saw Patrick Dinkeldein and Marco Seefried come out on top in a Proton Competition 991 GT3 R.

Patrick Dinkeldein

Michael and Johannes Kapfinger

MICHELIN

PORSCHE

yman GT4 CS

JERICH

718
CS MR
Class 1
3. SC

Mobil 1
Mobil 1

718
man GT
Class

MYLE

Open GT
1 GT3 CUP
Class 21
2. DR
3. BL

Open GT
Class 23

911 GT3
3. HA

PORSCHE
SPORTS CUP
SUISSE
Porsche Club
Zürich
WINNING CLUB
2
1
3

PORSCHE
SPRINT CHALLENGE
SUISSE
911
3 Cup
1. FERATI Ja
2. AEBERHA
3. BURKARD

BALLY
Mobil 1
MICHELIN

PORSCHE
SPORTS CUP
SUISSE
Heuer
ABSOLUTE RACING
WEC

SUISSE
911 GT3
Class

SPRINT CHALLENGE
SUISSE
obil 1

PORSCHE
SPRINT CHALLENGE
SUISSE
ORCHID
RACING TEAM

SUISSE
PDC
2. MEIS
3. PENA

AMAG First Rennsport
2
3

Andreas Greiling, Jens Richter

Frederick Jerich

Frederick Jerich

Alexandre Mottet

Nicola Garski

Jörg Dreisow and Manuel Lauck

Patrick Dinkeldein

DRIVER STANDINGS
CLASS 1, PORSCHE 992 GT3 CUP

POS	NO	DRIVERS	TEAM	POINTS
1	13	Jasin Ferati	Fach Auto Tech	305
2	17	Jürg Aeberhard	ANT Peformance	301
3	3	Gregor Burkard	Sportec Motorsport	174
4	4	Alexander Schwarzer	Fach Auto Tech	166
5	34	Ernst Keller	Sportec Motorsport	133

DRIVER STANDINGS
CLASS 2, PORSCHE 991 GT3 CUP II

POS	NO	DRIVERS	TEAM	POINTS
1	55	Luca Casella	Ortho Racing	256
2	59	Bruno Widmer	Widberg Motorsport	116
3	52	Joachim Günther	HMS	114
4	53	Marco Sacchet	ANT Performance	103
5	57	Bernhard Beutler	Widberg Motorsport	39

DRIVER STANDINGS
CLASS 10, PORSCHE 718 CAYMAN GT4 CLUBSPORT MANTHEY RACING

POS	NO	DRIVERS	TEAM	POINTS
1	102	Alexandre Mottet	Orchid Racing Team	248
2	114	Markus Lietzau	Amag First Rennsport	164
3	115	Detlef Schmidt	Allied Racing	136
4	115	Gero Bauknecht	Allied Racing	136
5	110	Giovanni Nladi	Amag First Rennsport	99

DRIVER STANDINGS
CLASS 11, PORSCHE 718 CAYMAN GT4 CLUBSPORT COMPETITION

POS	NO	DRIVERS	TEAM	POINTS
1	128	Andreas Greiling	MS Racing	313
2	128	Jens Richter	MS Racing	313
3	132	Remo Stebler	Porsche Basel Racing Team	241
4	130	Pierre Hirschi	Porsche Basel Racing Team	146
5	129	Balz Rüegger	Amag First Rennsport	93

DRIVER STANDINGS
CLASS 12, PORSCHE 981 CAYMAN GT4 CS

POS	NO	DRIVERS	TEAM	POINTS
1	154	Antonio Garzon	Orchid Racing Team	147
2	153	Stefan Kipfer	Widberg Motorsport	94
3	155	Arnaud Guillard	Orchid Racing Team	87
4	155	Pierre Melin	Orchid Racing Team	56
5	154	Cyrille Bagnoud	Orchid Racing Team	52

DRIVER STANDINGS
CLASS 19, PORSCHE CAYMAN GT4 CLUBSPORT MODIFIED

POS	NO	DRIVERS	TEAM	POINTS
1	181	Valerio Presezzi	Amag First Rennsport	271
2	182	Paolo Locatelli	Autorlando Sport	206
3	113	Nick Hirter	Widberg Motorsport	37
4	118	Günther Höge	Huber Racing	27
5	118	Stefano Höge	Huber Racing	22

DRIVER STANDINGS
CLASS 21, PORSCHE 992 GT3 CUP WITH ABS

POS	NO	DRIVERS	TEAM	POINTS
1	201	Loic Villiger	Orchid Racing Team	211
2	212	Zelijko Drmic	MS Racing	182
3	221	Dustin Blattner	PRE by Manthey Racing	173
4	225	Tareq Mansour	PRE by Manthey Racing	165
5	203	Jörg Dreisow	PZ 5 Seen	150

DRIVER STANDINGS
CLASS 22, PORSCHE 991 GT3 CUP

POS	NO	DRIVERS	TEAM	POINTS
1	251	Matteo Scapozza	Borradori Motorsport	31

DRIVER STANDINGS
CLASS 23, PORSCHE 991 GT3 R

POS	NO	DRIVERS	TEAM	POINTS
1	231	Philippe Menotti	ANT Performance	202
2	232	Patrick Dinkeldein	Proton Competition	182
3	231	Enzo Calderari	ANT Performance	122
4	233	Christian Voithofer	Wimmer Werk Motorsport	58
5	234	Simon Willner	Stadler Motorsport	57

DRIVER STANDINGS
CLASS 40, PORSCHE GT3 CUP MODIFIED

POS	NO	DRIVERS	TEAM	POINTS
1	276	Johannes Kapfinger	Huber Racing	290
2	264	Frederick Jerich	Huber Racing	177
3	268	Philipp Hagnauer	Porsche Basel Racing Team	158
4	262	Sebastian Schmitt	PZ 5 Seen	146
5	271	Nicola Sarcinelli	Dinamic Motorsport	117

DRIVER STANDINGS
PORSCHE DRIVERS COMPETITION

POS	NO	DRIVERS	TEAM	POINTS
1	705	Nicola Garski	Amag First Rennsport	236
2	707	Peter Meister	Stadler Motorsport	155
3	701	Xavier Penalba	Stadler Motorsport	145
4	739	Marius Hutmacher	Amag First Rennsport	132
5	719	Tommy Eriksson	Orchid Racing Team	97

(l.-r.): Jürg Aeberhard, Jasin Ferati, Alexander Schwarzer

PORSCHE
SPORTS CUP
CHINA
中国保时捷运动杯

PORSCHE SPORTS CUP CHINA

22.07.–24.07.2022 Ningbo, China
26.08.–28.08.2022 Tianjin, China
23.09.–25.09.2022 Zhuzhou, China

Liu Hangcheng

Zum vierten Mal fand der Porsche Sports Cup China statt, der neben der Sprint Challenge China auch erste Rennstreckenerfahrung für Motorsport-Neulinge ermöglichte.

Zunächst einmal gab es nach drei erfolgreichen Saisons jedoch einige Neuerungen in den Wettbewerben des Sports Cup China 2022: Die elektrischen Taycan-Modelle wurden in das Einsteigerprogramm „Introduction to Race Track“ aufgenommen und für die Gleichmäßigkeitsprüfungen Porsche Drivers Competition wurde eine Punktetabelle mit eigenen Podiumsplätzen und Preisen erstellt. Darüber hinaus durften Porsche 911 GT3 Cup vom Typ 992 sowie Porsche 718 Cayman GT4 RS Clubsport erstmals in der Sprint Challenge China eingesetzt werden.

Die Champions der einzelnen Klassen der Porsche Drivers Competition sowie der Sprint Challenge China wurden im Rahmen der Porsche Motorsport Asia Pacific Night of Champions in Shanghai geehrt. Gesamtsieger der Sprint Challenge China wurde Eric Zang von Toro Racing, gefolgt von Jeffrey Lee aus dem Team Shanghai Pudong & Waigaoqiao 69 Racing und David Szu, der für die Mannschaft BD Group ins Lenkrad griff. Yang Bo, Lin Weixiong und Deng Yi holten sich die Titel in den verschiedenen Prüfungen der Porsche Drivers Competition.

Eine neue Plattform, die im Oktober in China debütierte, ist der GT Trackday. Dieser ist zwischen der Porsche Track Experience und dem Porsche Sports Cup China angesiedelt und soll angehenden Rennfahrern den Einstieg in den Motorsport erleichtern. Die Premierenveranstaltung, die vom lokalen Partner Pirelli unterstützt wurde, war ein voller Erfolg, weshalb der GT Trackday auch 2023 wieder stattfinden soll.

Porsche Parade

Eric Zang triumphs for Toro Racing in the unique Sprint Challenge China

The Porsche Sports Cup China returned for its fourth season in 2022. The series visited five circuits in China, with four road car events and six rounds of the Sprint Challenge China. With three successful seasons behind it, the Sports Cup China shook things up for 2022, bringing Taycan models to its entry-level programme Introduction to Race Track, and adding in a season points table for the Porsche Drivers Competitions (Time Trial) that came with its own podium, points and prizes. What's more, the Porsche 911 GT3 Cup (Type 992) and the 718 Cayman GT4 RS Clubsport were introduced to the Sprint Challenge China for the first time.
The winners of each class of the Porsche Drivers Competition, as well as the winners from all Classes of Sprint Challenge China, were awarded during the Porsche Motorsport Asia Pacific Night of Champions in Shanghai. The overall winner of the Sprint Challenge China was Eric Zang from Toro Racing, followed by Shanghai Pudong & Waigaoqiao 69 Racing's Jeffrey Lee and David Szu from BD Group. Yang Bo won the Porsche Drivers Competition Tag Heuer 1-Lap Time Trial and also the Michelin 3-Lap Time Trial in the 718 class, while Lin Weixiong won the 911 Class 2 competition and Deng Yi won the 911 Class 3 championship, with both drivers taking the laurels for both the 1-lap and 3-lap competitions.

Podium at Tianjin

Organisation of Porsche Sports Cup China

Drivers Competition

David Szu

中国保时捷冲刺挑战赛 2022
Porsche Sprint Challenge China 2022
全场
Overall
年度季军
3rd Place
斯绍华
David SZU
年度总冠军
Champion
臧侃
Eric ZANG
年度亚军
2nd Place
徐岭谏
Jeffrey ZEE

718 组别
718 CLASS
杨博
YANG Bo
911 组别 I
911 CLASS I
杨浩宇
YANG Haoyu
911 组别 II
911 CLASS II
林伟雄
LIN Weixiong
911 组别 III
911 CLASS III
邓亿
DENG Yi
911 组别 IV
911 CLASS IV
周辰飞
ZHOU Chenfei
公开组
GUEST CLASS
黄颖
HUANG Xing

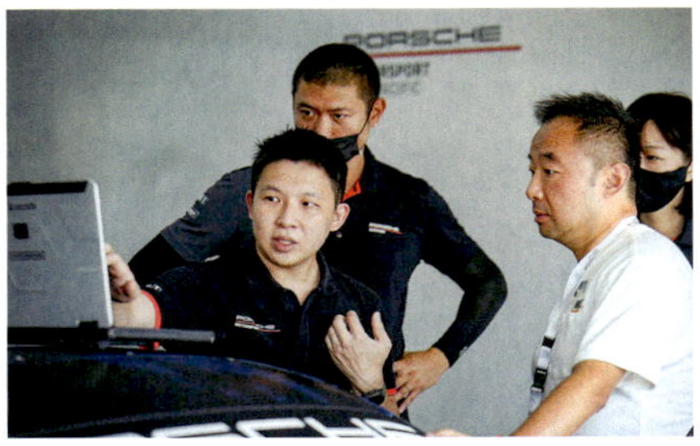

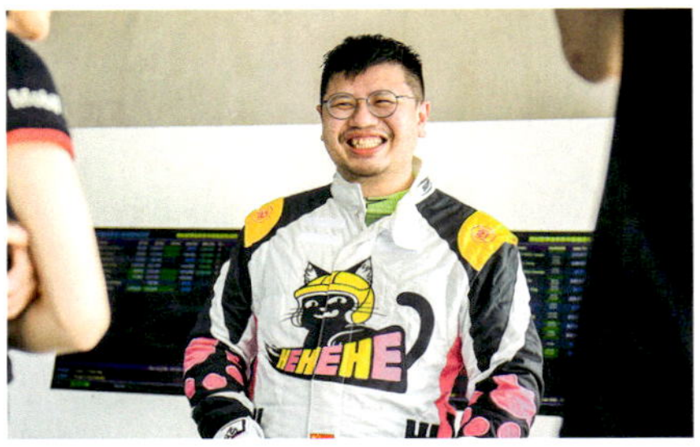

中国保时捷冲刺挑战赛 2022
Porsche Sprint Challenge China 2022
GT4 Clubsport 组别
GT4 Class - Clubsport
年度季军
3rd Place
杜宇
Yu DU
年度冠军
1st Place
楼端
Duan LOU
年度亚军
2nd Place
王翔
Xiang WANG
GT4 组别
GT4 Class
年度季军
3rd Place
俞元麟
Yuanlin YU
年度冠军
1st Place
斯绍华
David SZ
年度亚军
2nd Place
林伟雄
Weixiong LIN

Jeffrey Zee

With Carrera Cup Asia returning to international racing in 2023, the Sprint Challenge China is expecting a strong GTC Class grid, comprising the 911 GT3 Cup (Type 992) next season.

A new platform, launched for the first time in China this year in October, was the GT Trackday which is designed to cultivate motorsport culture. The Porsche Motorsport Asia Pacific Motorsport Pyramid is designed to accommodate all driver levels, from amateur to world-class professional. The new GT Trackday sits between the Porsche Track Experience and the Porsche Sports Cup China, adding in another level to help ease budding amateurs into the world of motorsport, getting behind the wheel of GT road cars or GT race cars. The inaugural event this year was a roaring success, supported by local partner Pirelli, and GT Trackday is planned to return once again in 2023.

DRIVER STANDINGS **OVERALL**

POS	NO	DRIVER	TEAM	POINTS
1	911	Eric Zang	Toro Racing	100
2	98	Jeffrey Zee	Shanghai Pudong & Waigaoqiao 69 Racing	72
3	2	David Szu	BD Group	61
4	69	Yang Ke	Shanghai Pudong & Waigaoqiao 69 Racing	54
5	868	Zeng Jianfeng	Shanghai RSR Racing Team	27
6	233	Sheng Jiacheng	Hehehe Racing	27
7	233	Lin Weixiong	Hehehe Racing	27
8	828	Han Lichao	Silver Rocket Racing	25
9	992	Liu Hangcheng	Absolute Racing	25
10	233	Yu Yuanlin	Hehehe Racing	22
11	21	Lou Duan	Blackjack Racing	20
12	5	Wang Xiang	Climax Racing	20
13	969	Du Yu	RSR GT Racing	16
14	91	Fu Zhenjiang	Blackjack Racing	12

DRIVER STANDINGS **GT3**

POS	NO	DRIVER	TEAM	POINTS
1	911	Eric Zang	Toro Racing	100
2	992	Liu Hangcheng	Absolute Racing	25

DRIVER STANDINGS **GTC**

POS	NO	DRIVER	TEAM	POINTS
1	98	Jeffrey Zee	Shanghai Pudong & Waigaoqiao 69 Racing	100
2	69	Yang Ke	Shanghai Pudong & Waigaoqiao 69 Racing	72

DRIVER STANDINGS **GT4**

POS	NO	DRIVER	TEAM	POINTS
1	2	David Szu	BD Group	86
2	233	Lin Weixiong	Hehehe Racing	52
3	233	Yu Yuanlin	Hehehe Racing	43
4	5	Wang Xiang	Climax Racing	36
5	233	Sheng Jiacheng	Hehehe Racing	30
6	868	Zeng Jianfeng	Shanghai RSR Racing Team	30
7	828	Han Lichao	Silver Rocket Racing	25
8	21	Lou Duan	Blackjack Racing	22
9	969	Du Yu	RSR GT Racing	18
10	91	Fu Zhenjiang	Blackjack Racing	14

DRIVER STANDINGS **GT4-718 CAYMAN GT4 RS CLUBSPORT**

POS	NO	DRIVER	TEAM	POINTS
1	2	David Szu	BD Group	86
2		Lin Weixiong	Hehehe Racing	50
3	233	Yu Yuanlin	Hehehe Racing	43
4	233	Sheng Jiacheng	Hehehe Racing	30
5	868	Zeng Jianfeng	Shanghai RSR Racing Team	30
6	828	Han Lichao	Silver Rocket Racing	25
4	91	Fu Zhenjiang	Blackjack Racing	30

DRIVER STANDINGS **GT4-718 CAYMAN GT4 CLUBSPORT**

POS	NO	DRIVER	TEAM	POINTS
1	21	Lou Duan	Blackjack Racing	50
2		Wang Xiang	Climax Racing	50
3	969	Du Yu	RSR GT Racing	36
4	91	Fu Zhenjiang	Blackjack Racing	30

Eric Zang

DEALER TROPHY **GT3**

POS	TEAM	POINTS
1	Toro Racing	100

DEALER TROPHY **GTC**

POS	TEAM	POINTS
1	Shanghai Pudong & Waigaoqiao 69 Racing	100

DEALER TROPHY **GT4**

POS	TEAM	POINTS
1	BD Group	100

NÜRBURGRING LANGSTRECKEN-SERIE

26.03.2022	67th ADAC Westfalenfahrt, Nürburgring Nordschleife, Germany
23.04.2022	53rd Adenauer ADAC Rundstrecken-Trophy, Nürburgring Nordschleife, Germany
25.06.2022	45th RCM DMV Grenzlandrennen, Nürburgring Nordschleife, Germany
09.07.2022	Rowe 6h ADAC Ruhr-Pokal-Rennen, Nürburgring Nordschleife, Germany
11.09.2022	12h Nürburgring Nordschleife, Germany
08.10.2022	54th ZEWOTHERM ADAC Barbarossapreis, Nürburgring Nordschleife, Germany
22.10.2022	PAGID Racing 46th DMV Münsterlandpokal, Nürburgring Nordschleife, Germany
05.11.2022	46th NIMEX DMV 4h-Rennen, Nürburgring Nordschleife, Germany

(l.-r.): Frédéric Mackowiecki, Laurens Vanthoor, Michael Christensen

Porsche glänzte auch 2022 in der Grünen Hölle

Die Marke Porsche war in der Saison 2022 der Nürburgring Langstrecken-Serie präsenter denn je. Grund dafür war die Porsche Endurance Trophy Nürburgring, die von Manthey-Racing aus der Taufe gehoben wurde. Neben der bereits etablierten Cup-3-Klasse mit Porsche 718 Cayman GT4 CS schlug die neue Cup 2 mit den neuen Porsche 911 GT3 Cup (992) richtig ein. Im Schnitt waren in beiden Klassen je rund 13 Fahrzeuge mit von der Partie und boten packenden Sport in der Grünen Hölle.
Nach ihrem Triumph im Vorjahr in der Cup 3, ist AVIA W&S Motorsport der Aufstieg in die große Cup-Klasse geglückt. Daniel Blickle sicherte sich den Fahrertitel, die Mannschaft rund um Patrick Wagner und Daniel Schellhaas die Teamwertung. „Wir hatten eine super Saison. Letztes Jahr der Titel und in diesem Jahr erneut Meister – besser kann man es sich nicht vorstellen", sagt Teamchef Schellhaas. „Der Kampf um die Meisterschaft war bis zum Schluss sehr spannend. Der Umstieg vom Cayman auf den Cup-Porsche ist uns gut gelungen, denn die Fahrzeuge sind komplett unterschiedlich. Mit dem Cup 2 fährt man in der Spitzengruppe der NLS viel weiter vorne – da ist es insgesamt dann noch etwas enger. Aber von der Competition her tun sich die PETN-Klassen nicht viel. In beiden Klassen wird um jede Platzierung hart gekämpft."
Die ersten Meister in der Porsche Endurance Trophy Nürburgring Cup 3 heißen Mauro Calamia, Ivan Jacoma und Kai

Porsche also shone in the Green Hell in 2022

Porsche had a bigger presence in the Nürburgring Endurance Series than ever before in 2022 with the introduction of the new Porsche Endurance Trophy Nürburgring, organised by Manthey Racing. The new Cup 2, for 992 GT3 Cup cars to complement the well-established Cup 3 class comprising the 718 Cayman GT4 CS, was an instant success. Both classes had average entries of around 13 cars for each event. Having graduated to the higher category following its Cup 3 title win the previous year, AVIA W&S Motorsport won the Cup 2 drivers' title with Daniel Blickle. His team, led by Patrick Wagner and Daniel Schellhaas, also sealed the teams' crown. Schmickler Performance powered by Ravenol drivers Mauro Calamia, Ivan Jacoma and Kai Riemer secured the Cup 3 title with one round to spare. The team scored points in every round and racked up three wins. Schmickler also won the overall Porsche Endurance Trophy Nürburgring title.

Alongside the two Cup classes, the Porsche 911 GT3 R also found success. Laurens Vanthoor, Michael Christensen and Frédéric Makowiecki won the opening round in the Manthey Racing "Grello". FALKEN Motorsports won the 6-hour race in the hands of Joel Eriksson and Sven Müller, and the inaugural 12-hour race with Eriksson, Müller, Jaxon Evans and Alessio Picariello.

The test races of the new 992 GT3 R in the SP-X class were further highlights in which the new 911 already hinted at its potential. During the maiden race, works drivers Frédéric Makowiecki and Julien Andlauer sensationally finished third overall for Manthey Racing. FALKEN Motorsport and Dinamic Motorsport ran the car in the other two test races.

Julien Andlauer, Frédéric Makowiecki

Karsten Krämer, Christopher Brück, Alexey Veremenko

Jaxon Evans, Thomas Preining

Tim Heinemann, Martin Ragginger

(120): Daniel Blickle, David Jahn - (30): Alessio Picariello, Adrien De Leener
(3): Tim Heinemann, Martin Ragginger

Riemer. Das Trio machte den Titel bereits ein Rennen vor Schluss fix. Das Geheimnis des Erfolgs war für Schmickler Performance powered by Ravenol die Konstanz. Das Team punktete in allen Rennen und fuhr dabei drei Siege ein. Einer davon war der wichtige Triumph bei den 12h Nürburgring mit doppelten Punkten. „Auch wenn wir mal Probleme oder Rückschläge im Rennen hatten: Wir haben nie den Kopf in den Sand gesteckt, sondern dafür gekämpft, das beste Ergebnis herauszuholen", erklärt Champion Riemer. „Hinzu kommt die Akribie von Teamchef Markus Schmickler, der nichts dem Zufall überlässt. Für ihn und seine Mannschaft freut mich der Titel besonders." Schmickler feierte zudem den PETN-Gesamtsieg.
Neben den beiden Cup-Klassen der Porsche Endurance Trophy Nürburgring war auch der Porsche 911 GT3 R in der Saison 2022 erfolgreich: Laurens Vanthoor, Michael Christensen und Frédéric Makowiecki holten im „Grello" den Auftaktsieg zu Manthey-Racing nach Meuspath. FALKEN Motorsports gewann mit dem ROWE 6 Stunden ADAC Ruhr-Pokal-Rennen und den erstmals ausgetragenen 12 Stunden Nürburgring die beiden wichtigsten Events des Jahres. Über die 6-Stunden-Distanz triumphierten Joel Eriksson und Sven Müller, beim neuen Saisonhighlight der NLS wurde das Duo von Jaxon Evans und Alessio Picariello unterstützt. „Für uns war das ein mega Rennen", sagt Teamchef Sven Schnabl, dessen Mannschaft damit nahtlos an den im Juli erzielten ersten Saisonsieg angeknüpft hat. „Das entschädigt für vieles, was zu Beginn der Rennsaison nicht nach Wunsch verlaufen ist. Wir dürfen rundum zufrieden sein mit diesem Ergebnis."

(l.-r.): Daniel Blickle, David Jahn, Tim Scheerbarth

(l.-r.): Kévin Estre, Michael Christensen, Laurens Vanthoor, Frédéric Makowiecki and Team Manthey-Racing

Start Nürburgring Langstrecken-Serie

(l.-r.): Jörg Bergmeister, Mike Stursberg, Mustafa Mehmet Kaya

Marcel Hoppe, Nick Salewsky, Michele Di Martino

Lars Kern, Martin Ragginger

Julien Andlauer, Klaus Bachler

Ein weiteres Highlight der Nordschleifen-Saison waren die Testeinsätze des neuen Porsche 911 GT3 R (992). Das Fahrzeug ging nur bei den letzten drei Rennen in der Klasse SP-X an den Start, da es noch nicht über eine finale GT3-Homologation verfügt. Der neue Elfer ließ dabei sein Potenzial bereits durchblicken. „Wir haben mit unserem neuen Porsche eine sehr gelungene Rennpremiere erlebt. Ich bin stolz auf jeden, der an diesem Projekt mitgearbeitet hat", fasste Projektleiter Sebastian Golz den ersten Testeinsatz unter der Ägide von Manthey-Racing zusammen. „Die Testrunden am Freitag auf der Nordschleife und der erste Renneinsatz haben gezeigt, dass die Basis des Fahrzeugs stimmt. Dank der guten Vorbereitung und Zusammenarbeit mit dem ADAC haben wir eine gute Vorstellung abgeliefert und ein positives Bild mit vielen Daten sammeln können." Bei der Rennpremiere fuhren die beiden Porsche-Werksfahrer Frédéric Makowiecki und Julien Andlauer sensationell auf Platz drei. Es folgten weitere Testeinsätze, betreut durch die Kundenteams FALKEN Motorsports und Dinamic Motorsport.

Robin Chrzanowski, Kersten Jodexnis, Peter Scharmach

Nicolas Raeder and Martin Raeder

Ivan Jacoma, Mauro Calamia, Kai Riemer and Team Schmickler Performance powered by Ravenol

Julien Andlauer, Matt Campbell, Mathieu Jaminet

Fréderic Mackowiecki, Laurens Vanthoor, Michael Christensen

(l.-r.) Alessio Picariello, Sver Müller, Joel Eriksson and Team FALKEN Motorsports

Sven Schnabl

Julien Andlauer and Matteo Cairoli

(103): Peter Ludwig, Noah Nagelsdiek, Maik Rosenberg · (104): Jörg Bergmeister, Mustafa Mehmet Kaya, Mike Stursberg · (114): Ben Bünnagel, Nico Otto

NIMEXX
PAGID

FALKEN

GP
BWK
L. ten Voorde

CAUTION
ACHTUNG
HAZET
FALKEN
ROWE
ROWE

MOTUL

FALKEN
FALKEN
FALKEN
FALKEN
ROWE

TEXTAR

WOLFOIL
FOUR MOTORS
cropenergies
PAGID
OMP
SMUDO

OFFICIAL

BLACK FALCON
H&R

H&R

PETN
2022
PETN
2022
PETN
2022

nürburgring
MANTHEY
Grello
MANTHEY
Grello
MANTHEY
Grello
#911
ADAC

H&R

ADAC

ADAC

nürburgring
BILSTEIN

BLACK FALCON

(l.-r.): Joel Eriksson, Jaxon Evans, Alessio Picariello, Sven Müller

Matteo Cairoli, Dennis Olsen

Klaus Abbelen, „Jules", Felipe Fernández Laser

DRIVER STANDINGS PORSCHE ENDURANCE TROPHY CUP3

POS	NO	DRIVERS	TEAM	POINTS
1	969	Mauro Calamia, Ivan Jacoma, Kai Riemer	Schmickler Performance	165,5
2	952/953	Christopher Rink, Francesco Merlini	Smyrlis Racing	133,5
3	949/959	Heiko Eichenberg	Sorg Rennsport	128
4	959	Fidel Leib, Philip Miemois	Sorg Rennsport	127
5	952/953	Philipp Stahlschmidt	Smyrlis Racing	118,5
6	976	Jens Moetefindt, Moritz Oberheim, Thorsten Wolter	FK Performance	103
7	955/956	Rüdiger Schicht, "Montana", Alex Fielenbach	Team Mathol Racing	102,5
8	949	Stefan Beyer	Sorg Rennsport	98
9	944	Leonard Oehme	Team Oehme	82,5
10	960/962	"Svittel", Marius Rauer, Daniel Bohr	W&S Motorsport	75,5
11	944	Niklas Oehme	Team Oehme	73,5

DRIVER STANDINGS PORSCHE ENDURANCE TROPHY CUP2

POS	NO	DRIVERS	TEAM	POINTS
1	120	Daniel Blickle	W&S Motorsport	163
2	112	Karsten Krämer, Christopher Brück	KKrämer Racing	146,5
3	120	David Jahn	W&S Motorsport	133
4	120	Tim Scheerbarth	W&S Motorsport	122
5	107	Arne Hoffmeister	Team Mathol Racing	97,5
6	104	Mustafa Mehmet Kaya	Black Falcon	97,5
7	104	Mike Stursberg	Black Falcon	86,5
8	123	Marcel Hoppe, Nick Salewsky	Mühlner Motorsport	80
9	102	Tobias Müller	Black Falcon	75

TEAM STANDINGS NLS-SPEED TROPHY

POS	NO	TEAM	CAR	POINTS
1	16	Scherer Sport Team Phoenix	Audi R8 LMS GT3 Evo II	210
2	5	Scherer Sport Team Phoenix	Audi R8 LMS GT3 Evo II	196
3	34	Walkenhorst Motorsport	BMW M4 GT3	130
4	3	FALKEN Motorsports	Porsche 911 GT3 R II	86
5	120	AVIA W&S Motorsport	Porsche 991 GT3 Cup	78
7	112	KKrämer Racing	Porsche 991 GT3 Cup	59
10	107	Team Mathol Racing	Porsche 991 GT3 Cup	38
12	25	Huber Motorsport	Porsche 911 GT3 R II	37
14	911	Manthey Racing	Porsche 911 GT3 R II	35
15	4	Falken Motorsports	Porsche 911 GT3 R II	34
15	102	Black Falcon Team Identica	Porsche 991 GT3 Cup	34
19	123	Mühlner Motorsport	Porsche 991 GT3 Cup	33
21	18	KCMG	Porsche 911 GT3 R II	29
22	111	Frikadelli Racing Team	Porsche 991 GT3 Cup	25
23	949	Sorg Rennsport	Porsche 718 Cayman GT4 Clubsport	22
29	959	Sorg Rennsport	Porsche 718 Cayman GT4 Clubsport	14
31	114	FK Performance Motorsport	Porsche 991 GT3 Cup	10
31	955	Team Mathol Racing	Porsche 718 Cayman GT4 Clubsport	10
35	125	Huber Motorsport	Porsche 991 GT3 Cup	8
37	101	RPM Racing	Porsche 991 GT3 Cup	5
38	944	9 und 11 Racing Team	Porsche 718 Cayman GT4 Clubsport	3
41	212	Schmickler Performance	Porsche 981 Cayman	1
41	976	FK Performance Motorsport	Porsche 718 Cayman GT4 Clubsport	1

DRIVER STANDINGS OVERALL

POS	NO	DRIVERS	CAR	TEAM	POINTS
1	500	Daniel Zils, Oskar Sandberg, Sindre Setsaas	BMW 330i	Adrenalin Motorsport	124
4	120	Daniel Blickle	Porsche 991 GT3 Cup	W&S Motorsport	106
5	969	Mauro Calamia, Ivan Jacoma, Kai Riemer	Porsche 718 Cayman GT4 Clubsport	Schmickler Performance	105
8	456	Lucas Daugard, Kaj Schubert	Porsche 981 Cayman	Young KRS Dames	89
10	112	Christopher Brück, Karsten Krämer	Porsche 991 GT3 Cup	KKrämer Racing	88
12	976	Christian Konnerth	Porsche 718 Cayman GT4 Clubsport	FK Performance	82
18	120	Tim Scheerbarth	Porsche 991 GT3 Cup	W&S Motorsport	77
20	952/953	Francesco Thor M. Merlini, Christopher M. Rink	Porsche 718 Cayman GT4 Clubsport	Smyrlis Racing	75
29	949	Heiko Eichenberg	Porsche 718 Cayman GT4 Clubsport	Sorg Rennsport	70
30	952/953	Philipp Stahlschmidt	Porsche 718 Cayman GT4 Clubsport	Smyrlis Racing	67

Mauro Calamia, Ivan Jacoma, Kai Riemer

C6 BANK MASTERCARD ENDURANCE CHALLENGE BRASIL

14.08.2022	*Termas de Río Hondo, Argentina*
16.10.2022	*Autódromo Internacional Goiânia, Brazil*
03.12.2022	*Interlagos, São Paulo, Brazil*

Alceu Feldmann and Guilherme Sales

Spannung bis zum Schluss in der Endurance Challenge Brasil, in der alle Entscheidungen beim Finale, den traditionellen 500 Kilometern von Interlagos, fielen.

Zum Auftakt der Porsche Endurance Challenge Brasil 2022 reisten die Teams und Fahrer nach Termas de Río Hondo in Argentinien, wo das Rennen erst beim letzten Pflichtboxenstopp entschieden wurde. Der Sieg ging letztendlich an Alceu Feldmann / Guilherme Salas. Die Führung in der Gesamtwertung übernahmen jedoch Christian Hahn / Diego Nunes, da das Duo das erste Segment gewann und im Ziel Rang drei inne hatte. In der Sprint Challenge war in beiden Segmenten niemand besser als die Paarung Nelson Marcondes / Renan Guerra. Das zweite Rennwochenende fand Mitte Oktober in Goiânia statt. Nach 79 Runden wiederholten Feldmann / Salas ihren Erfolg von Argentinien und kreuzten die Ziellinie erneut als Erste. Im ersten Segment jedoch konnte niemand die Rookies Enzo Elias und Adroaldo Weisheimer stoppen, die damit ihr Talent unter Beweis stellten. Carlos Renaux / Luiz Razia erkämpften sich in der Sprint Challenge Platz eins, auch wenn Ayman Darwich / Sergio Jimenez im ersten Segment die Nase vorne hatten.

Beim Finale waren noch alle ausgeschriebenen Klassen offen; das traditionelle, in diesem Jahr aber auch sehr verregnete 500-Kilometer-Rennen von Interlagos musste also die Entscheidung bringen. Am Ende setzten sich Hahn / Nunes durch und eroberten ihren ersten Titel. In der Sprint Challenge triumphierte auf der brasilianischen Formel-1-Strecke das Trio Ricardo Fontanari / Matheus Iorio / Christian Fittipaldi vor den neuen Champions Marcondes / Guerra.

Nelson Piquet Jr. and Rodrigo Mello

(8): Werner Neugebauer, Ricardo Zonta - (26): Christian Hahn, Diego Nunes

Christian Hahn and Diego Nunes crowned champions as Endurance Challenge title battle goes down to the wire in first season with the 992

Just like it was for the Sprint Series, the biggest attraction for Porsche Cup C6 Bank Mastercard Endurance Challenge was the premiere of the new generation of the Porsche 911 GT3 Cup. The 992 model came with more technology, traction control, ABS braking, and 510 hp. The car change brought a new level of competition especially for the endurance races, making the largest single-brand championship in the Americas even more interesting.

The first round of the 2022 Endurance challenge was accompanied by the return of Porsche Cup Brazil to international rounds. The modern track of Termas de Río Hondo in Argentina was the stage chosen after a three-year absence from the international scene due to the COVID-19 pandemic. The venue had already hosted Porsche Cup Brazil rounds in 2016 and 2017, but it had been a long time since the category raced there. The logistic challenge of bringing in the entire structure to abroad was worth the effort for the infrastructure of a brand new speedway, that also hosts the MotoGP.

On the track, there was news introduced to the rules book. Starting this season, with the intent of more teams to be in the hunt for the title until the very end and to intensify the battles and strategies, a new segmentation of the race was created. At the halfway point of the endurance race, 40 percent of the points would be distributed to the teams which completed the requirement of 75 percent of the initial segment, as long as the mandatory pit-stops criteria were met, with each driver at least having completed one lap.

The new points awarding system promoted balanced races, starting in Argentina, a race decided on the last mandatory stop, the victory ended with the team in car #1 of Alceu Feldmann and Guilherme Salas. However, the group which took the lead on the points' table was the duo of car #26 of Christian Hahn and Diego Nunes because their team ended up winning segment 1 and finishing the race in 3rd. On Sprint Challenge Nelson Marcondes and Renan Guerra won it all in both 1st segment and the race, obtaining the maximum number of points of the weekend to go back to Brazil in the championship lead.

Carlos Renaux, Luiz Razia

Podium at Autódromo Internacional Goiânia

Christian Hahn, Diego Nunes

(99): Jeff Giassi, Nicolas Costa - (9): Edu Guedes, Renan Pizii

Enzo Elias

Drivers of Porsche Endurance Challenge Brasil

Renan Guerra and Nelson Marcondes

Christian Hahn, Diego Nunes

Miguel Paludo, Dennis Dirani

Gabriel Casagrande, Rouman Ziemkiewicz

Cesar Ramos and Georgios Frangulis

Christian Hahn and Diego Nunes

The second round was held in mid-October in Goiânia. A hefty challenge for cars and drivers, with a temperature over 30 degrees that felt like 50 degrees on the track. After 79 laps the team of car #1 composed of Alceu Feldmann and Guilherme Salas repeated the success from Argentina and won once again, widening the gap in the points' table to the team in 2nd place. However, the 1st segment was awarded to car #73 composed of Enzo Elias and Adroaldo Weisheimer from the Rookie Class, showing the development of the newly assembled duo. For the Sprint Challenge, the victory was in the hands of the duo Carlos Renaux and Luiz Razia of car #145, even with #555 of Ayman Darwich and Sergio Jimenez having won the 1st segment. Yet the championship lead was still with the capable duo of Nelson Marcondes and Renan Guerra, who finished 2nd. The championship decision was held off until the season finale. With the titles in all six categories still up for grabs the traditional 500km race at Interlagos would define it all. In heavy rain, the race was a handful. In the end, a new team won its first title ever: Christian Hahn and Diego Nunes recovered from a poor result in Goiânia and prevailed as champs. Alceu Feldmann and Guilherme Salas went through some issues near the end when they were in conditions of finishing atop the table and ended up with 3rd place overall in the 992 category. As for the Sprint Challenge, the victory was of car #34 of Ricardo Fontanari, Matheus Iorio, and Christian Fittipaldi. With this combination of results, the title ended up with car #199 of Nelson Marcondes and Renan Guerra, who finished the race in 2nd. On top of that Marcondes also won the Sprint Challenge Overall title, which adds up Sprint Race and Endurance Challenge championship points.

(7): Miguel Paludo, Dennis Dirani - (70): Lucas Salles, Rafael Suzuki

DRIVER STANDINGS CARRERA ENDURANCE

POS	NO	DRIVERS	POINTS
1	26	Christian Hahn, Diego Nunes	181
3	73	Adroaldo Weisheimer, Enzo Elias	164
5	1	Alceu Feldmann. Guilherme Sales	161
6	99	Jeff Giassi, Nicolas Costa	145
9	888	Beto Gresse, Lineu Pires	130
11	80	Rouman Ziemkiewcz, Gabriel Casagrande	128
13	8	Werner Neugebauer, Ricardo Zonta	116
15	16	Renan Pizii	113
16	88	Georgios Frangulis, Cesar Ramos	109
18	77	Francisco Horta, William Freire	104
20	87	Nelson Monteiro, Alan Hellmeister	87
22	7	Miguel Paludo, Dennis Dirani	86
22	29	Rodrigo Mello, Nelson Piquet, Jr.	86
26	70	Lucas Salles, Rafael Suzuki	84
28	116	Marcelo Hahn, Allam Khodair	81
30	888	Vito Meira	79
31	17	Leonardo Sanchez, Átila Abreu	70
33	77	Pedro Aguiar	62
34	3	Franco Giaffone, Rubens Barrichello	58
36	25	Paulo Sousa, Galid Osman	52
38	9	Edu Guedes	49
39	17	Marçal Müller	47
39	85	Eduardo Menossi, Pedro Boesel	47
39	70	Fran Lara	47
43	33	Bruno Campos, Giuliano Losacco	42
45	44	Gustavo Farah, Sebastian Moreno	40
45	121	João Barbosa, João Gonçalves	40
49	87	JP Mauro	35
50	9	Carlos Ambrósio	32
51	5	Ricardo Maurício	26
52	25	Bia Figueiredo	25
52	9	Caio Collet	25
54	85	Sérgio Sette Câmara	23
55	16	Danilo Dirani	16
56	5	Sylvio de Barros	0

DRIVER STANDINGS ENDURANCE CHALLENGE

POS	NO	DRIVERS	POINTS
1	199	Nelson Marcondes, Renan Guerra	211
3	777	Josimar junior, Sergio Ramalho	182
5	555	Ayman Darwich, Sergio Jimenez	171
7	66	Sadak Leite, Fabio Carbone	145
9	145	Carlos Renaux, Luiz Razia	134
11	14	André Gaidzinski	132
12	002	Junior Dinardi, Yuri Alves	120
14	34	Ricardo Fontanari, Christian Fittipaldi, Matheus Iorio	103
17	74	Piero Cifali, Andre Bragantini Jr.	90
19	145	Pedro Costa	74
20	14	Nasser Aboultaif, Gabriel Robe	70
22	83	Marco Billi, Maurizio Billi	45
24	14	Ramos Artur, Ramon Alcaraz	38

DRIVER STANDINGS CARRERA ROOKIE ENDURANCE

POS	NO	DRIVERS	POINTS
1	73	Adroaldo Weisheimer, Enzo Elias	212
3	888	Lineu Pires, Beto Gresse	196
5	87	Nelson Monteiro, Alan Hellmeister	182
7	17	Leonardo Sanchez, Átila Abreu	156
9	25	Paulo Sousa, Galid Osman	139
11	9	Edu Guedes	133
12	33	Bruno Campos, Giuliano Losacco	123
14	44	Gustavo Farah, Sebastian Moreno	119
16	121	João Barbosa, João Gonçalves	118
18	888	Vitor Meira	103
19	9	Carlos Ambrósio	98
20	17	Marçal Müller	83
21	87	JP Mauro	82
22	5	Ricardo Maurício	81
23	25	Bia Figueiredo	67
24	9	Caio Colle	64
25	9	Renan Pizii	48
26	5	Sylvio de Barros	10

DRIVER STANDINGS CARRERA SPORT ENDURANCE

POS	NO	DRIVERS	POINTS
1	80	Gabriel Casagrande, Rouman Ziemkiewicz	208
3	77	Francisco Horta, William Freire	180
5	88	Cesar Ramos, Gregios Frangulis	175
7	116	Marcelo Hahn, Allam Khodair	169
9	70	Lucas Salles, Rafael Suzuki	163
11	3	Franco Giaffone, Rubens Barichello	145
13	85	Eduardo Menossi, Pedro Boesel	137
15	80	Renan Pizii	115
16	77	Pedro Aguiar	93
17	70	Fran Lara	79
18	85	Sérgio Sette Câmara	64

DRIVER STANDINGS ENDURANCE CHALLENGE SPORT

POS	NO	DRIVERS	POINTS
1	777	Josimar junior, Sergio Ramalho	222
3	66	Sadak Leite, Fabio Carbone	192
5	14	André Gaidzinski	180
6	002	Junior Dinardi, Yuri Alves	166
8	74	Piero Cifali, Andre Bragantini Jr.	125
10	14	Nasser Aboultaif, Gabriel Robe	97
12	83	Marco Billi, Maurizio Billi	55
14	14	Artur Ramos	53
15	14	Ramon Alcaraz	48

DRIVER STANDINGS ENDURANCE CHALLENGE ROOKIE

POS	NO	DRIVERS	POINTS
1	66	Sadak Leite, Fabio Carbone	210
3	83	André Gaidzinski	199
4	14	Yuri Alves, Junior Dinardi	185
6	2	Piero Cifali, Andre Bragantini Jr.	139
8	14	Nasser Aboultaif, Gabriel Robe	108
10	74	Marco Billi, Maurizio Billi	60
12	14	Artur Ramos	58
13	74	Ramon Alcaraz	53

GT4 America

PIRELLI GT4 AMERICA

15.04.–17.04.2022	Sonoma Raceway, California, USA
20.05.–22.05.2022	New Orleans, Louisiana, USA
17.06.–19.06.2022	Virginia International Raceway, Virginia, USA
22.07.–24.07.2022	Watkins Glen International, New York, USA
19.08.–21.08.2022	Road America, Wisconsin, USA
23.09.–25.09.2022	Sebring International Raceway, Florida, USA
06.10.–08.10.2022	Indianapolis Motor Speedway, Indiana, USA

Adam Adelson, Elliott Skeer

In der Pirelli GT4 America ging Porsche mit vier Titeln vom Platz: Sie stellte die besten Fahrer sowie das beste Team in den Kategorien Silber und ProAm.

Die stärkste Porsche-Leistung des Jahres in allen SRO-Serien in Nordamerika zeigte das Team RS1 in der Pirelli GT4 America: Die Fahrer Eric Filgueiras und Stevan McAleer teilten sich den Porsche 718 Cayman GT4 RS Clubsport mit der Startnummer 18 vom Auftaktsieg in den Straßen von St. Petersburg in Florida bis hin zu den beiden titelentscheidenden Triumphen auf dem Indianapolis Motor Speedway und sicherten sich damit sowohl die Team- als auch die Fahrertrophäe in der Silberklasse. Insgesamt gewannen sie elf von 14 Rennen. Im Gegensatz dazu war der Kampf um die Pro-Am-Ehren in der Pirelli GT4 America zwischen dem bisherigen Champion Nolasport und dem Herausforderer Premier Racing deutlich enger. Trotz eines schwierigen Finalwochenendes, an dem die Premier-Mannschaft gleich zweimal umfangreiche Reparaturen aufgrund von unverschuldeten Zwischenfällen durchführen musste, lief es auf ein Titelduell zwischen den Nolasport-Fahrern Scott Noble und Jason Hart sowie den Premier-Piloten Adam Adelson und Elliott Skeer hinaus. Ein Podiumsplatz von beiden Porsche-Teams im ersten Rennen sorgte dafür, dass die endgültige Entscheidung am Sonntag fallen musste. Ein Kühlerschaden am Premier-Cayman zu Beginn des Finaldurchgangs, der zum Ausfall des Renners mit der Startnummer 120 führte, brachte Nolasport gleich beide Titel: Noble / Hart wurden als beste Fahrer ausgezeichnet, Nolasport als bestes Team.

Race Action at NOLA Motorsports Park

Adam Adelson and Elliott Skeer

Jason Alexandridis, Derek DeBoer

RS1 walks away as top SRO Pirelli GT4 America Silver Champions.

The strongest showing of the year in any SRO America series came from the #18 Porsche 718 Cayman GT4 RS Clubsport of the RS1 team. Competing in the Pirelli GT4 America series, drivers Eric Filgueiras and Stevan McAleer shared the RS1 Porsche from a season-opening win on the streets of St. Petersburg, Florida through to a pair of wins at the Indianapolis Motor Speedway. These wins at the hallowed Brickyard secured both the Silver class Team and Driver awards. In total, RS1 won 11 of 14 rounds in commanding style.

By contrast, the battle for Pro/Am honors in GT4 America was the most hotly contested series of the year, with competition mainly coming from past champion Nolasport and upstart Premier Racing.

Despite a difficult final weekend, which called on the Premier crew to perform extensive repairs not once but twice as a result of incidents that were not of their own making, the title came down to a battle between Nolasport drivers Scott Noble and Jason Hart and Premier pilots Adam Adelson and Elliott Skeer.

A podium performance by each in race one pushed the championship decider to Sunday. However, a second punctured radiator of the day for the Premier Porsche at the start of the last race guaranteed the title to the Nolasport programme after a season that featured multiple wins.

Jason Hart, Scott Noble

DRIVERS STANDINGS **PRO-AM**

POS	NO	DRIVERS	CAR	TEAM	POINTS
1	47	Jason Hart, Scott Noble	Porsche 718 Cayman GT4 RS CS	NOLASPORT	191
2	120	Adam Adelson, Elliott Skeer	Porsche 718 Cayman GT4 RS CS	Premier Racing	177
3	8	Andy Lee, Elias Sabo	Aston Martin Vantage GT4	Flying Lizard Motorsports	161
17	71	Jay Logan	Porsche 718 Cayman GT4 RS CS	GMG Racing	11
22	319	Frank Sellforf, Travis Washay	Porsche 718 Cayman GT4 RS CS	Indian Summer Racing	3

DRIVERS STANDINGS **SILVER**

POS	NO	DRIVERS	CAR	TEAM	POINTS
1	18	Eric Filgueiras, Stevan McAleer	Porsche 718 Cayman GT4 RS CS	RS1	305
2	34	Gavin Sanders, Michai Stephens	Mercedes-AMG GT4	Conquest Racing/JWF Motorsports	244
3	68	Kevin Conway, John Geesbreght	Toyota GR Supra GT4	Smooge Racing	191

TEAM STANDINGS **SILVER**

POS	TEAM	CAR	POINTS
1	RS1	Porsche 718 Cayman GT4 RS CS	305
2	Conquest Racing/JWF Motorsports	Mercedes-AMG GT4	244
3	Smooge Racing	Toyota GR Supra GT4	191

MANUFACTURERS **SILVER**

POS	MANUFACTURER	POINTS
1	Porsche	322
2	Mercedes-AMG	223
3	Aston Martin	213

Stevan McAleer and Eric Filgueiras

DTM TROPHY

20.05.–22.05.2022	Lausitzring, Germany
17.06.–19.06.2022	Imola, Italy
01.07.–03.07.2022	Norisring, Germany
26.08.–28.08.2022	Nürburgring, Germany
09.09.–11.09.2022	Spa-Francorchamps, Belgium
23.09.–25.09.2022	Red Bull Ring, Austria
07.10.– 09.10.2022	Hockenheim, Germany

KÜS Team Bernhard setzt Achtungserfolge in seiner Debütsaison in der DTM Trophy – Premierensieg für Daniel Gregor im Regen von Spa-Francorchamps

Der Start in einer neuen Rennserie stellt Teams und Fahrer immer vor zahlreiche Herausforderungen – so ging es auch dem KÜS Team Bernhard bei seinem Einstieg in die DTM Trophy. Neben vielen Highlights musste die Mannschaft rund um Timo Bernhard immer wieder harte Rückschläge hinnehmen.

Der Saisonstart verlief für das Team und die Piloten Ricky Capo und Daniel Gregor vielversprechend: Beide Nachwuchspiloten fuhren gleich am ersten Wochenende mit ihren Porsche 718 Cayman GT4 RS in die Punkte. Auf den erfolgreichen Saisonauftakt folgte in Imola und am Norisring die große Ernüchterung. Das erste Freie Training beim Italiengastspiel musste gleich zweimal unterbrochen werden und beide Male war ein gestrandetes Fahrzeug des KÜS Team Bernhard der Grund. Während Capo mit einem technischen Defekt liegen blieb, schlug Daniel Gregor in die Streckenbegrenzung ein und beschädigte das Auto dabei so stark, dass das Wochenende für ihn vorzeitig beendet war. Nach den Problemen am Freitag lief es für Capo weiterhin nicht rund. Trotz wiederholt guter Leistungen im Qualifying konnte er beide Rennen nicht beenden. Ebenso schwierig gestaltete sich das dritte Meisterschaftswochenende auf dem Norisring. Während Capo erneut beide Male nicht die Zielflagge sah, stellte Gregor in den Qualifyings mit den Startplätzen zwei und drei sein Talent unter Beweis. Doch dem Youngster gelang es noch nicht, diese Leistung in ein gutes Resultat umzumünzen.

Nach der siebenwöchigen Sommerpause startete die DTM Trophy auf dem Nürburgring in ihre zweite Saisonhälfte – und das Porsche-Team schaffte den großen Befreiungsschlag. Aufgrund von Nebel ging es für die Nachwuchspiloten erst am Samstagabend ins erste Rennen. Eine Berührung zwischen den beiden Teamkollegen in der ersten Runde zwang Capo, seinen Porsche 718 Cayman vorzeitig abzustellen. Unbeeindruckt von dem Zwischenfall arbeitete sich Gregor kontinuierlich nach vorn und feierte mit Rang zwei den ersten Podiumserfolg der Mannschaft in der Serie. Noch besser lief es am Sonntag: Von den Startplätzen zwei und drei in den Lauf gegangen behaupteten Capo und Gregor ihre Positionen und feierten nach dem Fallen der schwarz-weiß-karierten Flagge ein Doppelpodium.

Beflügelt vom starken Rennwochenende in der Eifel reiste die Mannschaft von Timo Bernhard nach Belgien zum Circuit Spa-Francorchamps. Und hier drehte besonders der deutsche Youngster Gregor mächtig auf. Bei schwierigen Bedingungen auf nasser Strecke sicherte sich der 16-Jährige den zweiten Startplatz. Dank einer starken Leistung sicherte er sich und dem Team den allerersten Sieg in der DTM Trophy. Teamkollege Capo rundete das erfolgreiche Mannschaftsresultat mit Rang fünf ab. Die Stärke im Regen demonstrierten die beiden Porsche-Piloten auch beim letzten Auslandsgastspiel auf dem österreichischen Red Bull Ring. Im Qualifying für das Sonntagsrennen sicherten sich die beiden KÜS-Teamkollegen die erste Startreihe. Capo schied jedoch bereits früh im Rennen nach einer Berührung aus. Gregor hingegen fuhr mit Position vier ein weiteres starkes Ergebnis ein. Beim Finale in Hockenheim erlebte das Team einen schwierigen Saisonabschluss, der für beide Fahrer ohne Punkte endete. Am Ende belegt Nachwuchspilot Daniel Gregor in seiner erst zweiten Saison im Automobilrennsport Rang neun in der Gesamtwertung, Ricky Capo beendet das Jahr auf der 13. Position. In der Teamwertung landet das KÜS Team Bernhard auf Platz acht.

KÜS Team Bernhard with decent results in debut season in DTM Trophy as Daniel Gregor takes maiden win in the rain at Spa-Francorchamps

There were some highlights for KÜS Team Bernhard which had its maiden season in DTM Trophy, but there were also considerable setbacks in store. The DTM Trophy season started at Lausitzring where Ricky Capo and Daniel Gregor scored their first points in their Porsche 718 Cayman GT4 RSs. For Australian Capo, a front row grid slot was another highlight. However, the next two rounds, held at Imola and Norisring, were disappointing. At Imola, Gregor was sidelined after a crash in free practice in which his car got damaged beyond repair while Capo retired from both races. At Norisring, Capo retired twice once more while Gregor was able to demonstrate his speed with second and third place on the grid for the two races.

After the summer break, the second half of the season started at Nürburgring where the two Porsche drivers tangled in the first race. Capo was out, but Gregor worked his way up to finish second, the first podium result for the team in the series. In the race on Sunday, Capo and Gregor started second and third respectively and finished in the same positions.

Gregor, 16 and from Germany, shone at Spa-Francorchamps. On a wet track, he claimed second on the grid and secured the team's maiden win in the race, with Capo finishing fifth.

At the Red Bull Ring in Austria, the two Porsche drivers were also strong in the rain, locking out the front row for the Sunday race. Capo retired after a collision while Gregor finished fourth. In a rather difficult finale at Hockenheim, neither of the drivers scored points. In the final drivers' standings, Gregor ended up ninth, four places ahead of Capo. KÜS Team Bernhard was classified eighth in the teams' championship.

Daniel Gregor, Ricky Capo

(l.-r.): Thomas Preining, Timo Berhard, Daniel Gregor, Ricky Capo

(26): Ricky Capo - (25): Daniel Gregor

TEAM STANDINGS

POS	TEAM	CAR	POINTS
1	Project 1	BMW M4 GT4	275
2	Toyota Gazoo Racing Germany by Ring Racing	Toyota GR Supra GT4	231
3	BWT Mücke Motorsport	Mercedes-AMG GT4	209
8	**KÜS Team Bernhard**	**Porsche 718 Cayman GT4 RS CS**	**125**

DRIVER STANDINGS

POS	NO	DRIVERS	CAR	TEAM	POINTS
1	90	Tim Heinemann	Toyota GR Supra GT4	Toyota Gazoo Racing Germany by Ring Racing	235
2	47	Colin Caresani	BMW M4 GT4	Project 1	188
3	34	Theo Oeverhaus	BMW M4 GT4	Walkenhorst Motorsport	158
9	**25**	**Daniel Gregor**	**Porsche 718 Cayman GT4 RS CS**	**KÜS Team Bernhard**	**85**
13	**26**	**Ricky Capo**	**Porsche 718 Cayman GT4 RS CS**	**KÜS Team Bernhard**	**42**

Daniel Gregor

ADAC GT4 GERMANY

22.04.–24.04.2022	*Oschersleben, Germany*
20.05.–22.05.2022	*Red Bull Ring, Austria*
24.06.–26.06.2022	*Zandvoort, Netherlands*
05.08.–07.08.2022	*Nürburgring, Germany*
23.09.–25.09.2022	*Sachsenring, Germany*
21.10.–23.10.2022	*Hockenheim, Germany*

Drei Rennsiege und der Titel in der Trophy-Wertung – erfolgreicher Einstand für den neuen Porsche 718 Cayman GT4 RS Clubsport in der ADAC GT4 Germany

Zur Saison 2022 führte Porsche den neuen 718 Cayman GT4 RS Clubsport ein, welcher sich direkt großer Beliebtheit erfreute. In der ADAC GT4 Germany brachten gleich fünf Kundenteams das neue GT4-Fahrzeug an den Start. Zudem wurden im Saisonverlauf auch immer wieder ältere 718 Cayman GT4 Clubsport MR eingesetzt. Allied-Racing startete erneut mit drei Fahrzeugen in der Meisterschaft und durfte sich im Saisonverlauf über zwei Siege freuen. In Oschersleben kämpften sich die beiden Allied-Racing-Youngster Vincent Andronaco und Paul-Aurel König vom 17. Startplatz bis an die Spitze. Und auch beim Saisonfinale in Hockenheim war das Team erfolgreich: Andronaco sicherte sich gemeinsam mit dem Österreicher Leo Pichler den Sieg im ersten Lauf. Grund zur Freude gab es für die bayrische Porsche-Mannschaft auch in der Trophy-Wertung. Die beiden Luxemburger Christian Kosch und Tom Kieffer verteidigten erfolgreich ihren Titel in der Klasse. Moritz Wiskirchen und Alexander Hartvig waren im dritten Cayman des Teams im Saisonverlauf ebenfalls in der Spitzengruppe unterwegs und sammelten einen Sieg sowie einen Podestplatz in der Junior-Wertung.
Erfolgreich verlief die Saison auch für den AVIA W&S Motorsport-Piloten Finn Zulauf. Der Youngster entschied gemeinsam mit Teamkollegen Lukas Schreier den finalen Saisonlauf in Hockenheim für sich. Als Fünfter der Gesamtwertung ist Zulauf am Saisonende der bestplatzierte Porsche-Fahrer in der hochkarätigen GT4-Meisterschaft.

Darüber hinaus sichert er sich Gesamtplatz drei in der Junior-Wertung. Das zweite von W&S Motorsport eingesetzte Fahrzeug pilotierten Max Kronberg und Hendrik Still. Das Duo kämpfte ebenfalls um Podest-Ergebnisse und beendete die Saison letztlich auf dem zehnten Gesamtrang.
Bis zu drei 718 Cayman GT4 RS Clubsport setzte das bulgarische Team Overdrive Racing ein. Pavel Lefterov und Stefan Bostandjiev steigerten sich im Saisonverlauf immer weiter und kämpften in der Schlussphase der Saison ebenfalls um Topresultate. So reichte es beim Finale in Hockenheim zu den Plätzen sechs und acht. Im zweiten Porsche des Teams belegten Tano Neumann und Joachim Bölting Rang zwei in der Trophy-Wertung. Für einen prominenten Gaststart auf dem Hockenheimring sorgte Herberth Motorsport. Der Rennstall aus Bayern setzte einen älteren Cayman für Ralf Bohn und Alfred Renauer ein. Das Duo landete im Finallauf auf dem dritten Rang der Trophy-Klasse.

(23): Pavel Lefterov, Stefan Bostandjiev
(73): Aleks Stefanov, Alon Gabbay

W&S Motorsport Team

(l.-r.): Joachim Bölting, Tano Neumann, Axel Sartingen, Daniel Schwerfeld, Christian Kosch, Tom Kieffer

Three race wins and the Trophy title: successful debut for the new Porsche 718 Cayman GT4 RS Clubsport in ADAC GT4 Germany

Allied-Racing entered three new Caymans in the ADAC GT4 Germany, and racked up two wins. At Oschersleben, youngsters Vincent Andronaco and Paul-Aurel König won from 17th on the grid. Andronaco scored another win in the finale at Hockenheim, this time with Austrian Leo Pichler. The Bavarian team was also successful in the Trophy standings where Christian Kosch and Tom Kieffer, from Luxemburg, secured their second consecutive title. Moritz Wiskirchen and Alexander Hartvig raced the team's third Cayman and racked up one win and another podium result in the Junior class.

AVIA W&S Motorsport driver Finn Zulauf also had a successful season. Together with teammate Lukas Schreier, the youngster won the final race at Hockenheim. Fifth in the end-of-season standings, Zulauf was the best-placed Porsche driver in the high-class GT4 series. Moreover, he ended up third in the junior class. Max Kronberg and Hendrik Still drove the second car run by W&S Motorsport. The duo was also in contention for podium results and ended up tenth in the standings.

Bulgarian team Overdrive Racing ran up to three 718 Cayman GT4 RS Clubsports. Pavel Lefterov and Stefan Bostandjiev showed consistent progress throughout the season as was reflected in the finale at Hockenheim where they finished sixth and eighth. Tano Neumann and Joachim Bölting drove the team's second Porsche to runner-up position in the Trophy standings. Herberth Motorsport was a prominent guest entrant at Hockenheim where Ralf Bohn and Alfred Renauer drove their older Cayman to third in the Trophy class.

Axel Sartingen, Daniel Schwerfeld

DRIVER STANDINGS

POS	NO	DRIVERS	CAR	TEAM	POINTS
1	24	Hugo Sasse, Mike David Ortmann	Aston Martin Vantage GT4	PROsport Racing	185
2	007	Romain Leroux, Ben Dörr	Aston Martin Vantage GT4	Dörr Motorsport	154
3	69	Indy Dontje, Phil Dörr	Aston Martin Vantage GT4	Dörr Motorsport	140
5	31	Finn Zulauf	Porsche 718 Cayman GT4 RS CS	Avia W&S Motorsport	119
10	**30**	**Max Kronberg, Hendrik Still**	**Porsche 718 Cayman GT4 RS CS**	**W&S Motorsport**	**81**
16	44	Alexander Hartvig, Moritz Wiskirchen	Porsche 718 Cayman GT4 RS CS	Allied Racing	61
18	**23**	**Pavel Lefterov, Stefan Bostandjiev**	**Porsche 718 Cayman GT4 RS CS**	**Overdrive Racing**	**60**
19	22	Vincent Andronaco	Porsche 718 Cayman GT4 RS CS	Allied Racing	56
24	**31**	**Lukas Schreier**	**Porsche 718 Cayman GT4 RS CS**	**Avia W&S Motorsport**	**41**
25	32	Leo Pichler	Porsche 718 Cayman GT4 RS CS	W&S Motorsport	31
28	**22**	**Paul-Aurel König**	**Porsche 718 Cayman GT4 RS CS**	**Allied Racing**	**28**
32	26	Christian Kosch, Tom Kieffer	Porsche 718 Cayman GT4 RS CS	Allied Racing	21
37	**9**	**Joachim Bölting, Tano Neumann**	**Porsche 718 Cayman GT4 RS CS**	**Overdrive Racing**	**9**
45	33	Axel Sartingen, Daniel Schwerfeld	Porsche 718 Cayman GT4 RS CS	Black Falcon Team Textar	1

DRIVER STANDINGS **TROPHY**

POS	NO	DRIVERS	CAR	TEAM	POINTS
1	**26**	**Christian Kosch, Tom Kieffer**	**Porsche 718 Cayman GT4 RS CS**	**Allied Racing**	**512**
2	9	Joachim Bölting, Tano Neumann	Porsche 718 Cayman GT4 RS CS	Overdrive Racing	374
3	48	Yevgen Sokolovskiy	Aston Martin Vantage GT4	PROsport Racing	279
4	**33**	**Axel Sartingen, Daniel Schwerfeld**	**Porsche 718 Cayman GT4 RS CS**	**Black Falcon Team Textar**	**206**

(l.-r.): Joachim Bölting, Tano Neumann, Christian Kosch, Tom Kieffer, Ralf Bohn

GT4 European Series

GT4 EUROPEAN SERIES

01.04.–03.04.2022	Imola, Italy
03.06.–05.06 2022	Paul Ricard, France
01.07.–03.07.2022	Misano, Italy
28.07.–30.07.2022	Spa-Francorchamps, Belgium
02.09.–04.09.2022	Hockenheim, Germany
03.09.–02.10.2022	Barcelona, Spain

Das Porsche-Duo Mikhail Loboda / Andrey Solukovtsev holt sich den Am-Titel in der GT4 European Series – Porsche-Siege auch in der Pro-Am-Kategorie.

Fünf Porsche stellten sich dem Wettbewerb in der GT4 European Series. Die beste Klassen-Platzierung eines Porsche-Teams erreichten Mikhail Loboda / Andrey Solukovtsev, die die Am-Klasse für sich entscheiden konnten. Auf dem Weg zum Titel gewann das Duo von W&S Motorsport zweimal in Hockenheim sowie einmal in Spa-Francorchamps. Alle drei Am-Erfolge erreichte es von der Pole Position der Am-Klasse. Auch in der Pro-Am-Kategorie gab es Siege des Porsche 718 Cayman GT4: Alex Fontana und Ivan Jacoma vom Centri Porsche Ticino triumphierten im zweiten Lauf von Imola in ihrer Klasse, was dem zweiten Gesamtplatz entsprach. Sogar zweimal konnten Vincent Andronaco / Andreas Mayerl von der höchsten Stufe des Pro-Am-Treppchens jubeln: Im ersten Durchgang von Imola und im ersten Heat von Barcelona waren sie bestes Pro-Am-Team. In Spanien erreichte die Paarung von Allied Racing das Ziel sogar vor allen anderen Kontrahenten und gewann das gesamte Rennen.
In der Silber-Wertung schließlich war das beste Porsche-Resultat ein zweiter Rang von Alexander Hartvig / Moritz Wiskirchen in Misano.

Hendrik Still, Max Kronberg

(l.-r.): Hendrik Still, Max Kronberg, Mikhail Loboda, Andrey Solukovtsev

Mikhail Loboda, Andrey Solukovtsev

Alex Fontana, Ivan Jacoma

Porsche duo Mikhail Loboda / Andrey Solukovtsev claims GT4 European Series Am class title – Porsche victories in the Pro-Am class too.

Five Porsches took on the competition in the GT4 European Series. The best-placed Porsche team was the duo of Mikhail Loboda / Andrey Solukovtsev which won the Am class title. On their way to the title, the W&S Motorsport pairing scored two wins at Hockenheim and a victory at Spa-Francorchamps. All three Am class wins were achieved from pole position in class.
In the Pro-Am category, there were also victories for the Porsche 718 Cayman GT4. Second overall, Centri Porsche Ticino drivers Alex Fontana and Ivan Jacoma won their class in the second race at Imola. Vincent Andronaco / Andreas Mayerl even scored two Pro-Am class wins, in the first race at Imola and the first race at Barcelona. In Spain, the Allied-Racing pairing finished ahead of all the other teams and claimed the outright race win.
In the Silver standings, the best Porsche result was second place for Alexander Hartvig / Moritz Wiskirchen at Misano.

Andreas Mayerl and Vincent Andronaco

Alexander Hartvig, Moritz Wiskirchen

DRIVER STANDINGS **PRO-AM**

POS	NO	DRIVERS	CAR	TEAM	POINTS
1	87	Jean-Luc Beaubelique, Jim Pla	Mercedes-AMG GT4	Akkodis ASP Team	153
2	17	Kenny Herremans, Dante Rappange	Chevrolet Camaro GT4.R	V8 Racing	145
3	42	Gregory Guilvert, Fabien Michal	Audi R8 LMS GT4	Sainteloc Racing	142
4	718	Alex Fontana, Ivan Jacoma	Porsche 718 Cayman GT3 CS MR	Porsche Centri Ticino	139
5	22	Vincent Andronaco, Andreas Mayrl	Porsche 718 Cayman GT3 CS MR	Allied Racing	97
8	38	Hendrik Still, Max Kronberg	Porsche 718 Cayman GT3 CS MR	W&S Motorsport	78

DRIVER STANDINGS **SILVER**

POS	NO	DRIVERS	CAR	TEAM	POINTS
1	14	Roee Meyuhas, Erwin Bastard	Audi R8 LMS GT4	Sainteloc Racing	159
2	15	Enzo Joulie, Lluc Ibañez	Mercedes-AMG GT4	NM Racing Team	156
3	24	Mike-David Ortmann, Hugo Sasse	Aston Martin Vantage GT4	PROsport Racing	142
9	44	Alexander Hartvig, Moritz Wiskirchen	Porsche 718 Cayman GT4 CS MR	Allied Racing	60

DRIVER STANDINGS **AM**

POS	NO	DRIVERS	CAR	TEAM	POINTS
1	37	Mikhail Loboda, Andrey Solukovtsev	Porsche 718 Cayman GT4 CS MR	W&S Motorsport	157
2	61	Mauro Ricci	Mercedes-AMG GT4	Akkodis ASP Team	144
3	89	Julien Lambert, Wilfried Cazalbon	Aston Martin Vantage GT4	AGS Events	133

TEAM STANDINGS **PRO-AM**

POS	TEAM	CAR	POINTS
1	Akkodis ASP Team	Mercedes-AMG GT4	179
2	V8 Racing	Chevrolet Camaro GT4.R	151
3	Sainteloc Racing	Audi R8 LMS GT4	148
4	Centri Porsche Ticino	Porsche 718 Cayman GT4 CS MR	141
5	Allied Racing	Porsche 718 Cayman GT4 CS MR	97
8	W&S Motorsport	Porsche 718 Cayman GT4 CS MR	80

TEAM STANDINGS **AM**

POS	TEAM	CAR	POINTS
1	Akkodis ASP Team	Mercedes-AMG GT4	163
2	W&S Motorsport	Porsche 718 Cayman GT4 CS MR	161
3	Fullmotorsport	Audi R8 LMS GT4	152
8	Allied Racing	Porsche 718 Cayman GT4 CS MR	65

FANATEC GT2 EUROPEAN SERIES

GT2 EUROPEAN SERIES

01.04.–03.04.2022	*Imola, Italy*
20.05.–22.05.2022	*Red Bull Ring, Austria*
01.07.–03.07.2022	*Misano, Italy*
23.07.–24.07.2022	*Spa-Francorchamps, Belgium*
16.09.–18.09.2022	*Valencia, Spain*
14.10.–16.10.2022	*Paul Ricard, France*

In der GT2 European Series gingen die Ränge zwei und drei der Am-Abschlusstabelle an die Porsche-Piloten Gianluca Giorgi und Leonardo Gorini.

Der Italiener Gianluca Giorgi war der stärkste Porsche-Mann in der GT2 European Series, er holte für die Zuffenhausener zwei Siege – davon einen in Imola und einen in Spa-Francorchamps, drei zweite Plätze und zwei dritte Ränge. Damit kletterte der Schützling des Teams Ebimotors im Gesamtklassement der Am-Teilnehmer auf Position zwei, obwohl er den Lauf in Valencia ausgelassen hatte. Nur eine Stelle dahinter reihte sich der Schweizer Leonardo Gorini ein, der die komplette Saison als Alleinstarter auf seinem Porsche GT2 RS CS saß. Die besten Ergebnisse des Piloten aus dem Team LP Racing waren P2 im zweiten Durchgang von Imola sowie in beiden Rennen von Spa-Francorchamps. Alessandro Baccani bestritt nur drei Rennen der GT2 European Series: Eins an der Seite von Paolo Venerosi Pesciolini und zwei mit Giorgi. Mit ihm zusammen erreichte er mit den Plätzen zwei und drei auch seine besten Resultate. Außerdem klassierten sich noch Alberto Scilla auf Tabellenrang elf und Pesciolini an 13. Stelle der Abschlusswertung.

Gianluca Giorgi and Ebimotors Team

Gianluca Giorgi

In the GT2 European Series, Porsche drivers Gianluca Giorgi and Leonardo Gorini secured second and third place in the final Am class standings.

Italian Gianluca Giorgi was the strongest Porsche driver in the GT2 European Series as he claimed two wins, one in Imola and one at Spa-Francorchamps, plus three second and two third places. That enabled the Ebimotors driver to secure runner-up spot in the final Am class standings, even though he had missed the round in Valencia. One place further down, Swiss Leonardo Gorini ended up third, having driven his Porsche GT2 RS CS on his own in all the races. Second place in the second race at Imola and in both races at Spa-Francorchamps were his best results. Alessandro Baccani only participated in three GT2 European Series races: one together with Paolo Venerosi Pesciolini and two together with Giorgi. With the latter, he also scored his best results with one second and one third place. Other Porsche drivers in the final standings were Alberto Scilla in eleventh and Pesciolini in 13th.

DRIVER STANDINGS **AM**

POS	NO	DRIVERS	CAR	TEAM	POINTS
1	67	Henry Hassid	Audi R8 LMS GT2	LP Racing	212
2	7	**Gianluca Giorgi**	**Porsche 991 GT2 RS CS**	**Ebimotors**	170
3	911	**Leonardo Gorini**	**Porsche 991 GT2 RS CS**	**LP Racing**	138
7	66	**Alessandro Baccani**	**Porsche 991 GT2 RS CS**	**Ebimotors**	55

Gianluca Giorgi

Gianluca Giorgi

PORSCHE SPRINT TROPHY THAILAND

PORSCHE SPRINT TROPHY THAILAND

29.06.–03.07.2022	*Bangsean Street Circuit, Thailand*
25.08.–28.08.2022	*Chang Circuit, Buriram, Thailand*
30.09.–02.10.2022	*Singapore F1 Circuit, Singapore*
27.10.–30.10.2022	*Chang Circuit, Buriram, Thailand*
08.12.–11.12.2022	*Chang Circuit, Buriram, Thailand*

Yotsarun Sansuk, Hideharu Kuroki

Die thailändischen Porsche-Piloten Tanart und Munkong Sathienthirakul bewiesen auch in der Saison 2022 ihr Talent mit einigen Podestplätzen.

Die Porsche Sprint Trophy Thailand startete im Juli mit dem Auftakt der Thailand Super Series auf dem Bangsaen Street Circuit, an dem insgesamt neun Porsche in den Klassen GTC und GTM teilnahmen.

Die Brüder Tanart und Munkong Sathienthirakul, die für Mongkol Motorsports ins Lenkrad griffen, stiegen mit Rang zwei im ersten Lauf in die Saison ein, bevor sie sich im zweiten Rennen den GTM-Sieg sicherten. Tasanapol Inthraphuvasak gewann mit seinem Porsche 718 Cayman GT4 RS Clubsport den ersten Durchgang der GTC-Kategorie.

Auf dem Chang International Circuit erlebte Porsche dann insbesondere in der GTC-Kategorie ein erfolgreiches Wochenende. Aekarat Discharone gewann den ersten Heat, während Adisak Tangphuncharoen in Rennen zwei den dritten Platz ins Ziel brachte.

Im Oktober auf dem Marina Bay Circuit in Singapur war es an Tanart Sathienthirakul, für die größten Porsche-Triumphe zu sorgen. Mit zwei Klassensiegen ließ er keine Wünsche offen.

Mongkol Motorsports setzte seine starke Form auch beim vierten Stopp fort, als das Sathienthirakul-Duo auf dem Chang International Circuit beide Rennen auf dem Podium beendete. Zudem zeigte Pasarit Promsombat eine starke Leistung, als er in Lauf zwei die dritte Gesamtposition und auch Rang drei in der GT-Am-Klasse belegte. Das Finale der Porsche Sprint Trophy Thailand findet im Dezember (nach Redaktionsschluss) auf dem Chang International Circuit statt.

Sathienthirakul brothers show their class in TSS

The Porsche Sprint Trophy Thailand got underway in July as part of the Thailand Super Series campaign, which kicked off at Bangsaen Street Circuit. A total of nine Porsches were entered across the GTC and GTM classes.
Brothers Tanart and Munkong Sathienthirakul started their campaign with second place in the opening race, driving for Mongkol Motorsports, before securing the GTM class victory in the second. Tasanapol Inthraphuvasak was also victorious in the opening race of the GTC category, taking top honours in the Porsche 718 Cayman GT4 RS Clubsport.
Porsche had a strong weekend in the GTC category as the series moved to Chang International Circuit for the second round, as Aekarat Discharone took the win in the first of the races, while Adisak Tangphuncharoen secured third place in the second race.
Tanart Sathienthirakul was victorious in Singapore as the Marina Bay Street Circuit hosted the third round of the series in October, picking up class victory in both races.
Mongkol Motorsports continued its strong form as the Sathienthirakul duo finished both races on the podium at Chang International Circuit, while Pasarit Promsombat showed great pace to take third place overall and the GT-Am class in the second race for the YK Motorsports Billionaire Boy by Sunoco team.
The final round will take place in December at Chang International Circuit.

Kantadhee Kusiri

(14): Pasarit Promsombat - (63): Silapa Teeraniti, Grant Supaphong - (33): Jakraphan Davee, Phaophong Chanchalia

DRIVER STANDINGS **PORSCHE SPRINT TROPHY GTM**

POS	NO	DRIVERS	CAR	TEAM	POINTS
1	15	Munkong Sathienthirakul, Tanart Sathienthirakul	Porsche 992 GT3 Cup	Mongkol Motorsports	150
3	14	Pasarit Promsombat	Porsche 991 Cup	YK Motorsports	91
4	17	Kantadhee Kusiri	Porsche 991 Cup II	AAS Motorsport	75
5	88	Yotsarun Sansuk, Hideharu Kuroki	Porsche 991 Cup	Kuroki Racing	69
7	33	Jakraphan Davee, Phaophong Chanchalia	Porsche 991 Cup	Alpha Factory Racing Team	33
9	17	Nattachak Hanjitkasem	Porsche 991 Cup II	AAS Motorsport	33
10	17	Tasanapol Inthraphuvasak	Porsche 991 Cup II	AAS Motorsport	30
11	63	Silapa Teeraniti, Grant Supaphong	Porsche 991 Cup	Maxnitron Racing	20

after round 4 of 5

DRIVER STANDINGS **PORSCHE SPRINT TROPHY GTC**

POS	NO	DRIVER	CAR	TEAM	POINTS
1	26	Adisak Tangphuncharoen	Porsche Cayman GT4	B-Quik Absolute Racing Team	110
2	14	Tasanapol Inthraphuvasak	Porsche Cayman GT4	AAS Motorsport	40
3	11	Gregory S. Bennett	Porsche Cayman GT4	B-Quik Absolute Racing Team	30
9	99	Patchara Wutichat	Porsche 997 GT3 Cup	Diamond Motorsport Racing Team	24
10	99	Aekarat Discharoen	Porsche 997 GT3 Cup	Diamond Motorsport Racing Team	12

after round 4 of 5

DRIVER STANDINGS **GTM**

POS	NO	DRIVERS	CAR	TEAM	POINTS
1	**15**	**Munkong Sathienthirakul, Tanart Sathienthirakul**	**Porsche 992 GT3 Cup**	**Mongkol Motorsports**	**122**
2	29	Akihiro Asai, Ananthorn Tangniannatchai	Lamborghini Gallardo	Vattana Motorsport	96
3	24	Nattavude Charoensukhawatana	Lexus RC F	Toyota Gazoo Team Thailand	64
6	**14**	**Pasarit Promsombat**	**Porsche 991 Cup**	**YK Motorsports**	**60**
8	**17**	**Kantadhee Kusiri**	**Porsche 991 Cup II**	**AAS Motorsport**	**49**
11	**88**	**Yotsarun Sansuk, Hideharu Kuroki**	**Porsche 991 Cup**	**Kuroki Racing**	**40**
13	**33**	**Jakraphan Davee, Phaophong Chanchalia**	**Porsche 991 Cup**	**Alpha Factory Racing Team**	**22**
15	**17**	**Nattachak Hanjitkasem**	**Porsche 991 Cup II**	**AAS Motorsport**	**25**
16	**17**	**Tasanapol Inthraphuvasak**	**Porsche 991 Cup II**	**AAS Motorsport**	**16**
17	**63**	**Silapa Teeraniti, Grant Supaphong**	**Porsche 991 Cup**	**Maxnitron Racing**	**10**

after round 4 of 5

Munkong Sathienthirakul, Tanart Sathienthirakul

Yotsarun Sansuk, Hideharu Kuroki

IMSA MICHELIN PILOT CHALLENGE

27.01.–28.01.2022	Daytona International Speedway, USA
16.03.–17.03.2022	Sebring International Raceway, USA
29.04.–30.04.2022	Laguna Seca Raceway, USA
13.05.–14.05.2022	Mid-Ohio Sports Car Course, USA
24.06.–25.06.2022	Watkins Glen, USA
01.07.–02.07.2022	Canadian Tire Motorsports Park, Canada
15.07.–16.06.2022	Lime Rock Park, USA
05.08.–06.08.2022	Road America, USA
26.08.–27.08.2022	Virginia International Raceway, USA
29.09.–30.09.2022	Road Atlanta, USA

Alexandre Premat

Die Debütsaison des Porsche 718 Cayman GT4 RS Clubsport in der IMSA Michelin Pilot Challenge bringt einen Sieg für den neuen Porsche-Renner.

Der neue Porsche 718 Cayman GT4 RS Clubsport startete mit einem Erfolg auf dem Daytona International Speedway im Januar in die IMSA Michelin Pilot Challenge 2022 und alles deutete auf ein starkes Jahr des GT4-Boliden hin. Doch das Mittelmotor-Fahrzeug konnte danach keine weiteren Siege mehr einfahren, insgesamt aber fünf Podiumsplätze in der zehn Rennen umfassenden Saison sammeln. Acht neue Porsche Cayman traten in der GS-Klasse regelmäßig gegen starke Konkurrenz an. Die Autos waren schnell und standfest, aber weitere Trophäen wurden oft auf eine Weise verpasst, die sich der Kontrolle der jeweiligen Porsche-Teams und -Fahrer in der hart umkämpften Serie entzog. So beendete der deutsche Sportwagenbauer die Saison mit 130 Punkten Rückstand, auf die siegreiche Marke Mercedes-AMG, als Vierter der Herstellerwertung.
Beim Saisonauftakt konnte sich die langjährige Porsche-Truppe RS1 gegen harte Marken-interne Konkurrenz vom TeamTGM durchsetzen und mit den Fahrern Eric Filgueiras und Stevan McAleer am Steuer den ersten internationalen Triumph für den neuen Cayman-Renner erobern. RS1 war es auch, die 2018 den ersten großen Erfolg des damals neuen Porsche 718 Cayman erringen konnten. Das TGM-Duo Owen Trinkler / Ted Giovanis reihte sich auf Rang zwei ein, während die drittbeste Porsche-Mannschaft Tyler McQuarrie / Mark Siegel / Tom Dyer das Podest als Vierte nur um minimale 0,186 Sekunden verpasste. Insgesamt nahmen neun GT4 RS Clubsport am ersten Saisonrennen in Daytona teil, vier davon erreichten die Top Ten der Gesamtwertung.

Stevan McAleer,
Alexandre Premat

Debut season of Porsche 718 Cayman GT4 RS Clubsport sees single victory for road-based race car.

The new Porsche 718 Cayman GT4 RS Clubsport launched into international competition with overwhelming success at the Daytona International Speedway in January. All signs pointed toward a strong year in the IMSA-sanctioned Michelin Pilot Challenge after the first-round victory. While the mid-engine racer did not win again, it did accumulate a total of five podium finishes in the ten race season. Eight of the new Porsche machines contested regularly in the GS class with established teams and impressive driver lineups. The car showed speed and endurance in the hotly-contested road car-based series, but often had victory snatched from it in ways that were out of the control of the teams and drivers. Porsche eventually ended the season fourth in the Manufacturer standings, 130 points off the lead.
At the season opener, longtime Porsche entrant RS1 was able to stave-off heated competition from fellow Porsche privateer TeamTGM to score the first international victory for the 4.0-liter flat-six engined-sports car in the hands of drivers Eric Filgueiras and Stevan McAleer. It was also RS1 which earned the first win the then-new Porsche 718 Cayman in 2018. In total, nine GT4 RS Clubsports started the 2022 season, with four of them finishing in the top-ten overall.

Eric Filgueiras and Stevan McAleer

Nick Galante, John DuBets

James Sofronas, Kyle Washington

Andrew Davis, Michael McCann

Jason Hart, Mat Travis

Tyler McQuarrie, Sameer Gandhi

Hugh Plumb, Matt Plumb

James Sofronas, Kyle Washington

(69): Anderson Tanoto, Lars Kern - (47): Jason Hart, Mat Travis

DRIVER STANDINGS **GRAND SPORT**

POS	NO	DRIVERS	CAR	TEAM	POINTS
1	7	Alan Brynjolffson, Trent Hindman	Aston Martin Vantage GT4	Volt Racing	2760
2	56	Eric Foss	Mercedes-AMG GT4	Murillo Racing	2590
3	95	Bill Auberlen, Dillon Machavern	BMW M4 GT4	Turner Motorsport	2190
11	46	Hugh Plumb, Matt Plumb	Porsche 718 Cayman GT4 RS CS	Team TGM	1850
12	64	Owen Trinkler, Ted Giovanis	Porsche 718 Cayman GT4 RS CS	Team TGM	1830
13	8	Andrew Davis, Michael McCann	Porsche 718 Cayman GT4 RS CS	McCann Racing	1740
16	93	Tyler McQuarrie	Porsche 718 Cayman GT4 RS CS	CarBahn with Peregrine Racing	1550
18	28	Stevan McAleer	Porsche 718 Cayman GT4 RS CS	RS1	1520
21	22	Nick Galante	Porsche 718 Cayman GT4 RS CS	Hardpoint	1360
22	83	Spencer Pumpelly, Thomas Collingwood	Porsche 718 Cayman GT4 RS CS	BGB Motorsports	1320
26	22	Sean McAlister	Porsche 718 Cayman GT4 RS CS	Hardpoint	1230
30	93	Mark Siegel	Porsche 718 Cayman GT4 RS CS	McCann Racing	1020
31	47	Jason Hart, Mat Travis	Porsche 718 Cayman GT4 RS CS	NOLASport	1000
34	66	Alec Udell, David Brule	Porsche 718 Cayman GT4 RS CS	Kelly Moss	790
36	93	Tom Dyer	Porsche 718 Cayman GT4 RS CS	CarBahn with Peregrine Racing	680
37	28	Eric Filgueiras	Porsche 718 Cayman GT4 RS CS	RS1	670
39	28	Alexandre Premat	Porsche 718 Cayman GT4 RS CS	RS1	620
45	22,28	John DuBets	Porsche 718 Cayman GT4 RS CS	Hardpoint, RS1	450
49	93	Sameer Gandhi	Porsche 718 Cayman GT4 RS CS	McCann Racing	310
50	32	James Sofronas, Kyle Washington	Porsche 718 Cayman GT4 RS CS	GMG Racing	300
59	83	John Tecce	Porsche 718 Cayman GT4 RS CS	BGB Motorsports	140
61	540	Jeroen Bleekemolen, Tim Pappas, Sebastiaan Bleekemolen	Porsche 718 Cayman GT4 RS CS	Black Swan Racing	100
67	9	Derek DeBoer, Sam Owen, Sean Gibbons	Porsche 718 Cayman GT4 RS CS	Hardpoint	70
71	69	Anderson Tanoto, Lars Kern	Porsche 718 Cayman GT4 RS CS	Absolute Racing	50

DRIVER STANDINGS **GRAND SPORT BRONZE**

POS	NO	DRIVERS	CAR	TEAM	POINTS
1	11	Garry Ferrera, Kris Wilson	Mercedes-AMG GT4	Capstone Motorsports	3380
2	65	Brent Mosing, Tim Probert	Mercedes-AMG GT4	Murillo Racing	3260
3	09	Ramin Abdolvahabi	Aston Martin Vantage GT4	Automatic Racing	2080
5	32	James Sofronas, Kyle Washington	Porsche 718 Cayman GT4 RS CS	GMG Racing	620

MANUFACTURER STANDINGS

POS	MANUFACTURER	CAR	POINTS
1	Mercedes-AMG	Mercedes-AMG GT4	3030
2	Aston Martin	Aston Martin Vantage GT4	2980
3	BMW	BMW M4 GT4	2940
4	Porsche	Porsche 718 Cayman GT4 RS CS	2900

TEAM STANDINGS **GRAND SPORT**

POS	NO	TEAM	POINTS
1	7	Volt Racing	2760
2	56	Murillo Racing	2590
3	95	Turner Motorsport	2190
10	46	Team TGM	1850
11	64	Team TGM	1830
13	8	McCann Racing	1740
15	93	CarBahn with Peregrine Racing	1550
16	28	RS1	1520
18	83	BGB Motorsports	1320
21	22	Hardpoint	1230
24	47	NOLASport	1000
25	66	Kelly Moss	790
29	09	Automatic Racing	670
29	32	GMG Racing	300
34	540	Black Swan Racing	100
36	9	Hardpoint	70
39	69	Absolute Racing	50

Spencer Pumpelly,
Thomas Collingwood

YOKOHAMA DRIVERS CUP USA

01.04.–04.04.2022	*Spring Mountain Motor Resort, Nevada, USA*
22.04.–24.04.2022	*Circuit of the Americas, Texas, USA*
03.06.–05.06.2022	*WeatherTech Raceway Laguna Seca, California, USA*
24.06.–26.06.2022	*Utah Motorsports Campus, Utah, USA*
12.08.–14.08.2022	*Road America, Wisconsin, USA*
09.09.–11.09.2022	*Thunderhill Raceway Park, California, USA*
30.09.–02.10.2022	*Indianapolis Motor Speedway, Indiana, USA*
28.10.–30.10.2022	*Sonoma Raceway, California, USA*

Der Yokohama Drivers Cup USA 2022 zeigte wieder einmal spannenden Motorsport – die Titel gingen letztendlich an Jim Walsh, Joel Cortez und Dmitri Novikov.

Der Yokohama Drivers Cup USA lockte in seiner 16. Ausgabe altbekannte sowie neue Teams und Fahrer aus den gesamten USA und aus Mexiko an. Sie durften sich unter anderem auf zwei neue Austragungsorte freuen: das Spring Mountain Motor Resort in Las Vegas sowie den legendären Indianapolis Motorsport Speedway. Diese beiden Strecken vervollständigten den Kalender des Porsche-Markenpokals, der aus insgesamt acht Rennwochenenden bestand. Auf dem Utah Motorsport Campus und beim Saisonfinale auf dem Sonoma Raceway wurden 2022 erstmals Langstreckenrennen ausgetragen, um den Teilnehmern die Möglichkeit zu geben, neue Erfahrungen zu sammeln.

Jim Walsh aus dem Team Competition Motorsports holte sich mit seinem Porsche GT3 Cup 991.2 den Titel in der Platin-Masters-Klasse und sicherte sich zudem den Sieg in der Gesamtwertung des Yokohama Drivers Cup. Joel Cortez, der für Esses Racing an den Start ging, gewann mit seinem Porsche GT3 Cup 992 die Emerald-Klasse. Und schließlich war Dmitri Novikov aus der Mannschaft Rearden Racing in der Platin-Kategorie nicht zu bezwingen. Wie Walsh vertraute er bei seinem Erfolg auf einen Porsche GT3 Cup 991 der zweiten Generation.

(99): Jim Walsh - (74): Casey Dennis

The Yokohama Drivers Cup USA Series saw great achievements by all the competing drivers

Yokohama Drivers Cup USA Series celebrated its 16th season of Porsche one-make racing, attracting new teams and drivers as well as returning drivers from the USA and Mexico. Six current Porsche platforms, including the newly added Porsche GT3 Cup 992 platform, took to the tracks in 2022 to spark fierce competition and fun. Two new venues were added to the series, including the season opener at Spring Mountain Motor Resort, (Las Vegas, NV), and an invitation to the iconic Indianapolis Motorsport Speedway, (Indianapolis, IN). These two tracks completed the eight-round series. Drivers proved their talent over either two or three days of racing, on demanding racetracks around the US. Other events included Circuit of the Americas, WeatherTech Raceway Laguna Seca, Road America, Thunderhill Raceway Park and Sonoma Raceway.

The excitement of Enduro racing was introduced in 2022 at both the Utah Motorsport Campus and at the season finale at Sonoma Raceway. These longer races encouraged team building and the advancement of crew experience. Team success at executing clean pitstops was recognized with awards for Throttle Therapy Motorsports and Tatum Racing.

Jim Walsh, (Competition Motorsports) earned the Platinum Masters Class Champion title in his 991.2 GT3 Cup. He secured the overall 2022 Championship by driving with skill and consistency at every event of the 2022 season. Joel Cortez, (Esses Racing), new to the series and full-season driver for 2022, earned the Emerald Class Championship in his 992 GT3 Cup. Dmitri Novikov, (Rearden Racing), another new full-season driver drove aggressively to capture the 2022 Platinum Class Championship in his 991.2 GT3 Cup.

"On behalf of Yokohama Drivers Cup USA, Competent Motorsport is very pleased to have completed its 16th season of successfully supporting the Porsche Pyramid as a transitional series for teams and drivers to excel in Porsche racing," said Gregory Franz, Founder and President of Competent Motorsport.

(21): Jake Pedersen - (40): Tim Bidwill

(29): Dmitri Novikov - Platinum Class Champion

(99): Jim Walsh - Platinum Masters Class Champion/Overall Series Champion

(1): Joel Cortez - Emerald Class Champion

(14): Slade Stewart

DRIVER STANDINGS **PLATINUM**

POS	NO	DRIVERS	CAR	TEAM	POINTS
1	29	Dmitri Novikov	Porsche 991 GT3 Cup II	Rearden Racing	190
2	88	Kayden Kelly	Porsche 991 GT3 Cup II	Throttle Therapy Motorsports	182
3	33	Mark Wilgus	Porsche 991 GT3 Cup II	Competition Motorsports	123
4	45	Tom Haacker	Porsche 991 GT3 Cup II	Competition Motorsports	99
5	74	Casey Dennis	Porsche 991 GT3 Cup II	US Racing Dynamics	98
6	14	Slade Stewart	Porsche 991 GT3 Cup II	Competition Motorsports	94

DRIVER STANDINGS **PLATINUM MASTERS**

POS	NO	DRIVERS	CAR	TEAM	POINTS
1	99	Jim Walsh	Porsche 991 GT3 Cup II	Competition Motorsports	277
2	2	Michael Zuieback	Porsche 991 GT3 Cup II	Competition Motorsports	166
3	40	Tim Bidwill	Porsche 991 GT3 Cup II	Competition Motorsports	144
4	56	John McInnes	Porsche 991 GT3 Cup II	Tatum Racing	92
5	66	Steve Miller	Porsche 991 GT3 Cup II	Competition Motorsports	65
6	31	Will James	Porsche 991 GT3 Cup II	Migliore Motorsports	44

DRIVER STANDINGS **EMERALD**

POS	NO	DRIVERS	CAR	TEAM	POINTS
1	1	Joel Cortes	Porsche 992 GT3 Cup	Esses Racing	252
2	44	Sal Brogna	Porsche 992 GT3 Cup	BR Racing	160
3	63	Richard French	Porsche 992 GT3 Cup	BR Racing	147
4	21	Jake Pedersen	Porsche 992 GT3 Cup	Rearden Racing	111

PORSCHE
ENDURANCE TROPHY
BENELUX

PORSCHE ENDURANCE TROPHY BENELUX

14.05.–15.05.2022 Zolder, Belgium
05.06.–06.06.2022 Magny Cours, France
16.07.–17.07.2022 Spa-Francorchamps, Belgium
11.08.–14.08.2022 Zolder 24 Hours, Belgium
17.09.–18.09.2022 Nürburgring, Germany
08.10.–09.10.2022 Zolder, Belgium

Die Porsche Endurance Trophy Benelux sorgte auch 2022 wieder für tollen Sport, jede Menge Spannung und eine Titelentscheidung auf den letzten Metern.

Buchstäblich erst auf der Ziellinie des letzten von sechs Saisonrennen und nach einem Jahr mit mehr als 35 Rennstunden stand der Sieger der Porsche Endurance Trophy Benelux fest. Der Abstand zwischen den neuen Champions Hans Thiers, Frank Thiers, Christoff Corten und Jeffrey van Hooydonk aus der Mannschaft Russell Racing by NGT sowie Dylan Derdaele und Michael Cool, den unterlegenen Titelverteidigern vom Team Belgium Racing, betrug am Ende nur einen Punkt.
In der Saison 2022 gewannen beide Titelrivalen jeweils zwei Läufe. Außerdem triumphierten die Brüder Koen und Kris Wauters von Belgium Racing beim Saisonauftakt und Q1 Trackracing siegte mit dem Fahrerquartett Jan Lauryssen, Tommy Rau, Filip Teunkens und Florian Latorre bei den 24 Stunden von Zolder.
Der beste Porsche Cayman GT4 des Jahres war die Startnummer 63 von Tip Top Rent by NGT in den Händen des jungen Talents Arthur Peters und des Gentleman Gunter van den Bergh. Das Duo erreichte in der Gesamtwertung aller eingeschriebenen Fahrzeuge Platz sechs.

Michael Cool, Dylan Derdaele, Kenneth Heyer, Ziad Ger

Wim Meulders, Rik Renmans, Olivier Dons, Jurgen Van Hover, Pieter Ooms, Kurt Hensen, John De Wilde, Jos Menten

The Porsche Endurance Trophy Benelux in 2022 again provided plenty of action as the battle for honours was contested to the very end of the year. Russell Racing by NGT, with the brothers Hans and Frank Thiers, Christoff Corten and Jeffrey van Hooydonk, did just enough to claim the title, by a single point behind the wheel of the Porsche 911 GT3 Cup – Type 992.

After 35 hours of racing spread across six races, the fight for the Porsche Endurance Trophy Benelux went to the finish line of the last race. Defending champions Dylan Derdaele and Michael Cool, driving for Belgium Racing, came within a whisker of the title.

Brothers Koen and Kris Wauters, also driving for Belgium Racing, took an early lead by winning the opening round of the season at Zolder. Derdaele and Cool scored their first of two wins at the second race in Magny Cours, while the Russel Racing by NGT won the third race at Spa. The series then moved to the big race, the 24 hours of Zolder, which was worth double points to the winners. Q1 Trackracing took that honour thanks to their drivers Jan Lauryssen, Tommy Rau, Filip Teunkens and Florian Latorre.

Russell Racing won at the Nurburgring and even though Belgium Racing took victory at the final round, it was not enough. In the final classification of the Porsche Endurance Trophy Benelux, the title, therefore, went to Russell Racing by NGT, ahead of three crews from Belgium Racing, and Q1 Trackracing. The best-placed Porsche Cayman GT4 was the car of Tip Top Rent by NGT in the hands of the young talent Arthur Peters and gentlemen driver Gunter Van Den Bergh.

Winner Arthur Peters, Gunther Van den Bergh

Michiel Haverans, Jerry De Weerdt, Marc Goossens, Rodrgique Gillion, Nico Verdonck

Koen Wauters, Kris Wauters

Arthur Peters, Jurgen Gulicher, Luc De Cock, Gunther Van den Bergh, Laurent van Laere, Fernand Lancksweerd

Michael Cool, Dylan Derdaele, Kenneth Heyer, Ziad Geris

TEAM STANDINGS

POS	NO	TEAM	CAR	DRIVERS	POINTS
1	2	Russel Racing by NGT	Porsche 992 GT3 Cup	Christoff Corten, Hans Thiers, Frank Thiers, Jeffrey van Hooydonk, Glenn van Parijs	245
2	99	Belgium Racing	Porsche 992 GT3 Cup	Michael Cool, Dylan Derdaele, Kenneth Heyer, Ziad Geris	244
3	97	Belgium Racing	Porsche 992 GT3 Cup	Koen Wauters, Kris Wauters	176
4	78	Belgium Racing	Porsche 991 GT3 Cup	Michiel Haverans, Jerry De Weerdt, Marc Goossens, Rodrgique Gillion, Nico Verdonck	147
5	55	Q1-Trackracing	Porsche 992 GT3 Cup	Filip Teunkens, Jan Lauryssen, Florian Latorre, Tommy Rau	140
6	63	Tip Top Rent	Porsche Cayman	Arthur Peters, Jurgen Gulicher, Luc De Cock, Gunther Van den Bergh, Laurent van Laere, Fernand Lancksweerd	132
7	7	Speedlover	Porsche 992 GT3 Cup	Wim Meulders, Rik Renmans, Olivier Dons, Jurgen Van Hover, Pieter Ooms, Kurt Hensen, John De Wilde, Jos Menten	104
8	17	Rush Competition by Speedlover	Porsche 991 GT3 Cup	Toon Hugenaert, Dries Gelade, Pieter Ooms, Frank Geelissen, Frederic Bouvy, John De Wilde	66
9	77	BE Motorsports	Porsche 718 Cayman GT4 / Porsche Boxster	Stephan Beyens, Didier Beyens, Peter Sterken, Davy Suffeleers, Ines Lammens	34

P9 CHALLENGE

03.06.–05.06.2022 Red Bull Ring, Austria
24.06.–26.06.2022 Lausitzring, Germany
29.07.–31.07.2022 Hockenheim, Germany
26.08.–28.08.2022 Nürburgring, Germany
07.10.–09.10.2022 Dijon, France

Sechster Titel in Folge für Porsche-Ass Hermann Speck in der P9 Challenge, die in diesem Jahr ihr zehnjähriges Jubiläum feierte.

Bernhard Fischers Passion für Porsche in Verbindung mit seiner langjährigen Erfahrung im Rennbetrieb sorgte 2012 für den Startschuss der P9 Challenge. Die Serie ist im GT3- und GT4-Segment markenoffen: Lamborghini-, Mercedes-, Ferrari-, KTM- und Porsche-Fahrer kämpften in der vergangenen Saison Tür an Tür um Siege und Platzierungen. Austragungsorte für die beiden Bewerbe P9 Challenge Sprint und P9 Challenge Endurance waren 2022 die renommierten europäischen Rennstrecken Red Bull Ring, Lausitzring, Hockenheimring, Nürburgring und Djion.
Im Jahr 2017 erkämpfte Herman Speck sich seinen ersten Titel in der P9 Endurance. Der Nürnberger Unternehmer setzte sich damals in seinem Porsche 997 GT3 R gegen Jack Crow / Markus Alber durch. In den Folgejahren addierte er drei weitere Endurance-Trophäen. Ende 2020 wagte Speck den Umstieg auf den neuen Porsche 991 GT3 R und fügte seiner Vita in 2021 und 2022 zwei weitere Titel in der P9 Endurance hinzu. Dabei war Coach McKansy, der einen Lamborghini Huracán von HP Racing International pilotierte, im vergangenen Jahr sein härtester Rivale. Der Vize-Champion der P9 Endurance konnte sich im Gegenzug in der Sprintwertung der P9 Challenge durchsetzen und Crow sowie Jürgen Bender auf die Plätze zwei und drei verweisen.
Neben den Gesamtsiegern der beiden Kategorien Sprint und Endurance gab es in beiden Serien auch Klassen-Champions zu feiern. In der Klasse 2 hatte Philipp Schulz im Porsche Cayman GT CS die Nase im Sprint deutlich vor Marco Reinbold, in der Klasse 3 war Manuel Süßenguth im Sprint mit seinem Porsche 991 GT3 Cup Gen. I nicht zu schlagen – nicht einmal vom ehemaligen

Felix Neuhofer

Start at Hockenheimring

Sixth title in a row for Porsche ace Hermann Speck as P9 Challenge celebrates its 10th anniversary this year.

Bernhard Fischer's passion for Porsche combined with his many years of racing experience led to the start of the P9 Challenge in 2012. In 2022, the tenth anniversary year of the series, drivers with GT3 and GT4 cars of various brands competed in sprint and endurance races at Red Bull Ring, Lausitzring, Hockenheim, Nürburgring and Dijon.

Having won four P9 Endurance titles with his Porsche 997 GT3 R from 2017 until 2020, entrepreneur Hermann Speck from Nuremberg switched to a new Porsche 991 GT3 R and added two further titles in 2021 and 2022. Like in the previous year, Lamborghini driver Coach McKansy was his main rival and became runner-up in the Endurance standings, but came out on top in the Sprint classification.

Sprint honours in class 2 went to Philipp Schulz with his Porsche Cayman GT CS while Manuel Süßenguth with his 991 GT3 Cup of the first generation turned out to be unbeatable in class 3. With a 991.2 GT3 Cup, Petr Breka claimed the sprint title in class 4, just ahead of Hannes Lafix. Jack Crow won class 5b with his 991.1 GT3 R while Coach McKansy came out on top in class 6a and Oliver Huez (Lola B2 K40) was crowned in class 8.

Endurance title winners were Marco Reinbold (class 2), Süßenguth (class 3), Breka (class 4), Speck (class 5b), McKansy (class 6a) and KTM driver Uwe Schmidt (class 8).

Petr Brecka

Hannes Lafix

Manuel Süßenguth

Titelträger Wolfgang Triller. Petr Breka auf Porsche 991 GT3 Cup Gen. II ließ in der Sprintwertung der Klasse 4 äußerst knapp Hannes Lafix hinter sich, Crow gewann im Porsche 991 GT3 R Gen. I die Klasse 5b, McKansy die Klasse 6a und Oliver Huez mit seinem Lola B2 K40 die Klasse 8. In den Endurance-Klassen hießen die Gewinner Reinbold (Klasse 2), Süßenguth (Klasse 3), Breka (Klasse 4), Speck (Klasse 5b), McKansy (Klasse 6a) sowie Uwe Schmidt (Klasse 8), der einen KTM GTX bewegte.

Hannes Lafix

Start at Red Bull Ring

„Jack Crow“ and Hermann Speck

Hermann Speck

„Jack Crow"

Podium at Dijon

Kai Pfister

Podium at Nürburgring

THE TEXAS COMPANY

SPECK
pumpen

2
1
3

MICHELIN
MICHELIN

MAHLE
MAHLE
MAHLE
ALPQUELL

MICHELIN

Podium at Hockenheimring

DRIVER STANDINGS **ENDURANCE**

POS	NO	DRIVERS	CAR	POINTS
1	520	**Hermann Speck**	**Porsche 911 GT3 R II**	**105,34**
2	623	"Coach McKansy"	Lamborghini Huracán GT3 Evo	99,14
3	485	**Petr Brecka**	**Porsche 991 GT3 Cup**	**56**
5	490	Karel Neffe	Porsche 991 GT3 Cup II	42
6	206	**Marco Reinbold**	**Porsche Cayman GT4 CS**	**38,66**
7	423	Hannes Lafix	Porsche 991 GT3 Cup II	36
10	301	**Manuel Süßenguth**	**Porsche 991 GT3 Cup**	**28**
11	522	Boris Schimanski	Porsche 991 GT3 Cup	25,98
13	206	**Paul Hochberger**	**Porsche Cayman GT4 CS**	**23,66**
15	403	Manuel Zlof	Porsche 991 GT3 Cup	20
16	300	**Wolfgang Triller**	**Porsche 991 GT3 Cup**	**15,34**
16	569	Alois Rieder	Porsche 911 GT3 R	15,34
17	425	**Paul Hochberger, Marco Reinbold**	**Porsche 991 GT3 Cup II**	**15,34**
20	420	Markus Neuhofer	Porsche 992 GT3 Cup	1

DRIVER STANDINGS **SPRINT**

POS	NO	DRIVERS	CAR	POINTS
1	623	"Coach McKansy"	Lamborghini Huracán GT3 Evo	228,55
2	521	"Jack Crow"	Porsche 911 GT3 R	200,99
3	624	Jürgen Bender	Chevrolet Corvette C7 GT3	141,35
4	520	Hermann Speck	Porsche 911 GT3 R II	134,83
6	485	**Petr Brecka**	**Porsche 991 GT3 Cup**	**78,44**
7	423	Hannes Lafix	Porsche 991 GT3 Cup II	77,46
9	569	**Alois Rieder**	**Porsche 911 GT3 R**	**73,18**
10	204	Philipp Schulz	Porsche Cayman GT4 CS	70
11	425	**Marco Reinbold**	**Porsche 991 GT3 Cup II**	**53,52**
12	421	Kai Pfister	Porsche 991 GT3 Cup	52,62
13	522	**Boris Schimanski**	**Porsche 991 GT3 Cup**	**47**
15	420	Felix Neuhofer	Porsche 992 GT3 Cup	40,64
16	528	**"Jesse James"**	**Porsche 991 GT3 Cup**	**38,66**
17	490	Karel Neffe	Porsche 991 GT3 Cup II	36
18	422	**Harald Geißelhart**	**Porsche 992 GT3 Cup**	**33,08**
20	401	Mladen Pavlovic	Porsche 991 GT3 Cup II	30,99
21	206	**Marco Reinbold**	**Porsche Cayman GT4 CS**	**30**
22	301	Manuel Süßenguth	Porsche 991 GT3 Cup	29,33
27	426	**Matthias Jeserich**	**Porsche 992 GT3 Cup**	**23,01**
28	411	Manuel Süßenguth	Porsche 991 GT3 Cup	19,24
29	300	**Wolfgang Triller**	**Porsche 991 GT3 Cup**	**17,34**
30	403	Manuel Zlof	Porsche 991 GT3 Cup	17,28
31	402	**Michael Birkner**	**Porsche 991 GT3 Cup II**	**17,22**
32	825	Franz Lahmer	Porsche 992 GT3 Cup	12
36	858	**Gerald Hofer**	**Porsche 991 GT3 Cup**	**11**

DRIVER STANDINGS **CLASS 3**

POS	NO	DRIVERS	CAR	POINTS
22	301	**Manuel Süßenguth**	**Porsche 991 GT3 Cup**	**29,33**
16	300	Wolfgang Triller	Porsche 991 GT3 Cup	17,34
3	858	**Gerald Hofer**	**Porsche 991 GT3 Cup**	**9,66**

DRIVER STANDINGS **CLASS 4**

POS	NO	DRIVERS	CAR	POINTS
1	485	**Petr Brecka**	**Porsche 991 GT3 Cup**	**78,44**
2	423	Hannes Lafix	Porsche 991 GT3 Cup II	77,46
3	425	**Marco Reinbold**	**Porsche 991 GT3 Cup II**	**53,52**
4	421	Kai Pfister	Porsche 991 GT3 Cup	52,62
5	420	**Felix Neuhofer**	**Porsche 992 GT3 Cup**	**40,64**
6	490	Karel Neffe	Porsche 991 GT3 Cup II	36
7	422	**Harald Geißelhart**	**Porsche 992 GT3 Cup**	**33,08**
8	401	Mladen Pavlovic	Porsche 991 GT3 Cup II	30,99
9	4[illegible]0	**Josef Halwachs**	**Porsche 991 GT3 Cup II**	**27,92**
10	426	Matthias Jeserich	Porsche 992 GT3 Cup	23,01
11	411	**Manuel Süßenguth**	**Porsche 991 GT3 Cup**	**19,24**
12	403	Manuel Zlof	Porsche 991 GT3 Cup	17,28
13	402	**Michael Birkner**	**Porsche 991 GT3 Cup II**	**17,22**
14	825	Franz Lahmer	Porsche 992 GT3 Cup	12

DRIVER STANDINGS **CLASS 5A**

POS	NO	DRIVERS	CAR	POINTS
1	521	**"Jack Crow"**	**Porsche 911 GT3 R**	**200,99**
2	520	Hermann Speck	Porsche 911 GT3 R II	134,83
3	569	**Alois Rieder**	**Porsche 911 GT3 R**	**73,18**
4	522	Boris Schimanski	Porsche 991 GT3 Cup	47
5	528	**"Jesse James"**	**Porsche 991 GT3 Cup**	**38,66**

DRIVER STANDINGS **CLASS 2A**

POS	NO	DRIVERS	CAR	POINTS
1	204	**Philipp Schulz**	**Porsche Cayman GT4 CS**	**70**
2	206	Marco Reinbold	Porsche Cayman GT4 CS	30
3	201	Dalton Grant	Mercedes-AMG GT4	25,34

Kai Pfister

Paul Hochberger, Marco Reinbold

CARRERA CUP CHILE

PORSCHE CUP CHILE

26.03.2022	*Huachalalume, La Serena, Chile*
30.04.2022	*AIC Circuit, Codegua, Chile*
14.05.2022	*AIC Circuit, Codegua, Chile*
18.06.2022	*AIC Circuit, Codegua, Chile*
20.08.2022	*AIC Circuit, Codegua, Chile*
10.09.2022	*AIC Circuit, Codegua, Chile*
15.10.2022	*AIC Circuit, Codegua, Chile*
12.11.2022	*Huachalalume, La Serena, Chile*
10.12.2022	*AIC Circuit, Codegua, Chile*

Im Porsche Cup Chile 2022 wurde wieder guter Rennsport geboten mit starken Fahrern, top vorbereiteten Autos und immer größer werdenden Starterfeldern.

Der Porsche Cup Chile 2022 begann im März auf dem Huachalalume Circuit in La Serena. Carlos Ruiz erwischte den besten Start in die neue Saison und gewann die Pro-Klasse vor Alejandro Candida und Antonio Leiva, dem besten Lite-Piloten im Feld.
Für die folgenden Vergleiche traf sich der Cup auf der Rennstrecke von Codegua, wo die Zuschauer harte Positionskämpfe zwischen Candia, Ruiz und Carlos Ruiz Jr. sahen. Das Trio stritt in den Saisonrennen zwei bis fünf um die ersten drei Plätze in der Pro-Kategorie, dicht gefolgt vom besten Lite-Vertreter Leiva. Die Ränge zwei und drei der Lite-Gruppe eroberten Alejandro García-Huidobro und Juan Francisco Ríos.
Der sechste Heat wurde im Endurance-Format ausgetragen, bei dem die 105 Rennminuten entweder von einem Piloten allein oder von einem Fahrer-Duo bestritten werden konnten. Zudem war ein obligatorischer Boxenstopp vorgesehen und es wurden doppelte Punkte für die Gesamtwertung vergeben. Ruiz Jr. gewann die Kategorie Pro, während Candia Zweiter und Ruiz Dritter wurde. Der viertplatzierte Leiva sicherte sich zudem den Triumph in der Lite-Klasse vor Fernando Delfau und Ríos.
Durchgang sieben des Jahres fand auf der Strecke von Huachalalume im Norden Chiles statt, wo Ruiz in der Klasse Pro als Sieger, Ruiz Jr. an zweiter Stelle und Candia auf Platz drei abgewinkt wurden. Die Überraschung des Tages aber war der junge Joaquín Labra, der an diesem Tag den vierten Rang erreichte, was Position eins in der Lite-Kategorie bedeutete. García-Huidobro und Mario Chomalí mussten sich in der Lite-Wertung hinter Labra anstellen.
Der Porsche Cup Chile 2022 wurde im achten und letzten Saisonlauf (nach Redaktionsschluss) entschieden, in den Candia vor Ruiz und Ruiz Jr. als Spitzenreiter der Pro-Tabelle ging. In der Lite-Kategorie wurde der Champion zwischen Favorit Leiva und García-Huidobro ermittelt. Im Senior-Ranking schließlich reisten Delfau und Osvaldo Gaio mit Chancen auf den Titel zum Finale.

After a tense and exciting season, the Porsche Cup Chile title fight goes to the last round

The Porsche Cup Chile featured eight races during the 2022 season, starting in March at the Huachalalume track located in La Serena, 500km from Santiago. The circuit, located near to the sea, had changeable weather which posed some problems for the drivers of the series. There were drivers who were new to the category, including Felipe Barrios, the official ATC2000 driver in Argentina and the young Clemente Araya. In the Light category there was a nice surprise in store, thanks to the outstanding performance of Antonio Leiva. Leiva led the points' standings for the entire championship, heading a new driver in the shape of Alejandro García-Huidobro. Fernando Delfau and Osvaldo Gaio had the remarkable feat of not only taking part in the Lite category, but also being the absolute leaders in the senior category too.

Having completed the race in Huachalalume the series moved on to the Codegua circuit, 80km south of Santiago. There witnessed a fought fight between Alejandro Candia, Carlos Ruiz and Carlos Ruis Jnr. These three drivers were the class of the Pro field for three races, from the second to the fifth round of the series. They were followed over the line by the Lite category leader Leiva, who finished fourth overall. In class, he beat García- Huidobro into second place while Juan Francisco Rios finished third. What also made the race stand out was the performance of Delfau who, through consistent improvement to his lap times, managed to sit fourth in the standings.

The sixth race was an endurance format, 105 minutes of competition that could be done by a single driver, or by a pair with the two changing at a mandatory pit stop. The race was worth double points in the rankings so was one of the most important on the schedule. Strategy was extremely important and it was Carlos Ruiz Jr who played it best and walked away with the victory in the Pro class, with Candia following him over the line in second and Carlos Ruiz finished third. In fourth, and winning the Lites category once again was Leiva, once again putting in a strong performance. In his class, second over the line was Delfau and third place was claimed by Francisco Rios.

For the seventh round the series returned to the Huachalalume circuit in the North, where the race was held on a spectacular spring day. Once again the Pro category was won by Carlos Ruiz, and he was followed over the line by Carlos Ruiz Jr. in second and Alejandro Candia in third place. The surprise of the day was the young driver Joaquin Labra, who finished fourth on that day, and in doing so secured first place in the Lite category. Second in that category was Alejandro García-Huidobro and third was Mario Chomali. In the senior category the victory went to Osvaldo Gaio, while Delfau finished second and Sixto Ulloa third.

Carlos Ruiz jr.

Ernesto Rios

Carlos Ruiz jr.

Drivers of Porsche Cup Chile

Ernesto Rios and Antonio Leiva

Alejandro Candia

(l.-r.): Matias Chomali, Mario Chomali, Ernesto Rios JR, Juan Rios, Alejando Garcia-Huidobro

Carlos Ruiz jr.

(11): Enrique Feliu - (14): Eduardo Gonzalez

(17): Felipe Barrios - (1): Carlos Ruiz

Mechaniker Team Cup Chile

Juan Francisco Rios, Ernesto Rios jr.

The Championship looked forward to the eighth and final race before it could crown its champion driver. Following a series of strong results, Alejandro Candia led the class going into that final race, ahead of Carlos Ruiz second and Carlos Ruiz Jr. third. The Lite category will have its champion from one of two drivers, the favorite Antonio Leiva and Alejandro García-Huidobro. The Senior category will also go to the final race, and will be between Fernando Delfau and Osvaldo Gaio.
Porsche Cup Chile 2022 completed a full season, and it was a thrilling year with some outstanding performances from different drivers, wonderful racing cars and a record number of cars on the circuit.

(1): Carlos Ruiz - (3): Alejandro Candia

(17): Felipe Barrios - (1): Carlos Ruiz

DRIVER STANDINGS CARRERA CUP

POS	DRIVERS	POINTS
1	Antonio Leiva	171
2	Alejandro Garcia Huidobro	171
3	Ernesto Rios Jr, Juan Francisco Rios	100
4	Fernando Delfau	94
5	Mario Chomali, Matias Chomali	85
6	Cristian Labra, Joaquin Labra	61
7	Osvaldo Gaio	61
8	Lucas Machicao, Clemente Araya	57
9	Ernesto Rios Jr	52
10	Joaquin Labra	38
11	Felipe Barrios	45
12	Eduardo Gonzalez	40
13	Juan Francisco Rios	28
14	Mario Chomali	22
15	Matias Chomali	19
16	Sixto Ulloa	19
17	Sixto Ulloa / Matias Labra	15
18	Felipe Viñuela	14
17	Sixto Ulloa	1

after round 9 of 10

DRIVER STANDINGS CUP LITE

POS	DRIVERS	POINTS
1	Alejandro Candia	209
2	Carlos Ruiz	202
3	Carlos Ruiz Jr	185
4	Antonio Leiva	76
5	Alejandro Garcia Huidobro	74
6	Ernesto Rios	66
7	Ernesto Rios Jr, Juan Francisco Rios	48
8	Enrique Feliu	45
9	Felipe Barrios	44
10	Fernando Delfau	31
11	Ernesto Rios Jr	30
12	Cristian Labra, Joaquin Labra	27
13	Mario Chomali, Matias Chomali	25
14	Osvaldo Gaio	23
15	Joaquin Labra	20
16	Juan Francisco Rios	14
17	Lucas Machicao, Clemente Araya	12
18	Mario Chomali	9
19	Eduardo Gonzalez	8
20	Matias Chomali	4
21	Sixto Ulloa, Matias Labra	1
22	Sixto Ulloa	1
23	Felipe Viñuela	0

after round 9 of 10

Felipe Barrios

(l.-r.): Alejandro Candia Carlos Ruiz, Antonio Leiva

RUNDSTRECKEN-CHALLENGE NÜRBURGRING

02.04.2022	Bergischer Schmied, Nürburgring Nordschleife, Germany
07.05.2022	Preis der Schloßstadt Brühl, Nürburgring Nordschleife, Germany
26.05.2022	Feste Nürburg, Nürburgring Nordschleife, Germany
02.07.2022	Um die Westfalen Trophy, Nürburgring Nordschleife, Germany
20.08.2022	Nordeifelpokal, Nürburgring Nordschleife, Germany
03.09.2022	Rhein-Ruhr Pokal, Nürburgring Norschleife, Germany
09.10.2022	Preis der Erftquelle, Nürburgring Nordschleife, Germany
29.10.2022	Schwedenkreuz, Nürburgring Nordschleife, Germany

Der von Schmickler Performance eingesetzte Porsche Cayman Turbo feierte mit mehreren Piloten drei Gesamtsiege und gewann am Ende souverän den RCN-Gesamtsieger-Cup

Nach der schneebedingten Absage des Auftaktes feierten Stefan Schmickler und Carsten Knechtges beim zweiten Lauf einen Gesamtsieg. Der RCN-Meister von 2013 siegte beim fünften Rennen gemeinsam mit Fahrzeugeigner Volker Wawer und beim siebten Lauf ebenfalls – hier allerdings als Solist. Dazu kamen noch zwei sechste Gesamtränge für Stefan Schmickler.

Zu den Aufsteigern des Jahres zählten Routinier Andreas Herwerth sowie Junior Fabio Sacchi. Das Duo setzte sowohl auf einen seriennahen V5-Cayman als auch auf einen RS7-GT3 Cup. Teilweise sogar im gleichen Rennen und dann mit fliegendem Fahrerwechsel! Die beiden fuhren in fünf von sieben Läufen mit dem V5-Cayman in die Top 20 der Gesamtwertung und freuten sich bei der sechsten Veranstaltung über ihren ersten Gesamtsieg überhaupt mit dem 911 Cup.

Bei den Produktionswagen bis 3500 ccm (Klasse V6) tobte während der gesamten Saison das spannende Duell zwischen den beiden Cayman S des zweifachen Meisters Christian Büllesbach mit Lutz Marc Rühl sowie Sascha Kloft und Heiko Tönges.

Heiner Großeibl, Klaus Groninger

Run by Schmickler Performance, the Porsche Cayman Turbo scored three overall wins and sealed the RCN Winners' Cup

Stefan Schmickler and Carsten Knechtges started their season with an overall win the second scheduled round of the series after the season opener was cancelled due to snow.
The fifth race was also won by the 2013 RCN champion Stefan Schmickler, together with car owner Volker Wawer, and he also won round seven, driving on his own. Andreas Herwerth and Fabio Sacchi alternated between a V5 class Cayman and an RS7 category GT3 Cup. They finished in the top 20 overall with the Cayman in five of seven rounds, and claimed overall honours in the 911 Cup in round six. In the V6 class, the Cayman S pairings Christian Büllesbach/Lutz Marc Rühl and Sascha Kloft/Heiko Tönges battled all season long.

Marcel Haas, Stefan Gaukler

Lutz Rühl, Christian Büllesbach

Andreas Herwerth, Fabio Sacchi

Horst Baumann, Helmut Baumann

Sascha Kloft

Leo Glinz

DRIVER STANDINGS

POS	NO	DRIVERS	CAR	POINTS
1	300	Daniel Ostermann, Oskar Sandberg	BMW 330i	57,78
2	384	Peter Elkmann	BMW 325i	55,76
3	45	Daniel Odenthal, Julian Odenthal	BMW 325i	54,65
7	14	Sascha Kloft	Porsche Cayman S	51,71
8	**17**	**Andreas Herwerth, Fabio Sacchi**	**Porsche 981 Cayman**	**50,55**
9	212	Stefan Schmickler	Porsche Cayman	50,55

Christopher Brück

DUBAI AUTODROME
DUBAI AUTODROME

PORSCHE

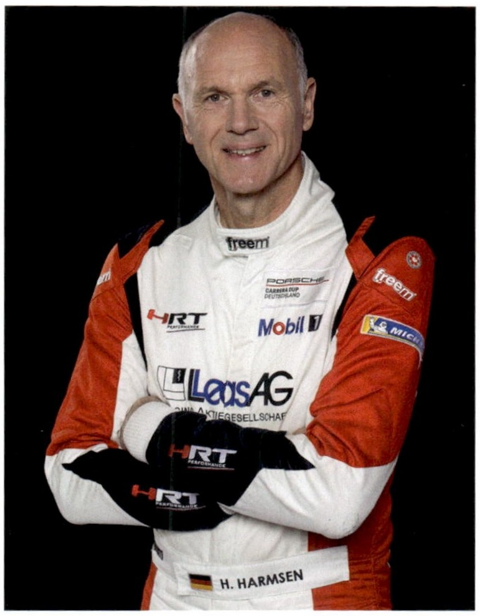
HRT
Mobil 1
LeasAG
H. HARMSEN

KÜS
1

HAZET
www.hazet.de

PORSCHE
MOTORSPORT
ASIA PACIFIC

REBELLION
TIMEPIECES
911
GOLD

16 SCHURING
P1

KRAUS
Immobilien
TEAM
WEAR
.AT

PRESENTED BY

IMPRESSUM - EDITORIAL

Herausgeber / Editor:
Gruppe C Motorsport Verlag

Projektleitung / Project leadership:
Tim Upietz

Projektmanager / Project manager:
Jan P. Brucke

Assistent Projektleitung / Assistant project management:
Lisa Hallmann

Autoren / Authors:
Laura Brunnenmeister, Andrew Cotton, René de Boer, Michaela Düngen, Markus Findeisen, Patrik Koziolek, Annette Laqua, Tom Moore, Jonas Plümer, David Tunnicliffe, Jörg-Richard Ufer

Übersetzung / Translation:
René de Boer, Celia Marshall-Bingler

Statistik / statistic:
János Wimpffen

Fotografen / Photographers:
Eric Alonso, Egidijus Babelis, Tom Banks, Luca Bassani, Dan Bathie, Guido De Bortoli, Fabio Brito, Jan P. Brucke, Bob Chapman, Ho Kean Chew, Malte Christians, El Cid, E. Clivati, Brecht Decancq, Dirk Michael Deckbar, Dirk Dekens, Paola Depalmas, DPPI, Wes Duenkel, Danny Dzenis, Ebimotors, Jakob Ebrey, Philippe Escalier, Alex Farias, Jorge Ferrari, Fotospeedy, Fernanda Freixosa, Lukas Fronk, Petr Fryba, Patrick Funk, Rafel Gagliano, Alex Galli, Rohan Ganapathy, Dom Gibbons, Charles Gill, Alexis Goure, Co van der Gragt, Armin Hadzic / A1 Work, Christian Hartung, Aaron Hermosilla, Mark Horsburgh, Nick Hrehor, IMSA Photo, Jerker Johansson, Qian Jun, Patrick Karbownik, Bank Kanchanavilai, Burkhard Kasan, Michael Kavena, Katsuyoshi Kobayashi, Bodo Kräling - Bildagentur Kräling, Jiří Křenek - HOCH ZWEI Photoagency, Michael Kunkel - HOCH ZWEI Photoagency, Daniel Laaksonen, Diederik van der Laan, Marcel Langer, Fritz Letters, Andrew Lofthouse, David Lord, Benny Luey, Fabian Lujan, Peter Malaise, Jack Martin, Andi Mayr, Justin McFarland, Jochen Merkle, Scott Mitchell, Manfred Muhr, Alvaro Naranjo, Lars David Neill, Klaas Norg, Ollivision. com Photography, Mattia Ozbot, Ari Paronen, Kevin Pecks, Giorgio Perottino, Adam Pigott, Angelo Poletto, Porsche Archiv, Porsche Motorsport North America, Kittawan Pothibut, Zhu Qianli, Joonas Raiha, Daniel Reinhardt, Silvia & Dirk Reiter - BRfoto, Peter Ritter, James Roberts, Jakke Röntynen, Sebastiaan Rozendaal, SACRED, Stephan Schmick, Julian Schmidt, Ingo Schmitz, Chris Schotanus - Essay Produkties, Leo Schulz, Kyle Schwab, Gianluca Sciarra, Michele Scudiero, Dan Sojeva, Sven Siebel, Richard Ström, Thomas Suer, Jürgen Tap - HOCH ZWEI Photoagency, Ivan Tarantsov, Angus Thompson, Georgi Todorov, Alexander Trienitz, Tim Upietz, USAC Racing, Lazenby Visuals, Xin Wang, Tubbs Wanigasekera, Nathan Wong, CW Yiau, ZimSpeed

Layout und Design / Layout and Design:
Jonas Hermanns – www.jonashermanns.de

Lektorat / Proofreading:
Tanja Altgaßen, Andrew Cotton, Michaela Düngen

Redaktionelle Mitarbeit / editorial cooperation:
Olivier Aerts, Valentina Albanese, Yannick Bitzer, Jan Bodenbach, Jingjing Chen, Laura Claesgens, Richard Craill, Fredrik Derkum, Anna Dostmann, Michael Dreiser, Kurt Ecke, Holger Eckhardt, Marc Eisenblätter, Bernhard Fischer, Flora Fornasari, Lukas Gajewski, Laurie Gautier, Alexandre Gibot, Benjamin Godau, Nadine Hafkesbrink, Kosho Ito, Jerker Johansson, Hari Kalsia, Hans Bernd Kamps, Patrick Karbownik, Oliver Köppen, Michael Kössler, Janis Kozloski, Robert Lechner, Walter Lechner, Marlis Linsner, Juhana Määttä, Charli Ma, Gianluca Mar, Mazzoli, Venceslas Monzini, Nicole Nagel, Arielle Neill, Lars David Neill, Giulia Olivari, Ari Paronen, Lars Plato, Dener Jorge Pires, Boya Qi, Raun Ratilainen, Johanna Reider, Oliver Schwab, Sebastian Seeling, Bernd Simmendinger, Hafeez Tahir, Angus Thompson, Patrick Vegeais, Felipe Vieira, Shirin Vollmer, Sven Wittich, Alexandra Yan, Flora Zhou, Ziyang Zhang

Produktionsmanagement / Productionmanagement:
Christoph Löhr – Produktionsteam, Düsseldorf

Produktion und Druck / Production and Printing:
Gunnar Kettler – DruckVerlag Kettler GmbH

Buchbinder / Bookbinder:
Integralis Buchbinderei